Someone Really Oughta Tell You™

A Life Strategies Manual for Young Adults and Life Renovators of any age

Di Gibson

ISBN: 978-0-9881471-0-2

Published by Tall Doors Press, Toronto, Canada

Cover photograph by Di Gibson

This book is dedicated to those who might find it helpful...
and to those who inspired it.

What's in this for you?

Generally self-help books are read only when something needs to be repaired, whether it's a faucet or your finances, your car or your credit report, your waistline or your relationships. *Someone Really Oughta Tell You* is not that kind of book.

Why is this book different?

It's pre-emptive. It's occasionally irreverent, pared down do-able information that works. And it comes in readily chewable chunks. It assumes that you may, like me, be a little impatient with how-to books that are too wordy, stilted, or somewhat patronizing. And it does not assume you're already in a jam, though you may be—or you may be heading for one and not realize it.

Who is this book for?

- For those who want to be able to see life as a joyful, meaningful adventure.
- For those who want to pick up some easy to implement practical tips that will help them live life on their terms.
- For those who'd rather avoid a rent-a-wreck kind of life and prefer instead a Porsche, a Bentley, a classic Harley, a Volt, a Tesla, or some other sweet ride. The analogy is not about the price or even the vehicle. It's about the quality of your life's journey, and the ease of care and maintenance along the way.

AVOID DENTS

It's so much easier to learn in ways other than from your own mistakes. Most of us gather a few dents that we'd love to have avoided. And could have. Ouch. But what if we aren't aware that there is something we really do need to know?

Life's a lot kinder and more fun when you learn the things you later wish you had known *before* you needed to know them.

Yet even the things we know we ought to do, we often don't—for a whole lot of reasons, and excuses—and it's often hard to tell the difference between the two. Sometimes it's simply that the "doing it" is not fun. But neither are the consequences of not doing it. Or we can't be bothered. "I'm special. It won't happen to me". Ya right. Why do you think they wrote a book about lousy things happening to nice people? Or is it that we're too embarrassed to admit we haven't a clue where to start? Yet if we remain naïve, we inadvertently set ourselves up for problems. Wouldn't it be nice if avoiding or solving hassles is easier than you think?

Someone Really Oughta Tell You this stuff!

AVOID the PILES and ALLIGATORS

It's a fact—S#*% always happens along the path to anywhere you'd like to go. Yet you can avoid stepping in it, at least most of the time. You just need to keep your eyes open. Remember the cliché, "It's hard to remember you should have drained the swamp when you're up to your ass in alligators." (Anonymous)

This book will help you avoid some dents, navigate the swamps, spot the alligators, and step in fewer little brown piles along your path. And it will help you create a happier, more meaningful life.

How to use this book...

Think of this book as a portable tool kit. Perhaps as one of those fabulous pocket-sized gadgets designed to fix, attach, snip, cut, or open things. Those gadgets, and this book, are designed to let you pull out the tool that's appropriate for the task at hand. Why not play with it a little? Familiarize yourself up front with which bits would be useful when, and for what tasks. In this book, those tasks are outlined in the Table of Contents as Sections and Chapters. Start wherever you want. What is your current need? What are you most curious about? Your choice. Hey, if you're not sure where to start, why not start at the beginning? But start somewhere.

Think of each **Section** of this book as a grouping of tools for similar tasks.

- You may want to tinker with your **Priorities.**
- Or get a better grip on how you spend your **Time** or **Money**. Or both.
- Maybe you need to do something more about **Covering your Ass...ets?**
- You may be hungry to know how you could boost your **Quality of Life**.
- The **Appendices** contain useful examples of some ideas we'll be playing with.

The **Chapters** explain how to use the various tools. Again, start where you want. Let curiosity and good sense lead you to the other Chapters and Sections.

The **Activities** (in gray boxes throughout the book) help you translate the *words* in the book into *realities* in your life. You don't become a competent, confident cyclist or biker by simply reading a how-to-ride-a-bike book—you've got to put those ideas to real use. So give it a go. And don't be surprised if you feel a little wobbly when you first start—these skills, like any others, will come more easily with practice. (By the way, I'm a realist about how much time you have. You could start with the activities that feel like play, or focus where you desperately need some help. It's your call—it's your life. You'll hear that more than once.)

Further Resources are included within each chapter. These are not intended to be a comprehensive list, just some good entry points into more information on the topic.

Some suggestions:

- Scribble anywhere. Do what you will with this book. (You should see my books when I've finished "reading" them. Librarians would hate me, so I buy mine. To me, for most books, it's the ideas that are precious not the actual pages.)
- Set yourself up with your favourite way of keeping "Notes to self". Digital or paper? Journaling, scrap-booking, sketching or doodling? Save your thoughts.
- It might be fun to bounce around some of these ideas with a friend.
- Keep in mind that you're the one in control here. Do as little or as much of this as you want. I'm simply giving you suggestions that work. Your life, your call.

Ah, perhaps you already know a lot of what's explained in this "manual". Awesome. Yay you! (Maybe your family and friends knew, and knew to tell you, and knew how to tell you in a way that you heard it. Or maybe the Education system did. Ya right. Or maybe, like me, you learned it on your own.) Congratulate yourself and them, and consider this a set of reminders. Yet, if you already know this stuff, are you actually DOING it?

You want to hit a home run? You gotta' pick up the bat.

Contents

DISCLAIMER

This publication is designed to provide useful information regarding the subjects covered. It is, however, sold with the understanding that the author and her publisher are not engaged in providing any form of legal, financial, or other professional advice. If or when such expert assistance is required, the services of relevant professionals should be sought. As each individual situation is unique, and since laws and practices vary with one's location and/or jurisdiction, questions should be addressed to an appropriate professional to ensure that the situation has been evaluated carefully and appropriately.

The stories and anecdotes are based on true experiences but the names have been changed, and some situations have been modified to protect privacy. Any possible slights to specific people, groups, or organizations are unintentional.

The websites suggested in this book are online at the time of publication. The author and her publisher do not claim that these sites provide the most appropriate information for your individual circumstances, nor guarantee the validity of the information they provide. We assume no responsibility for inaccuracies, errors, omissions or any inconsistency therein.

The author and publisher disclaim any liability, loss, or risk which is incurred as a consequence, directly or indirectly, of the use and application of any of the contents of this work.

Priorities

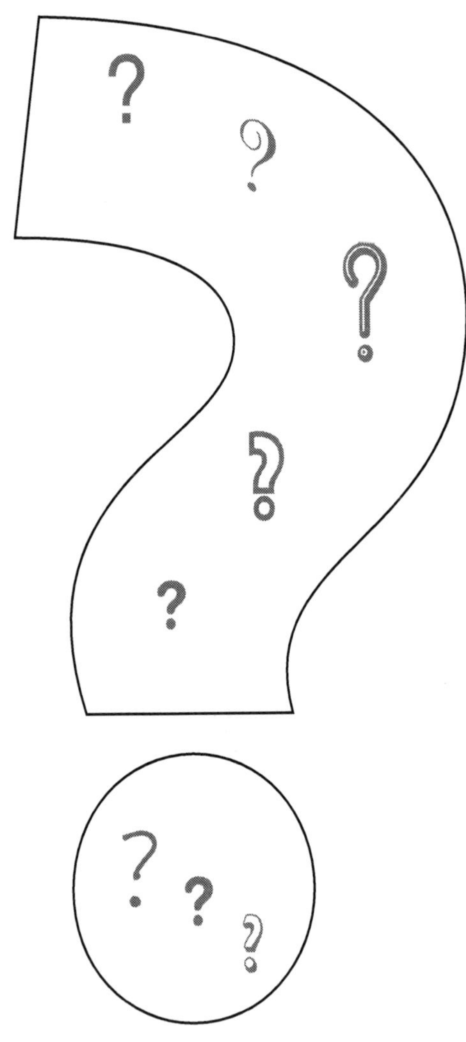

Chapter 1

Where do you want to go with this?

A Buddhist Proverb –
"If we are facing in the right direction, all we have to do is keep walking."

Where would you like your journey to take you?
What experiences would you welcome into your life?
What are your current priorities?

To these kinds of questions you get to, and need to, design your own answers. Others can only encourage you to ponder and explore, and perhaps prod you with questions that might spark ideas and insights. Occasionally, someone may make a suggestion for you to consider. So, prod, prod—here goes.

What do you want to do with your Time, Energy, Attention, and Money?

The Three Lists

Whether they love 'em or hate 'em, most people are used to making Lists. At least *writing* them—not necessarily *doing* them. Even if you don't much like lists, bear with me. These are not the "you must do" slightly annoying kinds of lists. These lists are simply to help you play with your possible wants, needs, and priorities.

Step ONE Creating your DO / BE / HAVE lists.

Use a separate page for each of the three lists. If you're using paper, leave a few lines between each item so you can later add details or insights.

Coming up with the first five on each won't be hard. Go for ten. (More ideas will likely come as you go through the rest of the book. Add them later. If you get on a roll, and end up with dozens of ideas, go for it. We're playing here.)
As well, write down any questions, thoughts, feelings that arise as you do these.

List ten things you'd like, during your life, to **DO.**

Want to travel the world? Have your music go platinum? Learn another language? Fly a plane? (You may wonder if such-and-such is a BE or a DO. Don't agonize. Just stick it somewhere, and keep going.)

List ten things you'd like to **BE.**

Be a good friend, a wonderful parent? Be better at not procrastinating? More confident? Classy *and* sexy?

Make another list of at least ten things you want to **HAVE.**

Some new gadget? A dog? A less pathetically saggy sofa?

Here are a few questions to prod your brain.

- You have a completely free day. What do you want to do with it?
- What absorbs you so completely that you lose track of time?
- Describe the people you'd like in your life. Who, what do you admire?
- What are you drawn to? What, whom, do you envy?
- Where do you want to live? What is needed to make a place your home?
- Now the familiar wish: You just won the lottery. A big one. Now what?

> Perhaps your life is great as it is—no changes or goals needed, at least not right now. Fabulous. Help someone else get there too. That's a superb goal.

Step TWO Debrief yourself

Did you find yourself censoring your lists because of what someone else might think? Because of what you think you "should" or "shouldn't" want? Because you think you're "not being realistic"? If so, put a gag on your internal critic. Let yourself daydream!

Did you include things you already do and things you already have? You weren't asked to do that, and there are likely a lot of those that you do appreciate. Add them now. We often take a lot for granted. What, if missing from your life, would be not only disappointing but problematic ... like food and a roof over your head? Remember the cliché: "You don't know what you've got 'til it's gone". It's too often true.

Step THREE What's the difference between a WANT and a NEED?

A.H. Maslow, one of the first social scientists or psychologists to study *healthy*-minded humans, published a now classic paper, "A Theory of Human Motivation" back in 1943. He described a *Hierarchy of Needs*, all of which must be satisfied in order to have a healthy life.[1] (Though this hierarchy is usually now presented as a pyramid, that was not how he expressed his ideas.) His intent was that the various layers blend and shift on an ongoing basis throughout life rather than manifest chronologically or one at a time. Yet, as with a ladder, the base—the physical survival needs—must be stable. For example, if one is starving, needs such as esteem and belonging seem less important, and those associated with self-actualization and transcendence are in serious jeopardy. (The outline below is not verbatim but the intent, I believe, is intact.)

Transcendence	Helping others become their best selves
Self Actualization	Creativity, Self-expression, Problem Solving Curiosity, a desire to know and understand Intellectual freedom Morality, Lack of Prejudice A good grasp of reality, self-awareness
Esteem	Self-respect, confidence, a sense of being capable Achievement, Recognition, Appreciation Mutual respect in interactions with others
Love and Belonging	Romantic attachment, Sexual Intimacy Family, Friendship, Community
Safety	Security of Resources, Property, Employment Security of the Family, of the morality of others Safety of, and shelter for, the body
Physiological	Homeostasis (balanced body functioning) Sleep, Excretion, Sex Breathing, Food, Water

Dear Reader, pay attention to each of those NEEDS, in your lists and your life.

You want to be sure to avoid getting less than you genuinely need while you're exploring and pursuing your wants.

Step FOUR **Prioritize**

Again ask yourself, are you letting "be realistic" get in your way? Don't.

Which items on your lists are the most exciting?
Which ones might be a little scary, but you want them anyway?

Which ones do you most want now?
Which ones do you most want always? Like food, friends, and clean air.

On the other hand, which ones might you be content to get to later, maybe.
(Is it simply an idle interest or something you'll later regret not having done?)

Step FIVE **Getting into Action**

We'll get more specific about designing and implementing goals in Chapter 10
As an appetizer, try this:

Pick ONE item from *each* of your DO, BE, HAVE lists.

First, blow off a little of that need-to-get-serious-about-this attitude.
(Leave winning the lottery out of this. You can be more creative than that.)
Get silly on purpose. Think up some truly goofy solutions. Maybe pretend you're setting up a sitcom. Suppose for example, you need a new sofa. And you also need someplace to store all those empty beer cases. Where you want the sofa, stack the beer cases two deep along the wall. Add more boxes for arms and a back. Throw on an old comforter or sleeping bag. More boxes? Want a bigger sofa? Or an arm chair?

Okay, now that your attitude's lightened up, your mind will have access to better ideas. (That's shown by research.) Brainstorm how you can, in the next few days, get started on a DO, BE, or HAVE. You want to go hiking in Costa Rica? Or night-life-ing in Vegas? Get online and look at trip options and costs.

Sure, there's likely to be some hurdles. So what?
When you're done this book you'll be better able to deal with many of those, including time, money, motivation, and cynicism.

Why not ask a friend to join you in this design-your-life activity? Share ideas. Companionship can make both the doing and getting there easier and more fun.

If you're excited about getting on with it *now*, jump to the Goals Chapter. You can read the intervening chapters later.

Not 100% sure what you want to get on with?
That's the next chapter...

Chapter 2

What matters?

When something is important, does it mean you must become oh-so-serious in your approach? No. It's actually better to adopt a playful mindset. The process of discovery will not only be more fun, it will be more effective! As you work—oops, play—your way through this chapter, keep in mind that you're simply clarifying your ideas here, not locking yourself into anything.

What matters to you will vary with your age and stage of life, and as your life and personal preferences shift and evolve. What matters to you now? What may matter to you later? Can you possibly know that? Even when you know where you're heading, you can't see the entire path. That's part of the adventure of life. Get to the first horizon of your journey, then look for the next. But do choose a direction or you'll most likely go in circles—or nowhere. You can, usually, change direction later[1] if you need or want to.

Don't care where you're going? Then it probably doesn't matter when or if you get there. But do you really want to wander aimlessly through life?

If you've no clue what you want, how are you going to recognize it if you do manage to get it? What if you already had a great version of whatever that is, but you didn't realize it? That truly would be sad.

How do YOU define success in life? Aha. Now that's no small question.

By understanding more clearly what you genuinely value, you're going to know better how to be, and feel, successful in all aspects of your life. And you'll be more able to recognize and adapt to your evolving dreams, to your new horizons and directions. Think of yourself as an explorer of life, as the architect of your reality.

Whether you're building a home or a life, keep your needs and preferences in mind. It's *your* responsibility—and your gift to yourself—to create the design, the blueprint, that allows for those. Include solid foundations, protective walls, a good roof, large windows to let light flood in and capture the view, and leave ample open space for movement, for joy and serendipity. Why settle for a life you don't choose? Design and build your own. Renovate when needed.

What needs some work? Your current context? Or a better understanding of your options? If, at some point, you find your life's not quite what you'd like it to be, get proactive. Perhaps simply freshen up a few things as you would freshen up a room with new paint. (Take up a new hobby, make some new friends.) Or knock down a couple of walls. (Open your mind to new ideas.) Or maybe you'd rather tear it all down and rebuild from scratch? Or sell and move on? (Change careers, continents, whatever?)

You and LIFE itself co-create your life. The interaction is the adventure.

As George Bernard Shaw said:

> "Life is not about finding yourself. Life is about *creating* yourself."

The next activity will help you explore what matters deeply to you. Some aspects of what you value may or may not change much over the years—we're all a blend of Core-Self and Growing-Self. If you can't describe your Core-Self in words, so what? (For some things, words are over-rated.) You likely have a pretty good sense of who that You is. Your Growing-Self? We are all works-in-progress, not statues carved in stone. How exciting! So enjoy—now and at any age—exploring who you are, and who you could become.

> When you hit your expiry date, how do you want to feel about yourself? What do you want to be able to say to yourself and to others about what you did while you were here?

What matters to you?

Here's a list of Values, in alphabetical order. Add one or two more if you like...

ACCOMPLISHMENT	ADVENTURE
AUTONOMY / SELF-DETERMINATION	COMFORT / CONTENTMENT
CONNECTION	CONTRIBUTION
CREATIVITY / INITIATIVE	ENTHUSIASM / PASSION
GROWTH / LEARNING	HEALTH
JOY / CHEERFULNESS	LOVE / INTIMACY
POWER / CONTROL	RESPECT
SAFETY / SECURITY	STEWARDSHIP / SUSTAINABILITY

Step ONE Notes-to-self

Jot down a few notes on your interpretations of each of the above. (If you do this with a friend, do these Notes-to-self separately first.)

For each Value, briefly describe two ways it would express itself in your life. Be as specific as you can. FREEDOM could mean having the money to travel anywhere anytime, or not to have to travel at all. It could simply mean leaving dirty dishes in the sink if you feel like it. COMFORT could be a day at a luxurious spa or a safe home. Or both. ADVENTURE? PASSION? Your call. What do *you* mean by each?

Questions and random thoughts will likely come to mind as you work through this. Use these to help you refine your interpretation of these values. POWER for example. What kinds of power are you talking about? Over others? Over circumstances? Over yourself?

Having a clearer sense of our priorities, as we and our lives evolve, will simplify numerous decisions we'll need to make. (More on decision-making in Chapter 5.)

Start by choosing your top three values. Then choose your bottom three. For those somewhere in the middle, pick your top half and your bottom half. Then further refine your priorities by deciding within each grouping which matters more, even if only slightly. If specific circumstances (if-then, only-when, and so on) might be part of your reasoning, note those.

Step TWO **Chew on this ...**

Are these values adequately expressed in your present day-to-day life?
Watch for ways to create opportunities to experience them more fully.
(You'll transform your values into specific goals later in Chapter 10.)

Are the ways you want to express these values compatible?
Perhaps COMFORT is right beside ADVENTURE. If you hate getting cold and wet, don't go back-packing in November in the northern Rockies.
What if you value CONNECTION but you're consistently working 70 hour weeks?

Make brief notes on how to avoid or deal with the potential problems. By not doing that, some people inadvertently create a less-than-happy life for themselves.

If you're doing this with a friend, ask each other questions, not to justify your choices, but to help each other clarify your own meanings and criteria.

Step THREE **Back then and much later ...**

Pretend you're a kid again.
  What did you like to do back then?
  How could you recapture some of that enthusiasm?

Assume you make it to a very old age.
  Which activities will you look back on with the fondest memories?
  Which values would you be disappointed with yourself for neglecting?

Heroes

Heroes don't have to be rich and famous. Include your cat who gets to sleep in when you don't, or your dog who's done a good job of training his two legged servants. Or some animated character with magical powers. (One of my heroes? Hobbes, of Calvin and Hobbes. Love the good-hearted savvy combined with a playful and irreverent, but constructive, attitude. What does that tell me?)

Why do you respect that person? What has he/she accomplished? In what fields? What about them intrigues you? Is there something in common about those you admire? In what ways might you already be somewhat like your heroes?

Do you think they succeeded because they were "just lucky", or had a perfect or an easy life? Check their realities. What was their personal life like? As a kid? As a young adult? When they were at their peak? Now? What obstacles did they have to overcome? How did they do that?

What could you learn from their mistakes, and successes, to help you with yours? How can you add into you more of what you admire in them?

(Told you I'd be giving you a lot of questions to ask yourself.)

Food for Thought … Basic Principles and Conflicting Values

Some **Basic Principles** in life are valid in pretty much any circumstance. Like gravity, they're realities not opinions. For example, being a jerk isn't likely to increase your popularity and yelling at your boss in public is probably not a good idea. Some things are just good sense.

There are many aspects of being a good person that don't have anything to do with religions, or the lack thereof. Don't eat your neighbour. Being helpful is generally considered a nice thing. (I'm sure you can think of other examples.)

However, some aspects of how-to-be and what-to-do are prescribed by context, dependent on circumstance. Don't eat with your left hand in some countries. Don't bow down to graven images in others. Wear a certain something on your head, or don't, if you want to fit in. Some of these may matter to you. Or not. Your choice. Or should be. Some of these you may choose to ignore, or disagree with. Some you might choose to fight to change or eliminate. Like apartheid. Slavery. Walls. And a lack of basic human rights. Summon the courage to help make a positive difference in the world.

How to be? What to do? Who decides that? That's why societies have laws—to determine its Shoulds and Shouldn'ts. And in some societies what is "acceptable" is quite different than in others. And within each of those cultures, who decides?

How do we acknowledge and respect other ways of being as valid, even if they would not be our personal choice? Should we? How do we become comfortable living side by side? With mutual respect. Or at least mutually benevolent tolerance.

Should we always accept what is viewed as the norm, for us or for others? Are there times when we shouldn't get comfortable? What about when the "values" of some are imposed on others? What about child soldiers? Child porn? Women as possessions? Genocide? Seeing other species on the planet as irrelevant?

Unfortunately, the boundaries between basic principles, accepted norms, don't-you-dares, and the maybe-I-can-get-away-withs can get blurred. Clarify yours.

Which values do you consider universally true? Which are culturally prescribed? Which are circumstance dependent? Is life all shades of gray, or all black and white? Or an HD picture with all the tonalities? No. It's so much more—it's intriguing, vibrant, multi-dimensional. It's our *reality.* And we help create it with *what we do.*

What are *your* core values? What are the basic principles you choose to live by?
What assumptions do you make about yourself, and about others?
What are the expectations placed on you by your current context?
Which might change for you, for the better, with a change of context?
What might you change, with a change of heart?

Sorry about making you think. (Ya right.)

Chapter 3

Gripes, Grumps, and Gratitudes

There's a British expression: "A stiff upper lip". It refers to being stoic, "calm and unflinching under hardship". Is a "stiff upper lip" like a "poker face"? So no one sees what's really going on inside?

"Be strong."	"Don't cry."
"Keep a lid on it."	"Be good."
"Be nice."	"Turn the other cheek."

Sound familiar? We're often told these things as kids—perhaps even occasionally as adults—when inside what we really want to do is wail and flail and throw a tantrum. But that's "not nice".

Do we need to "be nice" all the time to be genuinely good people? (Do we have to never snap at a sibling or our mate?) Can we not acknowledge, in honest and constructive ways, the disappointments and annoyances in life and still validate and appreciate the joys—those things we ought to be and are grateful for? Some of the puzzle pieces of life may be darker than others—we still see those that are light and bright. It's the combination that eventually builds the picture.

The reality is that "success does not depend on how you feel. Human moods have remarkably little to do with effective action." [1] Yet "somewhere along the line our culture has sold us the absurd idea that we've got to have a positive attitude to succeed."[2] Occasional negativity is realistic and human and we need to acknowledge that. By lying to ourselves, pretending that everything is nicey-nicey, we could end up depressed, incapacitated by a debilitating absence of energy and action. When things are getting us down, to re-energize we occasionally need to be able to vent—constructively—even if it's just ranting in a journal, or with a good gripe.

In their intriguing book, *Wishcraft,* Barbara Sher and Annie Gotlieb recommend "a good old fashioned gripe session raised to the dignity and status of a ritual".[3] This kind of constructive being-heard-without-intervention is a great stress reducer. "Real listening is the cure for chronic complaining."[4] To be truly listened to with the listener's full attention—even for a brief time frame—is a wonderful gift we can give each other.

Expressing one's annoyance, in a safe context, about certain bothersome aspects of life or the behavior of others is not the same as wallowing in self-pity. And it does not, as some fear, keep one stuck in the issue. In fact, it's energizing. "Get it off your chest." (There's another odd expression.) Let's do that.

Learning to Gripe—constructively.

With a trusted friend, you're going to complain—to Gripe—for three minutes, non-stop. To save your listener some discomfort, you *must* start with the vital comment: "You don't need to help me solve this. I just need to gripe." (There is an advantage for the listener, as well, in this. You, as a listener, have a chance to better understand your friend without the pressure of feeling that you're expected to fix the issue.)

A will gripe at B for three minutes. B says nothing, doesn't even grunt in sympathy. B just listens. This is *not* a conversation. That's crucial. Then switch.

When you've both had a good gripe, you're done. It may feel a little awkward the first time you try it. Yet it's surprisingly energizing to vent.

Then, if you want, switch to conversation mode. Discuss what you've been talking about. Brainstorm some possible solutions *if* you feel like it. (There are numerous suggestions throughout this book on how to influence what's going on around you. Be sure to visit Chapters 8, 10, and 30.)

More heresy—Forgiveness as bunk?

We all make unintentional mistakes. Forgiveness is warranted and beneficial. They screw up, you forgive them. You screw up, they forgive you. Maybe you really messed up—that's where atonement comes in. Do what you can to "fix it", to compensate for it. But what if someone seriously messes with your life and they did it intentionally? Forgive them? Sorry, guess I'm not that "nice".

Does "forgiving" them feel too much like saying it was okay that they did that? Does to me. Sorry—no, not okay. (I can hear the shrinks salivating.) If they did it intentionally or with callous disregard for the impact of their actions, are they likely to learn much from talking about it? Maybe. Maybe not. Maybe the consequences have been truly nasty. Ouch. That's why we have laws, shrinks, and healers.

Yet the more you fret, fuss, and fume, the more hold it has on you—and the more damage it will do—to you. Sure, see if you can learn something from the situation. You want to reduce the chance of it ever happening again. But don't get caught up playing detective in other people's minds and motivations. Don't get stuck in the drama and intrigue of trying to "understand why". Or in plotting how to get even. That's stupidly self-destructive, though it may be temporarily gratifying to fantasize a little. *Instead, do what you can, do what it takes, to LET IT GO.* Yes, that may take some practice, and some time. Move on. With some help if you need it. You don't need to "forgive" to let it go, so don't waste energy trying. Save your energy for solutions, not fixations, and for taking care of yourself.

Smaller Dents, and Atonements

Someone disappoints you or makes a mistake that negatively impacts you.
(Your brother forgot to call on your birthday? Any other examples come to mind?)
What would you like them to do to make it up to you, to "fix things"?
Did they, will they, do that? Did you actually talk about it with them? Why not?

You disappoint someone else or make a mistake that negatively impacts them.
Give an example or two. What could you do to rectify the situation, make it up to them? Would you? Why or why not? Go fix it.
What could you do differently to minimize the chances of similar disappointments?

Serious Dents

"Do unto others as you would have them do unto you." We all need to do what we can to prevent injustices. And we need to help remedy the negative outcomes of injustices, whether they were deliberately committed or not.

Some wrong-doers have truly pathological minds. Scary. Some "normal" people, as individuals or as a group, let loose their self-absorbed greed or anger, with nasty results. Yet perhaps surprisingly, others, with intentions that are originally benevolent, can set in motion long-lasting effects that are profoundly destructive. As "good people" who would not likely ever consider ourselves "wrong-doers", *we must give thought to what the impact will be on those who wear the consequences of our decisions.*

An example? I'm thinking of the Residential Schools inflicted on the indigenous populations of North America, in the name of "assimilating the natives" (who were already healthy, viable cultures). The self-righteous arrogance, and the methods used, became a shameful example of how not to treat our fellow humans, especially children. The Reconciliation Process, now underway, will attempt to address the needs of the multi-generational victims and the consciences of those who have inherited the responsibility of atoning for that unfortunate period in our history. It will not be a brief process, but hopefully it will help people find some peace and thus let them move on with their lives.

There is more to true Justice than punishment. Thankfully, there are now more places where other methods, and *prevention*, are being studied and implemented.

Enough of the heavy-hearted stuff! Let's switch to the upside!
Let's be grateful that—amongst the gripes, grumps, and occasional dents—most of us have so very much to be thankful for.

Gratitudes

Gratitudes

Make a list of at least ten aspects of your life that you're grateful for.
(We do take a lot for granted—like having a best friend, and toilet paper—not that I'd put them in the same category, but you get what I mean.)

Be inspired.

Find five quotes, sayings, or song-bites that make you feel good.
Put them where you will see them everyday.

Be kind.

Do one random act of kindness this weekend.

Compliment at least one person a day for the next week.
("I like the way you did such and such", or "That shirt looks good on you.")

Express your appreciation.

Tell two people at least one reason why you appreciate having them in your life.

Learn from others.

Collect stories from your friends, relatives, or strangers about what they're happy about and grateful for. Ask people from each of these age groups: your own age, middle age, over 65, and kids under 9 years old.

Ask them to describe an experience that pleased them. Perhaps a surprise party? Ask them to comment on other aspects of their life that they're grateful for. (Here's one we don't often think of—we have safe drinking water here that we don't have to walk miles to get.) If they say something that's very general such as "good health", ask them to elaborate a little. What's the benefit of that benefit?

Do they think that they had some input into helping that good-thing happen? If so, in what way? Do they think that it was just luck? Or a little of each? How could they help this good-thing happen again, or continue?

What you could do to contribute to someone else's sense of well being?

Briefly describe a way they could contribute to yours. Have you asked? Who knows, it might bring them considerable pleasure to do something that would bring you pleasure, if you actually communicated more clearly what that might be.

Gripes, grumps, and gratitudes—Good luck or bad?
Anything we can do about that?

Chapter 4

Creating Luck

Photograph by Di Gibson

Black cats, ladders, and broken mirrors. Lucky rabbit's feet, horseshoes, and rainbows....

Do you buy Lottery tickets? After all, if you don't buy a ticket, you're not going to win. But do you know what the odds of winning a million actually are? Statistically, you're twice as likely to get hit by lightning. Are you basing what you hope for and expect out of life on chance, luck, and wishful thinking? But hey, who knows? Someone wins these things. Why not you?

Serendipity does exist. Miracles even.

Were you born in a safe and beautiful place, or where bullets fly? Chance. Would you consider yourself a person who was "born with a silver spoon in your mouth"? Or was that spoon stainless steel? Or plastic? In other words, were you blessed with a financially secure and supportive family? Or not? Chance. Your early childhood path? Your neighbourhood back then? Chance.

Maybe you were amazingly lucky about where you started (great parents, lots of love, lots of money). Maybe so far your "road of life" has been remarkably smooth. Yet, if you're honest with yourself, some part of you knows that there likely will be potholes and detours, maybe heavy rain, or possibly even wash-outs en route. Some things in life you can't control. Ouch. Not that everyone has an interest in being a boy scout, but "be prepared" is a good motto.

Should we carry a rabbit's foot too? In a 1996 Gallup poll of 1000 Americans, 53% said they were slightly superstitious, 25% somewhat or very superstitious.[1] Why are we so superstitious? We know that there are times when luck, good or bad, can make or break us. And we know that surprises, both good and bad, are not rare. We'd feel safer in the world if we felt we had some influence over these. And we do, but not in the way we might initially think.

Why do superstitious beliefs and behaviors persist? "Throughout history, people have recognized that … a few seconds of ill fortune can lay waste to years of striving, and moments of good luck can save an enormous amount of hard work. Superstition represents people's attempts to control and enhance this most elusive of factors." It "comes from a time when people thought that luck was a strange force that could only be controlled by magical rituals and bizarre behaviors." [2]

Talismans and lucky charms may bolster our belief in being luckier. But do they actually work? Not in the way we think. *If* they open our minds to more and better possibilities, then in some small way, they might. Bona fide research, however, shows that superstition does not work. Luckily, there *are* ways to improve your Luck. Read on.

What's the difference between Luck and Chance?

Chance? An unforeseen event, often without assignable cause. A happening without premeditation or deliberation. Sometimes chance is thought of as a force in itself. There are truly rare events, like asteroids annihilating the dinosaurs. There are some forms of randomness that—once the occurrences are math-ed out—show a statistical pattern and hence some level of predictability. There are other times when a confluence of variables sets up a cascade of effects that no one could have seen coming. An example? A small number of computers being hooked together, simply to help a few researchers exchange data, morphing into the internet.

Luck? Richard Wiseman, a psychologist at the University of Hertfordshire in the UK, has spent almost two decades studying Luck and its influence in people's lives. To distinguish between luck and chance he uses the example of winning a lottery.[3] We have no control over that, other than to buy a ticket. While those kinds of chance events will have a major impact on someone's life, they are not frequent. He's found that when people consistently experience good fortune, good luck—or bad—it's actually because of something they are doing.

What's the link between risk and "bad luck"?

Risk can be defined as chance x damage, as the possibility of a negative outcome. Sometimes this is interpreted as "bad luck".

Just how risky is a particular risk? Sometimes that is harder to assess than we'd like. What can go wrong? How likely is a negative outcome? What are the potential consequences if it does occur? How extensive would the impact be to our work or to our personal life? To others?

Here's one example: the chance might be relatively small in terms of statistical probability, at least on this continent, that a new sex partner is HIV+. There is a chance too that they may not be aware of it themselves or that they may lie to you. The potential damage? Profound, debilitating, irreversible. Scary stupid risk. Bag it.

Other risks? Many people worry, justifiably, about the possibility of being exposed to H5N1, SARS, TB, or some other nasty contagion. Yet they're still smoking, still having unprotected sex, still texting while driving—all self-induced risks. Why is the risk of succumbing to a pathogenic microbe more frightening than the very real *and statistically more probable risks* inherent in the careless things we do to ourselves?

Are we more likely to accept the blame for a negative consequence resulting from our own actions, or to try to duck that responsibility by blaming it on "bad luck"? (Apparently we're better at re-writing history than at forecasting our futures.)

We need to have the courage to assess our own part, however small, in what happens to us. That includes the influence we might have by our actions or inaction over both the bad and the beneficial consequences of luck in our lives. For example, if you're foolish enough to drink and drive, you shouldn't have the right to sue your host or the bartender. Grow up! At your age, it's no one else's job to change your diapers. (For an adult, that's a medical condition not a motivational issue.)

When we do our best to assess and take steps, in advance, to counteract each of the possible downsides of a particular risk, we substantially decrease the chances of our experiencing "bad luck". In fact, we increase the opportunities to feel, and to be, luckier than most.

Creating your own luck

There are several kinds of luck.

Serendipity. Right place, right time. Purely coincidence.

Luck in hindsight.
You didn't know at the time that meeting so-and-so would turn out to be a wonderful break for your career or for your personal life.

Luck you have a hand in creating.
Be better prepared for opportunities that may show up. Improve the skills you would need for the context you want to move towards.
Know what you want. Or at least be able to recognize it when you see it.
Pay attention. Notice opportunities in whatever context you're in.
Use your initiative. Create opportunities if there don't seem to be any.

> Life is not a tidy process. It's an adventure. And making mistakes does not make you a fool or a failure. A fool? Someone who makes the same mistakes over and over. A failure? Someone who gives up before really trying. You're neither—you've chosen to learn how to get on with things.

Luck can't be controlled. Luckily, it can be influenced and harnessed.

"Luck isn't due to kismet, karma, or coincidence". Instead, "lucky folks – without even knowing it … think and behave in ways that create good fortune in their lives." [4]

Gems from Wiseman's Research

Wiseman and his group have shown that we have much more control than we think over the Luck in our lives. In fact, his research has revealed that lucky people help generate their own good fortune in a number of ways.

- Lucky people create, notice, and act upon chance opportunities. How? They build and maintain a network of people from various walks of life.
- Their relaxed attitude enables them to be more open to new experiences. They deliberately create more variety in their lives which increases the potential for serendipitous encounters. Routine, on the other hand, exhausts our opportunities.[5] People who see themselves as unlucky, sadly, tend to avoid the new or different which then, in turn, limits their possibilities.
- Lucky people respect, bolster, and listen to their intuition. They base their assessment of a need for caution, not simply on the facts, but on what their gut is telling them as well. And they don't ignore those warnings. Unlucky people instead "choose to continue with their wishful thinking and self-denial".[6]
  To better hear your intuition, give yourself quiet-mind-space. Perhaps learn to meditate.[7]

- Their positive expectations become self-fulfilling prophesies.[8] They actively seek solutions to problems and go after their goals even when the chances of success aren't high. (They do not set truly impossible goals.)
- They persevere when the going gets tough. They expect their interactions with others to be positive. (They're not, however, blindly naïve.) Their open and friendly manner and sensible attitude encourages constructive interaction.
- They learn to transform bad luck to good. How? They look at the bright side. They assume that bad luck is temporary, and that there's a reasonable chance something good might come of it, at least eventually.
- They don't fixate on the ill fortune. They do allow themselves some "Grr" and "Waa" time, but then distract themselves with something enjoyable. And they take constructive steps to prevent additional "bad luck" in the future by learning what they could do differently. (Three car accidents? Improve your driving skills![9] And pay attention to the road, not your gadgets.)

According to personality tests, unlucky people tend to be more anxious.[10] (Gee, I wonder why?) That anxiety, unfortunately, disrupts their ability to notice the opportunities around them. This is especially true if they expect that good things won't happen to them. (There's that self-fulfilling prophesy again.)

Whether we consider ourselves lucky or not, we need to realize that when we're too tightly focused on finding Exactly-what-we-want we can miss an awesome opportunity that's right in front of us.[11]

Another way that lucky people's mindsets are different is that they practice "counterfactual thinking". (That's what psychologists call our ability to imagine what might have happened rather than focusing on the facts of what did happen.) Wiseman says that lucky people will immediately imagine how things could have been worse. Ironically, this improves their mood and their overall outlook on life. This "find the treasure in the trash" attitude helps keep their expectations about the future high.[12] He emphasises that they don't dwell on the ill fortune and that they take control by improving their situation in whatever way they possibly can.

An example? A nasty car accident. You can't change the facts: something unfortunate did happen. "Lucky" people acknowledge that they had an accident but are happy that they weren't maimed or killed and that they didn't kill someone else. It would never occur to the "unlucky" people to see the situation that way. And they're certainly not likely to consider that this unlucky event, while a scary nuisance, may not even matter in the long-term. Interestingly, both ways of thinking—lucky and oh-poor-me—are unconscious and automatic. Luckily, you can learn to Think-and-Do yourself into actually being luckier. (More in a minute.)

(I don't much like the term "counterfactual". We're not countering the facts or denying the realities, we're choosing a different way of looking at the same outcome. I prefer the term "reframing"—reinterpreting the same situation from a different perspective. You've been diagnosed with cancer. Reframe—they caught it early. The next few months? Rough. But you do have the rest of your life to look forward to.)

When slammed by life, "Lucky people wobble, but they don't fall down."[13] Their attitude-of-gratitude and solution-finding mindset keeps them buoyant.

Learn to be lucky

Wiseman and his group have set up a Luck School where they teach people techniques to bolster their luck. First, they ask the participants to make a month long commitment to learning to be luckier. Here are some of their suggestions: [14]

- Keep a Luck Diary. At the end of each day, spend a few moments writing down the positive and lucky things that happened. Don't write down the unlucky stuff. After a month of accumulating an awareness of what's positive, it's hard not to focus more on the good things that are happening.
- Cut the occasional bad luck down to size by deliberately imagining how things could have been worse and by being grateful that they weren't. Be proactive about solving any issues that did arise and find ways to defuse or avoid similar problems in the future.
- Mix it up. Deliberately break daily routines and thus create new opportunities for potential lucky breaks.

The beneficial results of these techniques have been amazing. "The project ... is about encouraging people to move away from a magical way of thinking to a more rational view of luck." Perhaps most important of all, it is "using science and scepticism to increase the level of luck, happiness, and success in people's lives." [15]

> Not everything happens for a reason. But we can, with reason and a little courage, make something of what happened.

Three true luck-stories

Your job is driving you crazy, and you're looking for more suitable work. To de-stress, you take up boxing. (It's better than punching out your boss.) One of the guys who works out at the same gym just opened up a business and you're the perfect right hand man. (You were breaking out of your routines. And you had your eyes and ears open.)

All flights are grounded in Chicago because of a snow storm. People get chatting in the line-ups. A number of you go for dinner and end up talking well into the wee hours. Fast forward. You're married to the man who was standing next to you in line: twenty years later you're still nuts about each other. (Serendipity. Luck in hindsight.)

It's your first year at university. Your marks weren't the greatest so you weren't in the early acceptances. You're finally in, but most of the courses you want are already full. Do you just take whatever courses you can get? Work for a semester? Try to get in elsewhere? You decide to go part-time, taking courses you know you want, and find part-time work that'll help you build the skills you'll need when you eventually graduate. You take a couple of summer courses. The following year you get into the appropriate co-op program which, by the way, pays you. Five years later? You've no student loan debts. You love your work. And you were hired the day you finished school: you had not only the degree but real-world skills. (Luck you have a hand in creating.)

Further reading

The Luck Factor, Richard Wiseman
The Lazy Person's Guide To Success, Ernie J. Zelinski

Take This In ...

Yay! Luck is not something we're born with. Or not. We *can* get luckier in life! No superstition required—good luck isn't relegated to rainbows or rabbits' feet.

Our lives tend to be a mix of levels of luck, of intensities of both good and bad. And we may seem to be luckier in some areas of our lives, less so in others. What are we doing, or not doing, that impacts each of those? The point? We can influence our luck! We can tweak our thoughts. Shift our mindset. Change a few behaviors. There are realistic and researched ways to increase the good luck we experience in our daily lives. Fabulous!

Think of **Luck as *Awareness* plus Action[16]—relaxed creative *Action*.**

Awareness

- Know what you want now. Have a sense of what you might want later. That way you're more likely to recognize IT when it's right in front of you.
- Be deliberately aware of, and appreciate, the ways in which you already are so very lucky. (Have you done the Gratitudes Activities on page 21 yet?)
- Increase the chances of serendipity and synchronicity. Shuffle your deck. Play new cards. Get out of your rut more often than you currently do.
- Stay conscious. Be aware. Notice the possibilities around you!
- In which aspects of your life do you seem to have more luck? What could you learn from *how you do those* that might help with the lesser-luck areas?

Relaxed Action

- Be proactive. Pursue what you want, but in a relaxed rather than crazed way. Where did we ever get the idea that being uptight and anxious improved our effectiveness at anything?

When you are lucky, you come to expect good luck.
(That doesn't mean you're denying that sometimes less-than-lucky things will happen.)

When you consider yourself lucky, you notice more of the lucky aspects of your life. (And you're better able to roll with the occasional less-than-optimal or disappointing occurrences.)

Pay attention. Notice more of what's going on. "Count your blessings". Be proactive. And, as the research shows, you actually will become luckier. Sweet!

> That we have the OPPORTUNITY to take action and to make decisions for ourselves, is lucky in itself!

Luck and opportunities can show up both when we're prepared and when we least expect them. And they can disappear just as fast. So knowing IF and WHEN to seize the moment is a truly important life skill.

Decision-making strategies come next.

Chapter 5

Tools and Strategies for
Effective Decision-Making

How lucky for us, in this part of the world, that we can find or create our own opportunities and that we have numerous options to explore. How do we then narrow down those possibilities? Aha. There's not just one "right answer". There's not just one viable and enjoyable path-up-the-mountain. But how do we decide which path to take?

If you haven't yet done the "Three Lists" and "What matters to you?" activities in Chapters 1 and 2, please do them now. Knowing what you value is crucial in making good decisions. It helps you choose where to put your resources: your time, energy, attention, and money.

To improve your life, you don't need to make great decisions all of the time. You simply need to make slightly better decisions more of the time. "Just-a-little-better" implemented here and there, can create truly impressive results.

Facing a choice? Uncomfortable about some minor, or major, aspect of your life? That could be as simple as which apartment to choose or what to do for a holiday, or as daunting as whether to move to another country or leave your spouse. Perhaps life has imposed a need to explore other options—maybe your job just evaporated out from under you. Ouch.

What is the issue, the dilemma, you want or need to resolve?
Define it as well as you can. For example –

- You're surrounded by noisy rude neighbours. Your apartment is freezing in winter, baking in summer. Or your dad is getting too frail to live on his own.
- Or maybe it's a "problem" born of a happy circumstance. You need to upgrade your wardrobe because you just landed a fabulous job. Or you've been dating several nice people but have found someone really special, and you're wondering how to say "Sorry" to the others. Or you've been accepted at all three schools you applied to and now must make a choice.
- Maybe there are some changes that need to be made at work. Are you the one in charge? Or do you have to work with others to figure out what's going to happen when? Or are you at the bottom of the ladder, wondering what's coming down? Maybe you need to upgrade your skills. Maybe you already have because you want a promotion, or want out. Maybe you've been head-hunted and now have two very nice job offers. That's definitely a nice "problem".

Before deciding to decide ...

Decide if what you're dealing with is a PROBLEM or simply a CHOICE.
If it's a problem, is it a minor inconvenience, a considerable nuisance, life-altering or even life-threatening? The energy, time, and other resources we're willing to put into resolving the issue obviously need to be adjusted accordingly.

It's a PROBLEM if ...

- You're not clear, yet, about the criteria for the solution you'd prefer. Try this. Pretend the problem is no longer a problem. Imagine the situation as though things are going exactly as you want them to. What does that look like? (You can figure out later what changes need to be made and how to make them.) Do you and any others involved agree about what a viable solution would look like?
- You can't decide how important it is to even make a decision. Or when.
- You're unsure about whether there's adequate information on the feasibility of certain options, or how to get it.
- You don't yet have or can't get what's needed to implement the solution.

To transform the problem into simply a choice, resolve these ambiguities. But don't expect to be able to nail down all the contingencies and details before making a decision. There are times when we need to get comfortable with a little ambiguity—that's easier for some than others. (More later.)

It's simply a CHOICE when ...

- You're clear about what you want as a result.
- There is more than one viable solution. And ways to get reasonably good information about each.
- It's a choice between benefits, not right or wrong, good or bad solutions. (The potential for a downside is minimal, and the risk can be contained.)
- You and any others involved agree about the relative importance of the goal, and when to get moving on it.
- There are adequate resources available to meet the goal or, at the very least, ways to find them.

Do you need to make a decision now?
What might be the consequences of postponing action? Of acting too soon?
How could you assess these?

Examine the contributing factors...
Not only to what isn't working, but to what is. For both, think in terms of Who (including yourself), What, When, Where, Why, and How. In examining these factors, you're not looking to direct blame, but to find where all concerned can best direct their energy, time and other resources.

Are others going to share in the consequences of the decision?
If so, it's wise to involve them in the decision-making process, both to avoid backlash and to smooth the buy-in and implementation of the new ideas. Besides, they may see potential solutions and viable strategies that you haven't considered.

Play with possibilities.

Look for what does work and what could work under what circumstances. Look for how best to implement more of those ideas, actions, and contexts. Look for any one thing that if done a little differently or a little more effectively would set things off in a better direction. Get the ball rolling.

Interestingly, you don't necessarily need to "fix" a problem to create a solution. Implementing a slightly better way of tackling even a small component of the problem can often dissipate or dissolve it.

> Governments—want to cut our dependency on foreign oil? Instead of propping up wasteful business practices and environmental stupidity with big-business bail-outs, increase the rebates to better subsidize the taxpayers for the difference in cost between the stuck-think i.e. gas-guzzlers, and the new-think, i.e. hybrids and e-cars. (Americans, check out hybridcars.com: it outlines hybrid and e-car subsidies and perks. Canadians, see emc-mec.ca.) And encourage people to buy domestic cars by eliminating the purchase taxes on autos built here, but only if they have excellent fuel efficiencies. *Doing so would create and sustain more jobs in the long run.* And Businesses—large and small—there's good money to be made by *leading* positive change. Innovations that build a healthier world also build your business!

You don't want to get stuck in analysis-paralysis. Yet you also don't want to miss a viable first-rate option because you settle too soon. The most convenient or seemingly obvious option may not be the best. Brainstorm as many solutions as you can, even some seemingly quite silly ones. These at least may add a little laughter to the process. (Being more light-hearted expands the imagination and bolsters creativity.) For all of these possibilities—from the most practical and promising to the slightly hair-brained—generate ideas for "this might work if..." The best solution may in fact arise from a meshing together of those that initially seemed to be more than a little outside-the-box.

No matter what option you choose there will be a few hurdles to navigate. And you know instinctively, and from experience, that you're not likely to be able to foresee and control all the possible variations in the outcomes of any decision. "C'est la vie."

Yet better decisions do make for a better life. It's worth the effort it takes to improve your decision-making skills—you'll have more influence over your own life and in the world-out-there. How do we do that? How do we generate "the right answer"? What's the theory here? In the mid-1600's, mathematicians came up with Probability Theory. (How likely is it that a certain something will happen?) Fast forward. Now we have "Decision Theory" which considers humans to be "rational optimizers" who weigh various options and choose the "highest expected utility". Or not. In an international forum in 2011, scientists and other think-tank types pooled resources to further explore the other powerful forces that shape our decisions. Conscious and rational are only part of it. We need to take into account the effect of our "innate biases, emotions, expectations, misconceptions, conformity, and other all-too-human factors. While our decision-making may seem inconsistent or occasionally downright perverse, the truly intriguing thing is just how often these seemingly irrational forces help us make the right choice." [1]

Know that there isn't necessarily going to be just one "right answer". Consider Life as a write-your-own-adventure game with any number of possibilities. Your choices, your decisions, help you steer your adventure. Make them good ones.

In this chapter we'll be exploring a number of conscious and unconscious decision making strategies. They're listed below.

Decision-making strategies at the MORE CONSCIOUS levels:

Pairs and Apples
Pros, Cons, and Consequences with a Risk Twist
Head and Heart

Decision-making at LESS CONSCIOUS levels:

Habits
Memes
Blink

In the next chapter, we'll look at how to minimize overwhelm and angst while maximizing the benefits of better decision-making strategies, and at how we evaluate and interpret the results of our decision.

Keep in mind ...

- Like any skill, decision-making requires practice.
- The solution may be far simpler and easier than you think.
  Small changes can often solve big problems. Tug-boats move huge ships.
- Be your own captain. As much as possible, be the one steering your own life. And enjoy having a positive impact on what goes on around you.
- Get better at formulating good questions. Ask them, of the right people.
- Practice the skill of adapting as circumstances evolve.
- Know that you can't control everything. (Interestingly, that's not necessarily a disadvantage.) Yet you can control what you do in response.
- Again, the majority of the time, there is not just one right choice!
  (Perhaps you want a holiday with lots of sunshine and lovely breezes, and you want to be able to play and explore or to sit on a cliff and stare at a beautiful expanse of water. That's your criteria. The possible solutions could be in New Zealand, the Caribbean, Northern Ontario or any number of other places.)

Looking forward...

Pick any one decision you want to make in the next few months.
Briefly outline the issue that needs to be dealt with. Is it a problem or simply a choice?

Think back to a previous decision.
Was it a problem to be solved or a choice to be made?

Keep any notes you make on these; they might be useful examples to play with as you skill-build during this chapter.

Conscious Decision-making

Pairs and Apples

With this method, you're not required to sift through in advance the practical aspects of every option. You simply go with your gut reaction to your options two at a time.[2] Let's think desserts. (Maybe because my sweet tooth just kicked in.) Of course you wouldn't bother to use this formal a technique on a decision as simple as what dessert you're in the mood for. A more realistic use? Young people sorting through the colleges they might prefer, or soon-to-be parents choosing a name for their soon-to-arrive. Or perhaps for deciding who, of those you've been dating, you might want to build a more meaningful relationship with?

List your possible options. Let's do seven here, as a nice odd number.
Do more, or less, if you feel like it, and adapt the size of the table (below) to fit.
Our dessert example is listed on the left. On the right, list the options you're looking at for the decision you're currently contemplating.

1 - Poached Pear with whipped cream	1 -
2 - Apple Crisp with a little vanilla ice cream	2 -
3 - Key Lime pie	3 -
4 - Chocolate Ice Cream	4 -
5 - Banana split	5 -
6 - Crêpes with raspberries	6 -
7 - Crème brûlée	7 -

Pretend you're choosing between just two at a time.
In the chart below, for our dessert choices...

1 2 would mean you choose between Poached Pear and Apple Crisp.
1 3 between Poached Pear or Key Lime pie.
1 4 Poached Pear or Chocolate Ice Cream?
Etc.
2 3 Apple Crisp or Key Lime pie?
And so on ... (Yum...Getting hungry yet?)

Circle your choice for each pair.

1 2					
1 3	2 3				
1 4	2 4	3 4			
1 5	2 5	3 5	4 5		
1 6	2 6	3 6	4 6	5 6	
1 7	2 7	3 7	4 7	5 7	6 7

To arrive at your decision, count the times you have circled each option.

#1 __ #2 __ #3 __ #4 __ #5 __ #6 __ #7 __

Your preference is the option with the most circles.
Mind you, with that list of desserts, how could you lose? (Personally, I'd be eating Key Lime pie, and probably too much of it.)

Pros, Cons, and Consequences—with a risk-twist

What is the issue?

You're totally fed up with your job?
Or perhaps you need child care?

Briefly describe SEVERAL possibilities that might resolve the issue.

Sick of your workplace, your career? If you're independently wealthy, quit. (Ya right.) Look for ways to modify your current job to make it more palatable. Or look for another company to work for. Maybe get some career counseling and retrain for something more suitable and pleasing to you. (Visit Chapters 9 and 20 later.)

Need child care? You could find a full time nanny or a good day care center, call in the grandparents, or share child care with a neighbour.

Let's get started: What's the issue?

What are some possible solutions?

<u>Pros</u> List the advantages for *each* option.	For Option One 1 2 3	For Option Two	For Option Three
How *likely* is each advantage? Very, maybe 50/50, or unlikely?			
What do you need to KNOW and DO to **help this happen?**			
Where can you find this out?			

<u>Cons</u> List the possible downsides for each option.	Option One: 1 2 3	Option Two:	Option three:
How likely is each possible downside to happen? Very, maybe 50/50, or unlikely?			
What do you need to KNOW and DO to help this *not* happen?			
Where can you find this out?			

Work through the Pros & Cons of all the options, and make a preliminary decision. Then examine this preliminary decision with regards to the possible consequences.

Time frames
What will be the likely effect now? (Think days, weeks.)
In the long term? (Think months, years.)

Who will this impact?
What will be the consequences for you personally?
Who else will share the benefits or the fallout from this decision? In what ways?

What further thoughts, questions surface? What else do you need to know?
Do these considerations make you want to revisit your preliminary decision?
If so, revisit the other options and repeat the above steps.
Perhaps create a new option from the best parts of all the others.

Resolve any remaining concerns. Implement your choice.
Adapt, modify, as needed.

For the **Action steps** on how to do this, see Chapter 10, "Goals and A-LISTS".

Head and Heart

Spencer Johnson, an internationally respected MD and psychologist, produced an easy-to-read book and audio series called *Yes or No, The Guide to Better Decision Making*. As best-sellers, these have been translated into a number of languages including Spanish, Korean and German. His "decision map", presented as a short story, is useful for everyone—for both personal and career decisions.

Amongst his many valuable recommendations, I found two particularly useful.

- Logical decision making, "the Head", bases a decision on facts and figures. When *Yes or No* first came out in the 1990's, and even now, rational-and-logical tends to be the acceptable way, especially in the business world. Most did, and many still do, distrust using "the Heart", our internal self, as a component of sensible decision-making. Johnson reaffirmed how both, in any context, are crucial.
- He proposed a savvy and empowering strategy. Unless we are able to answer a clear "Yes or No" to certain questions we're not yet adequately ready, practically or psychologically, to make that particular decision. [3]

Before starting, ask yourself the following:

- What am I trying to solve? What are the facts? What feelings are associated with the issue?
- What do I want to do, if anything, about this? Do I really need to make this decision? If so, when? Do I need to make it now?
- Do I know what *not* to do? Do I know what to stop doing if it's taking me in the wrong direction, or preventing me from going in the right one? [4]
- If I made this decision my usual way, what would my decision be? Did this decision work well last time? Did it produce good results? Yes or no? [5]

To make a better decision, it's important to muster the courage to let go of what's familiar, and take a fresh look at the situation. [6]

We need to look at *both* the Head and the Heart, in either order. Each requires answers to three questions. (The outline that follows is a paraphrased summary of the *Yes or No* training, adapted with the kind permission of Dr. Johnson and his publishers.)

HEAD - The Practical Side

(1) Yes or No? Is this a real NEED? Or merely a WANT?

Remember that Needs must trump Wants. If we haven't met our genuine needs, even getting what-we-want can still leave us wanting. (We may want a fancy house, but we need a loving home.[7] Wants? "What do I wish I could do?" Needs? Later, what will you wish you had done?[8] Clarify what is that real need, and the desired result.

(2) **Yes or No?** **Have I informed myself of options?**

- Know you do have options. Your fears may be interfering with your ability to recognize and implement those options.[9]
- Figure out what information you need, and get it. Then carefully verify it.[10]
- Be patient with the process.[11] "It takes less time to make a better decision than to correct a poor one."[12] Just remember that not making a decision is a decision in itself, and often the wrong one.

(3) **Yes or No?** **Have I thought it through *all the way* to the results?**

- "The more clearly you see the results you need in the end, the easier it is to deal with whatever might happen along the way." [13]
- Which option is most likely to meet the real need? [14]
- Keep asking "Then what?" repeatedly.[15] (Decisions are rather like dominos.[16]) Anticipate possible problems. Then what? What would I do if that happened? What would be the best result? Then what? What would I do if that happened?
- Say NO to whatever won't help you get to the desired results. Avoid distractions.[17]

How do you measure your results? By how well they satisfy your *real* need.[18]

HEART - Our Internal Self

"Heart" is our internal private side. It's a combination of the conversations we have with ourselves, our beliefs and character, plus our intuition.[19]

(1) **Yes or No?** **Am I being honest with myself?**

"People with **integrity** won't fool themselves about a situation. They will cut through the nonsense and get through to the true core of things quickly."[20] Johnson defines "integrity as telling yourself the truth, honesty as being truthful with others." We may temporarily feel safer or more comfortable hiding from the truth.[21] But doing so has consequences that are much more inconvenient, and scarier, than facing our realities.

- What might I not be seeing? What might I *not want* to be seeing, and as a result am ignoring? "An illusion is a fiction we believe because we want to."[22] Do you feel angry when someone tries to tell you something? Are you angry because you're trying to hide from some uncomfortable aspect of your reality? Look at what you *want* to believe, then check out its opposite. The reality is somewhere in between.[23] Unfortunately, this is just as true for entire countries as for individuals.[24]
- Talk with close friends. What do they see that you might not be noticing? What are you avoiding? What bits of what they're saying just might be true? [25] (Genuine friends help each other not get trapped in illusion.)
- Check out your experiences and the consequences of your past choices. What is the reality there?

Search for hidden—or chosen—fictions and illusions. Find the truth. Base your decisions and actions on reality. Otherwise, things *will* fall apart. (If your house is riddled with termites, there's little point in simply repainting.) [26]
Better decisions, which are based on a better sense of reality, create better results. And the sooner you see the truth, the sooner you can make a better decision. [27]

(2) **Yes or No? Am I trusting my intuition?**

Intuition is our unconscious knowledge, partly based on experience. It's what's often referred as our "gut" sense about something. Intuition comes from the root word "to watch over, protect, teach". What is my intuition trying to tell me? [28]

- How do I feel as I'm making this decision? "Calm or anxious? Paralyzed or confident? Drained or energized? … Afraid or enthusiastic?[29] Clear or confused?"[30] If you're feeling peaceful, it's likely the right decision. If you're rattled, maybe it's the wrong decision—or maybe you need to get answers to questions you may not yet have asked.[31] Or maybe it's your Ego speaking. Ego likes to deny what we don't like about ourselves, and moving forward may require us to face whatever that is.
- Fear complicates our decisions and actions. And many emotions are fear in disguise, including anger and resentment. Don't base your decisions on fear. Instead, use that fear as a cautionary note and examine ways to prevent a negative outcome from occurring. Then ask yourself, "What would I do if I were not afraid?" [32]
- Minds often get confused—try listening to, and listening with, your body. Meditate, commune with nature, pray, or do whatever you do to become quiet inside. Is this decision generating fear or enthusiasm? [33]
- Does this decision feel right? Does it feel like meeting a dear friend? If not, there's a good chance it isn't the right decision. [34]

(3) **Yes or No? Am I acting as though I deserve better?**

Insight is rooted in genuine awareness—of our realities, and of what we tell ourselves. Sometimes it's not laziness holding us back, but self-limiting beliefs. Unconscious self-sabotage is like driving with the brakes on.[35] Of course it's illogical. Why would we do what we know is not in our own best interest? We do it unknowingly. Consciously we think we do deserve better but, at some level, we're uncomfortable letting ourselves have a better quality of life than we currently have. To gain some insight into your insight, look at what you usually *do.* [36]

- Do your decisions, past and present, show you actually do believe you deserve better? Or not? For some, this might apply to their personal life *or* work life. For others, both. For you? Where do you seem to feel more, or less, deserving?
- At some point, you've likely been hit with the spoken or implied question, "Just who do you think you are?" [37]
- What would I decide to do *now* if I truly believed I deserved better? Do I believe enough in this decision to act on it soon? [38]

You want to become "less naïve and more aware"[39] about both your external realities and your internal self. Use both "a cool head and a warm heart" [40] to both clarify and motivate.

Johnson advises that you think, believe, ACT AS IF you do deserve better, just in case at some level you unknowingly don't believe it.[41] I'll add YET.

I'm going to throw in a few more questions for you to chew on.

- If there was an I-Deserve scale, where would you put yourself on it? At one extreme, you think you shouldn't have to put in any effort whatsoever to get what you want. At the other extreme, you think nothing good is ever going to come your way. (That could be cynicism, or low self-esteem.)
- Are you afraid to admit, especially to yourself, that you believe you're not capable of getting what you want out of life?
- Were childhood expectations too high to meet? Or so low you thought others saw you as neither capable nor worthy? And what about bullying, then and now? And stereotyping? Are you still buying into imposed scripts?

What do you actually believe you deserve? Now, ironically, make that not matter. **Get proactive. Don't wait. DO the doing.** Continue to expand your capabilities.

Learning from our past decision styles.

Choose one decision you made in the **recent past**, and examine it thoroughly according to Johnson's Head and Heart criteria.

In retrospect, what might you change, if anything?
What might you have seen coming if you'd paid more attention?
Do I see better now how that decision revealed my beliefs?
What would I have done if I had "acted as if..."?
What would you choose—now—to do, if faced with a similar decision?

Now choose one decision you want to make in the **near future**, and try out his approach for making a better decision.

HEAD: Answer Yes or No to each:
Is this a real need?
Have I got the information I need and informed myself of options?
Have I thought it through—thoroughly?

HEART: Answer Yes or No to each:
Am I being honest with myself?
Am I trusting my intuition?
Am I acting as though I deserve better?

Use that "cool head and warm heart" to both clarify and motivate.

Decisions at the less conscious levels

Habits

Habits are the choices we've made, over and over again, to the point where we no longer need to consciously decide about whether or how to do those things. As habits, they're now ingrained, now below the level of conscious thought. They've become part of our autopilot system.

You probably brush your teeth daily and shower more than once a week. We hope. You probably put on clothing before you go out the door, at least when it's cold outside. You likely wear your seat belt. Even driving itself, with all the component skills that had to be learned and practiced and practiced and practiced some more, becomes habit, becomes second nature. Being able to hand off routine tasks and actions to Habit frees up our mind for those parts of life that require our more focused conscious attention—which is a major bonus, as long as they're beneficial habits.

ACTIONS as Habits

Name three beneficial habits.
Name three less than beneficial habits. (Like smoking?)
For each, ask yourself what got you started.
What kept you doing that particular activity until it became a habit?

What could you modify in your surroundings so that you're more likely to make slightly better choices? To decrease the likelihood of back-sliding? For example, throw out the trashy junk-food stashed in your cupboards. Instead, pamper yourself with delicious fruit, nuts, or high-quality chocolate which is also full of high-quality nutrients. (As with anything else, just don't overdo it!) If you feel a need for a bulk-snack to stuff your face, pop your own popcorn. Sprinkle on some herbs or spices if you want to zing it up.

IDEAS as Habits

This might be a little more of a challenge. **Think of beliefs as habitual ideas.**

List at least two of your beliefs that, at one point, were a *conscious* personal choice. Just as an experiment, pretend you think the opposite. What would you do differently if that were the case? (For example, "You're an adult when you're old enough to drink". Actually, you're more of an adult when you're savvy enough to know when not to.)

List three habitual ideas that you've picked up from others: from other individuals in your life, from your culture, or from society as a whole. These are referred to as MEMES. (No, not "me-me"—meme, pronounced like cream.) That's next.

Shake up your habits. Try something different. Who knows? Maybe sprucing yourself up with a new haircut will dislodge your resistance to cleaning out the garage or looking for that new job you think you want. You'd be surprised what a difference a small change can make. Even tiny improvements can transform into big motivators.

Memes

We inherit genes. We also apparently "inherit" memes. "Meme" is a term originally coined by Richard Dawkins in the late 70's. "Memes are ideas, skills, stories, songs or inventions that are passed from person to person by imitation." Indeed, "everything you have learnt by copying it from someone else is a meme." [42] The premise is that how we come to view the world, and ourselves, gets absorbed from the setting in which we are steeped—the norms and customs of our context become our view of how-things-are. Watch the 1995 movie *Babe*, if you haven't already seen it, for a fun and easily digested—the movie, not the pig—example of how-things-are.

Our interpretation of eye contact is one example of a meme. In one country, it might be considered invasive and rude. In another, lack of adequate eye contact is considered one of the signs of a sneaky person.

We are unaware, at a conscious level, of the pervasiveness of the impact of memes on our life and on our definition of self. Whether it's our culture or religion, our taste in music and fashion or our preferences for a certain lifestyle, we are profoundly influenced by our context. It's not necessary to get into a heavy academic discussion of memes. What is necessary is that we look at how our definitions of who-we-are and the choices we make are influenced, or hijacked, by how-things-are norms.

We owe it to ourselves to evaluate whether or not these hand-me-down ways of being are worthy of being how we view the world. How much influence are we going to let the various memes have over what we think, believe, value, and do? Unlike genes, we can make choices about our memes. Drag them out into the conscious light. Some we may be quite happy to incorporate into who we are. Others we may choose to modify, reject, or ignore.

Want an example? Why at Christmas these days (read Santa-mas) do people spend more money than they can afford to buy people things they don't want or need? Is it about genuine affection and wanting to please? Or is it now I *must* give? Has the custom become slightly tainted with a sense of obligation? Or is it an ego-need for status—an "I too can buy that" tantrum, even if you actually can't afford to? That's sad. And silly. Back off on the stuff. Why not show you appreciate someone by doing something for them or with them instead? I'm sure the Creator would approve even if the sellsters wouldn't. Of course I'm into some fun toys for the kids, but the best gift you can give your kids is helping them learn what really matters. And that isn't piles of more stuff.

Another unfortunate meme can be poverty. A few families and some social contexts unwittingly propagate a sense of "no you can't", "don't try you'll only get hurt", and "if I didn't get to, why should you?" That debilitating victim stance can be contagious. Hope gets replaced with frustration, jealousy, and anger. Ouch.

Yet opportunities do exist or can be created. And hand-ups are available. (Hand-outs may be temporarily necessary in some circumstances, but in the long-term they're counter-productive to self-respect.) Yet it can be hard to extricate yourself from your current circumstances and from the attitudes of your peers and family. It takes extra energy and effort to get on with life when you need not only to do-the-doing, but to take control of your own attitudes and beliefs so that you are able and willing to go after those opportunities. You owe yourself that.

Don't fall victim to your own stuck-think. The answer? Shake up your patterns. Play with other possibilities. You might be happily surprised!

- Travel. Experience other ecosystems, other cultures.
- Listen to music you've not tried before. Read a different style of novel.
- Play with some little kids. Recapture the joy and awe in simple things.
- Maybe try eating with your hands. Who says utensils are necessary?
- Assume someone else's role for a while. Walk that mile in their shoes.
- Volunteer somewhere new.
- Try thinking thoughts that are very different from your usual ones.
- "Act as if" and see what happens.

You're not trying to make yourself redecide everything in your life. That's unnecessary and would be overwhelming. Simply snip, here and there, the web of "choices" that have been imposed on you, unintentionally or deliberately, without you even realizing it.

Be wary of this one. Those-who-have are pushing the false belief that those-who-want can only "succeed" by thinking of the economy as a God whose "markets" are entitled to orchestrate all. We're told to bow down to the supposed "needs of the economy" at the expense of our own well-being and that of the environment. When we succumb to that coercion, inadvertently or voluntarily, we become subservient pawns in their make-*them*-money game. The environment is treated as no more than a commodity to be used, abused, irrelevant. And frankly, so are we. Look where that meme's gotten us. That "God" is anything but benevolent. And his minions are definitely more self-serving than they are wise or even competent. (There are times when I find the arrogance, ignorance, and short-sightedness of some humans absolutely astounding.)

The reality? "The economy is a subset of the environment not the other way around."[43] As are we. So value what is valuable. "Sustainability" and the "status quo" are not mutually exclusive as they would have us believe. In reality, without the first, there's no way we'll sustain the second. The economy needs to be our servant, *not* our master.

Who's writing *your* Script? (Or trying to?)

Your workplace?
E.g. Your boss is shipping you overseas, and not to a place you'd want to go.

Your peers?
E.g. They're into stuff you're not.
E.g. They love to whine and complain. You'd rather solve.

Your family?
E.g. Dad's a lawyer, Mom's an MD. You've finished school—you want to be a carpenter.
E.g. Your Mom's moving to England and she's insisting you do your degree there and that you live with her. If you go, she'll pay your tuition of $17,000 a year which she can't really afford. If you won't comply, she'll contribute nothing to your schooling here.
E.g. Your in-laws want you to start giving them grandkids, but you're not ready.

> *Write your own script.* Enjoy building who YOU are, and playing with who you want to become. Listen to advice, sure, but it is your life. As for "what's next?" Anticipate and plan, yes. But play with possibilities. The unexpected could become a joyful adventure that you wish you'd welcomed sooner.

Enough! Let's take a bit of a break from the serious stuff!

Here are some lighter-hearted "strategies" which, by the way, are also memes.

Roll the dice

Think of a decision you'll be making soon. List your options. Number them. If you don't have six, number those you do have. Roll the dice, and see what your reaction is to the number that comes up. If you're disappointed, keep rolling until you get a roll that doesn't disappoint you. It's not the result of the roll that's important—it's your gut reaction to that result that might be somewhat helpful. But is that really how you intend to create your life—by rolling the dice?

Coin tossing

Heads or tails? Your call. What is your reaction to the result of the toss? Disappointed or relieved? That reaction might tell you more than your conscious brain can. Instead of accepting and going with the results of the first toss, do you now find yourself wanting to doing 2 of 3, or 3 of 5 tosses? What results are you hoping for? Or perhaps you're resisting any "answer" because part of you isn't actually ready to make this decision—yet. Why not? (That's a genuine question, not a sarcastic one.)

Daisies

Instead of pulling off petals saying with each, "He loves me, he loves me not ...", ask yourself with each petal you pull, "I love him because ...?" And answer it. Then pull the next petal. "I love him not so much because..." See how you feel as you progress. (Obviously, substitute She for He in the above, as needed.)

Pendulums

Pick up something that swings. (No, not in a bar.) Maybe an actual pendulum, a fancy pendant, or meaningful amulet. Think about the question you're asking "the Universe". New age and Wiccan folks say there's a message for you in the way the object swings. Who knew?

Silly stuff? Seriously?

Consider the above techniques as a way to let your other-than-conscious mind off its leash to play for a bit. There are more ways to think than we think.

Think of a decision you'll need to make soon. Try out any two of the above techniques. Does "the answer" lie in what the results themselves are telling you? Maybe. Maybe not.

What is your gut reaction to the results? "Yay!" Or "Ohhhh..."
What wishes, what concerns surface? Is your off-leash Self growling, whining, barking a warning, cringing in fear? Or running around happily, and joyfully bouncing up and down?

Keep those off-leash wishes and concerns in mind as you work through the decision-making process.

Unconscious Decision-Making — Our "Blink"

The most familiar decision strategy, the conscious version, "is logical and definitive ... [but] it's slow and it needs a lot of information." Another strategy "operates a lot more quickly ... And it's really smart, because it picks up the problem ... almost immediately... It has the drawback, however, that it operates – at least at first – entirely below the level of consciousness". And it can "send its messages through weirdly indirect channels, such as the sweat glands on the palms of our hands. It's a system in which our brain reaches conclusions without immediately telling us that it's reaching conclusions." In the blink of an eye, we know. [44]

In Malcolm Gladwell's fascinating book, *blink*, he describes how the human mind's "adaptive unconscious"—not to be confused with Freud's version of the subconscious or with primitive urges—is crucial in our decision-making and hence to our survival. Our not-conscious mind is able to notice and analyze patterns in situations and behavior based on very narrow slices of experience. Some examples of this "thin-slicing"? [45] "Court sense" in basketball, "fist" in spy codes, and "giss" in bird watching. Another? The sense we get of someone's personality and habits by seeing their space, even if only for a minute or two.[46] And evidently, startlingly short videos of how a couple interacts are good predictors of whether the relationship will succeed or tank.[47] The pattern we pick up in a thin-slice provides the clues to the appropriate actions.

Personally, I loved it when science clued into the multitude of simple patterns in complex processes, be it in the contractions of heart muscle, music harmonics, or the paths of storms—rhythms in the seeming Chaos. The advent of computers facilitated the data crunching necessary to our being able to visualize those patterns. Our "adaptive unconscious" is our internal computer. Quietly in the background, and at mega-speed, it's processing and cross-correlating our incoming data, then it hands us the patterns to use to adapt to our realities.

Our adaptive unconscious "works out contingencies and relationships, and sorts through the mountain of information we get from the outside world, prioritizing it and putting flags on things that demand our immediate attention." It's a crucial part of our decision making, "a kind of mental valet" that takes care of all the minor mental details in our lives. It keeps "tabs on everything going on around [us], and makes sure [we are] acting appropriately, while leaving [us] to concentrate on the main [conscious] problem at hand". [48]

Timothy Wilson, in his fascinating book *Strangers to Ourselves,* tells us that "The mind operates most efficiently by relegating a good deal of high level sophisticated thinking to the unconscious, just as a modern jetliner is able to fly on autopilot with little or no input from the human, 'conscious' pilot. The adaptive unconscious does an excellent job of sizing up the world, warning people of danger, setting goals, and initiating action in a sophisticated and efficient manner... Nor is the unconscious a single entity with a mind and will of its own. Rather, humans possess a collection of modules that have evolved over time and operate outside of consciousness". These markedly improve "our ability to form quick evaluations of whether environmental events are good or bad." [49]

49 - Reprinted by permission of the publisher from STRANGERS TO OURSELVES: DISCOVERING THE ADAPTIVE UNCONSCIOUS by Timothy D. Wilson, pp.6-7, Cambridge, Mass.: The Belknap Press of Harvard University Press, Copyright © 2002 by the President and Fellows of Harvard College.,

People with damage to this part of the brain—our adaptive unconscious evidently lives just behind our nose, in the ventro-medial prefrontal cortex—are perfectly rational, but they lack judgment. There is a disconnect between what they know and what they do. They tend to endlessly run through options rather than get to a sensible choice.[50] They're caught in analysis-paralysis. (Relax. That doesn't mean that if you're currently caught in analysis-paralysis, you have brain damage, though some days it may feel like it.)

Why don't we trust our "blink"?

- "We are innately suspicious of this kind of rapid cognition. We live in a world that assumes that the quality of a decision is directly related to the time and effort that went into making it."[51] We feel we must be able to thoroughly and rationally justify our decisions. Yet the reality is that "If we are to improve the quality of the decisions we make, we need to accept the mysterious nature of our snap judgments. We need to respect the fact that it is possible to know without knowing why we know and accept that – sometimes – we're better off that way." [52]
- "If we make people try to try explain themselves, something very strange and troubling happens... Confusion overwhelms clarity." And we drop into "story-telling". We try to come up with explanations instead of trusting what some might call "our instincts". The reality is that we simply don't have a way to verbalize our feelings about that subject; we don't know how to explain *why* we know what we know. [53]
- In fact, introspection can destroy people's ability to solve insight problems. We need to simply say "I don't know" more often. Otherwise "we adjust our true preference to be in line with [a] plausible-sounding reason" and the advantage of the adaptive unconscious is then unnecessarily lost. [54]

When should we perhaps not trust our "Adaptive Unconscious"?

Surprisingly, short people are more likely to earn less money. And genuinely non-racist, non-sexist people can unintentionally demonstrate biases.[55] Why? "Our unconscious is a powerful force. But it's fallible.... It can be thrown off, distracted, and disabled. Our instinctive reactions have to compete with all kinds of other interests and emotions and sentiments."[56] For example, tall people, because they're physically more imposing, seem more commanding, more in control. They tend to get the more impressive jobs.

"We make connections much more quickly between pairs of ideas that are already related in our minds than ... between pairs of ideas that are unfamiliar to us", even though they may not be at all related from a cause and effect point of view. This sets us up to prejudge, unconsciously, based on associated rather than relevant information.[57] People "let the first impression they have about a person's appearance drown out every other piece of information they manage to gather in the first instant."[58] And it's actually the other criteria that are valid. The blink gets derailed by associations based, not on actual experience, but on our choices of what we watch and hear and by our tendency to pigeonhole in order to simplify our lives. And we can slip unwittingly into biases that we would consciously reject.

So, yes, there are times when we need to be cautious about this "dark side of rapid cognition".[59] Yet when our powers of rapid cognition run amuck, it's usually for specific and consistent reasons that can be identified and understood, and thus compensated for.

How do we improve the functioning of our "blink"?

- **With experience, practice, and with guidelines**
  In sports, the advantage of experience, of training and practice is obvious. And agreed-upon rules provide the "context" for the action. With Improv Theater which looks wildly spontaneous, the rule is that you-go-with-what-you're-handed. Here too there is much rehearsal, not of an actual script, but of how to communicate intended emotions and relationships. Again, there is a context and guidelines for what happens. [60]
- **By building relevant expertise**
  When we're outside our own realm of expertise, our snap judgments are not necessarily wrong but "shallow" and they're more vulnerable to being disrupted by our attempting to explain them. Without expertise and experience, we don't have the frame of reference, the terms, words, needed. Experts have a jargon, a vocabulary that enables them to better describe and explain judgments. And expertise comes with experience. [61] Deliberately seek relevant experience.
- **By not equating "different" with "weird" or "dangerous"**
  Great musicians who are later seen as icons of a new genre[62], superb products like ergonomic chairs[63], and innovative paradigm-shifting ideas are ignored because they're different, hence weird. Being unusual, unfamiliar, they make us nervous [64] and are shunned or even viewed as dangerous. Yet they're far superior to the conventional.
- **Ironically, by frugality of information**
  We've been thoroughly indoctrinated—by parents, the education system, employers, and the expectations of society—about the dangers of not knowing enough, and of not doing enough analysis. Yet the flip side, information overload, creates "enormous frustrations" [65] and ironically can make "picking up that signature [the pattern] harder, not easier . . . When we can't edit, or we don't know what to edit or our environment won't let us edit", we become less effective decision makers. [66] It's useful to "provide a context that does not clutter up the process with irrelevant information." For example, when musicians were auditioned behind screens so they were heard but not seen, orchestras were able to get past gender bias.[67] A simple solution to a complex issue.
- **By not confusing information with understanding.** [68]
  We need to accept that we can't know everything and that we can't see everything in advance. And drowning ourselves in data isn't going to change that. What are the truly relevant elements of what we seek? How can we reduce the sidetracking effect of the irrelevant? Just how do we pick out the components that would most impact the outcome? And what's the most appropriate action to take once we've hopefully figured that out?

I'd like to add a thought and a caution here. We're steeped in the cliché that "knowledge is power". Yet we ignore the reality that more and more information by itself, undigested, unedited, is neither. What do we need to glean from information, from knowledge? Wisdom. Good sense blended with conscience and heart.

When do we need to be truly cautious of our "blink"?

- **Under extreme stress** the judgment skills of rapid cognition break down tremendously. At a heart rate of about 175, the "mid-brain ... reaches up and hijacks the forebrain."[69] Your primitive animal self takes over. It's impossible to think clearly. You lose perspective. Even physical abilities can be impaired to the point where it's impossible to dial 911. "Arousal leaves us mind-blind."[70]
- "**Under time pressure**... [people] stopped relying on the actual evidence of their senses... When we make a split-second decision, we are really vulnerable to be guided by our stereotypes and prejudices, even ones that we may not necessarily endorse or believe." [71]
- **Yet extreme arousal and mind blindness are not inevitable** under stressful conditions. Citing rookie cops who might use their guns inappropriately, Gladwell explains that we can "develop our rapid decision-making with training and experience".[72] "To a novice, [an] incident may have gone by in a blur. Yet every moment – every blink – is composed of a series of discrete moving parts, and every one of those offers an opportunity for intervention, for reform, and for correction." Once a scenario is in motion it *is* possible to re-direct the potential outcomes. "This is the gift of training and expertise." [73]
- "**Our first impressions** are generated by our experiences and our environment, which means we can change our first impressions – we can alter the way we thin-slice – by changing the experiences that comprise those impressions."[74] Construct your life so that you can gain relevant experience in those concepts and contexts where you most want to improve your judgment.

"The task of figuring out how to combine the best of conscious deliberation and instinctive judgment is one of the great challenges of our time."[75] That applies to each and all of us—as individuals and as human societies.

So when to Blink, when to consciously Think?

While Gladwell does a wonderful job of helping us understand unconscious decision making, he cautions that—sorry—there's no simple answer here. Life's too complicated. We need to puzzle out the best mix for certain circumstances on a case-to-case basis.

For straightforward choices, especially when there is time to think, it appears that deliberate conscious analysis may be best. When it's a fast-moving situation or when many variables have to be juggled, perhaps the "blink" is best. Just perhaps.

Pattern finding is hard-wired into us, both at the conscious and unconscious levels. It evolved as a survival tool. What's safe? What's dangerous? What's beneficial, what's not? Some of the incoming information can be readily accessed, processed, and dealt with by the logical conscious mind either as simple pros-and-cons thoughts or in a manner that's much more complex. For example, now assisted by computers, we can figure out the patterns that were previously hidden in mountains of medical data, and design the best protocols for treating patients with various conditions.

But a lot of what makes for a good decision in daily life is highly complex. The clues are too subtle, the signals too fleeting, or not even measurable as data.

For example, how would you quantify someone's attitude, motivation, intentions? How do we mind-read? How do we get a sense of the safety of our environment? Our "blink", our speedy unconscious "computer" seems to be very good at processing this kind of information. And its optimal functioning needs to be protected. It can be messed up by too much introspection and by attempts to verbalize explanations, or overwhelmed by irrelevant information.

On the other hand, we can enhance this skill with training and experience. With the resulting expertise comes the confidence to better trust that you "just know".

Gut, hunch, instinct... You just knew.

Think of a time when a situation or a person instantly creeped you out. (Hopefully you didn't stick around long enough to find out if you were right.)

Think of a time when you were immediately drawn to an activity or a person. Hopefully you were right. If not, what can you learn from the experience?

Have you ever been wrong about either of the above? What did you learn from that? Maybe that you shouldn't ignore your "not-conscious" also-wise Self?

What do we need to keep in mind as we "make up our minds"?

Personally, I think humans are much too hung up on Either/or. It's not whether we use this OR that technique, this OR that part of the brain. We need to acknowledge that genuine wisdom, at any age, comes from blending *all* our ways of knowing. And, in my opinion, perhaps we're better off acknowledging that some of the most important things in life can't be hacked up into numbers, captured as words, or relegated to algorithms and what, on the surface, passes as logic.

We need, as well, the humility to realize there will be times when circumstances require us to decide and act without being 100% sure. How do we deal with that?

- Know what you want as a result of the decision. And do your best to gather what you need to know to help that happen. (You may not have all the puzzle pieces in your hand, but you can usually still "see" the overall picture.)
- What's your heart, your gut telling you? Kate Douglas calls our emotions "evolution's satnav". Disgust for example, "helps us avoid disease and shun people who don't play by the rules".[76] And fear evolved to keep us safe.
- Decide which is worse—no decision or *a* decision, even if it's not necessarily the "best" one. Then act. Or don't. See what happens. Either way, you may not be able to totally control the outcomes, but you can control what you do about those.
- You may not be able to stack the deck, but you can learn to play well the cards you're dealt. When to request other cards, and if or when to fold on that particular hand? That's up to you. But first of all, be sure you're playing the game *you choose*.

Pay attention to the following cautions:

- We tend to believe anything that confirms what we already believe or that we hope to be true.
- When unsure, we can skid towards what seems familiar or to the first thing that exceeds our current expectations.
- When information is limited, we seize on randomly linked events as supposed evidence. Or we follow the herd.
- Short term wants have a tendency to trump long range needs. And biological drives can hijack other priorities. (E.g. hunger, libido.)
- When we're run-down or trying to make too many decisions at once, we're unlikely to make good decisions. So take care of yourself, especially if you're facing choices that involve major life changes.
- And when in doubt, stop and ask yourself, "Does this path have a heart?" (Carlos Castaneda.) The quality of life is in the journey.

How do we evaluate the results of our decisions?
That's the next chapter...

Further reading

Blink, Malcolm Gladwell
SWITCH: How to Change Things When Change is Hard, Chip Heath & Dan Heath
"YES" or "NO" The Guide to Better Decisions, Spencer Johnson
A Primer on Decision Making: How Decisions Happen, James March
Do One Thing Different: Ten Simple Ways to Change Your Life, Bill O'Hanlon
Wishcraft: How to Get What You Really Want, Barbara Sher, with Annie Gotlieb
The Paradox of Choice, Barry Schwartz
The Lazy Person's Guide to Success, Ernie J. Zelinski

Evaluating and Interpreting our decisions...

Decisions with Less Stress and Better Outcomes

How do we avoid becoming overwhelmed by options, choices, decision-making? How do we avoid unnecessary angst and regret?

How do we better appreciate the results of our decisions?

Whether we base decisions on logic, heart, or gut, what criteria do we use to evaluate and interpret those results? And which matters more—the actual factual results or how we feel about the results of a decision?

Barry Schwartz, in *The Paradox of Choice*, outlines the psychology behind why we are feeling much less happy than a few decades ago, even though we have more choices available to us, each with objectively better potential outcomes. His observation is that too much choice forces a need for too many decisions, and the cumulative effect is overwhelming. It messes with our sense of well-being and peace of mind.[1]

How can we make more effective and happier decisions? (Below, I've sorted some of the ideas from the research according to before, during, and after we make a decision.)

Before

"When we are in a good mood, we think better... In general, positive emotion enables us to broaden our understanding of what confronts us."[2] Yet another reason to have a better attitude! Not that easy if you're engulfed in a problematic situation. Focus on knowing there is a solution—you just need to find it.

Want to drop your stress levels? Ask yourself whether—if the results are a botch and a bother—the decision can be reversed or repaired? Probably. Thankfully, fewer decisions than you might think are truly irreversible. Obviously, there are some painful exceptions. For example, while driving under the influence (drunk, stoned, or impaired by the side effects of a prescription drug) you kill someone. Or you have unprotected sex and become infected with HIV. *All it takes is once.* On some things there's no do-over, no reset. If you're making those kinds of choices, you should be stressed. "It can't happen to me." Ya right. Smarten up.

We generally weigh the advantages and disadvantages of various options by seeking and assessing the facts of a situation. Yet our interpretation of these facts can be distorted. We confuse the validity of the facts with the vividness or intensity of seemingly related memories. Familiarity or ease of recall gets confused with relevance or importance.[3] Try to be more objective about the potential and desired results of each option you're examining. Look for the need behind the need, the benefit in the benefit.

Choose *when*. That matters. Some things truly can be postponed, and in fact should be. (Yay!) Why check your work email late Friday afternoon if you can't or won't do anything about the issue until Monday? And research shows that being on call for your boss 24/7 is actually counter-productive for both you and the business. You have a life. You hope. Know and keep your personal boundaries. (Now there's a loaded topic.)

During

Timothy Ferriss, in *The 4 Hour Work Week*, tells us that we want to "learn to make non-fatal or reversible decisions as quickly as possible".[4] By "non-fatal" Ferriss means decisions that won't kill you or your business. "Fast decisions preserve usable attention for what matters."

Schwartz and others point out that we're "loss averse", and hung up on "sunk costs".[5] Whether it's leaving money in a bad investment or staying in an unhealthy relationship, we'll take a bigger risk not to lose something we already have than to gain something comparable. Once we've put in money, time, or energy, we're more likely to try to hold on even if, from a rational point of view, that's not a good idea.

We get hung up on the necessary trades-offs, on if-onlys, and on lost opportunities. We get ourselves stuck. We refuse to decide. Or we rob ourselves of the joy in even a well-made decision by constantly second guessing ourselves.[6] Or we let the resulting "negative emotional states of mind narrow our focus. ... And our decision making can be severely impaired".[7] So lighten up. That's sometimes easier said than done. As the cliché goes "Worrying is like a rocking chair. It keeps you busy, but doesn't get you anywhere." Sensible caution and endless fussing are not the same thing.

After

Avoiding regret.

Trying to explain, to justify in words, the reasons for your choices can decrease your satisfaction with a choice you actually would have been very happy with. And as the number of options goes up, so seemingly does your "need" to justify that choice. Yet, "what is most easily put into words is not necessarily what's the most important." That could be as simple as buyer's remorse about a certain car or as devastating as having to choose which cancer treatment to undergo. With some decisions, your life *is* on the line. People faced with very difficult choices are particularly susceptible to this justification nightmare. [8]

There's what we *thought* we'd feel, before we made the decision. And there's what we *do* feel at the time we are experiencing its effects. These don't necessarily match up. And then there's our view—in retrospect—as the consequences, and the feelings that go along with them, get absorbed into our memory.[9] In other words, "Regret is past tense decision making."[10] Coulda-woulda-shoulda. Unfortunately, these negative emotions only deplete the attention you can devote to improving the situation.

Improving appreciation

We adapt. Light a scented candle and soon afterwards you won't even notice its smell. Physiologically, though our nose still gets it, our brain doesn't. It's adapted so that it can focus on other potentially new aspects of our surroundings. That's a hard-wired survival tactic: notice the new movement in the underbrush or become some predator's lunch. Adaptation is vital. But at a more subtle level, it can be quite tricky. Adaptation at the emotional level means that even overt pleasure becomes simply comfort. We come to take for granted what once brought us considerable pleasure. Then we can get trapped on a "hedonic...satisfaction treadmill" where nothing holds it's value as "enough".[11] And that can apply to objects or relationships. A good antidote for this downside of adaptation? Take note of and truly appreciate the wonderful things that have, over time, become ordinary to us. We need to remind ourselves how lucky we are! Smell those roses!

Research has proven that "individuals who regularly experience and express gratitude are physically healthier, more optimistic about the future, and feel better about their lives than those that do not." They "are more alert, enthusiastic, and energetic than those who do not, and they are more likely to achieve their personal goals...." And unlike adaptation, which if we're not careful, can cause us to devalue what's beneficial and joyful, the "experience of gratitude is something we can affect directly."[12] (If you haven't already done the Gratitudes Activity on page 21 now would be a good time.)

SATISFICERS and MAXIMIZERS

Schwartz describes two fundamentally different decision mindsets.
Maximizers go for "the best". Satisficers go for a very good "good enough".

Maximizers put stress-inducing amounts of time and energy into checking out "all" options and every aspect of each. Satificers, on the other hand, set up their own criteria, their own high standards of what they want, and stop looking when they've found that. They're not compromising—they're just not falling into the trap of "diminishing returns" on the amount of energy, of "time, money, and anguish" it takes to make a decision. And in the long run, satisficers are happier with their choices than are maximizers.[13]
That's why it's so important to establish, and re-evaluate when necessary, our criteria for what matters in life.

"Time, effort, opportunity costs, anticipated regret, and the like are fixed costs that we 'pay' up front in making a decision, and then those costs get 'amortized' over the life of the decision." [14] **So where should we put our time, energy, and attention when it comes to decisions?** If it's a decision with major long-term implications, give the decision its due. Otherwise, ease your burden.

MAJOR MATTERS

What are the significant aspects of life that deserve your time and decision-making energy? Which ones can you use personally constructed "default settings" for? [15] The next activity, and the next chapter, will help you sort some of these out.

What has maximum meaning and the longest lasting implications?

Society's decisions used to be made with several generations in mind. And now? Politicians think in terms of their four year terms. Corporations? Quarterly profit, a lousy three months. And you? What are your time frames?

Life-altering decisions requiring careful consideration:

Changing jobs, moving to another country, choosing a spouse ...
List two more.

Decisions that aren't a big deal, certainly not in comparison to the above...

Get a dog? What kind of dog? Or maybe one of those bizarre hairless cats?
A different hair style, or colour? Or shave it all off to match the cat?
Who to date this weekend?
(Married, and the answer is not "spouse"? Consider that a *big* decision.)
List two not-so-biggies.

ROUTINES

People seem to love to read about 10-Steps-To-This, 5-Point-Programs-For-That. Why? Because it makes the process finite. And clearer. You figure out, find out, what works. The How-to process has been set up. The task feels much more do-able that way. It's simpler, and it satisfies. And you're not always arguing with yourself about getting on with it. You know that if you do such and such, you *will* get the results you want. Sweet.

Design your own "Steps to ... "

- Doing the weekly chores to keep your living space livable.
- What you would do during a typical week to stay fit.
- A favourite way to relax. (Put on your favourite music, run a tub?)
- Getting yourself and the kids, if you have any, out of bed, fed, and out the door.

These "Steps to" are malleable. Mess with them as you want. Mess up if you want—there are minimal consequences. But I do suggest you get to work with clothes on.

Checklists

Like a pilot readying for flight, you can create Checklists for specific situations. These can help you relax since you know you've got your bases covered.

Two examples of lists you might want to create:

What you need to have ready for a trip overseas. (E.g. You stand in line at the airport with all your gear, for ages and ages, only to discover at the check-in counter that your passport's still in your bedroom drawer. Oops.)

What's needed in the baby's diaper-bag. (Short list: diapers and wipes, or there's another Oops.) Keep the list in there too.

Our decisions impact Who-we-are and who we become...

Chapter 7

Who are you?

What kind of person do you want to be?

Your behaviors and beliefs become part of your identity. Choose wisely.
And enjoy the responsibility of making and implementing those decisions.

James March of Stanford University says that "when people make choices, they tend to rely on one of two basic models of decision-making: the consequences model or the identity model. In the identity model, we essentially ask ourselves three questions when we have a decision to make:

> Who am I?
> What kind of situation is this?
> What would someone like me do in this situation?"

We adopt and grow into what we perceive as our Identity. And we adapt our decision-making to fit that sense of who we are. Apparently "any change effort that violates someone's identity is likely doomed to failure".[1] The stick-or-carrot, or the analytical pros-and-cons approaches, are impotent in comparison.

> How would you describe yourself? How might others describe you?
> How do you relate to others?
> Who might you want to become?

Get a little more deliberate about these choices.
Let yourself grow towards being your best and happiest self—let that be your Identity.

WHAT WE DO reflects who-we-are.

Here are a number of activities for you to play with.
They'll help you get a clearer view of some of your behaviours and beliefs.

Habits

Closets can get cluttered with no longer useful items—so can heads.

If this were someone else's habit, would you approve?
If you were your own best friend, would you approve?
If you were *now* to deliberately choose this way of thinking or doing, would you?

Boundaries

Make a list of 10 things you'd NEVER do. They're either just plain wrong—or much too dangerous. (For some things, there are no do-overs.)

For any three of these, describe a circumstance in which you might break your own NEVER rule. (Wouldn't kill anyone? What if they were trying to kill your kids?)

Create your own Guidelines-to-live-by.

Make a list of five "rules" about how you treat family members and friends.
In what ways might these be different for people not as close to you?
In what ways would these be the same?

How will your everyday rules affect how you interact with your context?
In what ways might that choice impact your life?
(For example, you're punctual—you feel that shows respect for other people's time. Yet that premise varies. It's a meme. Some cultures are much more easy-going about timing, even for business meetings. In that context, you may find yourself occasionally a little frustrated.)

Movie Me

Describe a scene from a movie.
Ask yourself: "What might I choose to do under those circumstances?"

Now describe a scenario from your own life.
Imagine this situation as a movie script that you can write and rewrite at will.
What would you want the actor that plays you, as your best-self, to choose to do?
If the character that is "you" were going to make a real mess of life, what might he/she do? Avoid those actions. Keep the high drama for the movies.
It's better to have interesting and happy, not self-imposed torture, as your life script.
It's better to be your own hero, than the victim or villain.

What else reveals who we are?
Our EXPECTATIONS and ASSUMPTIONS.

Again let's use a movie as an example.

What are some of the assumptions made by one of the main characters about life and about other people?
What are some of the assumptions made about that main character? By other characters in the story? By you, watching it?
How do assumptions or expectations create situations the characters have to deal with?
What lessons might you learn from this movie about the impact of assumptions?

Tennis anyone? Your idea of a tennis game is to whack a ball around at the court in the park in whatever ratty shorts happen to be clean. Your colleague's idea of a tennis game is highly competitive, refereed, and "properly attired". You're each entitled to your version. But before you go out to "play tennis" together, you may want to sort this out. You're more likely to enjoy yourselves.

Perception and Identity

Get together with a couple of friends you respect and admire. With close friends you know you'll get honest and constructive feedback, after all, you have each other's best interests at heart. (If you don't, why call each other "friend"?)

Was there something on first meeting or early in the relationship that you had misinterpreted about each other? What caused this erroneous assumption? What helped you better understand, and clarify, what was actually going on?

Is there something a little "off" with someone you interact with? What assumptions are you making? Brainstorm other possible explanations for what's going on. How could you clear up what actually might be happening?

What expectations do you have of them?
How might they meet that expectation? Why should they?
What specifically would you like them to do differently? Have you asked for that?
What expectations do they have of you? Do you want to meet those? How?

Now pretend you are strangers to each other. What would your impression of "this person" be? If they—or you—are not coming across as your authentic-self and best-self, brainstorm some ideas on how to improve that.

Look at some of the following aspects:

How you present yourself visually ...

- **Grooming**: You smell okay, but do you need a more flattering haircut?
- **Appropriateness of clothing** to context and task, and to your shape. This bolsters comfort and confidence. Ever watch *What Not To Wear*?
- **Facial expressions**: Animated? Deadpan? Laugh lines, or grouch-mouth?
- **Body language**: Confident or aloof? Friendly and approachable? Or schlumpy, grumpy?

How you speak ...

- **Words and grammar**: If you want to be taken seriously, don't sound like the Trailer Park Boys, or some airhead cutie-pie.
- **Tone, intonation**: Again, to be taken seriously, don't whine. Don't squeak-speak like some annoying little mouse. As for raising your voice? That simply makes you louder, not more impressive.
- **Pace of speech**: Too slow drives some listeners crazy. Too fast can make you sound nervous or insecure.
- **Space makers**: Umm .. Like ... Duh.

How you walk ...

- Stride or shuffle? Skulk or strut?
- With a relaxed and confident pace? Or uptight and scurrying? Or as if you're paranoid or sneaky?

Your view of the world, its view of you, your view of yourself, all feed into each other.

Perception, awareness, meaning, identity...

You're *not* trying to convert yourself into someone or something you're not.
Quite the opposite.

You're trying to make sure that how you are seen is as close as possible to who you really are and who you want to become.

Match up as much as humanly possible, at least most of the time, your usual-self and your best-self. That may, on occasion, require a little tweaking. Like life itself, we are all works-in-progress.

Change strategies come next....

Chapter 8

Toddler Tactics & Strategies for Change

Life can feel like a tabletop puzzle: we figure out as we go which little piece fits where. And when we get stuck, we check once in a while with the Big Picture on the box. At other times, life may feel more like a kaleidoscope. Make one small move, shift one little bit, and the whole picture rearranges. Maybe you initiate the moves on purpose. Maybe not. Maybe life does.

- What changes have been imposed on you? By circumstances? By others?
- What do you *want* to change? About yourself? About your relationships? About your work life? About the world?
- What NEEDS (of the Maslow type, page 12) might need improving in your life?
- What WANTS are still an itch that need scratching?

Does this seem a little overwhelming? Admit it, it's also somewhat intriguing, enticing.

How can we improve our quality of life?

And just what do we mean by that? Social scientist Alex Michalos argues that our "perceived quality of experience" and our "standards of satisfaction" are based on the assessment of three gaps: "the gap between what one has and wants, the gap between what one has and thinks others like oneself have, and the gap between what one has and the best one has had in the past".[1] Psychologist Barry Schwartz adds a fourth: "the gap between what one has and one expects." [2]

Yes, having a sense of your perceived gaps may be useful. But be careful you're not buying into what you *think* others think you should want or think. They're not living your life, you are. (And vice versa.) Keep in mind that what we see is what others show us, not necessarily what's going inside them. We may see them as confident and well-off whereas they may be in a lousy relationship or up to their armpits in unmanageable debt. Instead, create your own criteria for success, for what has meaning in your life. In working through this Priorities section, you're improving your sense of what those priorities are, and are ramping up your skills for implementing them. In the next chapter, Goals, we'll explore these further.

Don't focus overly on the WHYS of what you need or want.

Excuse my heresy but articulating the Why, translating your reasons into words, is highly overrated. Toddlers don't list a dozen reasons "Why do I want that cookie up there?" before they have a go at getting it. Children simply harness cookie-passion to figure out a HOW. Yes, they may take a tumble. Even get a little bruised. But you can bet they're not likely to give up until they reach it. Sure it's easier once they have words to enlist the help that might be needed, but they still aren't going to be expected to explain why. They just need to ask for, or be shown how. If they can't get it by themselves, and can't get help, they may throw a tantrum. Not the best strategy if you're an adult. But you get the idea. No shortage of motivation. No need for articulated *Whys*.

Why do long lists of reasons WHY often fail dismally as self-motivators? The true reasons behind *why* can dwell in parts of the brain that can't be tapped into by what seems to be logic, and in parts that don't process thoughts as words. These parts of the brain are no less savvy about our well-being, in all the shades of the terms "well" and "being". **You want the cookie. Period.** As long as you're not doing damage to get that "cookie", go for it!

The awkwardness of change

A caution—**your natural response to a change**, even a good one, might be to feel slightly disoriented, disrupted, uncomfortable, perhaps slightly stressed, even distressed. Don't let that sidetrack you. Change, even when chosen rather than imposed, even when fun, beneficial, productive, feels different and our deeply primitive self knows that different might imply an increased need for vigilance. Heightened awareness kicks in, as a survival technique, as you shift out of familiar territory. Just acknowledge this and don't chicken out. (Try this simple experiment. Cross your arms. Now try crossing them the other way. Feels weird, huh. So does trying anything new.) As you become more accustomed to the newer circumstance, the newer better you, this temporary awkwardness will evaporate. Toddlers may be unsteady on their feet—for now. That doesn't mean they won't soon be running.

Newness and learning go hand in hand.

Here's another Maslow gem, popularized by Noel Burch and the Gordon Training International Organization—the "Learning Stages Model" which refers to being, in order, "unconsciously incompetent, consciously incompetent, consciously competent, then unconsciously competent".

- At the *unconscious incompetence* level you don't even know that you don't know something you need to. (Let me say that this is particularly tricky when it comes to life-skills. *Someone Really Oughta Tell You.* At least ask people in the know if there's something you should know at that particular stage of your life. Be proactive, preemptive.)
- At *conscious incompetence* at least you know you need to know, but don't—yet. But you're seeking the appropriate info and skill set. You're trying, practicing, and getting the hang of it.
- *Conscious competence* means that you know what and how but your skill level is not consistent. It's still not second nature, not a habit—yet.
- When you get to the *unconscious competence* level, you don't even have to think about it, it just works, it flows. You're in "the Zone".

You'll go through these phases with any skill whether it's speaking another language, playing a guitar, or such skills as goal setting, time management, and building a meaningful and successful life—your criteria for meaningful and successful.

"Success has been defined as the progressive realization of a goal. Based on this definition, are you successful?" [3] Note the progressive part. You're successful while you're in progress, not just if you get there. Nice. Hold that thought.

The quality of the journey is at least as important as the destination.

What changes would you be open to and welcome? For life to be just the way you'd like it, what changes might you be willing to initiate and implement?

Where do you fit in the world?

How we view life and what we value in the world, how alone or connected we feel, how confident or appreciative we are, depends significantly on how effective we think we are in influencing the changes we want to see. You as an individual are more influential than you think, especially if you combine with others of like mind. (I was once told by a marketing expert that for each complaint a company receives, they know that thousands of people feel the same way but haven't bothered to voice their concerns or annoyance. You, times a thousand. Use that power.)

"Never doubt that a small group of thoughtful, committed citizens can change the world. Indeed, it is the only thing that ever has." Margaret Mead

> Be careful you don't write off a goal as not being worthwhile because it's simple to achieve, or at least simpler than you initially thought. Contrary to popular belief, "everything that's worthwhile in life is hard to get" is *not* actually true. It's simply a thought that occurs to those who are tired or discouraged. You like clichés? Try this one instead, "the best things in life are free". For example, laughter and love.

Attitudes to change

There are obvious differences in how we view self-chosen change, negotiated change and imposed change. However, how well we deal with each of these is rooted in our attitudes and skill levels.

Spencer Johnson's now classic book, *Who moved my cheese?* is a fun and useful short read. Four mice named Hem, Haw, Scurry and Sniff, have very different behaviours in response to change. The cheese is gone. Eaten up so gradually no one noticed? Or was it suddenly moved, or removed? Do you wait, or go look for it? Where? How do you stay alive while waiting or looking? What if you find only crumbs, forensic evidence of previous cheese? What if you find a fabulous treasure load? What if you don't recognize this new cheese as edible, as even being cheese? If you do find it, do you help the others? Hem, Haw, Scurry or Sniff—which mouse would be your alter-ego? What is your change-response style? How adaptable and how proactive are you? Four mice and their cheese—a food-for-thought parable. [4]

Listen to yourself, not just to the self-talk in your head or to the words coming out of your mouth. What is your mood? What is your body telling you as you contemplate change? Whether responding to a change, or creating one, you could feel a little uncomfortable. And you'll definitely have a number of hoops to jump through. **Welcome to this adventure called Life.**

Revved up to get started? Yay! Jump to page 81 and go for it. You can read the rest of this chapter later if you need a hand up, or a kick in the butt, to get going again.

On the other hand, is some part of you still holding back? Is your brain saying "Yes, but..."? Acknowledge that knowing a change is needed is not enough to make it happen. And keep in mind that hope is a great motivator but not, in itself, a strategy.

DO what you can, DO what it takes, to help something good happen.

What gets us stuck?

- Does it feel as if it's just too much bother?
- Are the payoffs not immediate enough?
- Are you, at some level, not believing that you can be successful?
- Do you think that unless it's easy, you won't succeed?
- Or that unless it's hard to achieve, it's not a worthwhile goal?
- Are you a little nervous because you simply don't *yet* know how?
- Which obstacles are your own habits or mindset holding you back?
- Are fears masquerading as excuses? Is the possibility of failing too hard on the ego to risk really trying?
- Perhaps you have been disappointed too many times, or disappointed yourself and you're trying to avoid re-experiencing that nasty feeling. Failing here and there does not make you a failure. It's just part of being human, learning our way through life. (Dealing with and overcoming obstacles is one of the ways we grow, but only one of the ways.)

"People who have a growth mindset believe that abilities are like muscles – they can be built up with practice." [5]... "That's the paradox of the growth mindset"—you're more likely to persevere and to succeed when you realize that interim "failures" don't cause you to fail. Ironically, those occasional missteps and set-backs can help you succeed because they help you learn. "The growth mindset, then, is a buffer against defeatism".[6] See, told ya—toddler tactics. Fell on your face? Pick yourself up. Figure out a slightly better way to make that next step. And take it.

Fixed mindset people? Luckily they can grow a growth mindset—they just may not *yet* realize they can. Since you're reading this book, you're not one of them. Perhaps you can help someone else take that next step.

A Parrot Story

How did they, back in the day, teach a parrot to sit on a perch? (Sorry, no, not a joke.)

Here was the idea. You take a young bird, and attach a light-weight tether to its leg, and the other end to a perch. The bird tries repeatedly to fly away but can't get very far. You give it food and small rewards to help encourage it to stay put. Eventually, it learns that the most comfortable thing to do, and the way to avoid getting hurt, is to sit there. And sit there. And sit there. Even if its wing feathers have not physically been clipped, it stays put. It may turn around in circles, make occasional nice or nasty noises, and flap its wings because that's what birds need to do. The parrot eventually gives up attempting to do its thing which, being a bird, means to fly. Then you can remove the tether. *It has abdicated self-control and self-expression to an obstacle which is no longer there and to an ingrained habit that confounds and subjugates its true nature.*

You hopefully wouldn't abuse or neglect a parrot. You likely wouldn't leave it "tied down" by a mindset that's counter-productive. Have an honest look at your own tethers. Is it not a similar neglect, in this case of yourself, to not deal with the ingrained habits that are keeping you stuck? Where are the scissors?

What are the actual facts of your current situation? What is your fiction? "My dad was fat too, so it must be genetic." Possibly, but the genetic component of obesity impacts a very small percentage of the population. It's more likely that you eat too much of the wrong foods and do too little. Don't rationalize. Don't give yourself invalid excuses. In doing so, you're keeping yourself on that tether. (For-real excuses that take a little more effort to counteract? Search "obesogens" and "epigenetics".)

Some say there's a hidden benefit to anything we do, that even bad habits that verge on destructive behavior have a supposedly functional purpose. Personally, I'd rather think people aren't that daft. I'd rather believe that their staying stuck is probably just an unfortunate habit, a lack of awareness of or belief in better possibilities (perhaps their courage has been stomped on too frequently) or skills that aren't quite up to the task yet, rather than a strange and misguided unconscious intention. (Maybe that's me rationalizing. I do try to see, first and foremost, the best in people. Mind you, that's admittedly not always been the best idea. Enough said.)

Still stuck? Start on the dark side.

Choose one change you wanted to make in your life but didn't.
What did you do that caused you to blow it? Have you stopped doing that?
Or what did you *not* do that caused you to blow it? Do it.
What's the opposite of what tends to mess you up? Try doing that.
If you were to tell someone else how not to screw up, what advice would you give? Take your own advice.

A caution: Don't welcome or invent unnecessary obstacles so you can pretend that your life is "interesting". That really is a misguided mindset. Along the way, Life itself will hand you a few challenges, both good and bad, that will keep it interesting. Instead, *get deliberate* about creating and implementing the fun and productive changes you want to see happen.

External obstacles are those that are part of our current circumstance—time, money, obligations, and the possible negativity or resistance of others.

- Which of these circumstances are the results of our previous choices?
- Which are not at all our own fault? Although they may not be our fault, it is up to us to fix, or at least improve, the situation we find ourselves in.

Chip and Dan Heath in *SWITCH* explain several crucial and perhaps surprising aspects of either personal or organizational change.

- "What looks like a people problem is often a situation problem." [7]
- "What looks like laziness is often exhaustion." [8]
- "What looks like resistance is often a lack of clarity." [9]

What we perceive as **internal obstacles,** for example fatigue, anxiety, resistance or procrastination are often the result of ambiguity, a lack of clarity about what is wanted or how to get it. And "psychologists have discovered that self-control is an exhaustible resource".[10] When our brain has to consciously supervise everything we do, it's draining. (Have they got that right!)

If we reduce the need for self-control and tidy up some of the ambiguities, we're more likely to succeed at what we want and need to do. (Hopefully, this book will help clear up some of those ambiguities and make the What and How a little easier.) Life's more fun when you're not bogged by mistakes you didn't have to make! Luckily, many of the mistakes from the past can be rectified—if we do something about them.

Here's a happy caution:
You don't need to "fix" or "solve" your past to get on with positive change. Hooray! Face it. You can't change what's already happened. It's archaeology, ancient history. You may be able to learn a little from it or modify your interpretation.
Yet endlessly digging around in the less-than-optimal parts of your life so far?
Let it go. Rather than walking backwards, gaze fixated on what's behind you, put your energies into discovering and exploring the path forward, into modifying your present and designing your future. That's so much more productive. (If, at some point, you do find yourself needing a little help with a past-something that keeps chewing on you, I suggest the "Solution Therapy" approach, which could be more aptly named the "Solution Finding" approach.)

In *SWITCH*, the Heath brothers emphasize that "We need to switch from archaeological problem solving to bright spot evangelizing."[11]

Bright Spots—Shine a light on what works.

Think of a specific time in your life when things were going well.
What were you doing then? Do more of that.
Think of a specific problem you've faced in the past.
What was the obstacle? What did you do to overcome it or work around it?
What seemed to be the key things that helped resolve the issue?
What new strategy might help with what you're dealing with now, even if only slightly?

Rather than looking for the one-and-only right answer, *think of these possibilities as experiments.* Try something. Anything. (Well, maybe not quite anything.) See what happens and modify your approach as needed. (More on this in the Goals chapter coming next.)

A suggestion? Shrink the obstacle.

To help people decrease their fat intake, researchers got them to purchase 1% rather than whole milk.[12] That's a simple easy to implement and effective change that's more sensible than trying to coax or bully them into changing all their food habits at once.

When cleaning your home, don't think "spotless", simply think "cleaner".[13]
Or to start on your get-healthier goal, perhaps skip the donut with your morning coffee. Have a low fat bran muffin or a piece of fruit instead. Easy. And effective. One day at a time…

The up-beat side-effects of shrinking an obstacle down to something manageable? It reduces dread and decreases your resistance to starting. By making the doing simpler and easier, success is more likely.

Do you expect to be able to create the life you want? Do you expect success? (Yes, winning the lottery might help.) What do you say to yourself, inside your head? Would you say those things, or use that tone, with your dearest friend? Now, as if you were talking to your best friend, say several encouraging things to yourself. Preferably out loud. Right now. Be your own cheering section. Find your own bright spots, and create more of them.

Be kind to yourself

- Be willing to let go of your current, and possibly restrictive, ideas about who you are and who you could be.
- Be willing to let your usual-self become your slightly-better-self. That new-self is still you, just a happier version.
- Imagine one specific thing you'd admire about your better-self. Visualize it as already for-real. Hold that thought. (When driving, it's been shown that what we focus on is where we'll go. The same idea applies here.)
- Use the expression "I'm *letting* myself" not "I'm *making* myself." Again, a kinder, less intimidating, approach.

Back to the wisdom of toddlers. Toddlers have an insatiable curiosity and know how to have fun while they're exploring, learning, and skill-building. It's called Play. Remember that feeling? Play gets the job of learning done. (In many ways, toddlers are so much smarter than adults.) Find ways to have fun as you explore possibilities and implement your plans. Just because something's important doesn't mean you need to get oh-so-serious about it.

The Complete Idiot's Guide To Motivating People lists the following strategies: "Listen!, be sincere, use incentives, be a coach, promote camaraderie, encourage ideas and discussion, set clear goals, get rid of routines [that don't work], develop a purpose, discipline fairly, be a mentor, be a confidante, keep secrets, recognize and reward achievements, create security, inspire, offer a challenge, make work fun, encourage, recognize what's important to your team, be friendly, invest people in the cause, be optimistic, create satisfaction." [14]

Use some of those strategies on yourself, including "be friendly" and "discipline fairly". You wouldn't slap a toddler for dribbling juice down their chin or slopping food on their bib. Yet adults beat themselves up all the time when taking on and building new skills. And for most young adults and many not-so-young ones, goal implementation and the effective management of money and time are as much new skills as getting food into their mouths once was. Give yourself a mental hug, and keep at it.

Now imagine a toddler sitting quietly on the floor in serious contemplation. "I should learn to drink from a cup properly. I should learn to walk. I should learn to talk. I should do this, I should do that"... blah, blah. Laughing yet? "Shoulds" are your rational brain speaking. The "Want-to" side of you screams back. Ever feel that argument rage on inside you like a couple of squabbling siblings?

Jonathan Haidt uses an analogy to outline three major considerations for change strategies, whether related to ourselves as individuals or to large organizational structures: **the Rider, the Elephant, and the Path**. (Haidt is a psychology professor, researcher, and the author of *The Happiness Hypothesis*.)[15]

The Rider is the rational reflective conscious mind. It's small compared to the elephant, but has the reins and wants to direct, yet can easily get stuck in indecision and in analysis-paralysis.

The Elephant is our heart, our gut. It's our emotional and instinctive self and more into short term gratification, but it's strong, loyal, passionate and compassionate.

The rider and elephant often disagree about what to do and when, and thus trip each other up. Yet as allies, they're profoundly powerful.

To implement change we must appeal to both of them. And we must do our best to smooth the Path they'll need to take.

One way for the rider to motivate the elephant is to turn a Should into a Want-to, what I call a Cookie. (Just not literally, if you're already overweight.) For example, "I should walk more." (Aha, but will you? Okay, where did you go with that thought? Beating yourself up for lack of willpower, or whatever? Remember—don't slap that toddler. Everyone trips up once and a while.) Instead, be kind. Be helpful. Not just to your toddler self, but to both the Elephant and Rider parts of you.

My own get off my butt and go for a walk motivator? I love sunshine, fresh breezes, and bird song. They energize me. I think I'm solar powered. And, lucky me, I live near a lake and a park. Sweet. (Okay, see ya. I'm out the door. I'll come back to working on this later.)

Yes, expect success. And expect that some effort and focus, and likely a few interim missteps, will be needed. Welcome that chance to learn and grow. Utilize the bright spots, add a little hope, a dash of confidence, and ease the path.

Note that "willpower" hasn't been mentioned in this chapter. Perhaps because, frankly, I often don't seem to have a lot. What about you? I found an easier and kinder tactic to use on myself. I ask myself a simple question: **"Do I want THIS in this moment, or the accumulated results of making the better choice?"** For example: "Which do I want more? Not scaring myself in the mirror or this bag of chips?" Usually works just fine. One wee decision at a time. (My elephant side doesn't seem to have a lot of patience. Neither does my toddler self.) The great thing is that when you've actually tapped into a true passion, you can barely stop yourself from doing it. Like me chugging away, trying to get this book done and out there where it'll be useful to someone.

> Enthusiasm is much more fun than willpower. Enthusiasm is rather like the tasty herbs and spices added to a recipe for creating something yummy.
> It makes the whole experience—of planning, preparing, and enjoying the results—more delicious.

A few more thoughts...

- Sometimes life shuffles the deck on us. The change might be neither worse nor better, it just is. Yet it's different, so we stress. How do we respond? Do we consider it an adventure? A nuisance? An opportunity? The Chinese symbol for "crisis" is the same as that for "opportunity". Interesting.
- Life teaches us, not by talking, but by pushing us around. Each push is saying "Wake up. There's something I want you to learn". Responding by getting angry or by blaming is almost as counter-productive as giving up. Instead, "learn and move on". Otherwise we get pushed into submission. "The fear of losing" becomes "greater than the excitement of winning". [16]
- As I've said before, fear is our cautionary advisor. Pay attention to and deal with the concerns that arise, but don't let fear hijack, derail or cripple your ability to do what needs doing. Create a solution to the problem at hand.
- "Being effective – changing things, influencing things, making things happen – is one of the fundamental needs with which human brains seem to be naturally endowed.... From infancy onward... we...have a throbbing desire ... to make things happen." The more we lose our ability to control what's going on in our lives, the more likely we could become "unhappy, helpless, hopeless and depressed". Gaining, re-gaining control boosts both health and well-being.[17]
- "People need a sense of self-efficacy, strung together with resilience, to meet the inevitable obstacles and inequities in life."[18] **As with muscles, we can build and strengthen our abilities, our sense of competence and our resilience**. (One way you're doing that is by *doing* this book.)

Ya, there's OBSTACLES. So what?

When life shuts a door, find an open window. Or cut a hole in the wall—patiently if you must. Or hire a bulldozer. And if you trip up, don't give up. Re-group, modify your strategies, re-energize and get back at it. You don't see toddlers stay down. They may scream and fuss a little, but then they're back at it. *Toddler tactics.*

Shape your own life.

As Steven Covey says, "If we do not develop our own self-awareness and become responsible for [our] first creations [i.e. creating our own life-vision, first in our minds] we empower other people and circumstances outside our Circle of Influence to shape our lives by default." [19]

You've already had the "Three Lists" conversation with yourself (Chapter 1) and identified what matters to you (Chapter 2). You're well on the way to knowing what you *need* and *want*.

Give yourself permission to go after your dreams.
***Optimism* and *reality* can be used in the same sentence.**

To do that, I suggest you first have a look at your strengths and weaknesses.

Suggested reading

Do One Thing Different, Bill O'Hanlon
SWITCH, Chip Heath & Dan Heath

Flying frogs? Strengths and Weaknesses

A frog can't fly. Should it agonize over trying to learn how? Perhaps flight seems sexier. Yet can a bird or butterfly whip out a wicked and insanely-long tongue to slurp a speeding insect out of mid-flight? Or paralyze an attacker with a simple touch? These are pretty impressive capabilities. Not that I'm comparing you or me to a frog or a bird. My point? We all have and are entitled to our own strengths and our own weaknesses. So beware the common and misguided expectation that we should be spending annoying amounts of time and energy trying to fix what we, and perhaps others, see as our weaknesses instead of building and playing to our genuine strengths. After all, in the human world, the frogs, birds, and butterflies can team up or hire each other to get the job done.

How do we identify our strengths? What do we do about our weaknesses? Even seasoned adults have some difficulty with these questions. So if you're addressing these questions as a young person, you're ahead of the game. Knowing what your strengths are is obviously important for your career. It also goes a long way to helping you design a happier personal life.

Strengths

How excited, passionate are we about IT? How good are we at IT? What is our IT?

Over the years it's been a genuine privilege to watch the blossoming of numbers of young people ranging in age from late teens to mid-twenties. (They are the ones who inspired and encouraged me to write this book. I truly appreciate their vote of confidence.)

A student with attitude. Not trying, but smart. Annoyingly pushy, but charismatic. Athletic, but unmotivated. More interested in being the center of attention than in getting decent grades. Snarled at him, "Why would a Porsche deliberately behave like a rent-a-wreck?" Challenged him, if he "had the guts", to take himself out for a test drive, to actually try academically and to take charge of the following year's student council. He did. The spark there? He had a drive to make things happen, but that talent had never been focused or unleashed. It's eight years later, he graduated university admirably and is well on his way to becoming a successful sports entrepreneur.

A young woman, very bright, from a family where academia reigned goes off to university to take an Ivory-Tower-Bound degree. That was to be her first of three degrees. Prof-dom was her expected life-path. She dropped out after first year to go walk-about. By the time she came back, she had realized that the path she wanted was definitely not academia. Her spark? She's a natural problem solver and intuitive communicator. An experiential learner, she loved being physical not desk-bound. In high school she was a hospital volunteer working with injured kids, and loved it. Now she has a Master's in Physiotherapy and is truly passionate about her work.

Marcus Buckingham says "Strengths are made up of three separate ingredients… talents, skills, and knowledge." [1] However, a strength is not simply ability but ability plus appetite: "You actively look forward to it. While you are doing it, you feel inquisitive and focused.[2] …There is almost certainly effort, but it is seemingly effortless... You become immersed.[3] After you've done it, you feel fulfilled and authentic." He stresses that "the most direct way to identify your strengths is always to pay attention to how specific activities make you feel. No one can do this better than you." [4] (He's written several books on how to help us do just that.)

Do not confuse *talent* and *skill*. Too many people erode their own self-perception by mixing up the two. Talents or aptitudes are the things you are naturally good at. These are usually, but surprisingly not always, the things you most like to do. Tom Rath of the Gallup Organization, defines talent as your "natural way of thinking, feeling, or behaving".[5] If we want our talents to become full-fledged strengths, we need to invest time and energy to help that happen. How?

- Learn the related skills and behaviors, the physical How-To-s. And on an ongoing basis seek to improve these. Here good mentors and appropriate experience are pure gold. Some skills are transferable, like being organized and reliable, some less so, like operating equipment that's on its way out.
- Knowledge obviously also must be learned. And, like some skills, it too is often specific to certain contexts. For example, you wouldn't want a lawyer, even if he or she is very smart, doing brain surgery on you or your drama coach wiring your house.

Whether we want to drive a car or join a symphony, it's crucial that we take our newly absorbed knowledge and fledgling skills and if we are to achieve mastery, practice, practice, practice. Yet, as the cliché goes, "Practice does not make perfect, perfect practice makes perfect." We are engraining how we do things. So we may need to get a little coaching along the way, and be very conscious and conscientious with how we do what. Then we need to get very deliberate about noticing where and how to more frequently utilize and build each of our strengths.

I think of talents as seeds that could grow our joys. To grow those seeds?

- Healthy soil, of course, is best. (A proactive mindset nourishes ability.)
- And sunshine. The stored energy in seeds stirs in the encouraging warmth of sunlight. (Cheer yourself on. Maybe find a mentor.)
- Sunlight attracts leaves. (What pulls you, almost instinctively? What do you seem to crave doing? Shine more light on these talents.)
- Water them. (Put in the time to build the appropriate skills and knowledge.)
- Some seedlings need more or less of this or that, depending on the nature of that particular plant. (Deliberately look for ways to grow *each* of your talents.)
- As the wee leaves start to unfurl, make sure the context is appropriate. Where does it feel like your deepest roots could go down? (Where do you need to be, who with?)
- Keep the weeds cleared. (Don't let yourself get more-than-occasionally distracted. Rest? Sure. Give up? No. Instead, weed out the obstacles.)
- Add nutrients if and when necessary. (Add energy and resources, and keep feeding and building your base of knowledge and skills.)
- And prune away the bits that are growing in directions that aren't conducive to the optimum shape and health of the mature plant. (What form do you want that full-grown strength of yours to take?)

Current Competencies

What feels like you at your best?
List everything you can think of that you're already reasonably good at.
List a few things that you're proud of having accomplished.

At what level do we let ourselves believe we have built a strength?

There's competence, excellence, and then there's "perfect". Perfectionism can be as stunting a construct as procrastination. It's not how-you-are-now or "perfect".
This is a process, a progress towards excellence, which is not likely to be a straight line but a wandering path to mastery with both joys and frustrations en route. Yet when it's something you're enthusiastic about, it's well worth making that journey. Consider the effort involved a gift to your self.

"Gallup's research has shown that a strengths-based approach improves your confidence, direction, hope, and kindness toward others. So why isn't everyone living life with a strengths-based approach? One big problem is that most people are either unaware of, or unable to describe their own strengths … or the strengths of the people around them." [6]

What has, so far, built, bolstered, and shown you your strengths?

Your family? The education system?

Some families clip their kids' wings with too many cautions and "shoulds", ironically often with the best intentions. In what ways, subtle or obvious, might your wings have been clipped inadvertently or deliberately? Others stretch and strengthen their kids' wings with "Here, try this..." How did your family bolster your strengths? Which ones? Which did they—or you—not acknowledge or even notice, at least not yet?

"What's … disheartening is the way our fixation on deficits affects young people in the home and classroom. In every culture we [The Gallup Organization] have studied, the overwhelming majority of parents (77% in the United States) think that a student's lowest grades deserve the most time and attention. Parents and teachers reward excellence with apathy instead of investing more time in the areas where a child has the most potential for greatness." [7]

Does someone else's lack of belief in our abilities need to hold us back? No.
Get a large number of high-achieving adults in a room, and every one of them is likely to have a story about a relative or teacher who put them down at least once. We can choose to internalize that disbelief in our abilities and potential and let it hobble us, or we can harness our enthusiasm and rise above those disheartening messages. It helps if we have even one person who says, "Go for it!" That's who we should listen to. And if we find someone who will help with the How, that's even better.

Let's, for a minute, be perhaps politically incorrect and talk about raw brain power.
As with height, overall brain power, IQ, varies. This is *not* related to race or gender. It is impacted by, for example, Mom's nutrition while carrying the fetus, and by the health of Dad's sperm. (Habits do get passed forward, in ways we may not realize.) Interestingly, research shows that IQ is only minimally related to the family environment in which we're raised, unless it's been particularly inhumane or unfortunate. Thankfully, many (but not all) such consequences can be counteracted, at least somewhat.

Examples of harsh ones? Inadequate food (quality as well as quantity— we really are what we eat), serious neglect physically or emotionally (loving touch is vital, especially to infants), overt abuse, parental alcohol or drug abuse, or environmental toxins.

EQ, emotional intelligence? That's a whole other conversation. Apparently, there are genetic predispositions that hadn't been recognized until recently—combinations of a number of genes that steer us towards being "dandelion children" or "orchid children". Dandelion kids seem to do pretty well whether they're in fertile or more difficult surroundings. Orchid kids, on the other hand, do well if their early environment is nurturing, less so when it's less benevolent. They seem to be much more sensitive and responsive to their contexts, which seems to have overall benefits for the group. (The vast majority of us are not "either-or", but a blend of these tendencies.) Human evolution apparently needs both the hardy dandelions and the orchids.[8] The bottom line? From what I've read, though nurture is obviously important, it seems to have more of an influence on EQ than IQ.

Back to IQ and talents. Specific aspects of our inherent abilities can be tweaked and trained up by our family's input, but overall intelligence? Not so much, it seems. Studies on identical twins sent at birth to live in different families and neighbourhoods show that the IQ of each adult twin will be pretty much the same regardless of where each child grew up. So don't go blaming your "brain power" abilities, or lack of them, on your birth order or how you were potty trained.

> Nature picks our ball-park. Nurture coaches. The players all have their own differing talents. Experience and attitude determine how well we play the game.

Apparently, once a kid is old enough to start shaping their own choices of how and what they want to learn, their own chosen behaviors and nature outrank nurture. *Indeed, especially as adults, what we do with, for, and to ourselves holds a lot more sway in who-we-are and who-we-become than we might like to admit.* There are many people with moderate IQs actively building their talents into strengths and flourishing, while numbers of high-raw-IQ people sit about and ignore who-they-could-be. How sad. And truly stupid. (For a great short read exploring what is Intelligence and how to enhance and protect it, read *New Scientist*, the 2 July 2011 issue.[9])

Expecting more from those you have the privilege to mentor (or from yourself) is a compliment, not an imposition. Higher expectations—when combined with help and support in acquiring the appropriate skills—produces astounding results.
Some talents are obvious, some latent. Unfortunately we can confuse not being able to do something well *yet* with an absence of talent, rather than with *not yet* having acquired the necessary skills to fully realize that talent. What's gotten in the way so far?

- Lousy luck? Maybe you were sidetracked by health issues as a kid.
- Genetics? Maybe you're 5'0" tall and want to be in the NBA. That could be a problem. Why not become a jockey instead? You'd still be working with long-legged creatures.
- Your previous choices? Who did you hang out with? What attitudes might you have absorbed? Are they useful or counter-productive?

What did your friends tell you about what they saw as your strengths? Peer feedback—who we are seen as by those who know us—is very different in intent from peer pressure which tries to enforce conformity. Thankfully, peer *feedback* has a much more potent impact than peer *pressure* on who we become.

Before you were 10 years old...

What did you most like to do?
What did your friends tell you they thought you were good at?
What were your childhood dreams? (Still want to drive a fire truck?)
In what ways since have you explored those interests, indulged those passions?
If you haven't, at least not yet, when will you? That question is neither sarcastic nor rhetorical. If there's still some tingle of appeal to those, name a month when you actually will. (More in the Goals chapter.)

Did you, or do you, spend so much time playing with your thumbs or staring at a screen that you have little idea of what a big and wonderful physical world there is outside an electronic rectangle? How sad.

You owe it to yourself to discover and acknowledge each of your talents. At some point, you may have already tried out some aptitude and personality tests. These, by the way, don't tell you what you *are* good at. They simply point you in a direction that might be useful to explore. Since it's more fun to laugh at someone else's mistakes than make your own, I'll use myself as an example for you to chuckle at. (I'm hardly unique. Many adults have had career paths that are anything but straight lines. But then who says straight lines are the only, or the most interesting, paths up the mountain?)

In my first year at university, they ran us all through a series of aptitude tests to see what we might be both happy and good at, and to check out their research hypotheses for right brain / left brain, and gender differences. Their tests showed that I supposedly have a very "male-brain", and that I should be either a bush pilot or a minister. Well, I'm definitely a straight woman, so it must have been my math and spatial talents (I spent a lot of time running around in the bush and climbing rock faces and trees as a kid) that turned me into what, using their premises, was a stereotypical male-brain. As for the bush pilot bit? I think I was a bird in at least one previous life, not that I particularly believe in that stuff. But I really do love heights, clouds, exploring, and seeing the world from above, so they sure got that right. But the minister part? Personally, I'm not much into organized religion—no offense. But hey, here I am still trying to help if and where I can, which I guess is basically what ministers try to do.

Many years later, bored with work, and sick of being overworked and underpaid (sound familiar?) I was considering changing careers. (Maybe I should have paid more attention to those first tests and become a bush pilot.) I was accepted into law, film, and chiropractic. With two kids, a husband, and a mortgage there was too much at stake to make an unwise decision. And economic viability was a must. So more tests with a highly reputable career counseling organization to help assess my strengths... The results? IQ just fine, and divided up as visual this, logic that, etc. Personality tests—normal, more or less. Turned out my "deference score" was in the 3 percentile. The career counselor said that in 34 years of practice she'd never seen one that low. I asked her what that meant. She suggested that since I apparently had such an aversion to rules, why was I even considering law school? "There's a good chance you'd someday tell a Supreme Court judge to stuff it". Add to that my dislike for sitting still, for paperwork, and for performing (read courtroom), what was I thinking? A recipe for misery. And film? Though it's a true passion that fit well with my visual IQ, it seemed to me more like a happy way to starve given how inappropriately under appreciated the Arts are. Instead, I chose going back to school to do something that would allow me to be my own boss. I don't have any problem telling myself what to do.

Apparently, a lot of us may not be very good at seeing our own strengths. Often we take for granted what we think is typical, when it definitely may not be. Pay close attention, for a few weeks at least, to what you are drawn to and seem to be good at. Ask your friends, and people you work with and trust, to tell you what they see.

Here are a few strengths I had been ignoring about me.

- *Something I thought everyone could do easily, but apparently not—instantly seeing (i.e. creating and playing with) a fully-formed 3D design inside my head whether it's a garden, a house, or a schedule. And for some reason I seem to spot four leaf clovers, real ones, all over the place. (Like that's a useful skill. But it's that visual pattern recognition thing again.)*
- *Being organized, without getting anal or fussed about it. It just feels easy. For some, apparently, it's a small piece of hell.*
- *I knew that I loved learning and helping others get that same gee-wow feeling. I knew that I'm intensely determined to help young people not make the same mistakes as have many adults, including myself. But I had to be told that I'm rather funny and that I'm energizing and inspirational. That's not something I saw at all.*

On the other hand, you may already know the things you suck at, or are miserable trying to do. *For me, it's:*

- *Being told what to do by someone I have no particular respect for. (I know I'm not alone in that one.) And being expected to follow or impose rules I see as useless or counterproductive.*
- *Schmoozing at parties, particularly the more formal pretentious ones. (Sometimes it's a real drag being kinda shy.)*
- *And typing. Tried a number of times to learn, but apparently I'm slightly dyslexic. And here I am trying to write a book. Go figure. Definitely way more appetite than skill on that one.*

That's way more than enough about me. What about you? What feeds your heart or puts a smile on your face? What gives you the twitches or puts a kink in your day?

> The opportunity to explore is vital to identifying and building our strengths. And this is just as true for the entire span of adulthood as it is for kids. Deliberately take yourself out of your rut, on a regular basis. You might find you really like the view.

Finding your Strengths

List any number of things that you already know you're enthusiastic about.

What feels like play?

Which of these do you seem to have a knack for? What activities are your thing?

Which of these talents are you mildly or massively excited about exploring?

Which are your passions?

List several things you might want to try, just to see if they get you excited, with no thought as to whether or not you'd be any good at them. (For example, maybe you'd love to create sculptures, but you wouldn't want your income depending on that ability.) Sometimes there's simply more enthusiasm than aptitude. We're entitled to indulge that side of ourselves too. Giving ourselves permission to try new things, without worrying about looking "uncool", is a strength in itself.

On the other hand, sometimes we're reasonably good at something we're downright ho-hum about doing. Anything come to mind? (You may have fantastic balance. That doesn't necessarily mean you want to be a gymnast or to take up snow-boarding from helicopters. Maybe you're really good at math. That doesn't mean you want to be a statistician or accountant. Maybe you'd rather help others learn math, or do astrophysics.)

Numbers of strengths researchers say that when it comes to our potential strengths and weaknesses, a little self-examination goes a long way. The Gallup Organization's site strengthsfinder.com is a good place to get some help in assessing your strengths, and advice on building yours. (If you know some under-14s, they can try out strengthsexplorer.com.)

Give yourself a gift—the joy of achieving not only competence but excellence in at least one of your talents. And when you're appreciated for that strength, life is sweet indeed.

Building your strengths

Pick any one of your talents.

What new skills and knowledge are needed to unleash this desire?
How can you acquire these?
How will you practice and use these skills? When? Where?
What might maximize the joy in your indulging this side of you?

In the next chapter, you'll further design ways to implement such goals. Go there now if you want. Come back to this later.

There are multiple themes and facets to one's intelligence (spatial, verbal, etc.) as well as overall "smarts". And there are multiple learning styles: visual, kinesthetic, and so on. We're all a blend of all of these, not simply one *or* the other. And, for your own sake, do not mistakenly assume that "I can't", "I don't know how *yet*", and "I don't want to bother" are the same thing.

Clarifying your strengths and weaknesses

Experiment. It may not be so much what you're doing, but the circumstances.

Let's start with **Timing.**
What's your natural body rhythm? Are you an a.m. or p.m. person? What's your strongest time of day for specific activities? That may be different for your body than for your brain. When do you think best? What time of day do you most need or like to get some exercise? When are you most likely to sag? Adjust your schedule to suit your natural rhythms whereever you can. (Personally, my head works better in the morning. By 11 p.m., I'm running on brain stem. While I'd happily go dancing then, I wouldn't want someone's life depending on my intellect.)

Now let's play with **Context.**
Escape the cubicle. Why not take your laptop to the park to finish that report?
Need more quiet? Or, on the other hand, do you need a little hustle and bustle to better concentrate? (Some authors love to write in cafes. Tweens seem to like their music attached to their heads no matter what they do.)
Would getting your space more organized help?
Maybe you crave natural light and lots of it? Find a window. Get outside.
Some of us are more affected by physical context than others. It may be that, rather than the task itself, that's putting us off.

Who for? You likely find that some activities are easier to do for some people or causes than for others. Did you have a teacher or boss that inspired you to do your best? What causes matter to you? Which ones matter enough that you *actually will* do something to help?
Does it matter if others don't see the value in what you're enthusiastic about? No. If it's your passion, you're entitled to do something simply because you want to—as long as you're not hurting someone or something else.

Who with? Perhaps there's some goof you'd rather not get stuck doing anything with. (Think back to group work in high school.) But who knows, maybe they just come across that way because they aren't in a context that allows them to show their strengths. Or maybe they just are a goof. By the way, don't be that goof.

And what's in it for you?
Suppose a task is painfully un-motivating, but you truly do need to get it done. Is there something, anything, about that task that you could modify, even a little, to make it less gag-inducing? Maybe make a connection between that task and something that does matter to you. (Hate doing time-sheets? At least you get paid. Hate doing laundry? At least you know you smell better.)

> A CAUTION—Two extremes of mindset:
>
> Sometimes we bump into slugs in the workplace that do only enough to not get themselves fired. (They may even think that scamming the system makes them "smart".) Obviously that attitude's a weakness. Ironically, it may be one caused by their not getting to—or not choosing to—use their strengths.
>
> At the other extreme, there are people who are working so hard they don't have enough energy left to have a life. They mistakenly see that "dedication" as a strength. Busy-ness is not the same as competence or effectiveness. Confusing these is a weakness that burns people out.

Gallup poll studies "indicate that people who do have the opportunity to focus their strengths every day are six times as likely to be engaged in their jobs and more than three times as likely to report having an excellent quality of life in general."[10] Recent surveys of Canadians showed what's important to them at work. Respect is high on the list. And, overall, more important than the money were having a sense of accomplishment for doing interesting work, liking the people you work with, and having a passion for the cause. All of which would be considered working to your strengths.

Keep in mind that your strengths are great tools but you need to know where, when, and how to apply them. Perhaps you have a lot of initiative. If you're not tactful, that characteristic may have your bosses and co-workers concerned. They may come to see you as a loose cannon or prima donna rather than a creative and useful addition to the team. For how to work well with others, to mutual advantage, check out:

> *The Hard Truths About Soft Skills: Workplace Lessons Smart People Wish They'd Learned Sooner* by Peggy Klaus.
>
> *Difficult conversations* by Douglas Stone, Bruce Patton, and Sheila Heen.

You want to be in a context that enables and appreciates your strengths. Or place yourself in one that does. Or create one that would. (Have a self-directed or entrepreneurial mindset? Read *The 4-Hour Workweek* by Timothy Ferriss.) Which of your strengths are transferable to a different context?

Utilizing your strengths

Pick one of your favourite strengths.
For the next two weeks, watch to see where in your work environment, your personal relationships, your family dynamics, even your neighbourhood you could more frequently put this strength to good use.
Then do that. You'll like the results.

> You're certainly not going to be the only one who wants to see positive change. When people find a way to combine their strengths everyone wins.

Further reading

Go Put Your Strengths To Work, Marcus Buckingham
The Brain That Changes Itself, Norman Dodge
Mindset: The New Psychology of Success, Carol S. Dweck
Do One Thing Different, Bill O'Hanlon
Strengths Finder 2.0, Tom Rath

Weaknesses

Before we start, it's crucial to keep in mind two things. First, "when you confess that a certain activity weakens you, this does not mean that you disrespect the activity." [11] It simply means that you don't want to be the one doing it. (Not everyone likes math, can create music, or dance with the sensuous subtleties of Argentine Tango.) Second, do not consider yourself a failure because you have a few weaknesses. How boring if we were all good at the same things.

I like Buckingham's description of weaknesses. He calls them "your version of Kryptonite".[12] "Your weaknesses ... repulse you or scare you." The activity is "just barren and boring... you struggle to concentrate ... You feel not only physically tired but also emotionally and intellectually drained." [13] "This activity consistently creates in you negative emotional reactions." [14]

I'll add that weaknesses not only make you feel weak, they can make you downright grumpy, perhaps even anxious or ashamed. You may have tried repeatedly to improve this skill, with little success in spite of much genuine effort. In fact, if someone said you never had to do that again, you'd be buying champagne.

By the time you're a young adult, you likely have a pretty good sense of what repels or frustrates you. What others perceive as your weaknesses can be informative, but that's only useful if it enables you to see better how to work to your strengths. Perhaps there's a skill or two you need to improve to get on with it. Yes, you do need to be aware of your limitations. But do not invest extravagant and crazy-making amounts of time, energy, and attention—all of which are finite—into "fixing your weaknesses". Instead, give yourself permission to step away, to let go of these downers! You simply want to acknowledge and manage them so they don't trip you up.

Managing Weaknesses

The trick here? Distinguish between the specific skills that would boost your ability to use your strengths—even though you may not be enthusiastic about putting in the effort to improve them—and those where it's simply more efficient to work with or hire someone who's already good at them. (That goes for both the work-world and your personal life.) Or find someone to teach you a few useful tricks to get the task out of the way faster and with less irritation, whether it's cooking or doing your taxes.

By the way, congratulate yourself for working through this book. Some things you can't and shouldn't delegate. While many wouldn't put learning basic life-skills such as time and money management at the top of their Passions list, they do become increasingly enthusiastic about the results. Keep in mind too that by simplifying the pragmatics of life you're creating more time and energy for your true passions.

Gradually steer your tasks wherever possible, at work or at home, towards your strengths and away from weaknesses. Be gently self-protective, yes. But don't base your approach on Ego. Instead, think Team. Negotiate with the others. Think win-win. It's not you versus them. It's all-of-you-together taking care of whatever-needs-doing. You'll find too that there's a better outcome for everyone if each person does not "compromise" too soon. Productive compromise should not feel like settling.

What are you good at?
How can you best dove-tail that with the strengths of the others?

For example, at work I'd rather do all the scheduling than be the go-to-meetings-guy. I'm not very good at sitting still. And not particularly patient with the way that, too much of the time, the bosses of the bosses don't even listen to them, let alone to the rest of us. Sound familiar? I'd simply rather avoid hierarchies and the ladder-climbing mentality whereever possible, and just get on with it. For some reason, I find the scheduling easy. My colleagues are really good at numerous other things. We make a great team. Lucky us.

Yes, once and a while there are times when, even as a group, the task is no one's strength and we have to suck it up and get it done anyway. Negotiate who gets stuck with what. Consider it an Oh-poor-us team building exercise and perhaps all go out for a pint afterwards.

Frustrated with what you see needs doing in your organization? *Learn to lead from within.* It's possible to quietly instigate and implement beneficial changes even if the system is not particularly conducive to or initially supportive of what needs doing. Have a go at it. It's surprisingly effective and really quite fun, especially when others begin to realize they like your band-wagon.

I hate this!

Think of a task that leaves you feeling frustrated or incompetent.

Suppose you avoided doing that task. Would the required overall results actually be negatively impacted? Again, from a results point of view, which components of that task are the genuine musts?

Think of a way to negotiate some trade-offs with other people. We don't all have the same preferences, thank heavens.

If you must do it, how could you do it faster, yet adequately well?
Who could help you learn how?

What aspect of that task, specifically, do you find hateful? Is that affected by what, when, where, who for, and so on? How could you change the context or the timing to make doing the truly necessary bits less annoying? Some examples:

If you're your own boss, hire a highly competent person to do those things that you aren't good at or hate doing. That's definitely better for your business and your sanity and besides, it's a tax deduction.

If you're an employee, network with your colleagues. Together, negotiate to design constructive changes in what, how, when, who with, and where.

At home, who likes grocery shopping? Who'd rather do the laundry than cook?
Which days is who willing to do what?

Be particularly careful of these weaknesses…

A potentially incapacitating misconception? An overblown sense of entitlement. Too many, of all age groups, don't see it as their own responsibility to explore their talents and develop their strengths. It's annoying in adults. They should know better. It's sad in teens and younger adults. They need some help and encouragement to get on with it. Yes, have high expectations for your life, but expecting to have Life served up like a gourmet meal while you sit on your butt? That's counter-productive and daft.

Another toxic belief is that our current abilities are carved in stone. That leads to ego defensive patterns, turf wars, and having to put others down to make ourselves feel "okay". The result? A life in which who we *are* and who we *can be* are constricted by a narrowness of vision. Frustration and bitterness will not be far behind. Thankfully, this belief can be readily repaired, and should be. Beliefs are software, not hardware. Rewrite this one. It's debilitating and self-imposed. Fixed mindset people often don't realize that they can grow a growth mindset. Get some help with suitable strategies if you need to. (Perhaps start with the Further Reading list on page 77)

Speaking of ego-defense—does needing help with something mean we are weak or weak-minded? Of course not. Asking for help simply shows that we're smart enough to acknowledge we can't know all things. Don't let Ego get in the way of your becoming a wiser, more effective, happier person. (If you're worried about the dangers of exposing your underbelly, say at work, start by asking the advice of knowledgeable people you trust.) Occasionally needing help is human. The courage and wisdom to ask is actually a strength, at any stage of life. Indeed, asking for the appropriate help, appropriately, is a mature and masterful skill we should all aspire to.

Talent + Enthusiasm + Skill building => Strength

A profoundly valuable strength?

Knowing that you can expand who you are, and that you can adopt and develop the courage to help that happen. By stretching yourself, by playing and learning, practicing and gaining experience, you develop not only the parts of you that you currently value, but those that may be latent treasures just waiting to be unearthed and enjoyed.

Find and build your strengths and make your weaknesses irrelevant. [15]

You don't need to go it alone. Ironically, to best access and build your strengths and to be able to joyfully express your individuality, it's best to ask for help and to join forces with others. In reality, it's the Team (in a work place, a relationship, a family, even a tribe of friends) that needs all-the-strengths, not each individual. Encourage each other. Share ideas and useful strategies. Dovetail your strengths. You then can be each other's help-mates and mentors, if you want or need to, and by doing so smooth the path for all. As in *The Lord of the Rings*, become your own "Fellowship of the Tasks". And, of course, as individuals or as a group continue to improve your skills and seek relevant knowledge and experience. Keep growing.

Enjoy and appreciate the journey. Destinations are moving targets. Delicious goals get accomplished, desires shift, possibilities evolve.

Goals are the topic of the next chapter....

Chapter 10

Goals and A-LISTS

You're reading this book. Bravo! Yay you! And frankly, yay me. Indulge me for a moment, it's my first time. I've sometimes dabbled in trying to write poetry, but to write an entire book and publish it? Way outside my comfort zone. I had no clue where to begin, only a vague notion and a definite annoyance that we're not taught how to simplify and deal with practical realities nor how to build a quality life. Hence the title, *Someone really oughta tell you.*

I wondered what I should include. Things I'd learned over the years, many the hard way. Things I hadn't learned until recently. So many things I didn't know that I didn't know that would have made life so much simpler. Ouch. You likely have a few stories of your own to tell. What advice would you pass along to people ten years younger than you?

By the way, if you USE the material in this book, your life will be easier and hopefully happier. And since it would please me to think I've helped even a little, thank you for getting this far in your reading. As I said in the preamble, this book is not going to give you "all the answers". (Be justifiably suspicious of anyone who says they can.) But it's definitely a good start at the right questions to ask yourself and the appropriate others who will be able help along the way.

Since you're reading this, I got past a lot of decision and how-to hurdles. First, whether to bother doing this at all. Then which to do—a book, a website, or just blog it? Other hurdles? The perseverance to research and write it, and the obstacle course of compiling and organizing the material, then working with others to edit, format, design, and publish it. It's been a steep learning curve. (As I write this particular chapter, I'm still wading through all that.) And given that I'm pathetic at sales and have minimal extrovert tendencies, I cringe at the thought of the marketing process. (Can I hide under my desk now please? Oh, stop whining, Di.) My point? No matter what you want to do, there will be times when your energy and courage may sag. You will need to regroup and recharge. (How human of you.) It's a good thing that the thought of getting this done and out there where it can help someone, revs my engine. And it is an interesting though sometimes intimidating process. So I do this in chunks. A bit at a time. Until sanity melts, and I go play. Or I go to work. Writing is not my profession. It's not even my hobby. Right now, it's my cookie. What's yours?

What's *your* cookie?

In previous chapters, you've already spent time exploring what matters to you. Here's a little more food for thought to munch on. (We'll elaborate on goal implementation throughout the rest of this chapter. Consider this an appetizer.)

- You're told today you only have one year to live, in good health and with no financial constraints, then you just keel over. Pick five things you'd do with your only-one-year.
- What have you often thought you'd like to try but have been afraid to?
- Describe two situations that made you feel important or valued.
- What would you like to be more proud of or be more appreciated for?
- Name two changes you'd like to see in the world.
- When it's "too late", what will you most regret not having done?

Design, Create, and Welcome Your Best Possible Life

That's a tall order. It's not something you have to do all at once, and you can shift things around as you see fit later.

You want to cover all your bases. But how? It can be useful to sort your goals into Categories or Roles. Either way will do. (Or both if you want. Your call.)
Each goal will likely incorporate more than one value.

For example, you take up playing tennis with your kid brother:
The Categories: Health, Play, Relationships.
The Roles: Family member, Mentor.
The Values? Connection, Love, Health & fitness.

Priorities as CATEGORIES

Add one or two more categories to the list below if you want, but this is not a game of seeing how many categories you can list. You're just using these to help sort your goals.

Health
Career / Skill building
Play / Hobby
Relationships
Financial
Spiritual
Contributory (humanitarian, environmental, etc.)

Priorities as ROLES

How might you improve, i.e. be happier or more effective, in your role as:

Family member (spouse, parent, son or daughter, sibling, etc.)
Friend
Team-mate
Mentor
Employee / employer
Citizen (of a country, of the planet)
Any other roles ... ?

Now try this:

Write down one goal for each of the above Categories *or* Roles. (These will intertwine, so don't obsess over the process. The intention is simply to be sure you're covering your bases.)

From your current priorities, choose a total of not more than three goals for now. (Don't discourage yourself by tackling a lot of goals at once.) I suggest you choose:

- One that requires no money or very little money to implement,
- One that requires a short time frame and isn't too daunting,
- One that may be a little more intimidating, but that you find really exciting.

Suppose you've been a real slob lately and your home should be on a TV show about what-not-to-do. Don't try to get it ready for a *House Beautiful* photo shoot in one weekend. Go clean out one drawer. It's like trying to eat one potato chip. I dare you.

To energize each goal, create a notebook, file, or collage of representative pictures. It's not a corny thing to do. It's effective. Put pictures or notes where they're in your face everyday, perhaps on or around the bathroom mirror. (I've got travel books on the shelf just below my TV. Can't watch it without seeing those books. That helps me keep my self-proclaimed priorities straight.)

Now you've got a pretty good idea of the WHAT. Let's get on with the HOW....

ACRONYMS as advice for goals

There are lots of acronyms describing the steps for attaining Goals. Though they're all useful in their own way, frankly, I couldn't really get into any of them. For me, it all comes down to Ta-Da! (that "Yah!" happy dance of having succeeded) and the To-Do's to get there. (Could we turn that *Ta-Da-To-Do* into a drum beat? Then we could dance our way through the obstacles that always show up.)

Build your **A-LISTS.** Here's an overview of my A-LIST Acronym.

A What do you want to **A**chieve, **A**ccomplish?
What do you want **A**ccess to, want to **A**vail yourself of ...?
The clearer your vision, the easier it will be to hit the target.

L **L**ovin' it ! You gotta' be Lovin' it!
It doesn't matter if you can't put this into words. Just 'get it' in your gut.

I **I**nitiate and **I**mplement your **I**ntentions
Get off your butt. If you want the results, do the doing. Otherwise, resign yourself to sulking and to the pain of "shoulda-coulda-woulda".

S **S**teps to **S**uccess
Plan backwards from where you want to be to where you are now. At least, plan as much as you can. You may not know all the steps when you start, but don't let that stop you from getting underway. You can fill in the missing bits as you go. Think Here, There, and In-between.
Yes, there will be "yikes!" moments. Welcome to reality. You will learn how to navigate those. And you'll enjoy your new-found confidence and pride in yourself. How delicious is that!

T Put a **T**ime frame on the steps and the results, that "Ta-Da!" you're after.
And celebrate the little successes along the way. (Drum-roll please.)

S **S**upport , **S**ynergy, and **S**erendipity
Once you focus and commit to going for it, you'll notice coincidences and like-minded and/or helpful people all over the place.

Now let's get into more detail.

What do you want to Achieve, Accomplish, Access, have Available to you?

Your goal is real. Savour it. Experience it in your imagination. Describe it in intense detail, in doodles or pictures in your mind, if not in words. What are you doing? What does it look, feel, sound, even taste like? (I love to travel and have a thing about cliffs overlooking the ocean. I can feel the wind on my face, smell the salt air, hear the pounding surf, feel my skin sun-soaked as the day sinks into a mauve and orange horizon below my feet. Get the idea? Think that doesn't build my motivation to set aside travel-money?)

In your description, leave no room for **A**mbiguity. You need to be able to recognize when you've **A**ttained it.

What is that  ?

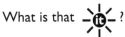

What's the goal behind the goal? Maybe there's a simpler way to get the same perk, to address the same need or want. Do you "need" that spiffy new car, or more respect from your colleagues? Do you "need" that slinky designer outfit, or to have your mate to pay more attention to you? Do you "need" that expensive vacation, or do you desperately need some time to yourself with no responsibilities?

Frame your goal in the positive, not the negative. For example, don't say to yourself, "I'm terrified of ending up a bag lady". Say, "I want to be a lady of leisure". And describe specifically what, for you, being a 'lady of leisure' means.

Don't let thinking "I can't afford it" get in the way of improving certain aspects of your life. (No, I'm not saying, "Go ahead, be foolish with your money".) The reality is that many, perhaps most of life's truly worthwhile ingredients require little or no money at all, like laughing more frequently (including at yourself), appreciating each other's company, being active with our bodies, being kind, and making a difference in the world.

The route to a goal may feel like a smooth freeway or a sequence of bumpy back-roads. Either way, the journey is likely to occasionally require perseverance and a little courage. The flat-tires of life are frustrating, but they're temporary set-backs. You're entitled to be proud of yourself for simply being underway.

It's often suggested that we start with smaller or more rapidly implemented goals. Small visible successes build skill and confidence, and with confidence comes momentum. Yet here's an intriguing and delightful surprise: *bigger goals are not necessarily harder to achieve than mid-size or mid-range ones.* They may in fact have more juice to them and hence be more motivating.

Yes, some things in life seem easier to do than others. A simple task like painting a wall? No problem. But it's often not the size of the goal that's the issue. If the goal involves modifying our ingrained habits or the dynamics of a relationship, that's a bit trickier. Which goals are the hardest? Those that might involve our needing to shift our sense of who we are. Hopefully, Who-you-are-now will welcome the realization that you are and will continue to be a wonderful work-in-progress. Embrace that wisdom.

L Lovin' it

You gotta be loving the thought of the end result. And skip the *whys*. Feeling that you need to verbalize *why* is too much like having to justify yourself. And, as we discussed in the Decision-making chapters, that can be quite counter-productive.

Your goal needs to spark your enthusiasm, ignite your engine, rev your motor.
If not, you'd be better off choosing a higher octane goal—one that has more meaning for you. It's not the size of the goal, nor how impressive it would be to others, that matters. How potent is the effect going to be on how you feel? Goals can be a massive *Wow,* like a trip around the world, or simply having more time for yourself, a clutter free work space or a nice juicy steak for dinner. (My mouth's watering. Ignite the BBQ.)

Imagine what your life will be like, look like, feel like when the goal is implemented. Again, you don't need to convert these imaginings into prose. (Unless that's your thing.) Pictures, doodles, or a bare few words jotted down, where you won't lose them, are fine. You're not writing and defending a Master's thesis—you're the one in charge here.

Think "If this ... then that.." Let your imagination take over. Follow the ideas through. See it in your mind as already-real. Be lovin' it.

Now visit the flip side. What would life be like, feel like if you don't follow through? Blah. Yuck. Ouch. Now harness the gap, the voltage, the charged energy in the contrast—the zap—to get on with it!

Initiate and Implement your Intentions

Enthusiastic and excited?

Great! Jump straight to the "Stages and Steps" on page 87.
Come back to this bit later.

Feeling some hesitation?

Getting started is frequently harder than the actual doing.
If you're a little intimidated by the process, start with baby steps.
Concerned because you know there will be a few obstacles? Ya, so?
Ha. Surprise, it may actually be easier than you think. There are tactics that work and there is help along the way.

What goals have you already achieved?

You're reading this: learning to read was itself once a goal whether or not you articulated it as such. You probably have a roof over your head: some things you just know you need to do. Those are goals too. And hey, you're already a goal-setter and a solver or you wouldn't have picked up this book.

What helped you sustain the momentum to get to your previous goals?
Which kinds of goals feel more do-able for you?
Which of your actions and thoughts seem to be most effective?
What circumstances, what contexts, seem to help you more easily get on with doing what needs to be done to get you there?

On the other hand, what goals have you, in the past, chickened out on?
Often the problem has more to do with not knowing how, or not believing we can, than with the actual difficulty of the goal. As we discussed in the Change chapter, that can manifest as procrastination, resistance, and fatigue—any of which could be misinterpreted as "laziness".

Ernie Zelinski, in the *Lazy Person's Guide to Success*, reminds us that perception can magnify an obstacle out of all proportion. "Excessive ... worrying about problems is like looking at nasty neighbours through high powered binoculars. The problems don't disappear; they end up appearing a lot larger—and nastier—than they really are."[1] When you see even small movement towards the desired outcome, dread will dissipate like a spooky night fog in the morning sun. Look for and create more of those "bright spots". (Revisit page 64 if you need to.)

It's useful but not necessarily easy to distinguish between genuine obstacles and the excuses that masquerade as "reasons". Excuses can be our jaded or scared, lazier or brattier, or too-tired selves putting us down, holding us back from initiating and implementing what we'd prefer in life.

The External Obstacles?

For most, these are money, time, and other people.

- Money we'll deal with in the next section.
- Time in the next chapter.
- As for other people? Sorry, you're on your own there. I did say this "manual" is not all-the-answers. (In the previous chapter I suggested *Difficult Conversations* by Douglas Stone, Bruce Patton, and Sheila Heen and *Switch* by Chip Heath & Dan Heath. I'm suggesting them again, hint, in case you didn't think I was serious the first time. They're truly useful reads.)

The Internal Obstacles?

Ironically, these are often trickier to solve, partly because we may not even be aware of them. Here are a few examples:

- Are you afraid that, if you set goals, you'll have to acknowledge that you're unhappy about something? (That's a surprisingly common one.)
- Are you disempowered by cynicism? Or by learned-pessimism? Are you afraid to hope? Or mired in blaming others?
- Do you think you're much too special to have to work for what you want? (Ya right. Sorry.) Are you feeling overly entitled? Or not enough so?
- Are you worried that "taking risks" is risky? Minimize risk by chewing off manageable proportions. Sometimes the worst risk is to take none.
- Think that being "mature" or "sensible" means you don't get to play and have fun? Hopefully, you'll reject that ridiculous idea with minimal effort.

- Are you assuming, wrongly, that what you do doesn't matter anyway? That nothing will come of it, even if you do try? It's sad and rather scary how many feel this way.
- Do you think that if you win, someone else loses? Or the other way around? (You just know you'd be the one voted off the island? Arg. You're watching too many "reality" shows.) Think win-win instead. Much more powerful. (Ah, a new program idea—no one wins unless everyone does.)
- Are you thinking you have to do it all by yourself? Or that asking for help is a perhaps embarrassing sign of weakness? It takes more guts to ask for help when you need it than it does to hide your insecurities. Besides, there are people out there who would love to have a chance to help where they can, and they consider it a compliment to be asked. It takes a village. Even the best didn't get there by themselves.

Do yourself a favour—decide you're not ready to do this, at least not yet, or get busy doing it. There's likely much less to lose by trying than later wishing you had. Shoulda-coulda-woulda—and didn't—BITES!

Is it easier on the ego to not really try than to risk discovering that maybe you're not up to that particular challenge? Why sell yourself so short? *Feel the Fear and Do It Anyway.* (Good book by Susan Jeffers.) Pay attention to what your scared brain is saying, deal with the issues that are worthy of caution, and get on with it. If you still want to. It's your life.

Babies, when learning to walk, stub their toes and take tumbles. Gradually, as their skills improve, they race and jump. Similarly, winners do trip on their way to winning. Losers, on the other hand, are the ones who are either so fearful or so hung up on having to "win", that they don't even try. You're not a loser so choose not to act like one. (Losers wouldn't have picked up this book.) A little help with skill building and a bit of hope as fuel, and you're good to go. So where do you want to start?

There's something surprising and delicious about having chosen a certain goal and decided to go for it. Even when you're not consciously thinking about it, your brain's unconscious, pre-conscious, subconscious, whatever you want to call it will be working away. Like bubbles out of fine champagne, good ideas will pop to the surface like heady little gifts.

S Stages and Steps to Success

You see the *Here*. You envision the *There*. Now you need to find, or create and build, the path. Think of this as planning backwards—before I can accomplish *that*, I need to do *this*. Or think of it as an end, a beginning, and filling in the in-between.

Break the HOW process into stages and each stage into distinct do-able steps. These may not all be visible at the outset. That's okay. In fact, in most cases that's typical. It's unlikely you'll anticipate every quirky issue that might arise, so don't get bogged down thinking you need to. Lay out the stages and steps as best as you can. Some you'll have to sort out as you go. Once you get to one horizon, you'll more clearly see the next.

Sketch a rough flow chart that you can add to as necessary. Do some research. Keep seeking the right questions to ask. And ask them. Keep good notes. Ask more questions. Keep doing the doing. Fine-tune as you go.

It's easier to focus once you have a game plan—then you can deal with one step at a time. You can get to those other tasks later. Give each of those "laters" a roughed out time frame. Roughed out. Goals sometimes seem to be moving targets. And this particular goal is not likely your only priority. (Parts of this book-process, for example, are taking me much longer than I anticipated. Yes, I set myself deadlines. But I'm not going to be mean to myself while trying to get this done. And neither should you.)

Rethink your tactics when necessary. There will be inevitable occasional frustrations but you'll solve them. Have faith in your ability to find the answers, some appropriate strategies, and people who can help. (See the **S**'s on page 90.)

Whether you're fixing the sink or your credit report, applying for that new job, painting a room or planning a trip, don't expect to do everything at once. By using Stages-and-Steps, you have a good sense of what you need to do *now* and what you need to do *next*. The process is then less stress-inducing or annoying. You may find yourself pleasantly surprised by feeling both calm and excited about what's happening.

An example of "planning backwards"? Moving. We all do it, some more often than others. You know the here-and-now. You decide the where-and-when. As for the in-between? What do you do when to keep the process as simple as possible? In Appendix A, there's a MOVING check-list to help you out.

Creating the Stages-and-Steps for Accomplishing a Goal

You'll use these at the end of this chapter.
For now, simply read them over and let your brain chew on them.

Visualize and Plan – Your first horizon.

What is the result you want?
What information is needed? Where can you get that?
What actions are involved?
What materials are needed? Where and how do you get those?
If you'll need some help, arrange that too.
What concerns do you have? How could you resolve these?
Address, in advance, as many of these as you can.
Block out the time frames for each stage.

Prepare
Fine-tune the timing for each step of this phase of the project.
Get the materials together. Have your how-to information handy.
Arrange for the necessary help. Be specific about what needs doing and when.
Do whatever prep work is required.

Do DO the doing. (Each stage. Each step.)
Adapt to, and solve, whatever kinks and quirks show up.

Tidy up afterwards. Physically, and otherwise.
Thank whoever helped along the way.

Smile Enjoy the results. Pat yourself on the back! You did it!

Get on with the first few small steps and the momentum will build.
(You may want to revisit the Change chapter if you find yourself getting stuck.)

Don't get yourself too regimented. *Look for the joy in the journey, not just the destination.* It's all part of the experience. Remember to take breathers.
And reward yourself for accomplishing each stage.

At least once a week, ask yourself:

- What's working? What are you doing well? Do more of that.
- What could be done a little better?
- What should you do less of, or avoid doing?
- What one thing, if done more regularly, would improve the situation?

T Time frames

For each of your steps to success, set an approximate time frame. How hard-core you choose to be about those deadlines is up to you.

Still procrastinating? Is it confidence or the how-to skills that you're lacking? You're entitled to be occasionally lazy or scared. (How human of you.) Perhaps, if you're honest with yourself, you just aren't interested enough in the results to be bothered with the process? Surprise, you're entitled to that too. It is your life. But you're also entitled to the consequences of not following through. (Want to quit smoking? Time frames. Maybe you get down to half a pack by next month? Down to four cigarettes a day by the month after that? And reward your small successes, just not with another cigarette. Or you could choose to continue procrastinating and die of lung cancer. Your call. Your life. Some habits are more difficult to change than others, some consequences more devastating than others.)

"If at first you don't succeed, try, try again". When is perseverance appropriate? When is it simply silly? Suppose the obstacles are, at least for the moment, piling up. That will happen occasionally. How do you know when to bail? When to reassess and modify? When to just keep on chugging? Einstein's definition of insanity: "Doing the same things over and over again and expecting different results". Ouch. So what do you do? How do you "wrestle an obstacle to the ground"? Figure out what you're not doing quite right yet, then try again. I like the word YET—YET tells your brain that you can and expect to succeed. YET gives your frustrated-self a little incentive to keep working to solve the puzzle. That's more fun than fuming and fretting.

Be a little flexible with your timelines. Or take a bit of a break.
Perhaps enlist some friends to help or to at least be your cheering section.

> The final hour of any journey seems to last as long as the entire rest of the trip. Hang in there!

Recapture the initial excitement. Revisit **A** and **L** above as motivators when the momentum drags or the energy sags. If the intended results have lost their luster or you decide you're not willing to pay the price, it's okay to let that goal go. It is your life. But, again, be sure you're okay with paying the price of not doing it.

A little frustrated? What modifications to your current strategies or new tactics might be useful? Do you know how to implement these? You may want some knowledgeable and experienced help.

Support and Synergy

Get practical advice.

What information do you need to implement your goals?
What questions do you need answered? Who might be able to answer them?
Check out several sources of advice. Try a few of their suggestions.

Find a mentor, a coach.

Learn from the successes, and mistakes, of others. Who is doing or has already done something similar? (Ask around. Maybe read some autobiographies.)
Find those who have overcome the same issues that you're dealing with.
How did they do it? Would they be willing to mentor you?
And be a mentor. Be a buddy. Whose life can you improve?

Enlist moral support.

Find those who will encourage you. Seek out those who can and will help with your dream, not clip its wings before it can fly. Too many parrots—sorry—people have been conditioned to curtail their dreams. Even those who love you may try to "protect you" from possible disappointment. Others may envy your gumption for going for it. Watch out for these naysayers—sensible caution is one thing, corrosive negativity is quite another.
Find a buddy who's going after a similar goal. Be each other's allies. Be accountable to each other, on an ongoing basis, about your progress. Acknowledge and celebrate each other's small successes along the way. There is strength in companionship and synergy.

Create a "Fellowship of the Tasks".

Synergy: one-plus-one is more than two. It is useful to team up with others with a similar goal, yes, but deliberately seek out those who have *different* task-tackling styles. Work done by Kathy Kolbe, an eminent and intriguing learning strategy specialist, shows that there are Four Action Modes ® :"Quick Starts" (jump right in types), "Fact Finders" (info junkies who can get caught in analysis-paralysis if they're not careful), "Follow Thrus" (highly organized people with methodical systems) and "Implementors" ("tool" makers and real world modelers). Each of us possess different talents in all four Action Modes.[2] When we team up with those who are skilled in what we're less than fabulous at, we are as a group more effective in taking on what needs doing. We can then help each other achieve our goals, and with less stress and fuss. (For more information on Action Modes, or to learn more about Kolbe and the good work she does for individuals and for organizations, go to www.kolbe.com.)

Serendipity

"An apparent aptitude for making fortunate discoveries accidentally".[3]
Not magic. (Supposedly. Well, probably.) But definitely real and wonderful.
Be AWARE. If you haven't read the chapter on Luck, I suggest you do that now.
Life will occasionally drop a sweet in your lap. Recognize, enjoy, and appreciate it!

Helping Good Things Happen

When you put in the effort, when you plan and act on your ideas, you improve your productivity and chances of success. Even a small taste of that success boosts your confidence and energy levels. That, in turn, fosters better quality and more frequent inspiration, and the willingness and ability to put in more effective effort. Throughout, you're increasing your skill levels at whatever you're doing. Up goes your confidence, and your chances of being even more effective and successful. Sweet.

The magic? *Effective* effort. Not killing yourself.

Putting together a Play-by-Play for achieving your Goal

Let this feel like a game, like you're going to *help* your goal happen. ("Make" it happen can sound like too much work.) Enthusiasm is much more effective than willpower! And think of ways to help the process of getting-there be more fun.

Refer back to the three goals you chose in the previous "Categories and Roles" activity. (Page 82) For now, pick one of those.

The Play by Play

- What is the desired result? Describe it in detail. Lots of detail. Not necessarily in words. Use doodles, pictures, a collage if you'd rather.
- Map out the path. Maybe do scattered circles on a page at first. (Some call this Mind-mapping.) Or set up a flow chart. Add details as you figure it out.
- Refer back to the Stages-and-Steps on page 88.
- Choose one specific thing you can do today to start the process. If you "can't" today, pick a day and time later this week and hold yourself to that.
- How long might it take for each step? What's your overall timeline? (There's more on Time-and-Task management in the next chapter.)
- Who could help with good advice, skills, or even simply as moral support?

What are some of the obstacles you will, or could, face?

- What might this goal cost? When? Can you deal with that in stages? How?
- What are your current time constraints? What could you cut back on to create more time for this?
- Who else is involved? Who do you need to negotiate with? About what?
- What internal issues might be tripping you up? (Revisit page 86)
- What strategies could you use to overcome each of the external and internal challenges? (Time we'll deal with in the next chapter. Money in the next section. Those nagging internal issues? The tactic "Act as if..." seems to work wonders.)

> "Great deeds are made up of small steady actions, and it is these that you must learn to value and sustain." [4]
>
> Barbara Sher

Your home as an example of a manageable goal...

Whether it's modest or extravagant, whether it's a cave or a penthouse, a condo or a private island, your place of residence can and should be adapted to your lifestyle and your taste.

Even if you currently live in a basement bachelor apartment, you can begin in some small way turning your dream—if you know what that is—into reality. Then upgrade parts as you go. Ratty linens and towels? It's not expensive to replace a few. With nicer ones, you'll feel every day like you're taking better care of yourself. For bigger items, e.g. a new flatscreen, start saving and watch for sales.

Start with some basic aspects that are independent of money:
Is your place tidy? Is it clean? Is it organized so you can conveniently find things?
Do you have too much stuff? Clear out the redundant and seldom used. Make room for the more meaningful and aesthetically pleasing.

What items would improve your day-to-day living? (Maybe some extra shelves or an under-bed storage box?)

What practical needs and personal preferences do you want your home to satisfy and support? For more on designing and outfitting your home, see Appendix C.

What thoughts and feelings have been surfacing while you've been thinking through and working on your goals?

Dismantle the counter-productive ones.
Examine the cautionary ones.

And note and celebrate the energizing thoughts.
Harness their energy to help you move forward !

Be aware of what's going on around and inside you. Learn. Strategize. DO.
Reassess. Do more of what's working. Less of what doesn't.
Along the way, acknowledge and celebrate your progress.
And **welcome success**.

"Sure I have goals and dreams, but I don't have enough time!"

There are solutions to that...

Time

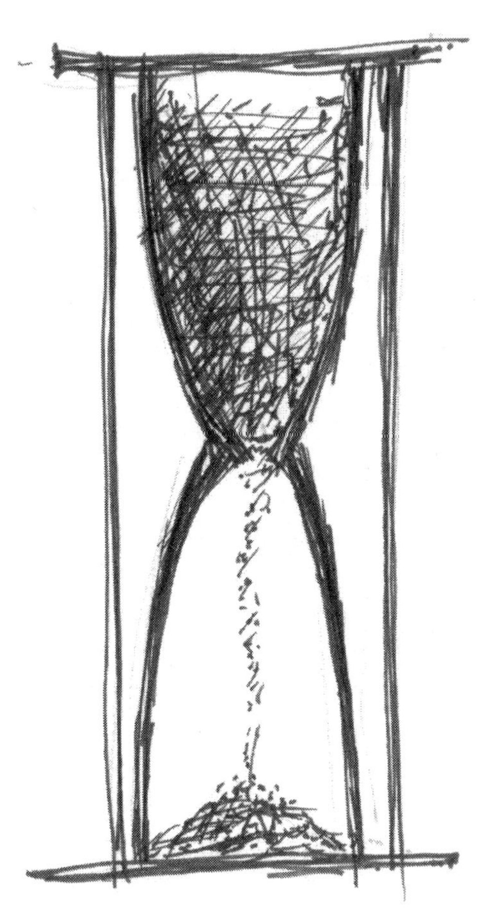

Chapter 11

"I don't like planning. It's boring."
"Planning takes the spontaneity out of life".
"There's never enough time anyway."
"It's a waste of time."

Ya, whatever...
Planning is not wasting time—it's making time for what *actually matters* to you.
It's life-affirming skill building. Keep reading.

Everyone's got 24 – 7

There are 168 hours in a week, 8,760 hours in a year.
The number of years in our lifetime we don't know.

Some have too much time on their hands and don't know what to do with it. Endless hours at their disposal. Others would consider that a nice problem—their day feels like an overstuffed suitcase that they're having to stomp on to make everything fit. They're worn down, discouraged, annoyed because they need 34 not 24 hours in a day. The well-lived life lies somewhere in between.

Do you find yourself resisting even trying to plan your week because getting-it-all-done feels oh-so-impossible? Does it feel like the weeks and months stretch on and on? That it's all just too hectic, or too bland? Or both? That there's never time for just being you? Are you feeling, not like the driver, but like a bound and gagged hostage in the trunk of your own life? Okay, I'm getting carried away here. Let's lighten up.

Think of time simply as a puzzle to be assembled, not as a straight-jacket. Here's the fun irony of planning your time:

- You do it, not to tie up every single minute, but to **free up hours**.
- You do it, not to nail down every minute as some fear, but the opposite—to **create space for spontaneity and guilt-free play-time**.
- You do it so you can **put boundaries on the Musts and Shoulds**.
- You do it to **enhance your ability to do what matters**, in the short and long term, and to **make room for what brings you joy and meaning**.

For the discouraged and the cynics—no, we can't plan it all. No, you can't see every detour or contingency that may unfold. So what? You can't see, all at once, every inch of highway for your entire trip, yet I doubt you'd choose to drive blindfolded. The journey is finite. Time is finite. Open your eyes. If you can see what matters most in your life, you'll get less side-tracked by what matters least.

The rest of this chapter will help you with the following:

What to do? What *not* to do?
How long do things take?
When to do what?
What about when Life throws a curve ball?

Let's get you in that driver's seat. Keep your A-LIST Goals handy. By the way, the more you feel yourself resisting trying these time-related activities, the more likely it is you need them. Think of them as dating possibilities, not marriage to one plan.

What to do? What not to do?

Personally, I've never responded very well to being told "you must …" (Ask anyone who knows me.) And I hardly think I'm alone in that. We want to be in charge, not dictated to by an imposed exhausting and exasperating To-Do list whose supposed benefits are in question and that we're not sure we signed on for anyway. (Feeling a little grouchy are we?)

It's more fun to be gently guided and inspired by our personally designed A-LISTS. And the more constrained our time is, the more diligent, even fierce, we need to be about sorting out our priorities perhaps generating, as well, a Not-to-do list. "No", tactfully stated, is a very useful word. We can be both self-protective *and* generous hearted.

That being said, whether you aspire to be a saint, a hero/heroine, an earth-mother/father, a warrior, or a bad-ass, there are things you need to do to take care of yourself. Avoiding these, pretending they don't matter, will bite you at some point. Does that mean we resent doing them or consider them part of respecting ourselves?

- There's self-care as a biological entity, like enough sleep and healthy food.
- And taking care of the practical stuff allows us to have a kinder, more fun life. (Unless you want to wallow like a hoarder or enjoy sleeping under the bridge.) Whether its chores or money management, there are ways to make these pragmatics easier to do *and* have them produce better results.
- Then there's the downright fun stuff. Play is not a waste of time or energy. Consider it regeneration time. You're recharging your batteries and even the Energizer Bunny needs those.

Yet so much of what we do is a waste of time and energy. As with overstuffed and disorganized closets or garages, the best place to start is with a good purge. What can you let go of? The activities in this chapter will help you decide that.

Speaking of wasting time—evidently the average executive, as reported by the Wall Street Journal, spends on average almost an hour a day searching through cluttered desks and files. That's a whopping total of about six weeks per year!

How long do things take?

Not everyone takes the same amount of time to get a certain task done. Some people like to putter in the garden and blast through the bills. Some, like me, like to jack-rabbit through the grocery store. Others consider it a relaxing outing.

Get better at guesstimating, then noticing the reality of how long specific tasks take you. You're entitled to your preference of how-long. But there may be things you'd like to get faster or better at. You can learn to minimize the time it takes for such practical tasks as organizing your finances, doing laundry, or cleaning up. And you can learn to minimize your time wasters. That way, you'll free up more time for the fun stuff. (More on that shortly.)

When to do what?

Not everyone has the same natural body rhythms. You may be a night owl or a morning person, or more energetic and efficient when it's not dark and dreary out. SAD, Seasonal Affective Disorder, is more prevalent than researchers originally thought. Perhaps as many as 15% of people deflate without adequate sunshine. Including me. Get outdoors more, especially in the morning. Take some Vitamin D. Even buy one of those special bright-light lamps. Mine's on right now. It's February.

Adapt your what-to-dos to *your* best *whens* for that particular kind of activity. When does your brain work best? Your body? When do you have the most patience with others? The least? When do you most need a bit of time to yourself? My younger daughter calls this "budgie-cover time". When tired, over-done, over-stimulated, some birds can get down-right squawky, uptight, agitated. Throw a cover over the cage and let them hide out for a little while, and they calm right down. Build in some budgie-cover time for yourself. It's good for you and for those around you.

What about when Life throws a curve ball?

Let's acknowledge the cliché that "even the best laid plans" can get fouled up. However, once you've gotten a handle on what overall rhythm makes a "normal" week work for you, you can more easily get back on track when life messes with your plans and your head. Once you've built your priorities into your week, you can breathe a little easier knowing you're "taking care of business", and taking care of you and yours. Then, ironically, you can schedule more time when you won't be scheduled! Sweet.

The Puzzle Pieces

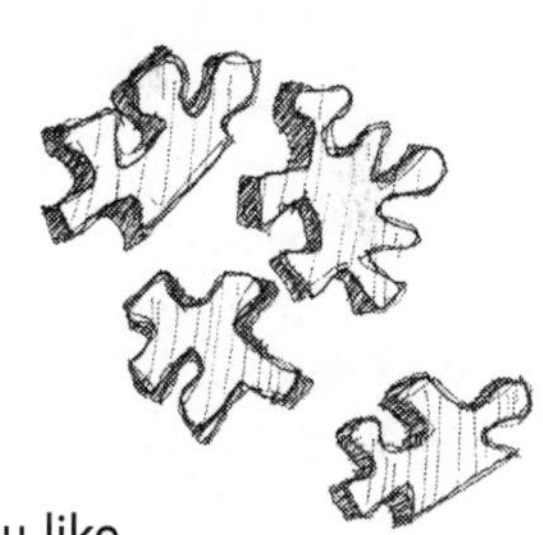

Here are some categories of what you do with your time…

- Sleeping (Lack of sleep actually is a torture technique.)
- Getting up and ready for your day.
- Eating
- Commuting
- Time on paid work. Subdivide this into typical tasks, if you like.
- Living space chores: tidy and organize, clean, do laundry, make meals, get groceries, and other errands. Lawn, garden…
- Taking care of pets. And things like your car, which for some is a pet.
- Doing for and with others: your romantic partner, the kids, other family members, friends. And possibly some volunteer-time.
- Hobbies. List them and how much time you spend on each.
- Taking care of you. Staying fit, some R&R.
- Taking care of your money, now, and for the long term.
- Moving forward with the goals you designed in the previous chapter.

Some things have a daily or weekly, a monthly, or seasonal repeat pattern. (Hopefully paying bills is not the latter.) The yearly stuff? Paying your taxes, getting a full physical on you, the kids, your car. And maybe a vacation? At least a stay-cation. And longer range stuff such as improving your work skills, and building towards your freedom from hand-to-mouth working for a living. And Big Picture aspects like Contribution, Meaning, and Spirit. Don't forget those. They matter too.

Enough. Too much talk. Let's get on with it. And patience please—you're spending maybe an hour now to save yourself many hours on an ongoing basis. Consider this a time tune-up.

GET REAL - Build your own Time Machine

There are three time charts, "puzzles", for you to play with in Appendix D.
If you figure that you're already quite good at Time Management (some call it Task Management), jump straight into designing your Preferred Week. If not, to improve your skill at knowing how long things take, and to see more clearly how you use your time, guesstimate your "typical week" and then compare it to an "actual week". Either way, please read the rest of this chapter. You may in fact have yourself over-planned and over-scheduled. Or not.

Typical Week Chart (pages 296-297)

What do you typically do when? There are some "suggested categories" down the side of the page. Add any others you want. If you work shifts or your weeks vary a lot, just do a best-guess about the upcoming week and see how that works out. How much time do you think you typically spend on each category?

Actual Week Chart (pages 298-299)

Day by day, fill in the Actual Week chart. When done, add up the hours for each category. You'll then have a better sense of how you spend, invest, or waste your time, and a better idea of how much time each activity really does take. Knowing that puts you more in control. Nice.

There are the genuine Musts, such as getting enough sleep, going to work, paying the rent or mortgage, feeding yourself and probably the kids and maybe your mate who's been nice to you today. And doing some laundry before your socks walk off by themselves, or replacing the car's now tar-ish oil.
There are meaningful Shoulds, such as getting some exercise and phoning Mom.
There are the oh-so-boring "Why am I bothering?" things, and those "OMG, I'm too dead to get off the sofa" times.
And then there are the sneaky Time-Wasters.

Time Wasters

- Just how disorganized are you? Do you spend ages looking for stuff?
- Do you have to food shop multiple times a week, instead of once or twice?
- Do you actually like talking to telemarketers and survey takers?
- Are you checking emails numerous times a day? Answering even unnecessary ones? Texting or tweeting incessantly? Are you that afraid everyone will forget about you? Or so bored (or boring) because you've got nothing better to do?
- Are some activities, like video games and 'social' media, fun and interesting but you're really overdoing them?

What time wasters clutter up your day, your week? List at least 3.

How much time is actually going into what truly matters, into what interests you and brings you joy, and towards your future? That's next.

CHEMISTRY and BIG ROCKS

Don't worry, this is not a chemistry lesson. Bear with me for a minute. How do elements (the chemistry, not the stove version) fit together? Usually, the bigger bits or higher energy items arrange themselves in the space first. The effects these have on the other atoms then orchestrate the sequence of what happens next, and determine both what the end-result will be and whether or not the whole thing holds together. To create the right "chemistry" for your life, you want the right ingredients and the necessary space. And you want the elements with the most impact in there first.

Here's another analogy. You have a container. And three piles. Rocks, pebbles, and sand. If you fill that container first with sand, you won't get any rocks or pebbles in. Here, size does matter. Do you want the big stuff, the important aspects of Life in there, or to have your years chock full of grit and sand?

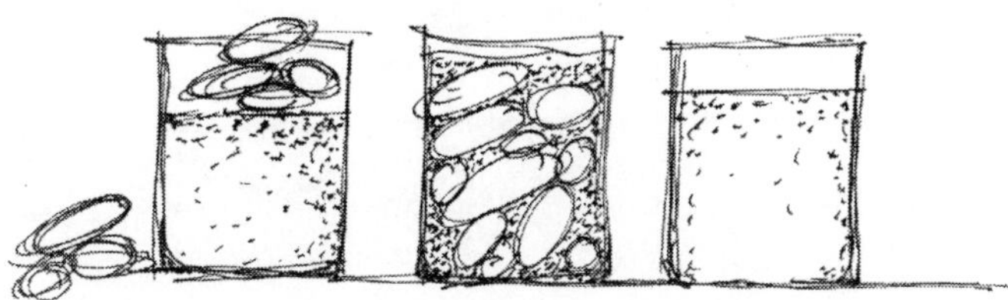

Think of what we do with our time as the rocks, pebbles, and sand that we're putting into the big container called our Life. (The clarity of this useful analogy was harnessed and popularized by Stephen Covey's Group in *First Things First.*)[1]

Be more deliberate about getting those rocks and larger pebbles in there. We need to focus first on **what matters most**—the truly important ingredients of life—those with long-term timelines and/or profound consequences[2] such as taking care of our health, our relationships, and our individual and collective futures.

Unfortunately, the **value-based** aspects of life are often set aside or ignored, drowned out by our typical day-to-day doing. They don't seem as immediately urgent, so we mistakenly treat them as being less necessary. We let them get swamped by the more in-our-face demands on our time and energy.

Our **roles and goals** are the larger pebbles. They go in next. While not necessarily as crucial or as vital, these do have meaning. Include the goals you've designed. And include the stay-afloat practical tasks such getting some food in the house and paying the rent. The must-do-it-now tasks, such as changing that stinky diaper, will be obvious.

The **time clutter** (the time wasters we spoke of earlier) think of as sand, as grit in the gears or the underwear of your life.

Again play, rejuvenating ourselves, is important. Recharge your batteries.

"To be highly productive and still have plenty of time to rest and play – this is where true genius lies." [3]

Ernie J. Zelinski, The Lazy Persons' Guide to Success.

So into your life, your container, your week, place the rocks first then the pebbles. Sand will trickle in anyway, and the more sand (those activities of minimal or no importance) you let in, the less space there is for the happy-making things that can "rock" your world.

What happens if you shake a container of sand, rocks, and pebbles? The large bits rise to the top. What if life shakes up your world? You'll very quickly notice your "big rock" priorities. (Ask anyone who's been in a bad accident or who has a loved one with cancer.) Take the time to develop a good sense of what really matters without Life having to hand you a wake-up call.

More? Or less?

Be more effective, productive, and have more fun. Sound good?

Step ONE
For each of the things you do, what's your **interest level**? Which are annoying, boring, not so bad, mildly interesting, or exciting? Make yourself a few notes on that.

Step TWO
For this part of the exercise, "interesting or not" needs to be irrelevant. Just figure out if it is **useful, i.e. productive and effective**. No, only sort of, yes, very?

Step THREE
Choose two things you want to **DO LESS OF**. How can you do that?

Just don't do it.

- **Eliminate** tasks. Would there be many, if any, negative consequences?
- **Learn to say "No", tactfully.** Just because something needs doing doesn't mean you're the most appropriate person to do it. That doesn't make you "selfish". You don't have to save the world single handedly. Yes, of course, help, contribute, volunteer, but for those things that have meaning to you. That's much more effective and energizing. Encourage others to do the things that have meaning to them. If we all did even just a little, a lot of wonderful things would get done. And don't constantly rescue people who would be better off being helped to learn what they need to know: self-reliance is good for their well-being and self-respect.

Pass it off.

- **Delegate** tasks. If you don't have the official authority to do that, negotiate.
- **Hire someone** to do it. Sometimes trying to do it all yourself is a waste of both time and energy. (I could do my own taxes. Ick. And I could try to learn InDesign to get this book ready for the publisher, but it makes more sense to pay someone who's experienced and use my time to improve the content. If I take on too much, I might just give up on the whole project.)
- **Trade expertise.** You scratch my back, I'll scratch yours.
- **Arrange to share** a certain task with someone else, preferably with someone you respect and whose companionship you like. Or take turns doing something that neither of you likes doing, but the task truly does need to get done.

If you must do it yourself ...

- **Decrease the time it takes.** Improve your skill level for that particular task, or don't be such a perfectionist. There are plenty of times when "good enough" *is* good enough. Or diddle less, focus more.
- **Make the doing more palatable.** There's always going to be some things that are a little boring that genuinely need doing. (That doesn't mean that everything that needs doing is boring.) Perhaps listen to your favourite upbeat music while doing those.

Step FOUR

Choose two things you want to **DO MORE OF** or put more energy into. They're **more exciting, more productive and effective** at improving the quality of your life.

What's interesting or exciting? Your call. No justification required.

What's productive and effective? Pick one or two things that if done even just slightly better, or a little more frequently, would make a positive difference in your life. It could be as simple as eating one more piece of fruit a day or getting to bed twenty minutes earlier.

Build these into your schedule and protect them from the Sandstorms! That's why you custom design your Preferred Week. (That's next...)

The 80/20 Rule

In 1906, Vilfredo Pareto noted that most results come from a much smaller percentage of our actions than we might anticipate. In the 1940's, Dr. Joseph Juran developed and popularized this idea as "the vital few and the trivial many."
This is now known as the 80/20 Rule: 80% of your results come from 20% of what you do. What does this mean? **Rather than "working hard" on something, you want to be working smart, and on the right things**. Seek out and place your emphasis on those vital few. Interestingly, the 80/20 Rule seems to apply to your effectiveness in your work context and to what brings you joy in your personal life. And it seems to apply whether it's your energy, time, or other resources.

A CAUTION about Multi-tasking

Studies have shown that **multi-tasking is not efficient** for your work context or your personal life. And it's certainly not conducive to a healthy mindset or body.

Don't split your focus by combining *Tasks*.
Emailing someone else while discussing a work problem with a colleague? You don't look important-because-you're-busy, just rude. Or texting while you're supposedly having "quality time" playing with your kids or your date? You're saying that who you're with doesn't matter that much. Focus. Memories are built of moments—opinions are built on both.

Instead combine *Values*.
You want to get more fit *and* have time with your favourite squeeze? Take up hiking or dancing together. Or boarding, blading, climbing, whatever. That way you can enjoy each other's company while sharing a common focus. It'll build closeness and fun memories.

> "For all of the most important things, the timing always sucks… The stars will never align and the traffic lights of life will never all be green at the same time. The universe doesn't conspire against you, but it doesn't go out of its way to line up all the pins either. Conditions are never perfect. 'Someday' is a disease that will take your dreams to the grave with you." [4] Timothy Ferriss

Designing your Preferred Week

You can be anal-retentive crazy-organized and efficient, but if your current priorities and actions aren't taking you where you want to go, what's the point? Instead, with your Preferred Week, **set up time frames that:**

- **help you get to the things that actually do matter,**
- **create space for guilt-free play time,**
- **are flexible enough to allow for spontaneity.**

What to do?
These come from your A-LISTS (Chapter 10) and your practical-tasks categories. And you now know what you want to DO MORE of.

What not to do?
You're aware of the time-waster grit that can trickle in.
You know what you want to DO LESS of.

How long do things take?
You've explored this too. How long is your commute? How much time does it take to pay the bills? (That will become much easier and quicker after you've done the Money section.) You know it takes about two hours to buy groceries and put them away, and you've planned that for this afternoon. But you get a last minute invitation to hang out with a couple of friends who are in town only for the day and you haven't seen them in months. That obviously trumps when you food-shop. Groceries? Tomorrow.

When to do what?
Morning person or night owl? Respect your own rhythms and preferences when choosing what to do when. The needs of those we care about can make this a little trickier. And so does shift work. However, you might be able to make some minor modifications that would let you get a slightly easier rhythm going.

SHIFT WORKERS obviously need some special consideration, and more tailored self-care strategies. Search "shift work sleep disorders". Some schedules and how they roll are less disrupting to your life and health than others. Two of many useful sites: cdc.gov/niosh/topics/workschedules
webmd.com/sleep-disorders/tc/shift-work-sleep-disorder-topic-overview

If this Time-Design process feels like a bit of a nuisance right now, so what? Humour me. Hang in there. Be nice to yourself. It'll be worth it. And it will get a lot easier. *You're doing this FOR yourself, not TO yourself....*

Let's start with those ROCKS.

You have to be functional. Assign the practical necessities their blocks of time: sleeping, eating, working, getting the little ones to school and so on. You've gotten better at guesstimating how long these things take, so you're less likely to find these frustrating.

Another big rock—making the time to take care of your health and sanity, and your current and future financial well-being. (The money section, next, will help with this.) Now add your shorter range goals, the **Pebbles**. Paint the living room, purge your files, learn to play an instrument...

Look for the **flexible pieces of time** in your day, week, month, year. What might you do with these? Listen to an audio-novel on the way to work? Go for a walk? Plan a holiday? Clean out your car which, at the moment, looks like a travelling garbage can?

There's a big difference between **play and relaxation** and wasting time. Set aside time each week to happily do "nothing", to just chill. But do not be tempted to let back in those time-wasters you worked to weed out. Instead, add in something more distinctly fun (like going on a date with your honey) or that's genuinely relaxing (like hanging out by a pool, listening to your favourite music, or getting a massage).

Try out this version of **your Preferred Week** for a couple of weeks. Modify it as needed. **You are its master, not the other way around.** When designing your "Time-maps"[5] don't worry about "getting it right" the first time. (Realistically, there is no 'perfect' plan. You just want to come up with one that works for you most of the time.) You'll gradually get better at this. It's not genetic, not carved in stone. It's simply a skill you improve on like driving, playing the piano, or good sex.

Once you've gotten a few of the kinks out of your "preferred week", let it guide you. There will be times when you don't feel like doing what you promised yourself you'd do. But do it anyway. Like trying out a new sport, it's a little awkward at first. Give it a chance for a few weeks—that's roughly how long it takes us to modify a habit. **What about when life throws a curve ball?** Things go awry. You've got a big project at work *and* your dad's in hospital *and* one of the kids has the stomach flu. To get back on track, use what-usually-works—think of it as your week's default-settings.

Your Preferred Week (pages 300-301)

Start by sketching in the less negotiable, less flexible, "must" blocks of time in one of the charts in Appendix D. (E.g. work times, commute times. And are you getting enough sleep? Unfortunately, many are not, for any number of reasons.) Then build from there. (Rocks, then pebbles.) *You're creating productive task-time and guilt-free play-time!*

After you've done that, get out your paper planner or electronic time-tracking gadget.

If you don't yet have one you like, go buy one. Today. Now. No planner is going to be perfect, and you may need to do some experimenting before you find one that suits your style and your circumstances. (A colleague looks tattooed by the end of the work day. He writes all over his hands—calls it his "palm pilot"—and later transfers the info to his electronics.) As I said before, try out this version of your time-plan for a few weeks, modifying it as needed until you get a reasonably comfortable fit.

Life evolves. So will what you need and want to do with your time.
The skills you're improving here will both build resiliency and give you more effective control over what is, literally, your Life-Time.

OBSTACLES? Of course.

Some things that get in our way we can control. Some we must roll with.
We can improve our skills for dealing with the EXTERNAL obstacles.

You're disorganized. And wasting time has you stressed and frustrated.
Either make the time to get organized, or hire someone to help get you there.

You've got f**requent interruptions**, whether it's kid-care, phone calls and emails, your fellow workers, or the demands of your bosses or clients.

- You can't sell your **kids**, though there may be days you'd like to. But you could hire a sitter or take turns with friends minding each other's small humans.
- **Phone calls**? That's what voice mail is for.
- **Emails, texts, tweets** are like dirty dishes. They wait for you. Choose when to answer them. And make that not every two minutes.
- **Your fellow workers**? Perhaps post times. "I'm available between…"
- **Your bosses**? Negotiate, if you can. If you're good at what you do, they're more likely to be open-minded. And learn some better negotiation skills.
- For **your clients**? Stipulate and, if you must, negotiate access times.

Then there's **the unexpected**. A newly laid-on "Do this *now*" project at work.
Or your flight gets grounded (arg!). Adapt. Cope.

What about our INTERNAL obstacles?

You can't get motivated. Have you taken the time to clarify your goals?
You're constantly exhausted. Are you taking care of your health?
You procrastinate. But why?

Some thoughts on procrastinating might be helpful here:

- The hold-up, the indecision, is often not about whether-to but how-to.
- Dreading or avoiding a task can take almost as much energy as getting it done.
- The further away our deadlines, the more likely we are to give in to distractions.
- Adrenalin junkies supposedly like the intensity of last-minute. Or are they just giving their egos the excuse of "If I'd started earlier, I could have done better"?
- Perfectionists have trouble both starting and finishing projects, knowing in advance that they won't think the result is "good enough".
- I think there's another layer to it. Is it partly an attempt to put it out there that we're the one in control, rather like a little kid dragging his feet and screaming "I don't wanna!" Is some part of you saying that is not your path?

- Or is it possibly a passive-aggressive attempt to tick someone off?
- Ask yourself if the results of your procrastinating are solely yours to wear, or if the results might also bite someone you care about. Is that more motivating?

Julie Morgenstern, an experienced and remarkably wise time management specialist, says that psychological obstacles are particularly tricky when you're not aware of them. For example, you may actually get off on conquering crises so you create them, though quite likely unintentionally. Or you are unaware that you fear failure, or success, so you don't try. Or you fear structure will stifle creativity.[6] Recognize yourself in any of these? The number of people I've seen, over the years, trip themselves up with any or all of these obstacles is astounding. (If you haven't done Chapter 9 on building your strengths, I suggest you do that now.) If you still find yourself frustrated or stressed, resisting or resenting, or screwing up your time-for-what-matters puzzle, I strongly suggest you read Morgenstern's book, *Time Management From the Inside Out.*

Parents, take the time to build and encourage COMPETENCE.

A simple example? Healthy food choices and food prep are part of self-reliance. Make that fun and interesting. Parents, go explore a farm or the local farmers' market with your six year old. Fruits and veggies don't grow in aisle three. At that age, they're not "too cool" to hang out with you in public and they find mucking about in the kitchen fun.

Training the frontal cortex of one's brain is not an easy task for kids, tweens, and teens, or for their parents/guardians and teachers. Research has shown that there seems to be a very real neurological disconnect in that age group between behaviour and the perception of consequence. Growth, both physical and intellectual, is bumpy at times. Teens genuinely do misread faces and intent and often don't have—yet—a sense of who they are or could be. (Makes for good comic strips, but less than optimal family dynamics.)

A tough but necessary life lesson is **getting to see that what one does actually does have something to do with what happens**. (Obvious? Apparently not.) That goes for many adults too, not just for kids and teens. Help the young-uns out with that. Don't, even with the best intentions, do everything for them. Instead lead by good example. Show them how. Do things with them. Let them practice. You wouldn't hand over the car keys to a 12 year old and say, "Here, you figure it out. Drive". But we do seem to expect that with other important life-skills.

Create a healthy context where they are encouraged, enabled, and expected to gradually build valuable self-reliance skills whether it's changing a tire, cooking a decent meal, or managing their money. Give them and get them good advice. Competence and self-reliance build confidence and resiliency, and we all need both.

Parents, to do *for* rather than teach *how* is unintentionally clipping your fledgling's wings. And it's inadvertently trampling on their self-esteem. And if they layer an inappropriate sense of entitlement over that incompetence and lack of self-reliance, they're set up for being miserable and for being miserable to be with.

Teens, don't assume your folks have control-freak intent. Maybe they actually do have something on the ball. Or maybe not. Maybe there should be, not just a Nanny 911, but a Teen 911 to help out with daft parents who don't help you learn *how*. But if they themselves don't know, didn't learn or weren't helped either, maybe you could learn some of this stuff together. If they're not interested, you must anyway. It is your life. You're also then in a position to help them out, if they need it. If they'll let you. But that's another book—one that someone else can write.

Blending Time and Goals - Planning Backwards

"If we want to accomplish that … then we need to do this …"

A fast review:

What do you want the end result to be?
What are the steps?
Establish the time frames for each step.
Put into your planner when you will do each of these steps.
And DO them.

Some examples?

- **Moving.** (We touched on this briefly in the Goals Chapter.)
  How do you organize a move with the least effort and irritation?
  What do you need to do when? See the time-line in Appendix A.
- **Too much to read?** Getting a little frazzled?
  There's a big difference between savouring a delicious novel, reading to absorb ideas, and scanning for information.
  To learn? Scan read, then re-read. Highlight. Make brief notes on the crucial bits, then do something with that info so you'll keep it in mind, literally.
  For bulk info-reading? Reduce the time it takes. Scan. Learn to Speed-read. Check out for example, revitupreading.com.
  When reading for pleasure, don't rush. This is gourmet dining, not fast food.
- **Getting a good education.**
  A teen or an adult wants to get a good education or maybe simply finish high school. By when? With what courses? What marks must you achieve to get on with what you want to do next?
  To do this? Well, showing up for class is generally a good idea as is doing the work and writing the exams. Duh. But time management and motivation might be an issue. Luckily, you can improve both.

SOAK THIS UP…

Your belief in yourself, and in what's possible, will catch up with you one way or another.

Instead of wishful thinking, act-as-if you're the person who could and would. And DO the doing. As your results improve, so will your mindset, and your possibilities. You're entitled to ask for help along the way, but it's not other people's job to do that doing for you! So get on with it! As I keep saying, it is your life...
Keep that thought in mind for the next Section—MONEY.

Money

Chapter 12

Get Sea-worthy

Are you a sailor? (Even if you're not, read on Matey, the analogy's useful.)

Don't run aground. Learn where the reefs are.
Don't get swamped by high seas. Learn how to set the sails for the various weathers of life, the doldrums, the sweet breezes, the lashing gales.
Choose a destination, and know you will need to make corrections along the way.
Be sure to take along your compass, a map, and a GPS. The compass is your values. The map, your goals. The GPS, your reality checks. And, Sailor, get on board and cast off or you're not going anywhere!

In the next few chapters, you'll learn how to steer your hard-earned money and how to create better money habits. It's not only about building a better future, it's about having better todays.

Life is wonderful and interesting but not always smooth sailing. Get sea-worthy. Otherwise, you could get caught out there listing heavily, taking on water, your sails shredded. Or, heaven forbid, get washed overboard or go down with the ship. On the other hand, you might find yourself permanently moored, too fearful to ever leave the harbour. Wouldn't you rather get yourself ready to have a great adventure?

Know the ropes. It's so much better to control your money than having it—or rather the lack of it—control you. Wishful thinking won't get you where you want to go. Better habits and a better attitude will. **What works? Getting things organized, simplified, and automatic.** Yes, that takes a bit of effort to set up. So what? It'll save you a lot of stress and hassle on an ongoing basis. Your new mantra? *"I'm doing this FOR myself, not TO myself"*.

Once you understand your cash flow, you can more easily manage and improve your finances. It's not budget-and-binge like some nasty strict diet spiked with fat-food chasers. And you won't be starving yourself either. (If you would, go get some help.) Starvation, whether physical or financial, is not a motivator. Helping your finances get fit and healthy is. Cash flow planning—**getting more conscious and conscientious about money**—is more like eating for optimal health and energy. You will be able to say YES to yourself about what truly matters to you, and without guilt, once your game plan is in place. Sweet. Guilt-free sweet.

Most people are stuck where there's more month than money, and that's not just those living on minimum wage. In the research done for her book, *The Difference,* Jean Chatzky discovered that in the USA, while 3% are truly wealthy and 27% are financially comfortable, 54 % are living paycheck to paycheck, and 15% are going further into debt each month.[1] The crazy thing is that paycheck-to-paycheck happens even at the six figures per year level. Yikes.

On the other hand, here's an encouraging surprise. Nearly all of the upper middle class did not start out wealthy. Neither did three-quarters of the rich families in the USA. Only 2 to 4% of the rich inherited their money; 96% are first-generation millionaires, that is, they built that million themselves.[2] Were they just lucky? Fewer than 4% say luck had even a partial hand in it. So how did they get there? By knowing and doing what most people don't. (More on How-To's later.)

No, a huge bank account will not guarantee you happiness. But neither will poverty or constant struggling. You don't need to be rich to be happy, but you do need to be able to meet your basic needs such as food, shelter, and safety.

Even if you don't care about being extraordinarily wealthy, at the very least, aim for financial peace of mind and the ability to do a lot of what you want, when you want, for yourself, for others, and for good causes. That itself is a superb form of riches.

As a reality check for those who think they can "have someone take care of them", here are two more stats. According to the National Marriage Project (2002) in the USA, 15% of current young adults will never marry. And for the first time in Canadian history, there are more unmarried than married people, ages 16 and upwards (CBC News, Oct. 4, 2010). Money skills are vital for *everyone*. You need to wear your own financial pants.

On the upside, it's much easier than you might think to learn good money skills and habits. You don't need to be a Newton, Einstein, or Hawking. We know that gravity works whether we understand it or not, so do the not-so-complicated fundamental laws of money. And they work against us or for us, no matter who we are. You can come from better or worse circumstances economically or geographically, but what your life becomes, for the most part, is more dependent on what you DO than you might like to think or admit. That's both intimidating and exciting at the same time.

Let me say it again. Believe it or not, it's not complicated. *Someone Really Oughta Tell You...* **Just DO the basics. Do them first, and do them well.** Those basics are the engine and the generator of financial viability—the rest, the "fancy stuff", is just icing or fluff.

> "The irony of youth is that while as a group young people could benefit the most from a wise program, they are the most unlikely to pursue one. It takes genuine maturity to become sophisticated and humble enough to believe in a simple system. Our egos would rather we live thinking that we accomplish great things by our own might or cleverness ... Perhaps we feel cheated or at least embarrassed when, after a long struggle, we find out how simple things really are..." [3] Jon Hanson

Life is so much easier if you get off on the right foot with your finances. If you didn't, let's change that now. Once you have an appropriate system set up, rather than have to worry or constantly argue with yourself, you can relax about money. Sound good? **By working through this section of the book, you'll develop some sensible, straight forward, and effective money strategies. One do-able step at a time.**

If you're keen to start on that right now, skip to the next chapter.
The next three pages are for those who might need some help getting underway.
If any part of you is saying, "Yes, but...", I suggest you read them.

Hesitant to leave the harbour?

Stress manifests as fight, flight or freeze. And with money, most of us experience all three at some time or another. I know I sure did, a lot. And I'd like to do whatever I can to help you have a smoother journey. When sailing, you need to know-the-ropes. Those ropes, if left lying around in tangled heaps on the deck, can trip you up, or worse, send you overboard into very cold water. Let's tidy them up.

$$$ OBSTACLES: Our attitudes and habits? Definitely.

Jon Hanson in *Good Debt, Bad Debt* describes financial obstacles in terms of D's and I's.[4] The validity of each is obvious, if we have the courage to look at ourselves, and so are the potential consequences.

The D's: **Discipline**: actually, the lack of...
Deferral: procrastinating
Discernment: a difficulty in sorting the true from the false

The I's: **Indifference**: not caring, for any number of reasons
Immediacy: of genuine needs, or impulsive self-gratification
Ignorance: in the true sense of not knowing What or How.

To Hanson's **D's**, I'm going to add three more: **Disdain, Doubt, and Denial.**

Disdain

- Some seem to think that money issues are beneath them. They are, of course, too special for gravity to affect them, and the world, after all, does owe them a living. (Many of us know at least one of those people.)
- Others think that caring about money means that you're materialistic, shallow, less-nice, perhaps even ruthless and uncaring. Wrong! It's not the knowledge itself, but the character of the person with that knowledge that determines its use. Why would we want to leave that knowledge primarily in the hands of those who care little about what truly matters, or in the hands of those who love to take advantage of the uninformed? Don't set your self up to be one of their victims. The more of us that have good hearts *and* money savvy, the better off we'll all be. And so will the planet.
- And don't be your own victim. Don't be someone who blames and sulks rather than solves. You're better than that. Like so many, you're not "stupid", just uniformed. And that's solvable.

Doubt

- You don't know how. So you think you can't? Maybe you don't know how *yet*. You're reading and learning. You're on your way.
- You choke at the thought that if you really were to "give it your best-shot" and still messed up, it would be too tough on your ego. Be kinder to yourself. Everyone screws up once in a while.
- Family patterns or peer attitudes might be such that we've learned, not how to accomplish what we want, but that *we* (that is, "our group") can't. Or that "there's no point in trying." (Besides, if you did try and succeeded, where would that leave their egos?) Try trusting that they do care about you. They may, based on their own belief system, genuinely just be trying to protect you. Succeed anyway, with integrity and legally, then show them how.

Denial

- Some are "too busy", and maybe genuinely so. Perhaps on a treadmill going nowhere? Money-care, along with self-care, is a must. Chances are you could work less and be a lot less stressed if you directed more effectively where both your money and your time are being spent.
- Others are "too busy" but with the insignificant or irrelevant. Re-arranging the deck chairs on the Titanic? Perhaps they're too afraid to have an honest look at their life and their finances, and are using "busy" as an excuse. Easier to pretend that it's all okay? **Ostrich syndrome. Head in the sand, butt in the air. Careful—Life's got a big boot. Wise up!**
- What happens if you ignore gravity, pretend it doesn't exist? Splat.
  If you ignore your financial realities? Or refuse to learn and adapt?
  Are you really willing to accept the consequences if you don't DO something?

A few more questions to ask yourself:

- Do you expect failure, success, or mediocrity?
- What's settling? What's enough? What pleases you?
- Whose criteria are you using for what matters?
- Just what does money do-for-you?

"We are still a long way from knowing why some people go crazy over money, while others seem to pay so little attention." For some it's like a drug, and they may seem pathologically addicted to it. "Some may be greedy, and others just needy – thirsty for status or using money to compensate for social short-comings." It may seem a little weird, but it appears that we may process our money ideas through the same neural pathways that evolved to think about food.[5]

Perhaps with money as with food, we—sadly—can become gluttonous, or like an anorexic, deny its relationship to our well-being. We can choose instead to do what is genuinely satisfying *and* makes us healthier now and in the long run.

$$$ OBSTACLES: Our circumstances? Only to a certain extent.

You didn't get to choose where you were born or to whom, and you can't change the past. But you can change what happens now and as you go forward. You can LEARN and DO what's needed to rectify the situation. Not from the silver-spoon set? So what? Gripe about your current circumstances if you want, but don't let that Sad-Mad-You become your self-image, your chosen identity. (I've had that conversation with myself, believe me.) And go after useful ideas rather than sympathy. Much more gratifying and effective.

Remember that so-called "laziness" and procrastination may actually be pessimism or fatigue in disguise (Chapter 8). And a lack of clarity creates and aggravates both. That's solvable. Let's clarify the HOW. That way, it'll take less time and courage than you think to learn what you need to know and do. Let's be realistic, self-control is finite. Thankfully, it's renewable.

Toney Fitzgerald, in *Don't Bitch, Just Get Rich,* explains how people choose their money beliefs and money mindset as either "have not" or "will have". Rather than put energy into re-writing their self-imposed script, they use their up-to-now circumstances as part of their self-definition and become unhealthily attached to it.[6] Instead, write yourself a life-story as you want it to be, as one that is more authentically you, and get on with making that happen. You're the script-writer, the director, the actor, and the editor. Fitzgerald goes on to explain why and how to write your own rulebook for your life choices, competencies, and outcomes. It's a good read. His advice?

"Replace the pain of bitching with the joy of self-mastery." [6]

> "Money will be your friend—like all friends—only if you treat it with respect." [7]
>
> Ernie J. Zelinski, *The Lazy Persons' Guide to Success.*

The next chapter will help you GET REAL about the facts of your current financial circumstances. You want just the FACTS. Skip the whys. Frankly they don't matter. Solutions lie in the HOW, not the why.

Before we get into that, please clear your head of any nasty self-talk. It's one thing to bad-mouth your circumstances. It's even more counter-productive to be continually snarling at yourself.

No guilt. Don't beat yourself up for not having known any better. Let that go. Now you're learning. You're doing. Be pleased with yourself for that.

No blame. Frankly, it doesn't matter if the mess you're in is someone else's fault, mostly. Sorry, no victim badges allowed. They don't help solve anything. Instead, think self-defense. Learn from it, move on, and don't repeat your mistakes.

No excuses. Waa. Sure, whine a little if you want. Just don't get stuck there. And don't wimp out. Get on with it. Get the appropriate and competent help if or when you need it. Solve the issue. That's very good for your confidence and self-respect.

So, now what? What's the magic?

Spend somewhat less than you make, and do smart things with the rest. The usual response to that? An annoyed groan, or comments such as:

"Like I haven't heard that before."
"My income sucks, so there goes that."
"Oh, piss off. Being 'smart' means I don't get to have any fun."

Grump. Grump. Okay, I hear ya'. But what did I just say about Doubt and Denial? Does it sound too simple? Too straightforward to be for real? (Oops. If it's not all that complicated, there go our excuses.) And, surprisingly, "making it" depends only partly on what you make. It depends more on your willingness to learn some simple and readily do-able fundamentals. Wish someone had taught me those way-back-when. And I'm certainly not alone on that one. *Someone really oughta tell us.* You've chosen to learn sooner rather than later—my compliments.

Direct your dollars toward what truly matters to you, both short and long term. Then your life and your dreams won't stay stuck in the what's-left-over, if anything, at the end of the month.

For more help with getting to a better emotional and pragmatic place about money issues, here are some great additional resources:

The Difference, Jean Chatzky
Don't Bitch, Just Get Rich, Tony Fitzgerald
The Courage To Be Rich, Suze Orman
Your Money Or Your Life, Vicki Robin, Joe Dominquez & Monique Tilford
The Cure For Money Madness, Spencer Sherman
Debt Free Forever, Gail Vaz-Oxlade
You're Broke Because You Want To Be, Larry Winget

Chapter 13

Getting Real

KISS: "Keep it simple stupid." Unfortunately, many people feel and frankly too many of us are, or have been, stupid about our money. But that's because we're not taught this stuff at a time when it can matter most—when we're young. The earlier we develop better money habits the fewer mistakes we'll need to recover from. And there's a lot of magic in compound interest over time.

Here's some good news—the Know-how is, thankfully, not all that complicated. (Believe me, if I could get better at this, so can you.) You don't need to be math competent, let alone be a math wiz, to manage your money well. You just need some help to simplify the game plan.

Whether playing a sport or doing your finances, get the fundamentals down first.

Three Vital Money Fundamentals

(1) **What you earn is not what you get to take home.**
What gets deducted from your income, and for what purpose? (Taxes are only one deduction.) What's left?

E.g. You're in a 50% tax bracket: for every $2 dollars earned you take home $1. And each after-tax dollar not wasted is worth $2 of what you had to earn.

E.g. In a 30% tax bracket, you keep about two-thirds of what you earn. (For each $1.50 earned, you keep about $1. Flip that around. Every dollar you don't spend is $1.50 you don't have to replace. Get the idea?)

GROSS Income is what you make in total, without any deductions.
NET Income, i.e. your Take Home Pay = Gross – taxes and other deductions

(2) **The Rule of 72.**
Math phobic? No worries. (The 72-bit assumes "compounding annually", but you can ignore those kinds of details, the rule still works. You don't need to be able to tune your own car to be able to drive.)

You can use *The Rule of 72* to determine how long it takes your money—or your debt (ouch)—to double. It works FOR or AGAINST you. And like gravity, it can not be ignored.

E.g. Credit card debt, at about 18%.
72 divide by 18 = 4 Your debt doubles every 4 years!

E.g. An investment averaging 6% return per year:
72 divide by 6 = 12 In 12 years your money doubles.

E.g. Inflation, which is how much the cost of living tends to rise each year.
The Average inflation since 1994 has been 2.5 to 3%.
72 divide by 3 = 24 Living costs will double in about 24 years.

(3) **Don't drive blindfolded**—steer where your money goes.
Removing those blindfolds, opening your eyes, getting real, is what this chapter is about. Let's call it Search and Rescue.

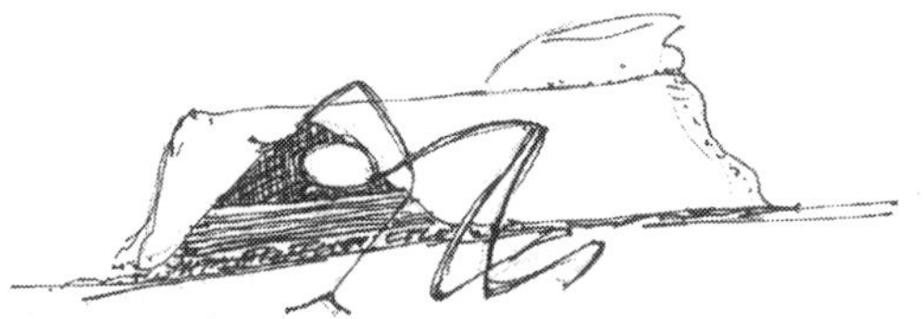

Search and Rescue

Get organized. No, don't groan. Or whine. Show a little more respect for yourself and for what you want out of life. Yes, it may be a bit of a pain to go through this organizing phase. The upside? Afterwards, taking care of your money—now and later—is SO much easier! Less stress and more time to play. Sweet.

Let's keep this phase as simple as possible. Do it in stages.

Stage ONE

Get the following items. They're a one time purchase and worth every penny in stress reduction.

- **A small moveable solid file box (perhaps 12" x 16") that's both lockable and fireproof** for your most important papers, i.e. those related to your identity and other legalities.
- **A regular file box and hanging files, or an expanding file.** Get a system that appeals to you, and is sturdy. You could use some space in a file cabinet, but an expanding file is just easier to move around.
- An inexpensive **shredder.** When you get rid of any paperwork, even utility bills, you must shred them! Each year almost 10 million Americans and Canadians are the victim of identity theft. It's all too easy for crooks to sort through your garbage and become "you". All they need is one back-trackable piece of paper that can serve as an entry point. Here a little paranoia is highly appropriate. (See, as well, Chapter 28.)

Stage TWO

Label the folders using the following categories as a place to start. Refine your layout as you need to. You may or may not have kids or other dependents (such as aging parents) at this stage of your life. If you do, add these categories as needed. If you have your own business keep separate files for that.

NOTE: The upside of a safety deposit box is also its downside—no one else has access to it. What if you're seriously injured, sick, or dead? Officially designate a highly trusted person as a co-signer on the box, "just in case". Go together to your bank and do the appropriate paperwork. For legal papers such as Living Wills, Directives, Wills, and so on, keep the originals with your lawyer and the executor of your Will. Keep copies of all these in your firesafe lockable file box. Be sure a close relative, and a BFF know who these people are and where your file box is—just in case. (More on this in Chapters 22 and 25.)

The CATEGORIES

Keep *at least* those items marked with *** in your firesafe lockable file box.

IDENTITY & LEGALITIES ***

These are your most crucial papers. Keep them ALWAYS.

- Social Insurance card, Birth Certificate, Passport, Immigration papers (Do not carry your SIN or SSN card around in your wallet.)
- A photocopy of your driver's license
- Marriage certificate / Cohabitation Agreement, Divorce papers
- Copies of the most recent version of your: Living Will, Powers of Attorney, Directive, Will, Trusts, and any other Estate planning documents. The originals should be kept with your lawyer.
- Perhaps, sadly, Death certificates for close relatives.

EDUCATION and SKILLS (Keep always) ***

- Certificates, degrees
- Letters of recommendation, job performance reviews

PERSONAL INSURANCES: (Keep only the current policies.) ***

- Medical
- Disability, Critical Illness, Long Term Care
- Life
- Travel insurance

WHO's WHO *** Keep a How-to-Contact list of ...

- Your MD, dentist, and other health care professionals
- Your insurance agent, accountant, lawyer, the proxy for your powers of attorney, and the executor of your will.
- Include a list of your closest next of kin, and perhaps your best friends. (If you were in a serious accident, who would need or want to know?)

INCOME and other TAX related items

- Pay-stubs and records of any other income sources you may have. In January, check your last pay stub for the year against your W-2 (States) or your T4 (Canada) and if all is well, shred old pay stubs.
- Charitable donation slips suitable for current year tax deductions.
- Paperwork related to retirement investments. (See "Investments" next page.)

What qualifies as a deduction, and how long you need to keep tax-related paperwork, depends on where you live. Check the details online or better yet, with an accountant. In general, **keep these for seven years.**
For the sake of space, use large envelopes, labeled by year, in a separate box rather than in this file. Note: there is no seven year statute of limitations if the government thinks you've been frauding them. (Is that a new verb?)

ACCOUNTS

- A list of which accounts are where.
- Bank statements for each account. (ATM slips can be shredded once you've checked them against your bank statements. Thankfully, having to balance your cheque book manually went out when on-line banking came in.)

ASSETS and INVESTMENTS

- Documents showing what kinds you have and which company each is with.
- The print-outs the companies send showing what transactions you did when. These are needed, not only for your own information, but for tax purposes. (Include contributions you've made to your retirement funds.) At year-end, transfer these to that year's tax file.
- And Net Worth statements (see page 182) which should be updated annually.

DEBT

- Current Loans (e.g. student loans, car loans)
- Keep documents that prove you've paid off previous loans.*** (E.g. student or car loans, previous mortgages, etc.)
- Your most recent credit reports and credit scores. (See pages 161-164)
- Credit card agreements showing their rates etc.
- Credit card statements for the current year. Shred the receipts after checking them against the statements

WARRANTIES and RECEIPTS for larger purchases.

- Include serial numbers. And take pictures of the items, in case you someday need to make an insurance claim.
- Keep receipts for large purchases. (Needed to return or repair a defective item.)
- Keep only the warranties and manuals that are relevant to things you currently have. Pitch the others. Pitch these manuals too if you can find the relevant info online.
- Keep receipts for tax-related purchases for 7 years. Transfer these to your appropriate tax file at the end of each year.

HOUSING

- Leases, or mortgages. Year-end updates of mortgages.
- Property tax statements
- Utility bills (heat, electricity, water) preferably each in its own slot.
- Property Insurance – the most recent version

TRANSPORTATION

- Car loans, leases, purchase papers, copies of ownership
- Car insurance (if it's with the same company as home insurance, note that here)
- Receipts for car maintenance and repair, useful for re-sale later
- Parking bills, toll fees, transit pass costs for that year (if these are tax related, keep them for seven years)
- Alternative transport: bike repairs, taxi receipts, car rentals.

COMMUNICATION

- Keep only current contracts.
- Bills: land-line, cell phone, internet, cable. Shred the bills after a year, unless they're tax-related as with a home-based business.

ADD CATEGORIES as needed …

For kids, parents, a home business?
Make a list of these here. Label your file accordingly.

Stage THREE Find, sort, and purge your papers.

A bit at a time, if you'd prefer. Just don't do a "maybe someday" to yourself—that we both know, realistically, means *never*. You deserve better than that.

Put on your spy-guy/spy-gal or search-and-rescue hat, and dive into your piles, files, and junk drawers. Look under the bed or where ever else you might unearth the necessary contents for your new system.

As you find things, drop them into the appropriate slots. Have a large envelop or shoe box on hand to hold any items that don't fit directly into the current file categories. You can decide what to do with these later—give them their own labeled slot or shred them. Anything with identifying information of any kind (e.g. bills or tax documents) *must* be shredded!

Again, you don't need to do this all at once. That can be crazy making. When done, have yourself a "Yay Me" mini-celebration. You've earned it!

Once a year, maybe at tax time or the end of the calendar year, go through this file and purge and shred the materials that are no longer needed. Boring? So what? *You're doing this FOR yourself, not TO yourself.*

With the filing system you just created, keeping track of your important papers and rescuing your money will be much easier.

Stage FOUR Removing the Blindfolds—the Reality Check.

Where is your money *actually* going?

Please note that in the following charts, there's a "What's real now" and two Revision columns. As you go through the following chapters, you'll get much better at rescuing and redirecting your hard-earned money. For now, you're just seeing where it and you are at. A bit apprehensive? Have courage. Keep at it. Having now sorted your paperwork, you'll find this a less irritating task. Getting "money management" in hand soon will feel more like a speed bump than Mount Everest.

The approach for the next activity?

If you're an employee, get out your pay stubs. If you're self-employed, use last year's tax forms. Establish your per-month Take-Home-Pay. Then fill in the charts that follow.

- Dig through your bills. Work through the Living Expenses (the first two pages). If you haven't been keeping all of your receipts recently, do that for the next month. It'll be a useful eye-opener for fine-tuning your charts later.
- List all debts other than your mortgage. (Your mortgage, if you have one, goes under "Living expenses".) What's the total of those debts? What are you currently paying per month to service (i.e. carry) them?
- Dig out the records for what you've already set aside for your short-term and long-term goals. (If anything.)
- Figure out what you're putting into Play Money per month.
- Find the receipts for your charitable deductions.
- Now grab a calculator.

LIVING EXPENSES – monthly	What's real now $$?	Revision One	Revision Two	
HOUSING				
Rent or mortgage				
Property taxes				
Home / Tenant Insurance (liability and contents)				
Maintenance / Major repairs / Fees				
Heat				
Electricity				
Water bills				
Housing Total				
FOOD, etc.				
Groceries & Misc. Household				
Food out (when truly necessary e.g. business related, otherwise it's Play)				
Food Total				
PERSONAL INSURANCES				
Medical / dental / eye care, etc				
Disability Critical Illness Long Term Care				
Travel Insurance				
Life Insurance				
Personal Total				
COMMUNICATION				
Phones, internet				
Postage, courier				
Communication Total				
CLOTHING				
"Everyday" clothes for *each* person (Clothing related to specific hobbies should be included in "Play", not here.)				
Business / Work related				
Laundry, dry cleaning, repairs				
Clothing Total				

LIVING EXPENSES continued	What's real now $$?	Revision One	Revision Two	
PERSONAL				
Grooming e.g. hair				
Vitamins & over the counter medicines				
Health costs insurances don't cover				
Other				
Personal Total				
TRANSPORTATION				
Car payments				
Car registration & insurance				
Gas, maintenance, repairs				
Parking & toll fees				
Transit				
Taxis, car rentals, bike & repairs				
Transportation Total				
BANK & MONEY FEES				
Account fees				
ATM fees				
Overdraft expenses				
Misc: NSF fees, wire transfers, etc.				
Accounting services, Tax prep				
Bank & Money Management Total				
OTHER EXPENSES e.g. Day care for the kids? e.g. Alimony?				
"Other" Total				
DISCRETIONARY SPENDING (not quite the same as play money)				
Pets: food, vets, etc.				
Household help e.g. cleaning service, lawn mowing				
Miscellaneous				
Discretionary Total				
TOTAL OF ALL LIVING EXPENSES				

"OUCH" fund for Financial Resiliency *How much do you have now?* ___________ (Build to 3 months worth of take-home-pay.)	*How much is going into this per month?*	Revision One	Revision Two	

PAY DOWN DEBT	*How much is going into each of these per month?*			
Credit cards: *List each & amount owing*				
Student Loans: *List each & total amount owing*				
Other Loans: *List each & total amount owing (e.g. for vehicle?)*				
Sum of all Non-Mortgage Debt ___________				

LONG TERM goals Respecting Future-You	*How much is going into these, per month?*			
Skills development, Further Training *What would be useful? What might that cost?*				
Long Term (Savings, Assets, & Investments…) *List types and totals here:*				

CONTRIBUTION	What's real now $$?			
List causes you do or want to contribute to. If you can't yet afford to give money, contribute some time.				

SHORT TERM GOALS: A-LISTS List below any savings you have already accumulated for each.	How much are you setting aside, per month, for each?	Revision One	Revision Two	
Savings for gifts				
Savings for vacations & adventures				
Savings for a vehicle				
Savings for a home down-payment				
Savings for *voluntary* household upgrades List and cost them NOTE that major *necessary* repairs are to be included in Living expenses under Shelter, not here				
Moving? Moving in together? Wedding plans?				
Want kids? Have kids? Their goals?				
Other				
Total savings for Short Term Goals __________				

PLAY MONEY per month	Per month			
Dining out				
Going out *e.g. Movies, concerts, clubs*				
Staying-in entertainment *e.g. movies, music, reading material, cable, gadgets & games, etc.*				
Pampering *e.g. spas*				
"Above and Beyond" Clothing (20 pair of heels, or 40 shirts? That's *Play*, not Necessity.)				
Hobbies, recreation *List each type and the cost per month, including equipment, hobby related clothing, fees*				
Not-so-good Habits ** *e.g. Smoking? Gambling? Over-drinking? Etc.*				
Play Money Total per month __________				

**** If you put yourself in a position of having to choose between bad habits and fun, you're more likely to improve your habits.***

Stage FIVE
Summarize what you've figured out so far:

[ ]	Your monthly take-home-pay?
[ ]	Any other income?
[ ]	The total of your living expenses?
[ ]	Of that, how much goes to housing costs?
[ ]	The amount you currently have in your Ouch account?
[ ]	How much are you putting into that per month?
[ ]	How much debt do you owe, other than your mortgage?
[ ]	How much are you putting, per month, into paying off those debts?
[ ]	How much do you have saved for your long-term goals?
[ ]	How much are you putting, per month, into those?
[ ]	How much do you have saved for your short-term goals?
[ ]	How much are you putting, per month, into those?
[ ]	Contributing to your favourite charity or cause? Volunteering?
[ ]	How much do you spend per month as play-money?

So, where are you now? Grinning or groaning? Gain or pain?

- More expenses than income? (Ouch.)
- Perhaps your expenses and income almost match up, but you're not getting ahead, *yet*? (Note the word YET.)
- Maybe you've more income than living expenses, but you aren't taking your future into account, yet.
- Maybe your money is already going exactly where it needs to. It's creating and enabling choices now and for your future. Sweet.
- Maybe your money is already working hard for you, so you don't have to? Impressive.

Okay, maybe you're not quite where you want to be YET. You can fix that.
If you're a little discouraged at the moment, hang in there.
Use the prospect of financial peace of mind and guilt-free play-money as motivators.

You'll make major strides in the right direction over the next few chapters. You'll **revise where the money goes**, gradually over a few weeks or months, to give yourself a chance to adjust to your new and better habits.

- You'll see how to **build a good credit rating, credit score**. (Arg, I thought when we left school we were done with Report Cards.) Think of it as your reputation—your financial reputation.
- You'll **make everything automatic** so you don't need willpower or a good memory.

- You'll **make your cash flow more visible and much simpler** with online banking and an easy tracking system. Pencil and paper are okay too, but it's more work. I'd rather be lazy and just download. Once you've got it set up, it takes ten minutes, not ten hours.
- At least once a year, perhaps around your birthday as a great gift to yourself, revisit each of your living expenses to see where you can **redirect money from what matters less to you to where it matters more.**
- With each major life change or goal accomplished, you'll **revise** your automated game plan.
- Always keep in mind the value of respecting your Future-Self. You'll learn to **build rather than mess up your Long Term financial resources**. It's truly astonishing how fast the future becomes the present!

> What you're doing with your money—and the time it takes to earn it—needs to be taking you closer to your priorities, not farther away! And you want, as well, to be able to have fun en route.

Sometimes I get asked "What's typical?"

I'll give you typical financial stages rather than typical habits. Typical money habits are, sadly, rather grotesque. Forget typical. You want optimal.

Here are the typical *stages*:

- In your 20's, you're figuring out who you are and are getting your life on track.
- In your 30's, you're probably juggling mortgage and car payments, possibly along with kid-costs, and you need to be paying down debt. It's not an easy time financially. By the way, knocking down debt is, indirectly, saving for your future.
- In your early 40's, you're likely still chopping away at the mortgage and any other debts you may have accumulated. You need, as well, to be building assets—*genuine* assets—not a bigger pile of toys. (If you're sinking deeper into debt to buy toys, smarten up.)
- By your late 40's, the kids likely will be finished school. And your mortgage, hopefully, is almost paid off. Get much more serious about saving, investing, and building assets for your Future-You. Get some sensible help to revise and crunch your numbers.
- By your early 50's, go nuts on further building up your Retirement Portfolio. Get unbiased professional help: you need to maximize what you get while minimizing the tax bite. If you started sooner than this—which you certainly should have—all the better.
- The average retiree will likely need to make their retirement money last at least 30 years. The recommendations for how much you'll need vary widely and depend, of course, on the lifestyle you'll want.

As a young adult, your main priority is to LEARN about what works and to reduce debt which indirectly and very effectively contributes to your financial future. As well, sock some into savings and into genuine assets, sooner rather than later.

When you've done this book, you'll be way ahead of typical. Yay you!

Chapter 14

Taxes

Notice that I've put the "Taxes" chapter between "Getting Real" about your cash flow, and "Flushing Money". Tell you something?

We all hate paying taxes. The average Income Tax rate is 35 to 50 %. Most people work January to May just to pay their taxes. The middle class hands over about half of what they make. Ouch. And we all have other slices out of our pie such as government pension plans and social security, employment insurance and so on. (No, we wouldn't want to do without these.) Yet when all the various deductions are added up, they do take a bite out of the old pay check. What you make, your "Gross Income", is not actually what you make.

> Taxes differ considerably in types and amounts depending on where you live or earn. So check these aspects for your location. If you're thinking of moving, whether you're changing countries, provinces, states, you'd be well advised to look into the possible variations.

Types of taxes

- **On Business income**
  In general, business tax rates are lower because businesses pay their bills from their income, then they're taxed on what's left.
  I.e. Income – Bills => Taxable income – Taxes => Profit.
- **On your Personal income**
  There are both federal and provincial or state taxes. And they're smart—they take their bite first to make sure they get it. Then, unlike with businesses, you pay your bills with what's left.
  Gross Income – Taxes and other Deductions => Take Home Pay – Bills => $$?
- **Retail taxes** on pretty much everything you buy. And **service taxes** on what you have done for you whether that's a plumbing repair or getting your nails done. How much, and on what, varies with your location.
- **Property taxes**
  What kinds of Property are taxed varies considerably with the country, state, province, and municipality. For example, in Canada you aren't taxed on the value of your car; in many states you are. In the States, you can claim your mortgage interest as a tax deduction; in Canada, you can't unless you're renting out part of your home, in which case the tax deduction is proportional to the percentage of your space you rent out.

BE SMARTER with your taxes.

You want to pay what you must, but *only* what you must.
Otherwise, you're flushing money! Just keep your minimizing legal.

- You organized your paperwork in the last chapter. Now, as tax related items come in—your pay tax stubs (e.g. T4's in Canada, W2's in the U.S.) and receipts for retirement plan contributions, charitable donations, and so on—simply slip them into the tax slot of your files so they're easy to find at tax time.

- Use one of the many online tax calculators or buy a tax program. Or hire an accountant. (Accounting fees are tax deductible.) Bureaucrats are always finding new and clever ways to stick their hands in your pocket. It's easier to let the professionals keep up to date on all the rules, and it's likely to be cheaper than missing deductions or making a mistake.
  Examples of inexpensive programs:
  Canadians: ufile.ca, drtax.ca or turbotax.ca
  Americans: icanefile.org or turbotax.com
- If you e-file, especially without mailing in your paperwork at the same time, you're more likely to get audited. Yes, you'll likely get your return a little faster by e-filing, but if you submit your paperwork early or on time, the difference in turn-around time is minor.
- Have you heard the cliché "You can't beat City Hall"? Here it is again. If you file late and owe the government money, they charge you an interest penalty. File on time even if, when you file, you can't pay what you owe. The penalty will be somewhat less. If you're behind on your taxes, you'll have to negotiate a payment schedule, and it's definitely better to call them than have them come after you.
- Keep good records. Keep anything to do with taxes, in most places for seven years. If they question or audit you, you need to be able to prove how and why you did things. This is realistically a guilty-until-proven-innocent scenario.
- Don't make the mistake of thinking that "saving" on your taxes is more important than upgrading your income.

Now you see it, now you don't.

If you're an Employee...
Get out your paycheck. Make a list of all the deductions, both the types and amounts, coming out of your gross earnings. Do you know exactly what each of these is for? If not, find out. Call your Human Resources department and talk to the Benefits person.

If you're Self-employed...
How much will you have to set aside from your gross income to pay the tax-man? How much do you need to cover your own benefits, to pay into government pension plans, and so on? If you don't know, get help from a good accountant to structure this.

You employ others?
Sort this one out with your accountant and a business lawyer.

GRIPE - The History of taxes

Taxes were originally introduced in the late 1800's, and it was the rich that were taxed. Then, believing the Robin Hood myth[1]—that it would be the rich who would be called on to "help the people"—the middle and lower classes voted in taxes as a permanent political reality. However, having gotten used to that steady flow of income, governments began to tax farther and farther down the income levels. Meanwhile the rich were inventing ways to avoid being taxed.

Now it's primarily the middle classes that are sagging under the weight. And while the infrastructures supported by taxes are valuable and important, it's sad and annoying that there is little reward for government departments to be frugal or efficient. Money not spent is re-possessed by the higher ups, and that dollar amount often deducted from future budgets. The default mindset of "spend it even if you don't need to or lose it" makes it hard for conscientious government personnel to do their best and to plan ahead. Now even well-intentioned governments are juggling the priorities of we who elected them and the vested interests of big-bucks profit-driven lobby groups.

So what did the rich do as the taxes gradually dug deeper? They invented the Corporation. A Corporation is considered a legal entity unto itself. And for Corporations, the tax rate is usually considerably lower than it is for individuals. As a corporation, business owners have two advantages: they pay their business expenses in pre-tax dollars which means less taxes overall, and they have more safety from liability. If you have a reason to incorporate how you earn your living, do it. You'll get rich a lot quicker.

"A 'Corporation' is simply a legal document that creates a body without a soul".[2] Yet, contrary to a common and unfortunate assumption, you don't have to be cut-throat or evil to succeed financially as either an individual or as a corporation. **It's vital that people realize that money can be made, and a lot of it, by doing the right thing the right way.** (Overseas, I once met three German guys in their early thirties who, believe it or not, were almost ready to retire. They had made a not-so-small fortune installing reliable high-quality solar panels on upscale hotels in West Africa where consistent power is a common problem.)

But to do the right-thing the right-way you need not only good business savvy, you need a conscience and a sense of social responsibility. The people who lack these love to keep others thinking that to "make it", one needs to be ruthless and ignore all other values. That's a nasty control tactic on their part—keep the population discouraged and scared to the point of apathy and acquiescence. Then they and their greedy-ass cronies can get away with doing whatever they want. In the name of supposedly "saving the economy" and "saving jobs", they use their fellow citizens as grist for their profit mill. Grrr. Come on people. Wise up! And that goes for both the "99%" and the "1%". (Okay, enough ranting. I'll shut up now... Well, maybe for a little while.)

GRATITUDE - for Taxes?

I had a conversation with a cabbie in Ghana a while back. We got chatting about how-things-are in each other's countries. Of course, the topic of incomes came up, and despite the huge disparity, we started comparing notes about where the money goes. It was hard to absorb how hard he worked for the little he made. He, on the other hand, couldn't believe how much we need to spend, especially for housing. Digits of difference in the income but also digits of difference in the expenditures.

I mentioned taxes. He asked "What's taxes?" And he freaked out that the government keeps on average about a third of our income. But he also couldn't believe that we all have free education, and here in Canada, virtually free health care. He had eight kids, and he, his wife, and their oldest five (ages 18 to 11) were all working full time so they'd have the money to get one or two of the youngest ones into school. Not an upscale private school, any school—all schools cost money over there. (The 9 year old was the "day care" for the 3 and 5 year old kids.) They hoped to be able to afford to get the wee ones to at least grade four so they'd "have their reading and numbers".

There are definite advantages to paying those taxes. So, to those reluctant kids and teens living here, stop thinking of your education as an irritating imposition. Instead recognize and appreciate it for the wonderful opportunity it is!

We take way too much for granted. How lucky for us that we can.

Chapter 15

Flushing money

The less financially savvy you are, the more likely it is that you'll make silly unintentional mistakes, or be taken advantage of. Why be willing to flush away your money?

You're investing time to become wiser. By doing this book, you are getting a savvy yet simplified bang for your buck. Think of this chapter as a "treasure hunt"[1] to reclaim your money. (I like analogies. That one is courtesy of Ramit Sethi, *I Will Teach You To Be Rich.)*

We're going to look at **five ways to avoid wasting money**.

ONE	**The hamster wheel of debt load**
TWO	**Ego feeding and retail therapy**
THREE	**Not knowing, not respecting what's important to you**
FOUR	**Paying too much**
FIVE	**Sneaky little leaks**

It doesn't matter how much or how little you make, if you don't pay attention here, you're still in trouble. Some may have an extra digit in their pay check, but they likely have an extra digit in their debt as well. Being daft with money happens at all income levels. It's a short trip from short-term "gain" to long-term pain.

"Most people never see the trap they are in."[2] Money is running their lives. Two cruelties lie in wait here. One is to lose ourselves in working hard for money, "thinking that money will buy you things that will make you happy.... Fear and greed and desire always there. Don't let them control your thinking..."[3] The rat race is a result of trying to balance that greed and fear. The result of rampant hedonism? A toxic anxiety about the possible loss of a ramped up lifestyle. The other cruelty? "To spend your life living in fear, never exploring your dreams."[4]... "Self-inflicted fear and ignorance ... keeps people trapped."[5]

Denying the impact of money—or the lack of it—on our lives is just as whacked as an addiction to it. Many will work ridiculously long hours, even two jobs, but they're supposedly "not interested in money". Ya right. Denial, avoidance, and fear are a vicious cycle. Luckily, it's one that can be broken. Let's get started. So what if this is a bit of a nuisance? *You're doing this FOR yourself, not TO yourself.*

Are your financial records so messed up that you haven't a hope of pulling up much useful info from the last couple of months? Instead, track your money going forward.

Forget perfect form right out of the blocks. No four minute miles required. Crawl, walk, jog a little. Some training and practice, then enjoy those runs.

Ya, I know, you don't have any extra money. Neither did I, or so I thought.
I dare ya.... have a go at this.

WASTE # ONE The Hamster Wheel of Debt

There's good debt and there's bad debt. A reasonable student loan to get yourself better educated, good debt. Buying stuff you don't truly need, on credit, bad debt.

Most Americans spend one-quarter to one-third of their take-home income paying the interest on their debts. That figure doesn't include their mortgages. Yikes. Let's translate that: every eight-hour work-day they hand over at least two hours worth of their day and pay to the money lenders, solely for the interest on their consumer debt. Paying down the principle (the amount they originally borrowed to buy that stuff) and all their other living expenses, including their mortgage, has to come out of what's left. Gross.

If your mortgage, car, and credit card payments eat up 40% or more of your gross pay, you're in serious financial jeopardy. Between 1998 and 2007, the number of households above this 40% mark rose (from under 10% to about 13%) for the $60,000 to $98,200 group, and more than doubled (from 3.5% to over 8%) for the $98,200 to $140,000 group! And more and more of the $140,000 plus group are also getting into trouble.[6] That's a lot of people with major problems that you'd think should have been financially just fine.

DEBT becomes your personal hamster wheel. You'll be getting nowhere, no matter how fast or hard you work. In *Good Debt, Bad Debt*, Jon Hanson describes the effects of debt as "loss of freedom, loss of cash flow, loss of time, loss of opportunities".[7] Unfortunately, when they get more money, most people still find excuses to spend more than they make, and simply sink themselves into more debt.

CREDIT, the ability to borrow money, is obviously useful. But credit is money you can access, *not* money you have! And credit once accessed is DEBT. Too many ignore that fact. They're walking out onto quicksand. Even before you graduate, the credit card companies will start trying to entice you. They'll make you feel it's a privilege to have a card, a right of passage to adulthood. Yes, credit cards are convenient, but if you don't have adequate self discipline, they're a TRAP. Don't get seduced into thinking it's your spending money. A little something here, a little there—those $10 and $100 expenditures quickly become thousands. You're actually being seduced into servitude to the money lenders. Instead, learn to use their game to your advantage. (For how to do that, see Chapter 17.)

Why make the banks and credit card companies rich?
Here's an example of how they make Billions in interest per year.
Suppose you owe $5000 in credit card debt at an interest rate of 20%.
Try these scenarios:

Amount you pay off per month	# months to pay it off	Charged on card	INTEREST paid	Total costs
A $100	109	$ 5000	**$ 5840**	$ 10840
B $ 200	33	$ 5000	**$ 1522**	$ 6522
C $ 300	20	$ 5000	**$ 907**	$ 5907

In scenario A you paid more than double what you charged on your card. Imagine how much you pay when you only pay the minimums each month! Yikes.

Remember the Rule of 72 from page 115?
72 divided by the interest rate = the number of years until the debt doubles.

At 20%, 72/20 means that your debt doubles in 3.6 years. Interest costs bite. What could you have done with that money instead? That "Instead" is what's called an "Opportunity Cost". You could have put that $5840 you flushed as interest (in A above) into a nice safe investment. Or you could have had a great trip, or a lotta Play Money. Instead, silly you, you handed it over to the credit card companies to fill their pockets instead of your own.

How to avoid flushing money when using credit cards.

(For more on how to be smarter with your cards also see pages 161-164)

- You shouldn't be paying an **interest rate** of more than prime plus 7 or 8% if you have a good credit rating. For example, if prime is 3%, the max should be 10%, not 20 %. Ask them to lower it if they want your business and they do, *if* you have a good credit rating. (*Prime* is the interest rate that banks charge their most reliable customers, and it's related to what they charge each other. In 2012, it's about 3%. In 2000, it was about 6%. By 2020? Who knows?)
- Be cautious when they tempt you to transfer your current balance to a new card to get a "low **introductory rate**". Surprisingly, that's not the best option. First of all, these rates are just teasers. Some intro-periods are shorter than others. Read the fine print. Secondly, when you card surf it bites your overall credit score. (There's more on protecting your credit rating in Chapter 17.) Try this:

  Option one: Let your current company know you've been offered a lower rate and see if they'll match it. They'll likely at least agree to drop their rate a bit, *if* you have a good credit rating. (Notice a theme here?)

  Option two: *if* you can afford to pay off the entire balance while the "intro rate" is still in effect, you might consider switching cards. (But, if that is the case, why haven't you been doing that already?)
- Do not use **store cards**, even if they offer incentives like "10% off your first purchase". (Say "No thanks". They may look at you funny. Like you care.) Store cards have insane interest rates, often 10% higher than the regular credit cards. At around 25 to 30%, they're almost up there with the knee-breaker guys. If you're buying a whole living room's worth of furniture? Well, maybe. Just pay it off right away then cancel the card. (There's a good chance that stuff would have been on sale soon anyway.) There's too great a temptation to continue using that store card and they know it. You may save 10% on your first purchase but, from then on, you're paying them 30% interest on whatever you purchase on that card. Who got the better of that deal?
- Do not take **Cash advances** on your credit card. Card holders take out a staggering $100 Billion a year in cash advances. For the majority of cards, the interest starts accruing immediately and the rate on a cash advance can be 3 to 10% higher than the usual rates. (Some even charge a flat fee in addition to that.) Cash advances earn the card companies Billions a year, over and above the interest they charge you on your purchases. So buy the item using the card rather than withdrawing cash from your card to do so. Better yet, if you can't afford to pay off the entire balance within the next couple of weeks, don't make the purchase until you can. You want out of a hole? First, stop digging.

Stats Can recently put the average Canadian household debt at greater than 150% of its income. That's dangerous. In 1990, it was 91%

- Do not buy **credit protection insurance**. It actually insures them against your not being able to pay if you're hurt, sick, lose your job, whatever. Instead, put this amount into paying down the debt faster.
- Do not use one card to pay off another. If you try to play a **shell game** with the big-boys, you're not going to win. They've got deeper pockets and a bigger machine than you.
- Avoid short **grace periods**. When you buy something, there's a certain amount of time before the interest charges kick in. That's the grace period. The shorter the grace period, the more they make. Most are fairly similar, but ask. When you pay off your purchases before the grace period ends, you don't accrue any interest. This way, the card company does your book-keeping and you're not paying them to do it. Nice. Keep it even simpler— if you're paid biweekly, pay off your card each time you get a paycheck. If you can't do this, you're not alone, but you really need Chapter 17.

Bigger debts => bigger hamster wheels.
Credit cards are not the only place you're paying interest to service debt. Whether it's cars or condos, a little planning goes a long way. A one or two percent difference in the interest rate and/or a slightly different time frame will save you many thousands. (More on that in the next Chapter.)

WASTE # TWO Ego feeding and Retail Therapy

Are you spending money so you don't feel poor, inadequate, or left-out?
If you buy into retail therapy, you're simply creating an illusion of wealth. Your illusion, their wealth. Why volunteer to be the prey of big business and the credit card industry?

John F. Schumacher, in *New Internationalist* [8]

"As human beings continue to be reshaped by consumer culture into restless, dissatisfied, and all desiring economic pawns, greed is being re-defined as a virtue and a legitimate guiding principle for economic prosperity and general happiness. In the process, it is steadily eating away at the cornerstones of civilized society and undermining the visions, values, and collective aspirations that made us strong... The commercial exploitation of false needs... even the commercialization of childhood is being lead by greedy corporations that put profits before social responsibility and children's health..." [So what if your kids are fat and hyper? The soft drink companies want their profits.]

"Greed is beginning to overwhelm conscience, reason, compassion, love, family bonds and community. Moreover, existing levels of constant greed are causing clinical depression and despair in many people." He goes on to show that chronic greed will "tarnish a person's overall experience of life" and that extreme greed ironically "makes the economy sick" not healthier, and by laying waste the environment, a greed economy is highly toxic to itself. In other words, short term "gain", long term pain.

So, do you want a more fulfilling life, or just more stuff? Are you trying to "keep up with the Joneses", going along with the crowd, instead of establishing your own priorities? Have you joined the ranks of what I call the "Obsessive Consumptive"?

Successful marketers are skilled at bringing your feelings to the surface. You may have an unfulfilled need to feel special so you're easily convinced to shop in upscale stores, even if the quality's not much better and you can't really afford the prices. Maybe you feel guilty about not making enough time for your kids or other loved ones? Buy them something. Preferably something expensive. Then buy them more. In actual fact, what they really want is some time and attention, neither of which cost you anything. But that doesn't make the corporate sell-sters any money. So shame on you. (Excuse the sarcasm.) Now neuroeconomists (a new breed of researchers) are attaching electrodes to people's heads to figure out what makes certain products more enticing, even if we aren't consciously aware of that ourselves.[9] Groan. I have great respect for good research, but researching how to play more effectively with our heads and pockets rather puts me off. You?

Improve your spending smarts.

- Remember that you're buying things with after-tax dollars. So when you're considering a purchase, look at the cost in terms of your actual Take-Home-Pay, not your Gross Income. (Depending on your tax bracket, you might need to be earning $2 for every $1 you spend.)
- Consider the total cost of the purchase, that is, the initial cost plus the total amount of interest you're going to pay. To see what purchases really cost you, use the calculators at
  bankrate.com/brm/calc/minpayment.asp or bankrate.ca
  calculatorweb.com
- Say no to impulse buying. Decide what you need in advance and watch for deals. At certain times of year, there are really good discounts, e.g. air conditioners in the fall, winter tires in the spring.
- Buy less, but buy better quality. And take care of what you have. (Don't get sucked in by hype. Most gee-wow features simply add to the price, not to the usefulness or quality of the product.) Which items have the features and reliability you want, at a price you want to pay? Always comparison shop to get the best deal on what you *genuinely* need. See consumerreports.com and/or consumerworld.org
- Don't hang out at the mall. Shopping is not recreation. It's temporary therapy at best, but therapy that bites when the bills come in.
- Don't purchase extended warranties on gadgets and appliances, unless it includes a guaranteed gift certificate for the unused portion when the warranty expires. (That's a new and nicer version of an extended warranty.) Some credit cards give you a free extended warranty on anything you buy with your card, so check to see if yours offers this benefit.
- Don't let emotions overrun your good sense. Put a limit on spending for gifts. Avoid the holiday hangover, the financial version. And encourage your family and friends to do the same.

Shopaholic? Put the same rampant, sometimes even rabid, enthusiasm with which you buy stuff into building a financial safety net instead. That way, you'll be taking care of all your YOUs—the kid within that maybe never had enough, the Now-You who needs to show more self-respect by getting your act together, and the Future-You who'll be thanking the You-that-you-are-now for the peace of mind and the comfortable lifestyle.

Stuffed?

Check out your wardrobe.

What do you need for what you do?
What's actually useful and appropriate for work, play, and day to day life?
Do you have more than you actually use? The wrong things?
Or exactly what you truly need? What functions well for you?
(See Appendix B.)

Check out your gadgets and gizmos.

Which of these have you not used enough to have justified that purchase?
Add up what these items have cost you over the last year. At least guesstimate... What could you have done with that money instead?

Clutter Cash

Feeling deprived? Want some guilt-free play money? Or a head start on paying down those depressing bills? Maybe you realized in Chapter 12, when you were searching for your materials to file, that life might be a little easier if you cleared up and unloaded some clutter. Often when one aspect of your life is disorganized, chaotic, so are others.

Let's solve a couple of things at once. Turn your clutter into cash.
Make a list, or a pile, of all the things that have some value but you no longer treasure. Many garages can't even fit a car in them these days. What about that drum-set you never seem to get around to playing or the exercise gadget that's now a clothes rack? E-bay, Craigslist, Kijiji, or garage sale them.

If something has sentimental value, like that collection of stuffed toys, take a picture of the group and keep that, along with a few favourites, instead of the whole crew.

Want more ideas?

Give the stuff to charity. Someone else then gets to enjoy what you no longer need. In some cases, you can get a charitable donation receipt to hand over to the tax man as a deduction.

With good friends, you could pre-arrange to "pass-along" where appropriate. For example, you know your friend Sally covets your jade necklace. It's her birthday soon. (Besides, now you have a different favourite.) *New is not the only Nice.*

The bigger things - Need, greed, or reward?

A comfortable home or a status address? The difference can be 5 or 6 figures plus. A sensible and reliable vehicle or an ego-mobile? The difference? Easily over $20,000. What else could you do with that money?

Other luxuries?
Some you maybe feel you can afford to buy, but can you afford to own them?

- I'd love to have a dressage horse. But... Buy, yes. Shell out for ongoing keep, no. Much as I love riding, it's cheaper and just as much fun to dance. And besides, I'm saving to do more traveling.
- My friends and their sailboats? One couple, in the summer, spends more time sailing than at home. Yes, it costs, but it's their passion and their together-time. So they keep the rest of their life simple. The other couple gets out on the boat only three or four times a season. But, at this point in their lives, they can afford the wishful thinking. Both couples got their financial pragmatics in hand first. And guess what, the first couple are not bankers, but middle aged custodians. With purely legal incomes, I might add. Priorities.

WASTE # THREE — Not knowing what truly matters to you. Not respecting what does.

If that's the case, you're probably wasting not only money but time and energy.

In the Priorities Section, you learned more about what matters to you. By respecting those values and goals you're showing respect for yourself. If you leave those deeper needs and meaningful dreams unexplored and unfulfilled, it won't matter how much you spend, how much stuff you accumulate, you'll still have an emptiness echoing somewhere inside.

Interestingly, some studies have shown that even the winners of large lotteries often return to their previous levels of happiness after a couple of years. So don't assume that more money necessarily translates into more happiness. (I bet you, like me, wouldn't mind a chance to check that out.) Ironically, it often just translates into a fear of losing the up-scaled lifestyle. As well, "the grass is greener on the other side of the fence" kicks in. There's always someone with more. And less.

Understanding—or not—what truly matters is not tied to income levels. Look at all the rich-and-famous people whose lives are a mess. Sure, for most of us "Average Joes", more stuff seems tempting. But stuff cannot fill emotional black-holes. What is the true need behind the supposed need?

The authors of *Your Money or Your Life* caution that we seem to have lost our imagination about how we might meet many of our deeper needs *without money*. When we know how much is Enough, when we have defined *for ourselves* what is fulfilling and meaningful, our choices—from how we spend our time and our money to whom we hang out with—will reflect that mindset and create a context that meets those deeper needs. "For these people there is wealth beyond money; there is 'Enoughness', a stance of material sufficiency and spiritual affluence."

Your Money or Your Life is a transformative must-read. It takes time and personal energy to earn your money. "Spending money…in ways that might bring superficial happiness but don't contribute to lasting fulfillment", in reality, means you are not adequately valuing yourself. "It's frittering away…precious, one-way life energy."[10]

The authors suggest you ask yourself three questions for each spending category: "Did I receive fulfillment, satisfaction and value in proportion to the life energy spent? Is this expenditure of life energy in alignment with my values and life purpose? How might this expenditure change if I didn't have to work for a living?"[11]
By consistently asking yourself these questions, you'll come to see that you can *choose and enjoy what is Enough*, rather than waste energy on what's simply More.

So I ask you, how much are you contributing per month to your dreams, towards your short and long term goals? Is your wasteful silly-spending eroding your chances of realizing these? If so, you can change that.

How sweet it would be to get to a place where you can say YES to what deeply and authentically matters to you—without guilt, without worry!

Another rant:

The alternative to materialism is not a primitive existence. That either/or mindset is promoted by the self-serving greed of too many unscrupulous corporations. Unfortunately, that fear-mongering is willingly swallowed by a gullible public. And it's absurdly counter-productive to our individual and collective well-being. Stuff => status? The result is our harried frenetic work style. We wear ourselves out to purchase, house, and protect more and more stuff while having to pay for more and more services to counteract the stress. All in the name of "having more fun" and thinking we're "more worthy" or "impressive". (Ya right.) Meanwhile, CEOs with eight figure incomes and wealthy shareholders are laughing all the way to the bank while they ship jobs overseas to further increase their profits. With more sensible priorities, we can afford to gift ourselves more time instead. And, with more time, we are much more likely to discover and create more *genuine* joy and meaning in our lives. And that is priceless!

WASTE # FOUR Paying too much for things you do need.

More Search and rescue ...

Revisit your Current Cash Flow pages from Chapter 13. If you guesstimated the amounts you entered, go through your Expenses lists and, over the next month, figure out your actual costs.

How could you reduce some of your expenses? Brainstorm and research alternatives for each category. Implement your better strategies. This may take a little time. So what? You're worth it.

Get smarter.

- Look for better rates for phone and long distance plans, internet and cable, at least once a year. Avoid long term contracts where possible, unless it's a really good deal.
- Food should be primarily groceries, not eating out five times a week. And cut back on the junk food you buy. Want sweets? Buy yummy fruit such as blueberries, mangos, organic bananas. Make that the whole comes-in-it's-own-skin kind rather than the processed stuff-in-a-box. Your body will thank you.
- When you buy clothes, get washable items rather than those that must be dry cleaned. Buy what you actually need, and love. Buy fewer items, but good quality ones that really suit you and how you live. (For more, see Appendix B.)
- Avoid getting something just in case you might need it. And don't settle for something simply because it's on sale.
- Renters: Several months before your lease is up, compare your current rental costs to other places in your area. Would there be an advantage to moving? Maybe, at least for now, cut costs by getting a roommate?
- Owners: Are there better mortgage rates out there? If so, explore what it might cost to switch over and get unbiased advice on whether it would be worth it. (See also pages 155-159.)
- If you're near decent transit, do you really need a vehicle? For the two-car families—do you really need the second car? Instead, check out Autoshare, Zipcars, or the like for the occasional run you need to make. They rent by the hour or day, at very reasonable rates.
- Be sure you've got the right kinds and amounts of Insurances: Health, Disability, and/or Long Term Care, Critical Illness, Life. (See Chapter 22.) You don't want to be truly wasting money while you hope you're wasting money. Let's face it, no one actually wants to have to use their disability or fire insurance.
- To cut insurance costs somewhat, raise the deductible (the amount you pay of what it costs to repair the damage) from $500 to a $1000. And with some insurance companies, if you pay upfront annually rather than monthly, they'll give you a bit of a discount.
- Look for ways to cut your taxes. And pay the taxman on time to avoid the late-filing penalties. Get the advice of an accountant or at least a certified tax-prep person; it will likely save you more than it costs.

As you go through your expenses list, groan, snarl, or cry if you want to, then pat yourself on the back. You are reclaiming money you were previously flushing away. Your Smarter Self and Future-You say thank you. You're on the path to peace of mind, higher self-respect, and guilt-free play-money.

For more ideas, read David Bach's *Fight For Your Money.*

> Small indulgences are delightful. We just need to have $$ boundaries on these, and to be sure that the indulgence chosen creates genuine enjoyment. The better we are at not flushing our money, in big and little ways, the kinder we can be to ourselves and to the people and causes we care about.

Small Indulgences

Which of your current small indulgences are authentically meaningful and enjoyable? Which ones, maybe not so much? Those are simply leaks.

WASTE # FIVE Sneaky little leaks... that can add up to hundreds per month.

Money processing fees

- Credit Unions and internet banks charge less in fees than the regular banks. Shop around.
- ATM fees can really add up if you're not using your own bank's ATM.
- NSF (non-sufficient funds) charges are often $40 plus, each. Ouch.
- Avoid the extra costs you incur when you don't pay a utility bill on time.

Bad habits

How much do you spend per month on your not-smart habits, like cigarettes? Smoking doesn't only impact your health. You'll see why in the examples to come.

The "Latte Factor"

You could have a normal coffee, a regular cuppa-joe, but why when you deserve to spoil yourself, right? We "latte" money away, almost unconsciously, on day-to-day little things. Each of these, individually, seems fairly inconsequential. Ha. Add it up over a month. Apparently, for the average 30-year-old, these smaller expenditures add up to about $300 a month. (What about yours?) Again, it's important to distinguish between the occasional small indulgence that truly satisfies and those that, in reality, do not. In that case, you'd be better off and happier by re-directing that money to something more genuinely fun and meaningful.

Let's play with some numbers here.

Keep in mind that we're talking about money that, at the moment, you're basically *wasting*. Math phobs, relax. I've "done the math" for you. (The following uses the calculators at ingdirect.ca/en/tools. There are many others.) We're going to try several scenarios using currently realistic numbers.

- Straight savings at ZERO percent, pretty much what most banks give you.
- Very safe investments called Guaranteed Investment Certificates. (A five year GIC, right now, gives you about 2%.)
- The Market: Some years, some decades are better or worse than others, and some sectors do better than others, for varying amounts of time. That having been said, between the 1920s and now, if you average out the whole timeframe, it comes out at about 10% a year. Inflation has chewed away at about 2 to 3%. That's an average increase in the market, *as a whole*, of 8%. If you're investing in mutual funds you may be paying 3% in fees for them to "manage" your money. So let's use 5% as what the market *might* (emphasis on *might*) make. There are certainly NO guarantees. Are there predictable patterns? Some patterns, yes. Predictable? No. If you are curious, see econbrowser.com and search "long term perspective on the stock market". And some strategies for investing in the markets are, apparently, safer and more effective than others. (More ideas on that in Chapter 19)

Example ONE

Suppose you cut back on your silly-spending even a little bit, perhaps by $100 a month. Set aside that $100 a month *for 5 years.*

- Even at ZERO percent interest, you'll have $6,000.
- At 3% interest, $6,480.
- At 5% interest, $6,800.

Set aside that $100 a month for 10 years at 5% and you'll have $18,416. You put in $12,000. The interest paid to you contributed $6,416 *you didn't have to work for.*

Example TWO

Eliminate $200 a month of wasteful spending, for example by quitting smoking. Set that $200 per month aside for 20 years. (Maybe for your midlife crisis?)

- At ZERO interest, you'd have $48,000.
- At 3% interest, $65,850. ($17,800 of which is interest they paid you.)
- At 5% interest, in an RRSP or 401K, you'll have about $82,550 of which you put in $48,000. You did not have to earn the other $34,550. Sweet.

Are you telling me that for a free, tax free, work-free, and legal $34,550 you wouldn't quit smoking? Are you getting this? You're burning money with every cigarette. So butt out, butt-head. Your body and your future will thank you. (No, quitting is not easy. Neither is earning that extra $34,550.)

Example THREE

Revisit the example on page 132 in which you owe $5,000 on a credit card at 20% and are currently paying it off at only $100 per month. We saw it would take 109 months to pay off the $5,000 you borrowed plus the $5,840 in interest, for a total of $10,840. More than double the value of what you bought.

Try this. Reduce your wasted-spending a little and add an additional $100 a month to that $100 you're currently paying. With $200 a month now going in, it's paid off in 33 months rather than ten years and costs you $1,522 in interest rather than $5,840. You saved yourself $4,318 (i.e. $5,840 – $1,522) in interest. Money in your pocket, not the credit card company's.

Example FOUR

Rescue $300 a month. Most people, apparently, waste at least that not including the bigger mistakes that are all too common with debt mismanagement. (The $$ values in the following chart are approximate.)

$300 per month for this # of years	**You put in** a total of …	@ 0 % Interest you have …	@ 3 % interest you have …	@ 5 % interest you have…
5	18,000	18,000	19,442	20,480
10	36,000	36,000	42,027	46,780
20	72,000	72,000	98,740	**B*** 123,800
30	108,000	108,000	**A*** 175,258	250,700
40	144,000	144,000	**A*** 278,510	**C*** 459,700

A* Even at only 3%, as time passes, the interest *they pay you* substantially adds to what you put in. Remember I said earlier you were going to learn to play their game to your advantage? SROTY.

B* At a rate of 5%, let's say in a tax-deductible retirement savings plan (an "RSP"), as either an RRSP or 401K, in 20 years you've already almost doubled what you put in. The interest *they pay you* (instead of the other way around) has now contributed close to half of your nest egg.

C* At 40 years at 5% you have a cool half million! And here's the kicker. Of that, *they paid you* $315,700 in interest—way more than the $144,000 you put in.
No, not crazy. For real. If you're not interested now, you're the one that's crazy.

Okay, let's make your head spin. Take that interest rate up to 8%.

Put $300 a month for 40 years into an RSP. If that, over time averages 8%, you've got $1,054,000! Yes, 40 years is a long time. So what? Take your current age plus 40 years, and some money you're likely *wasting* and ZAP, you're a Millionaire. And you put in only $144,000. The interest provided over $910,000. Wow. Between years 30 to 40, your money actually doubles. So, even if you pull it all out 30 years from now, you've still got a cool half million to play with. The power of compound interest. *Someone really oughta tell you...* Besides, if you're 20 now, in 40 years you'll be 60 which is earlier than many people get to retire. Sweet.

Can you be guaranteed 8% or more in the Markets? Of course not.
Want to feel nauseous? Imagine what you're paying out, to carry your debts, over 20 or 30 years at only 5%, let alone the 20 to 30% rates charged by credit cards or pay-day-loans. Ouch. So if you have DEBTS, pay them off as fast as you can. That's a guaranteed investment in your sanity and your future. If your credit card is running at 18 to 25%, paying that off is just as good as earning that rate in the market—which would be awesome—and the beneficial results are *predictable and guaranteed*, which the market is not.

Interest, when used in *your* favour, is money you get that you don't actually have to work for. Ya, I know. I didn't believe the numbers either. The magic is time. Sure wish someone had pointed this out to me in my twenties!

Which will it be? Interest on your debts going into *their* pockets or a growing interest in—and on—money you were previously wasting now going into *yours*?

You now know you can *generate many thousands by not wasting hundreds.*
Isn't it worth taking a little time to find some ways to stop flushing your money?

Okay, how? Obviously, you want to decrease or avoid interest costs wherever possible. As well, ask yourself which of your Discretionary Expenses and Play-costs really matter to you. No, I'm not advocating you stop feeding your dog or stop having fun, just that you get a little wiser about where you're directing your money.

Negotiate with yourself. What are you willing to cut back on or perhaps eliminate? This is likely to take some trial and error as well as some planning. Give up the *Whatever* for a month and see if you really do miss it.

Think of this as an experiment to help you figure out what truly matters to you, and what's simply become a habit.

- Rather than curtail the activity, look to reduce the cost. You love movies? Perhaps go a little less often or skip the popcorn and pop. Rent movies, join a by-the-month group, or borrow them from the library. Same goes for games.
- Take a bag lunch to work a couple of days a week. And instead of frequent fast-food dinners, go out for a good meal once a month. Likely cheaper overall and you'll feel as though you're truly pampering yourself.
- If you have a seldom used gym membership, get rid of it. Take up running or cycling for cardio, and buy a rubber band or a few weights for resistance training.

What suggestions would you have for your friends?
What suggestions might they have for you?

A couple of times a year at least, weed your financial garden.

There's a great analogy from a motivation guru, Tony Robbins, which paraphrased goes something like this: You can't simply look out your backdoor and say "There are no weeds in my garden". Then a week later, do the same thing. "There are no weeds in my garden." By the end of the summer, what shape is your garden in? So much for only positive *thinking*. Instead, go for positive *doing*. Each week get out there and pull some weeds. Then there *will* be no weeds in your garden.

I think the same idea applies to money—*denial only gets you in more of a mess.* If you want to be able to enjoy your garden-of-life, you need to take some time to plan the layout, plant what you want where, and weed, water, and fertilize.

Here's a blunt reminder from Larry Winget: "Affirmation without implementation is self-delusion."[12] Go Larry. I like his no BS style.

Get on with it! Refine where your money's going—gradually—a little each month. And if you backslide a little here and there, so what? Think Toddler Tactics. Get back up off your butt and at it again. It's one step at a time. And praise yourself for even the small successes.

> Take a long view of your life.
> Ask yourself: If I keep going in the same direction, where is it likely to take me?
> And in the meantime, what is the quality of the journey?

The idea is not to deprive yourself, but to **re-direct your money to that which matters most.** Once you've freed up some of the money you've been wasting, put it instead towards something that truly matters to you. STOP FLUSHING IT!

- Trade ego-feeding and retail-therapy for what genuinely brings you joy. That probably has much less to do with money than you initially thought.
- Stop paying more than you have to for what you do need.
- Sweat the small "latte" stuff? Limit these, yes. Eliminate totally? No.

Now what? Sweat the BIG stuff!

You'll set up a game plan to deal with both good debt and bad debt.

And you'll learn to how to better respect your lazy self, your fun self, *and* your sensible self.

Further Resources:

If you need more help with the reasons for and how to defeat your not-so-beneficial money attitudes and habits, I suggest you read any of the following:

Your Money Or Your Life, Vicki Robin, Joe Dominguez, Monique Telford
Good Debt, Bad Debt, John Hanson
Money Madness, Spencer Sherman
You're Broke Because You Want To Be, Larry Winget
"Put Equality First - Fair Economy", Vanessa Baird, *New Internationalist,* March 2012

Big Ticket Borrowing

When is borrowing a good or a bad idea? If you're borrowing to enhance your ability to make money, such as for a student loan or a more reliable truck for your carpentry business, it's good debt. That having been said, **caution is vital** no matter what type of loan you're after. We're going to look at loans for upgrading your education, for vehicles, and for homes.

Education / Student Loans

If you need these, get them. Your education will pay for itself many times over, especially if you're smart with your money. That doesn't mean getting that education is going to be easy, academically or financially. Many of us have to earn our own way through school with part-time jobs, scholarships, or grants, instead of help from Ma and Pa. Not all families can afford to help. One option, depending on what you're studying, might be a Co-op Program in which you alternate school terms with work terms. Not only do you make money along the way, you graduate with appropriate real-world experience, hence a better skill set and a better resume.

Before you take out a student loan, check out all the possible scholarships and grants. Every year, many thousands of dollars go unclaimed by people who would have been granted the money *if* they'd applied. How sad!

How much are you likely to need? Take out as little as possible. This is your education loan, not a party fund. Avoid borrowing anywhere near what you will *likely* make your first year out of school. More than that tends to make life-after-school unnecessarily difficult. Even at modest interest rates, you could end up paying back almost twice what you took out. For example, the typical total student loan for an undergrad program in Canada these days is about $25,000. Paying that off at $300 a month for 10 years, at current interest rates, will cost about $40,000. Taking longer will cost you more. About 10% of American grads are carrying more than $35,000. Ouch. *Be very frugal.* Consider a part-time job. Or get creative.

Two friends headed off to first year at the same university. They'd taken a year off after high school to work in construction and save. A cousin was starting second year. Instead of going the residence route, the three of them decided to pool their resources and put a pathetically small down payment on a rather pathetic but good-bones house. The cousin's best friend worked in town and had enough of an income that, by all of them signing together, the bank gave them a mortgage. Fast forward. They worked their butts off—at school, at summer jobs, and to fix up the house, one project, one room at a time. (Yes, money and time were tight, but it was not all work and no play. Those guys knew how to have fun.) When they graduated, they sold the now-nice house. That paid off the mortgage, gave the working friend his share, and paid off all their student loans. They started "adult" life with no debts. Impressive.

Here are some useful sites for exploring the ins and outs of student loans, grants, scholarships, schools, and for saving for your own kid's education:

In Canada	studentawards.com, scholarships.com, and canlearn.ca
In the USA	finaid.com, ed.gov and nslds.ed.gov

Useful student loan repayment calculators can be found at
canadastudentdebt.ca or dinkytown.net.

Before signing up for your loan, be sure to clarify the following.

- What interest rate applies? What circumstances might change that rate?
- Understand the required repayment steps. To whom, when, how, and where do you make your payments?
- When will the repayments need to start? How soon after graduation? (The interest charges likely start as soon as you finish school.)
- What happens if you drop out? Or if you drop to part-time studies? Will that trigger the "pay us back now" requirement?
- Check out the circumstances that might allow "deferments" and "forbearances". (You lose your job. They may let you temporarily decrease the amount you pay on your student loans. Ask.)

Already have student loans?

- List them all. Who are they with? How much do you owe on each?
- Ask your lenders if your current method of repayment is the most efficient. Ask what options are available for reducing the interest rate.
  For example, ask for a slightly lower rate in exchange for giving them automatic withdrawals from your account. They love reliable and predictable.
- If you have more than one loan with the same institution, see if they'd send you a "unified bill" each month to simplify the payment process and the paperwork.
- How much extra will they let you pay off here and there, if and when you can afford to?
- The interest on student loans might be tax deductible. Ask your lender or your tax advisor.
- Though it's rarely the case, there may be some provisions for forgiving part of your loan. For example, nurses who work in areas with severe nursing shortages may get a break.

Oops. In trouble with your student loans?

Call your lenders right away and negotiate whatever palatable changes you can. You need to be proactive, especially if you're having difficulty with your payments. This is definitely one of those "You can't beat City Hall" things. And the default consequences are nasty. The collectors will come after you and your credit rating will get slammed, which has its own cascade of unpleasant consequences. The government can garnishee your wages and/or keep any future tax-refunds to "help you" pay off what you owe them. Even if you have to declare bankruptcy, you are still required to pay off your student loans[1], at least in part. How much you pay is your lender's call, not yours. Bankruptcy follows you for at least seven years. Avoid it as you would Ebola.

In Chapter 13 ("Getting Real") you already, I hope, listed all of your debts along with the amounts and the rates on each. Your student loan's interest rate is, almost surely, less than your credit card's. So kill off the highest rate debts first, while just paying the "musts" on your student loans. Then attack the latter. (For more on how to efficiently reduce your debts, see pages 167-168)

Vehicles – buy, lease, or rent-as-needed?

Do you actually need a vehicle?

If you live in an urban center with reasonable public transit, use it, at least for now. Use taxis when necessary, Zipcars and Autoshares for local errands, rental cars for the occasional trip. Say you're spending about $600 to $800 a month or more on car payments, insurance, maintenance and upkeep, and various fees and taxes—that's easily the equivalent of a transit pass, a lot of taxis, and a couple of weekend rentals a month of whatever new car you happen to be in the mood for. If you live in way-out-there suburbia or in the country, that's another matter. You may have limited options for getting around without a vehicle.

> Caution: Offers-to-purchase and leases are legally binding contracts. There's no backing-out period or do-over once you've signed one of these.

So you've decided you do want your own vehicle. Now what?

To avoid a lot of potentially expensive mistakes, spend some time on the sites mentioned in this section *before* you go vehicle shopping. They cover a range of buying and leasing advice for both Americans and Canadians, and will help you understand and explore your insurance options.

To lease or not to lease?

Yes, the smaller payments may be a temptation. The short answer? Don't lease—unless you're a corporation, in which case, there *might* be some tax advantage. (Sorry, leasing companies.) Still tempted? Check out leaseguide.com.

What do you actually NEED your vehicle to do for you?

Sounds ridiculously obvious, but many don't figure that out in advance. Do you want reliable, suitable, fun transportation, or are you looking for an ego-mobile? Are you hauling around tools, toys, kids, or just you and your groceries? And what options are the musts? Which simply the would-be-nice ones?

How much are you able and willing to put into this?

- Decide in advance how much can you *sensibly* handle per month. It's not only the payments you're taking on. (See the point below.) Upscale cars come with upscale repair bills and upscale insurance costs.
- **Total vehicle costs per month** = loan payments + insurance + gas, oil etc. + routine maintenance + repairs + licenses + taxes + parking + optional CAA or AAA fees. Ballpark *each* of these *before* buying. (E.g. insurance for a young male can be $400 a month plus, depending on your driving record.)
- How much are you likely to have to pay for the vehicle you want? Check out edmunds.com, kbb.com, or autotrader.com or .ca.
- There's a decent chance you'll get a better interest on your loan if you've saved up a down payment of about 20% of the vehicle's value.

A caution, especially for Americans or those driving to the States:
You really must have "uninsured driver" protection included in your policy. You're insured but the other guy may not be. Incredibly, if there's an accident, you're likely to find yourself on the hook for their lousy driving or bad luck, and perhaps even their medical bills. Yikes. These fools take out insurance to get their license renewed then cancel it. In Canada, the penalties are such that Canadians aren't so short-sighted as to let their insurance lapse. Some bone-heads in the States try to "save money" by doing just that. The law should deny non-insured vehicle owners access to the other driver's insurance. You can't afford any insurance? Don't own a vehicle until you can.

"The quickest way to financial ruin is to shortchange your insurance coverage." [2]

Suze Orman

Vehicle Loans

- Before you shop for the actual car, shop around for your car loan. And before you do either, get your credit reports and credit score and keep them handy. Why? The loan companies and dealers will otherwise try to stick you with a higher interest rate than you should have to pay. This bias is particularly tough on young people who haven't had previous car loans. I suggest you read the advice on carbuyingtips.com.
- Get pre-approved for a loan you can handle comfortably. What's the point of having a spiffy vehicle if you then can't afford to do anything?
- See such sites as bankrate.com or lendingtree.com. Ask a couple of banks and credit unions for their rates.
- To figure out how much a loan (principle plus interest) will actually cost, try edmunds.com or http://ca.autos.yahoo.com/p/1881/5-car-loan-mistakes-that-cost-you-money.
- As with any loan, pick the shortest loan time frame (the "amortization period") you can manage. If you can't pay a car off in four years max, buy a less expensive car.
- Zero-percent financing is reserved for those with excellent credit ratings, which is, unfortunately, not the average person. That's yet another reason to maintain a good credit rating.

What if you want to trade in a vehicle you still owe money on? The short answer? Don't. The change-over can get messy. Clear the lien (aka loan) on your current car first. You'll get a better deal on the new car.

Buy new or used?

- Whether you're buying new or used, check the reliability, safety, gas usage, and resale value of the make and model you're interested in.
- Some useful sites: iihs.org, safercar.gov, consumerreports.com, carinfo.com, edmunds.com.
- With new cars, dealers generally have about a 5 to 15 % profit margin to play with. Get quotes from the so-called no-haggle dealers as well.
- New cars depreciate up to 20% the minute they're bought and another 20% in the second year. You'll save many thousands by buying slightly used.

Suppose the current model costs $25,000—you could save $10,000 by buying the comparable model that's two years old. If someone handed you a legal no-strings attached $10,000, wouldn't you take it? As an added bonus, the insurance on a slightly used vehicle is noticeably less. This is particularly important for young males who are charged more because, as a group, they have higher accident rates.

- Consider a "demo" (no, not "demolition", "demonstrator") car from a dealer. It's just nicely broken in, with minimal mileage, and will have virtually a full warranty.
- When to go looking? In late summer the next year's models are starting to come in and dealers are more motivated to clear out their sales lots. On weeknights, salespeople have more time to show-and-tell than on weekends.
- Don't put up with biases about gender or age. (I once had a patronizing salesman tell me that "Women don't drive stick-shifts." I quietly and politely reminded him that he was paid on commission, and walked out. As I left, I could hear his manager growling at him. "What did you say to her?" Young people often get the same kind of crap.) Learn as much as you can before you start the process. And find a dealership where the sales people are more evolved. Perhaps, while you look, take along an experienced friend who'll help you not get sucked into the manipulative hype.
- When test driving a vehicle, do *not* leave them your actual license. And do *not* give them your social security number. They will want to make a copy of your license, but write on the copy, "No credit checks allowed". (The more credit checks that are made on you, the lower your score slips.) Credit checks come after you've made a deal, *not* while you're looking.

Purchasing tactics

Negotiate from an informed stance. Do ALL of the above FIRST. Then...

- Whether you're buying new or used, privately or from a dealer, you must get the car's inspection history and pay an independent mechanic to thoroughly check it out.
- You must see proof-of-ownership of the vehicle before buying, especially if you're buying privately.
- Buyer beware. Make sure there are no liens against the vehicle: if the owner borrowed money against the car and you buy it, the car can be seized from you and sold to pay *their* debt. Ouch. Also check to see if it's been in any accidents, floods, etc. Take the Vehicle Identification Number (aka VIN, a 17 character code on a small plate on the dashboard between the steering wheel and the windshield) to your nearest Dept. of Motor Vehicles, or run it through:

  In the States autocheck.com or carfax.com;
  In Canada carproof.com

Until you have negotiated a final price…

- Do not tell the dealer what you're willing to pay for the vehicle.
- Do not tell them what you can afford per month. They'll try to get you to spread the payments over a longer time frame to get you "into more car". The result is more money flushed in interest.
- Do not tell them if you have a trade-in. They'll fudge the final price to their advantage. Besides, you'll probably get more for yours by selling it privately.
- If they even once say "the deal is only good for today", walk out. Reputable dealers won't do that. They want happy customers and repeat business.
- Never give a deposit until you have a final price, in writing, signed by the manager of the dealership. (And when you do, leave a deposit of a few hundred dollars, not a few thousand. Preferably use your credit card for that. If there's an issue later, you'll have a better chance of sorting it out.)

There's more good advice on vehicle How-To's, both buying or selling, on your provincial or state government sites. For example, at mto.gov.on.ca in Ontario.

Other websites you might want to check out:

Automobile Protection Association: apa.ca
carbuyingtips.com
carcostcanada.com
carquotes.ca
dealfinder.org

HOME – Rent or Buy?

There are mixed opinions, even amongst experts, about "what's right" financially and what's right emotionally. What's right depends on how long you intend to live there, your life-stage, your personality and goals, and "location, location, location".
All this hinges on your ability to financially carry whatever you're taking on.
You shouldn't be going over 25 to 30% of your Take-Home-Pay to rent or buy.
That's sometimes not easy.

Renting

Renting may seem less stable but perhaps it's simply more flexible. If you're likely to be relocating for a new job in the next couple of years, or if your income fluctuates, it's probably better to rent. If you're self-employed, you may need to rent, at least for a while. If you're moving to a new community or a different country, you might want to try out the new context before putting down roots. Rent for a while first.

Generally the experts seem to agree that unless you're planning on being in that home for at least three to five years it's usually better to rent, even if you could afford to buy. By the time you've paid the costs of buying ("closing costs") plus selling costs (real estate fees and so on), there's a good chance renting is the better option. However, if renting costs less than owning, you should do something sensible and constructive with the difference, like paying down debt.

Let's use 25 to 30% of your take home pay as your housing expenditure. Suppose that's $1500 a month and your rent would be $1250. Put that $250 per month difference, plus what you would have used as a down payment on a home, into reducing debt and into savings and assets. Will you later kick yourself for not buying? Maybe home values will go up faster than you could have saved, or faster than what you would have gained in other investments over that time frame. Maybe they won't. There are only averages and trends, not crystal balls.

In *Money Madness,* Spencer Sherman gets more specific about how to decide between renting and owning. He says that if the annual renting costs are less than 5% of the purchase price of an equivalent home, be it a house or condo, it's better to rent.[3] Huh? I ran an example to see if I understood what he was saying.
Bear with me here. Let's assume we're looking at a $300,000 house.
5% of that would be $15,000/year or $1250/month.
Could we rent a comparable place for $1250? Would owning it cost more than that?

Rental costs = rent + tenant insurance + utilities + cosmetic fix-ups.

Ownership costs = mortgage payments + property taxes + home insurance + utilities and water + maintenance and repairs + major upkeep savings.

For maintenance and repairs, Sherman suggests we save about 1% of the price of the house per year. For major upkeep, such as a new roof, save another 0.75% per year.[4] (I'm lazy, so let's round those off.) On that $300,000 house, 1% is $3000.
For both, that means we need to set aside about $6,000 a year, i.e. $500 per month, in addition to the more obvious costs. Are we still under that $1250? If not, Sherman would say "rent".

That having been said, David Bach has a different opinion. In the *Automatic Millionaire Homeowner*, he says that between 1984 and 1999 the wealth of home owners increased 29 to 70 times that of renters.[5] No, it's not quite the same housing market these days and values in some areas have sunk more than in others. But home values usually do grow over time and many areas have already rebounded significantly. Looking for fast money, whether it's in real estate or the market, is less likely to produce positive results than slow and steady.

It used to be that a home would cost two to three times a family's annual income. Now, in many urban centers, it's five to ten times that or more. So be realistic about your cash flow. However, Bach cautions that "You can't get rich renting... the fact is, you aren't really in the game of building wealth until you own some real estate." [6] The name of the game is EQUITY.

What is **Equity**? You buy a place. Over the time that you own it, it goes up in value. (You hope, and that is the usual case.) Meanwhile you or your tenants are paying the mortgage and carrying costs. Value up, mortgage down. Whenever you choose to sell the place (minus the various buying, carrying, and selling costs) that difference is equity. And you do have to live somewhere. Are you more comfortable paying off your own mortgage or someone else's?

There is an upside to the downside of the slide in home prices in some areas. IF you want to and IF you genuinely can afford to purchase and carry the running costs—now and in the foreseeable future—it's perhaps a good time to buy. Prices are down. Mortgage rates, at least for now, are down. (Canada's mortgage and real estate rules are quite different than America's, and frankly—no offense intended—more sensible. That's why the American housing meltdown was more severe than here in Canada.)

So, I repeat, is buying a good idea? That depends on some factors you can control, like paying attention to the local market and to demographics, the location you choose, and how long you'll live there. And on some factors you can't, such as the overall economy and bank rates. Be sensible and self-protective. Don't overextend. That way, you can ride out the occasional downturn.

Ah, there's the number crunching and there's the what-do-you-really-want. I own a house. I don't like having to ask permission to do things with the space I'm in. Bit of a brat that way. My tenant in the upstairs apartment could afford a house, but he can't be bothered with the hassle of upkeep. Win-win. The rent money helps carry the mortgage, and I get a tax write-off on half the cost of running the place. Nice.

So you've decided you want to buy. Now what?

It's crucial in the searching and buying process that you have good help. (And that doesn't mean just your favourite know-it-all relative.) You need a reputable real estate person helping you look, a knowledgeable and thorough home inspector and a real estate lawyer. But get your financial ducks in a row first.

Before you start looking:

- Know your cash flow patterns and habits. Track these for at least three months. (Revisit Chapters 12 and 13.)
- Save up a decent down payment, i.e. 10% to 25% of the estimated cost of the kind of home that interests you, plus enough for "closing costs" which can be $10,000 or more. (More on that in a minute.)
- Next "pre-qualify". Get mortgage approval *before* you go home shopping. The lender assesses your ability to pay the principle plus interest and taxes, and promises you *in writing* a certain dollar amount at a certain rate for a certain length of time, say three months, while you look. Rates aren't likely to stay this low forever.

Figure out what you think you can afford.

In your 20's & 30's, don't assume your first house needs to be your dream home. You will likely buy and sell several places before you're 40. So don't go dream-house crazy or be pressured into buying more house than you can afford *comfortably*. The banks may qualify you for more than you can actually handle. You want to have a life, not just a roof over your head. Being house-poor curtails your lifestyle and stresses your sanity and your relationships.

> Real estate agents are paid a percentage of what you're paying for the house. Usually there are two agents involved—your agent who helps you look and the seller's agent. Each negotiates on their own client's behalf. The seller is responsible for paying the commission which is shared by both agents.

Buy a home that's appropriate for your current life stage—perhaps for the next six to ten years. Young singles, young couples with a wee one, larger families, and retiring folks have **differing housing needs and preferences. What are yours?** Larger or more expensive homes won't necessarily provide what you genuinely need. (See Appendix C)

Banks will say that your total housing costs (including mortgage, taxes, utilities, etc.) should be less than 30% of your Gross monthly income (i.e. the total before taxes and deductions). If you make $4000 a month gross, that's a housing maximum of $1200. That's why it often takes two incomes to buy a home. Again, if you want a life, keep your housing costs (whether buying or renting) below 30% of your take-home-pay, not 30% of your gross. Not always easy, but it's much safer financially and much kinder to yourself.

> Do not assume that the banks or other lenders have your best interest at heart. They care more about their bottom line than yours.

Aha. How much can you *really* afford?

How much do you have set aside in that OUCH fund for emergencies? That safety net has to be your top priority.
How much debt are you already carrying? How much is that costing you a month?
How much have you saved as a down payment? (25% of the cost is a good goal.)
What amount have you been pre-qualified you for? (Remember, you really oughta' *not* maximize that amount.)

Again, home ownership costs = mortgage payments + property taxes + home insurance + utilities and water + maintenance and repairs + major upkeep savings. What would be your total carrying costs? Is it under 30% of your take home pay?

Where might you want to live with that dollar value in mind?
Only now should you start looking at actual homes.

Thinking of commuting farther so you can afford what you want? Add in the cost of the commute. It may be cheaper to live closer to work. And better for your sanity.

Some good calculators for "how much" are
mortgagecalculator.org, cmhc-schl.gc.ca, mortgage101.com.

PLAN FOR THE UPFRONT COSTS

Home Inspection

Any offer you put on any property must be contingent on a thorough home inspection done by a certified and reliable company. (Be sure to include a mold, termite, and radon inspection.) That few hundred dollars could save you mega-bucks. Otherwise you may find you've bought yourself a money pit. Also have your lawyer check with City Hall to make sure there are no "Stop work" orders on the place. The present owners may be trying to unload a nightmare that didn't pass the reno-permit inspections. If you buy the place, those become your problem.

Closing Costs

These include appraisal fees, the cost of an up to date survey (if your lender won't accept the seller's version), mortgage insurance (see below), land transfer tax, provincial fees and title transfer, legal fees, taxes on the sale, fire insurance, and possibly title insurance. (The latter insures you in the event the seller didn't actually own the house they sold you. It happens, though infrequently. You buy it, that's now your problem. How's that for an Ouch!)

Down payments, rates, and insurances

Generally, the smaller the down payment, the higher the interest rate you'll pay. And with less than 25% down, you're usually required to carry, with your lender, life insurance that would cover the mortgage. This usually costs a bit more than comparable "term insurance" from outside sources. And it adds up over the years. Once you've built some equity in your house, do some cost comparisons with other insurance providers and renegotiate this. *Have the new policy in place, in writing, signed, and in your hands before you cancel any current policy.* (More on insurances in Chapter 23.)

GO MORTGAGE SHOPPING

Before you go home shopping, carefully assess a number of mortgage options. This is likely to be the biggest expense of your life and you can throw away, unnecessarily, many times your annual salary by not choosing wisely.

You'll need to figure out:

- the dollar amount you need to borrow to make the purchase (the principle),
- the overall length of time of the mortgage (the amortization),
- the renewal period/term,
- whether the mortgage is "closed" or "open",
- the interest rates (and whether they're "fixed" or "variable"),
- the payment frequency,
- and how much extra one can pay towards the principle per time period.

Sound complicated? Keep reading—it'll make more sense shortly.

What is considered "standard" in the way mortgages are handled varies slightly for different countries and between mortgage providers. However, the effects of interest rates and time frames on your costs, as described below, are fairly similar.

Amortization periods

When you take out a mortgage, you select a maximum number of years in which to pay it off. Most people go for a period of 25 years, though 30 years is fairly common in the U.S.A. (35 years is crazy. Buy a less expensive place.) Though the monthly payments are less with a longer mortgage, the increase in the total interest paid is *huge*. You'll save tens of thousands or more by amortizing for 20 or even 15 years, if you can afford the payments. If not, amortize for the 25 but pay off as much extra as you can afford, as often they'll let you. (Maybe that's 10% once per year. Negotiate perhaps 15% or 20%, or a more flexible time frame.) Specify that the extra goes directly to the principle.

When your mortgage comes up for renewal (that's the next page) you can decrease the amortization period if you want, but that means you'll have a larger payment you *must* make. You might be more comfortable leaving the amortization as it is and put extra into the principle when you can. *The earlier you do this, the more you'll save in interest.* During the first 10 years of a 25 year mortgage, up to 90% of the money goes to interest, only 10% to the principle. That proportion shifts more in your favour as the years pass, so your dollars become more efficient at paying down the principle. (See also p. 158.) If you're a landlord paying off a rental property, there are other ideas and subtleties you need to discuss with your accountant.

Here's an example showing how amortization periods affect your costs.
Let's assume a $200,000 mortgage @ 5% interest.

- Amortize for 30 years => you pay $1074 monthly. The total *interest* cost over the 30 years is $186,000, almost doubling the cost of your home.
- Amortize for 15 years => you pay $1582 monthly, which is half again as much, but you're mortgage free in half the time. The total interest paid? $83,900, not $186,000. You just saved yourself over $100,000. Sweet.

Renewal Periods / Terms

These are the time intervals between negotiations with your mortgage provider. In Canada, you can choose from a number of variations from 6 months to 10 years. Many Canadians will choose, for example, a fixed mortgage with a 5-year period. That means that, for the next 5 years, your payments are predictable and in five years you renegotiate the details with your lender. Fixed rates for 5 year terms are generally 1 to 2% higher than variable rates or shorter terms but, since they're predictable for that time period, you can sleep at night. In the States, the framework is a little different and 30 year terms are common. Their "amortization period" and "term" are pretty much the same, so you are not having to renegotiate with your lender within the amortization period.

In a fixed mortgage, if rates drop before your term is up, you can negotiate with your lender but you'll pay a penalty. (Often its three months interest, but that can be considerably more depending on the difference in rates and the length of time left on your term. Discuss the details and number crunch with your lender and a couple of their competitors to see if it's worth doing.) On the other hand, if rates go up, in a fixed mortgage you're won't need to worry, at least for now.
In a variable? Rates may cost you sleep or put a smile on your face. Who knows? (More in a minute.)

When it's time to renew, the bank will want to charge a renewal fee. Refuse to pay this. Some other bank or mortgage lender would likely be happy to take over your mortgage and would waive the fee to do so. Lenders these days compete for your mortgage but only if you have a good credit history. (Notice a theme here?)

You must shop around for mortgages months in advance of either buying a home or renewing your mortgage. The choices you make have costly and far-reaching implications.

Closed or open?

Closed means that you can't get out of the mortgage before the specified period is up, at least not without paying steep penalties. You have a payment schedule as a specified amount at a specified time (monthly, biweekly, or weekly), within the chosen term or renewal period (e.g. 5 years). And you can pay a certain percentage (not large, compared to the total mortgage) extra towards the principle each year. That pays off the principle faster and, dollar for dollar, rids you of the mortgage more efficiently.

With an open mortgage you can pay off any amount, even the full amount, at pretty much any time, all without penalties. Open mortgages generally run at slightly higher interest rates and can be harder to get. Lenders see them as less predictable for their bottom line.

Rates - Fixed or Variable?

A small difference in rates makes a huge difference in long-term costs. A 1% rate difference on $100,000 with a 30 year amortization is about $25,000 difference in your interest costs. A 1% difference on a $300,000 mortgage? Huge.
"Posted rates", such as those you see online, can often be negotiated downwards *if* you have a good credit rating.

With a **variable rate**, the interest you pay fluctuates on an ongoing and frequent basis with the bank rate which is something you have no control over. Variable can be a percentage or more lower than fixed which helps pay off your mortgage faster, but it's more unpredictable. That uncertainty can be unnerving. Some lenders will keep your payments the same but how much of that payment goes towards the principle versus the interest then varies. That may shorten or lengthen your mortgage.

A **fixed rate** keeps your payments the same until it's time to renew at the end of your current term. (It's that crystal ball thing again.) Whether fixed or variable is better *for you* depends on your circumstances and how financially resilient you are. Talk to an unbiased financial advisor, and get several options from competing lenders.

Yes, variable rates are lower, but most advisors advise against *closed* variable mortgages for other than very short time frames, e.g. six months to a year. (If rates start to climb and you want to "lock in" a rate, you won't get to negotiate. The lender gets to dictate the new rate and you might not be happy with it. You could break the mortgage if that happens, but you'd pay some likely punishing penalties.) An open variable would be better, if you can get one.

"Convertible" mortgages (as either variable or short-term fixed) allow borrowers to move into a fixed rate at any time without paying a penalty. Usually you need to choose a term that's longer than you currently have. (If rates seem to be coming down, the lender lets you wait before committing to a longer term.) It's a useful option to have.

Some Mortgage Statistics

- 68% of Canadian household debt is residential mortgage. 20% is from lines of credit. About 5% is credit card debt. (Bank of Canada, Financial System Review, 2010)
- 47% of those who will likely buy a home in the next 2 years will be first time buyers. And 1/3 of mortgages paid off in the last 20 years were paid off early. (Canadian Association of Accredited Mortgage Professionals, *Stability in the Canadian Mortgage Market*, April 2011)
- 60% of people who took out a mortgage went with a fixed rate. 31% went with variable. (CAAMP, *Annual State of the Residential Mortgage Market in Canada Report*, November 2011)

Payment frequency: Monthly, bi-weekly, weekly?

Your choice, your call, fairly easily changed at any time. Usually it's as simple as a call to your lender.

Bi-weekly (every two weeks) has a couple of advantages over monthly. It's the time frame in which most people get paid so automatic withdrawals, once set up are easy and predictable.
Accelerated biweekly will pay off a 25 year mortgage several years sooner, and saves you a delicious amount of interest. For example, simply switching from monthly to accelerated biweekly on a $200,000 mortgage saves you about $40,000. Wow. Wouldn't you rather be putting that forty grand in *your* pocket?

Paying that little extra ...

Again, in an open mortgage you can pay off any amount at any time. Even with a closed mortgage, most lenders let you to pay a certain percentage extra. How much and how often depends on the lender and can be negotiated. It's often 15% a year. Again, *the earlier you pay these extras, the sooner you'll be free of your mortgage*. We're not talking saving hundreds here—we're talking tens of thousands.

Let's once again assume a $200,000 mortgage, amortized over 25 years, at 5% interest. Below are some possible variations. (You can modify your approach at each renewal period. For simplicity here, I've used the same game plan for the full 25 years of the mortgage.)

(A) The basic version—you're required to pay $1163 per month.
It takes the full 25 years to pay it off.
You'll have paid $149,000 in interest plus the $200,000.

(B) Pay that $1163 per month *plus $100 extra* => $1263/month.
You're mortgage free in a little over 21 years.
Interest paid? About $124,800. You saved yourself about $25,000.

(C) Pay the $1163 *plus* $250 per month extra => $1463/month.
You have knocked more than seven years off your mortgage!!

Your turn...

Go onto one of mortgage-calculating sites suggested. Try a $200,000 mortgage. Run the following scenarios, and compare the numbers with those above.

(1) A **20 year** amortization. 5 year term. **5% APR**. Use "accelerated biweekly."
What's the cost biweekly? How long until the whole thing's paid off?
What's the total interest you'll pay out?
Compare that to (A) above. How much do you save yourself?

(2) A **25 year** amortization. A 5 year term with a **4%,** not 5% APR.
What's the cost *per month*? How long until the whole thing's paid off?
What's the total interest you'll pay out?
Try the same 4%, but "accelerated biweekly". Get the idea?

Refinancing

This is not the same as renewing. Refinancing means that you pay off the old mortgage and start a totally new one. It's only sometimes a good idea, and is definitely not a simple decision. Is it worth it? That depends on the difference between the old interest rate and the new rates, the penalties they will charge (which can be substantial), and your life circumstances. Discuss this with a mortgage broker, your financial advisor, your current lender and a couple of their competitors.

Portable mortgages

Some mortgages can be portable, and that's often a good feature to specify. The mortgage behaves more like it's attached to you than your place. Then if you want to sell and buy a new home (as in new to you, not necessarily brand new) before your current mortgage expires, you can take your mortgage with you as long as the new place meets your lender's criteria. This way, you can avoid both the costs of taking out a new mortgage and the penalties for getting out of the old one. If your old rate is better, that's an obvious advantage. If you need a bigger mortgage than what's left on your current one, you can get a "blended rate" which is a combination of what you have now and what you need.

When you're ready, visit any of the sites suggested below and do some number crunching. It's not hard, even for math-phobes, and not particularly time consuming. You'll likely save yourself mega-bucks!

Try out some variations at:

ingdirect.ca ('tools')
dinkytown.net
moneytools.ca
intuit.ca
tmacc.com
mls.com
mls.ca
mortgagecenter.com

For a list of mortgage advisors: Canadian Institute of Mortgage Brokers and Lenders www.caamp.org.

Big Borrowing... ?

Whether it's for a student loan, vehicle, home or any other large purchase, comparison shop. (You may get sick of hearing me say that. I'm not apologizing.) Just be sure you're comparing apples with apples. You want the best you can get—at a price you can afford—*not* the cheapest one. (You'll hear me say that again too.)

Get the appropriate advice from knowledgeable and *unbiased* sources.

When you're doing your exploring—both for what you're purchasing, and how you'll pay for it—*never* assume anything, about any aspect. ASK! And get it all in writing.

Make sure everything is thoroughly clarified, and get the legalities checked out *before* you sign anything, ever. There's too much at stake—for your finances, your stress levels and your lifestyle—if you mess up.

Chapter 17

Money - Using it well

Isn't it premature, a little backwards, to be discussing how to use money before discussing how to make it? No. People may have a small, average, or enviable income yet most, including those who are very well-off, still think it's not enough. So if or when you do ramp up your income, chances are the not-enough syndrome will still be there. Learn to be wiser first.

Becoming wiser involves learning how to:

ONE	**Build and protect your credit rating.**
TWO	**Respect your lazy self.**
THREE	**Build an OUCH account.**
FOUR	**Reduce debt AFAP** (No, not a typo—As *Fast* As Possible).
FIVE	**Respect your needs and your Future-Self.**

Step ONE Build and protect your Credit Rating.

I'm going to "state the obvious" here because many seem to forget the following reality. **Credit** is the potential to borrow someone else's money, if they'll let you. And you're going to have to pay them interest for the privilege of using that money. That interest is their profit. The total of what you borrowed, plus that interest, is your **debt**. The lower the interest rate, the less it's going to cost you in the long run.

Your **Credit Rating** is your financial reputation, so make it a good one. Why?

- First, the better your credit rating, the more likely you'll get the loan you need, and at a better interest rate. A poor rating => unnecessarily high interest rates => many thousands in wasted money.
- Second, a good credit rating improves your chances of getting a better apartment or even better insurance prices. As well, potential employers may check to see if you're reliable and sensible which they believe is reflected by your credit rating.

What if you're just starting out?
Get on the radar of the Credit Bureaus and start building a good credit history. How?

- Choose a convenient bank or credit union and set up both a checking and a savings account. Even kids can have accounts. But until you're the legal age at which you be held to a contract, you won't be given a credit card or granted a loan. Usually that's 18, depending on the type of contract and your jurisdiction.
- When financial institutions offer you credit cards, don't take it as a compliment—they make billions a year on us. And be careful—for the first year at least, pick just one card and have a low maximum on it, perhaps $500. To build a credit rating, you do need to use the card. But consider this a short term loan to yourself and pay it back fast. And on time, all the time. If you're not offered a card, arrange to get a "secured card". You pay the limit upfront so they know they're covered, then use it as you would a credit card. This too will build your credit rating. Replenish the amount you've used as you go. After a year, ask for a regular credit card.

> **Shred card offers that come in the mail.** Do NOT throw them out. Identity thieves sort through trash and can use these as entry points to your records.

- Once you have an income, take out a small loan (maybe a few hundred dollars) with a short time frame (say six months). Pay it back faithfully, every payment on time. Don't use the money. Stick it in a separate account and set up automatic repayments. The whole point of this loan is to build your reputation with the Credit Bureaus. To build your rating, it's well worth the few dollars in interest you'd pay on a small loan.

Credit Ratings have two components: a Credit Report, a Credit Score.

Your **Credit Report** is a summary of your identifying information and your accounts, your history of bill payments and the inquiries into your credit status.

Your **Credit Score** is a three digit number they calculate based on your behavior. Low 600's, bad. High 700's to 850 range, good.

Here's how that number is calculated:

- About a third of it comes from your payment reliability and promptness. Do you make your payments on time, within 30 days, 60 days, or longer? The later you pay your bills, the lower your score drops.
- About a third is based on your *utilization rate,* which is *how much you actually use* compared to *what you can access.* When you frequently max out your credit, you are then seen as more of a risk. It's good to keep your utilization rate under 30%.
- The rest is based on how long you've had a credit history (one year, ten years?), how long you've been with the same bank or credit companies (longer is better), and whether you have different *types* of credit. They like to see that you've not only got a credit card, but that you've had and are reliable in paying off a student or car loan, for example, or a mortgage.

Credit bureaus don't include your net worth (the sum of what you have that has monetary value) as part of the calculation directly, but they will have a more favourable view of you if you have property, savings, or other valuables as *collateral.* (Collateral is whatever can be seized and sold if you default on your payments. There's more to this than a car company repossessing your wheels. Banks and governments, for example, can tap into your other assets to get their money.)

Check your credit reports now if you're just starting out. You may already be "on file" and you need to be certain that the information they have on you is correct. Everyone should get an updated copy, each year, to check for possible errors. These can range from simple spelling mistakes, readily corrected, to more serious ones. (You could discover that, because of mistaken identity, it was recorded that you defaulted on a loan you never took out!) If you find an error, do not wait. Contact the credit agencies immediately. And beware Identity Theft! The impact of that can be disastrous, both financially and emotionally. (For more on Identity Theft, see Chapter 28.)

Credit Reports: You're entitled to a free report annually from any of …

Canada:	Equifax.ca	1 800 465 7166
	Transunion.ca	Quebec 1 877 713 3393
		Outside Quebec 1 800 663 9980
USA:	annualcreditreport.com	
	equifax.com	1 800 685 1111
	experian.com	1 888 397 3742
	transunion.com	1 800 916 8000

Credit Scores:
Make any necessary corrections to your Report then buy your Credit Score at myfico.com. It costs under $20. It's worth every penny to know your score and to understand how to improve it. To get an approximation of your credit score, and simulate what you could do to improve it, try creditkarma.com.

For more sensible use of credit cards…

- Your card statements **help you track your purchases** more easily. Check them each month for accuracy, and to see where you may be overspending. (Cash can just seem to evaporate out of your wallet.)
- In some circumstances they can be **used as ID**, which can be handy. But that's even more reason to immediately call the card company if you lose it.
- For your **personal use**, have at most two credit cards. (More is cumbersome and likely to be the edge of a spending slippery slope.) Have each with a different company in case there's an unforeseen temporary glitch in either one. (Perhaps you're traveling and discover that company X's system is temporarily down, or that the place you're in doesn't like company X's cards. Use Z's.)
- If you have your own **business**, use a completely separate card for that. It makes your bookkeeping much easier.
- If you're **part of a couple**, each of you should have your own cards (a max of two each), and perhaps one joint family-and-home-expenses card. (There are more ideas on couple-money in Chapter 27.) Both of you need to be willing to communicate about money, to learn more, and be able to trust each other.
- Choose a card with a **low interest rate** (Annual Percentage Rate = APR) and a low annual fee. Once you've developed a good credit rating, ask them to lower your APR and waive or reduce the annual fee.
  For USA card comparisons: bankrate.com, mint.com
  For Canada: Canada.creditcards.com or ratesupermarket.ca
- Get a card with the **perks and features** you actually will use.
  Prefer cash back? Or perhaps, like me, you want travel rewards?
  Don't scatter and fragment your points by having more than two cards. (You could have travel points on one, cashback on another.) And be sure to use those rewards. Evidently there are a ridiculous number of unused points floating out there in never-never land. What a waste.

Certain cards have more **subtle benefits** at no extra cost, such as extended warranties on your purchases or rental car insurance. Keep any differences in annual fees in mind, as well as the differences in benefits. (A travel card may cost you $120 a year, but you might each year generate hundreds off your travel costs.)

Protecting your Credit Rating

Reliability

Again, pay all your bills on time. It's best, of course, to not put more on your card than you can pay off completely each month. If once and a while that's not realistic, pay what you can that month, even if it's just the minimum, but *do it on time*. (If you're overextending regularly, you really need to rethink and rework your finances.)

Utilization rates

Is it sensible to immediately cancel a seldom used or high interest credit card? Surprisingly, it's not. By doing that, you decrease the total amount of credit you have access to which technically increases your "utilization rate". Your credit rating as a result *goes down*. (To protect your credit rating, keep *what you owe* compared to *what you have access to* as low as possible.) Instead, you could use the card occasionally (say, once every three months) to keep it active. But it's better to simplify your life—if you have multiple cards, choose two with the features you most like, preferably with the companies you've been with the longest. Ask them if you were to cancel the excess cards, would they increase by that amount the limit on the ones you want to keep?

Predictability

From the credit bureaus' point of view, the longer you've been with a company the better. If you want to switch to a card with different perks, say travel points, use the same company. (E.g. switch a TDVisa to a different kind of TDVisa card.) Each time you switch *companies*, you're modifying your history and your score drops a bit. So don't card surf, even to access those introductory (but very temporary) low rates. Instead, ask your card company to match the lower rates of their competitors. They will want to keep your business *if* you've got a good credit rating.

Keep inquiries to a minimum.

The credit bureaus assume that the more inquiries made about you, the more over-extended or less reliable you may be. They're then more likely to charge you higher interest rates or flat out deny you a loan. So set up a sensible system for yourself (we'll get to that shortly) and only mess with it when you must. If you're planning to ask for a loan within the next six months, don't make changes to your credit status, for example by getting a new card. Avoid new inquiries on your record until after you'd made the application and have been granted that loan.

Half of a couple?

Each of you must cultivate your own credit history. Have your own cards. Have your own accounts. You may want to have as well a joint account and a joint credit card for joint expenses. Downside? The other person can clean out the joint accounts, max the joint card, and leave you stuck with the full cost of paying it all off. It's not two names equals half the debt each. Its either of you owes all of it, if one defaults or takes off. Banks and other lenders come after whoever they can get the money from. "Upside"? If one of you dies, a joint account "with right of survivorship" (this must be specified when you open the account) transfers to the survivor. Individual accounts will be frozen until the will is dealt with. (See also chapters 25 and 27.)

NEVER EVER co-sign loans for anyone—not family, not friends, especially not lovers. If their finances are wobbly enough that they need a co-signer/guarantor, chances are too high that they will default. That leaves you responsible for the debt and, in the process, trashes *your* credit rating. There is an alternative. If you really do want to stick your neck out for them, take out the loan yourself for the specified amount. At least you can then control the repayments to the bank, even if you get stuck having to make some or, groan, all of them yourself. Set up a written agreement with the person who is requesting your help, including a repayment schedule (outlining specific dates and specific amounts) and have a couple of people witness you both signing it. By being in charge of at least the timing, you're not putting your hard-earned credit rating in the guillotine along with your hard-earned money. And think twice—assume there's a chance you may never see it, even if their intentions are good. $%#*& happens. At least do what you can to avoid stepping in it.

Step TWO Respect your LAZY self.

It's easier to be kind to your lazy-self than have to fight with it. It's easier to put a little time into getting organized up front than to have to argue with yourself on an ongoing basis. And it's easy to set up and use automatic deposits and online banking to save yourself the hassle and stress of having to remember what-and-when. As David Bach says, "Protect yourself from yourself."[1] The taxman has it figured out. He gets his cut before we see it. Do the same for your less-than-perfect self.

You're going to set up a system that helps you direct your money to where it needs to go to do you the most good, in the easiest way, by making the process automatic. It's remarkable how much less effort is required to take good care of your money when more of what needs doing is on autopilot.

How do you do set up your Easy-system?

(1) Set up a chequing account.

Have your employer deposit your paycheck directly into a chequing account at the bricks-and-mortar bank or credit union of your choice. Choose one that balances convenient hours, decent customer service, and low fees. And go in or call in to set up online banking with them. It's magic—it makes it so much easier to get and stay smart. Worried about scams and identity theft? You're in more danger if you don't shred your paperwork, or have your wallet stolen, or aren't cautious when making purchases from online sites than you are with online banking. Frankly, if we can't steer and track our money easily, the odds of our messing ourselves up financially are much higher than our being messed up by some crook.

Have your student loan, car loan, mortgage, and other predictable bill payments come directly and automatically from your bricks-and-mortar chequing account. (Remember, reliability is major. Build a financial reputation that's stellar, not sleaze.) Further, to avoid paying overdraft fees, negotiate an overdraft allowance or keep an extra half-month's worth of expenses in the account. The great thing about online banking is that it's all visible to you 24/7. No more "balancing your cheque book" or wondering where your money is at. With the click of a few keys, it's all right there in front of you.

(2) **Set up savings accounts.**

For your savings accounts, choose an online bank. They usually give you a better interest rates. (They have minimal bricks-and-mortar to pay for.) And they're covered by all the usual banking requirements and laws. INGdirect is one example. (No, they don't give me a kick-back.) The only downside is that it takes a couple of days for your money to shift back and forth between the bricks-and-mortar and the online banks. But this isn't impulse money—these are goal-oriented accounts. Supposedly you're taking money out only for a planned-something anyway, so plan. A couple of days should be a no-brainer.

Set up separate accounts for your Ouch savings and for *each* of your short and long term goals. With separate labeled accounts, it's easier—and more fun—to see where you are en route to that particular goal. Link each of these to your chequing account for ease in transferring your money. The online banks don't charge you for these transfers, another nice perk.

(3) **Carefully and regularly watch all your accounts.**

This is really easy once you have on-line banking set up. It takes only a few minutes a month. Call to fix any accidental errors within 60 days. Catch hints of identity theft as fast as possible. If you're the least bit suspicious of anything, call immediately. Banks hate ID thieves and the impact of those scams too.

(4) **Consider a money tracking system.**

This is optional but helpful. Some of the most popular systems are mint.com, moneydance.com, or quicken.com. They give you typical categories for this-and-that, but I suggest you personalize your system by setting up the same categories as used in Chapter 13, "Getting Real". You can then easily adjust, refine, and improve your game plan. From there, fine-tune your categories to suit your own needs. Get as detailed (or not) as you want. It's easy to download from your bank sites into your tracking system, and reports can be built and printed for any time frame and for a variety of purposes. To track and steer your money then takes minutes per month, not hours. Sweet.

Step THREE Build up an OUCH account.

Call it a Peace-of-mind account if you prefer. Again, remember that life is not all smooth sailing. Protect yourself. Build a lifeboat.

Don't think left-over money here. Belt tighten. Drastically, if you need to. Get one month's worth of take-home-pay into that account. In the meantime, if you have to, pay just the minimums on your debts and bills. Try to put in at least 5 to 10% of your gross income, preferably more. If you can't do that yet, get started as best you can. But get started. Life's storms can hit without warning—job losses, health issues, accidents, etc. Can't get motivated? Go to disabilitycanhappen.org and check out the stats.

Once you get one month's worth in place, you'll continue building your Ouch account, but perhaps a little more slowly since you'll be starting to focus as well on reducing your debt. Keep going until you've got at least three months worth set aside. OUCH money needs to be in a totally separate yet easily accessible account.

Do not use this for anything other than a *genuine* emergency. If you really must dip into it, pay it back as fast as possible or you're stealing from your own peace of mind. A little financial resiliency goes a long way towards reducing stress, as does perspective. (My furnace, though serviced regularly and not old, died mid-blizzard. There went a good chunk of my Ouch-account, and the holiday I'd been saving for. Waaa. But I'm looking on the bright side. A dead furnace is a minor issue compared to a serious health problem, or a job loss, as faced by so many these days.)

Step FOUR Reduce Debt AFAP - as fast as possible.

I was going to say ASAP, but *soon* is too nebulous, too *someday*.
ASAP too often becomes someday, *maybe*. You want warp-drive on this one.

Gather up the following information.

- What debts do you have? List them. All of them. If you didn't do that in Chapter 13, do it now.
- Which debts are tax-deductible? Unless they're related to a business expense, most debts are not. If in doubt, ask a tax-prep person.
- Which ones are the largest?
- Which debts did you take on for constructive reasons? (Student loans?) Which ones when you weren't being your smartest self? (Party animal? Shopaholic?)
- Which of your debts have the highest interest rates? Store cards and credit cards are usually the worst. If you don't know the interest rates, look online, or call the companies. Try to negotiate a lower rate. And minimize your card use. Better yet, stop using them, at least for now. (To get out of a hole, first stop digging! If you have minimal willpower, shove the card into some raw ground meat or mashed tofu, and put the ugly lump in the freezer. By the time that icky goo thaws out, hopefully your better sense will have kicked back in.)

Again, don't mess with your utilization rate. Rather than canceling cards outright, reduce the debt by paying them down, then off. And don't switch cards, renegotiate limits and so on, until your debts are reduced, your financial habits are better and, as a result, your credit rating has improved. At that point, you'll have more negotiating power.

Slaying the Debt Demons

Create a plan for reducing debt by making a table of all your debts as follows:
(Don't include your mortgage yet, if you have one.)
Add rows as needed (Hopefully that won't be many.)

Who you owe	Interest rate	Amount you owe on each	Minimum monthly payment	✳ (See the next page)

The first demon to slay? There are several approaches.

(1) Stomp on the littlest twirps first. They're irritating and the easiest to do in. Makes you feel more potent and powerful, and that's a motivator.

(2) Or start, not with the largest demon, but with the nastiest—the one with the sharpest teeth and worst breath, i.e. the highest interest rate. If all the Debt-Demons run at the same rates, kill off the smallest first, i.e. the one with the lowest balance.

(3) Or you might slay first those you're most annoyed with yourself for having taken on in the first place. These can be the most emotionally toxic. Besides, they're usually the higher interest consumer debts anyway.

Now become your own hero.

Think of yourself as a Ninja. If you're into gaming, these debts are the bad guys. Pick a target on that chart. (For now, pay the minimums on all the other debts.)

Ninja, fling every Dollar-star✳, shoot every arrow you've got into Demon #1 until it's down, done in, and can't slash, gash, and bleed you anymore. Be aggressive! Next, take the same number of dollar-darts or more—not less—and go after the next foul-breathed long-fanged menace. Soon the air will begin to smell a little fresher and you'll breathe a little easier. This may require month after month of persistence. Your arm and your willpower may get tired on occasion. (Mine sure did.) So give yourself small rewards along the way. The big reward is the sense of relief and freedom you'll feel—and the expanded life options you'll have—when you're not hiding from the demons and dragging all that debt around with you.

Decreasing debt is arguably the best investment you could make.

Paying off debt at, for example, 18% is like making 18% on an investment. In fact, it's better than 18% because it's in after-tax dollars. So it's more like 24 to 35%. That's a fabulous return! Better yet, it's **predictable and guaranteed,** unlike the stock market, in that you can't lose your money. How sweet is that especially these days! What's even better? Don't build up so much debt in the first place, especially for "stuff".

Debt consolidation

Considering a consolidation loan to pay off your debts? Be careful! You want help from *unbiased* professionals to see if, and how, to do this. If consolidation would drastically reduce the interest rates on your current debts, perhaps. But extending the length of time you take to pay it off? You may pay less per month but you'll have higher total interest costs in the long run. This is where the number crunching help comes in. Figure out what time frame and monthly amount would work in your best interest, literally.

Be cautious about the consolidation and debt-aid services that you have to pay for. There are some really unscrupulous folks out there. Here it's actually better to use the free services. The folks listed below have seen it all and will give you excellent, effective, and practical help at little or no charge.

For advice on dealing with debt, you could start with:

In Canada creditcounsellingcanada.ca
In the USA debtadvice.org

Do not use your home's equity to consolidate debt unless you have proven to yourself beyond any doubt that you can trust that your dumber-habits won't take over. If you don't make your payments, they'll foreclose and you'll lose your home on top of all your other problems. You must be financially *very well disciplined* and have a *secure* steady income. Otherwise, a home equity loan to consolidate debt is way too risky. (See also page 192.)

Disastrous Debt → Bankruptcy?

Sometimes, not because of poor choices but because of catastrophic life events, people are left struggling with bills that are impossible to pay off. They empty themselves inside out financially and emotionally trying to dig their way out when, realistically, there's no hope for financial recovery. In that case, bankruptcy is the appropriate option. "Some got slammed with accidents, disease, job loss, divorce or other set-backs. There's usually plenty of blame to go around, and some of it belongs to a system that keeps spewing out credit to people clearly unable, for whatever reason, to handle it." [2]

Bankruptcy follows you for at least seven years and seriously messes with your financial reputation. Consider it only as the very last resort. Bankruptcy is like a black hole. Do whatever you can to avoid getting close to that no-coming-back "event horizon". Get credit counseling *now*. If you truly must go through that crushing experience, you want competent advice on how to survive and how to recover on the other side.

An often unforeseen complication? If anyone has co-signed a loan for you, you can not declare bankruptcy. Yet another reason to never co-sign a loan. It can bite both ways.

USA	thebankruptcysite.org or abiworld.org
Canada	creditcanada.com or legalsuggest.com/bankruptcy-law-11.html

Step FIVE Respect your needs, goals, and your future-self.

Change. It can be the inconsequential "ya, whatever" kind. Or delightfully wonderful. Or shall we say, euphemistically, less than optimal? Some change is predictable, some not-so. But face it, change is gonna happen. Rather than hope or dread, prepare for it. You want to be able to roll with it. And you want to be able to capture the upside of changes that come your way or that you create.

"How do you get a secure financial future? It's simple. You buy it."[3] How?

- Build resiliency first. Get sea-worthy. Build that financial lifeboat. (At least have a life-preserver.) Build a healthy Ouch account, have appropriate insurances, and build long-term savings and assets. Without these, life's occasional nasty surprises can turn into long-term enslavement, sadly self-imposed because you didn't think ahead or were naïve or arrogant enough to think "it can't happen to me". Ya right.
- When you get a raise, don't immediately ramp up your lifestyle. You won't feel that deprived if you live the same way just a little longer. Instead, use that extra money to create more in genuine assets, then use a little of the new money generated by those as a reward to yourself.

- Learn the difference between an asset and a toy. Otherwise your possessions will own you. This is not about "denying yourself" constantly and forever. It's about knowing how and when you can indulge in the treats and luxuries. (More in Chapter 19.)
- Instead of thinking "I can't afford that", think "perhaps not quite yet". And ask yourself "How can I afford it?" which "opens the mind to possibilities and action".[4] And congratulate yourself. By working through this book, you're learning how to better implement those Yes-es.

Don't fritter away money on the meaningless and unproductive instead of building a happier present and a freer future!

In the early 80s, Canadians were saving about 20%, Americans about 11%. By 2005, American savings were down to 0.5%. In 2009, Canadians only saved between 2.5% and 4.5% of their income, at all levels of income, modest or major.[5] In 2010, American saving was climbing, and back up to about 6%.

Surprisingly, those with the bigger incomes aren't necessarily any smarter with their money than the rest of us. (Yes, the economy's not in its best shape. But, in the past 20 years, saving has gotten harder for most folks partly because spending has become easier.[6]) And unfortunately, the middle class is getting painfully squeezed. But that's too big a topic for discussion here. What do these saving rates mean? That we're working about twenty minutes a day for ourselves. The rest is going to pay bills and service debts.

Robert Pagliarini, in *The Six Day Financial Make-over*, says people mess up their investing because they stick everything in one awkward investment account which is supposed to do all things. That's de-motivating. Each goal should have its own time frame and its own strategy attached to it.[7] You need to see and savour progress, so have a title and a date attached to each account. (Newer Car, Trip To Europe, Kids' College Fund, Flying Lessons, and so on.) But first build up that Ouch money. Then once you're in the process of slaying your debts and have begun taking care of Future-You, more of your money can go towards these other goals *without fear or guilt.*

So daydream. Let your imagination loose. Design those goals. Savour the feelings of how it will be *when, not if*, you'll be enjoying those experiences—that's a great motivator for helping good things happen. Again, what matters to you? What do you want and need?

The authors of *Your Money Or Your Life* state that "consumption is rooted in changing a feeling state, which is signaling a need isn't being fulfilled" and "most of our needs are not material".[8] Robin, Dominguez, and Telford pull a wonderful quote from Donella Meadows' book *Beyond the Limits*:

> "People don't need enormous cars, they need respect. They don't need closets full of clothes, they need to feel attractive and they need excitement and variety and beauty... People don't need [more] electronic equipment; they need something worthwhile to do with their lives. People need identity, community, challenge, acknowledgment, love, and joy. To try to fill these needs with material

> things is to set up an unquenchable appetite for false solutions to real and never satisfied problems. The resulting psychological emptiness is one of the major forces behind the desire for material growth." [9]

Your Money or Your Life points out that both "self-denial and self-indulgence" need to "yield to self-awareness, which ends up being a much bigger pleasure."[10] So don't say "No" to your deeper needs. Look below the surface to what those needs actually are, and find a way to meet them in a more precise, personally targeted, and less expensive way. In reality, "more stuff" isn't going to do the trick.

Just how much is ENOUGH for you to live a fulfilling life?
If you don't know what matters to you, how are you ever going to feel satisfied?
And how do you juggle the energy and time needed to generate the income you think is necessary with your ability to enjoy life?

Here's another great question to ask yourself:
"Other than winning the lottery, how can I afford to never have to work again?"
As I've said before, your chances of winning that million-plus in the lottery? Statistically less than your chances of getting killed by lightning.

Here's another statistic: the majority of millionaires are made, not because they're brilliant business wizards, but because they've lived slightly below their means and built their assets slowly and surely.

> "The world is always providing us with instant feedback. We could learn a lot, if we tuned in more." [11] What is Life telling you about your money skills?

As life evolves...

Once a year at least, revisit your living expenses and pull out the weeds. Get rid of any undesired and unnecessary expenses that deplete the vitality of your garden-of-life.

Re-evaluate your financial progress. See whether what you're doing with your money and time still fits your goals. Maybe you want a house, a spouse, and kids. Or maybe you want decades of singledom. Maybe you've decided to work overseas, for now. Or later. As your life evolves, your priorities will shift.

And dynamics change within families:
Parents—you may be trying to decide between saving for the kids' education or your retirement. Yes, it's nice to be able to help your kids out, a bit. But saving for your retirement must be a top priority. Your kids will have other options, and time to pay off their loans. "They don't hand out scholarships or grants for retirement."[12] You're the one without options if you get to retirement and don't have the funds for it. In return, you may have to live off your kids. Some favour you did them.
Young people—you may not be aware of the potential long-term impact of sponging off your folks. That too can bite both ways.

The capacity for self-reliance boosts dignity and self-respect, at any age.
It's best if you're all standing on your own feet, financially, as much as possible.

You want more freedom, more control over your life, better possibilities?

- Create alternatives. Explore options. Make a decision about those. Then DO something about them!
- Want a better life? Make better decisions. Notice I didn't say perfect decisions. Just better ones. A bunch of just-a-little-betters add up to big benefits.
- Be careful—sometimes we spend money we don't have so we don't feel poor or so that we don't look less successful than our egos would like us to be. That applies at all income levels. Don't overextend. And don't buy luxuries on credit.
- Juggling priorities? (We usually are...) Which goal, if deferred, would create more problematic consequences? Which goal, if implemented, would create the most benefit for the most people? Include yourself of course.
- "Living within your means" really does pay off. If you don't like your means, ramp them up. (We'll visit how to make money in the next chapter.)
- Maybe this is all rather frustrating, even depressing, because your income isn't up to the task at the moment. Perhaps even your basics aren't covered and you're doing the best you can. Refuse to be your own victim—don't give up. Here especially creativity is a must. Just keep your creativity legal.
- **Need some inspiration?**
  Francis O'Dea, who along with Tom Culligan built the Second Cup chain from scratch, was a street kid.
  J.K. Rowling of Harry Potter fame was an impoverished single mom.
  And for her first book, she had been turned down by numerous publishers.
  (Bet they're crying in their beer. Nya, nya.)

> What if it's easier than you think? Try this. Negotiate a $1 an hour raise. That's an additional $40 a week. If you work another 35 years and never get another raise, that $1 per hour upgrade would turn into over $192,000 if you invested it and earned 5% a year. Little things can make a BIG difference. Pay attention to them.

Life could be SO much easier...

Unfortunately, there are times when we haven't a clue there's something we really need to know—and *now*. I'll include myself in that one. And take my own advice about our not beating ourselves up. *No guilt. No blame. No excuses. Instead, just get on with solutions.*

Let's just say I have a soft spot for dedicated and hard-working people, especially the single moms out there. Yay you! Keep reading—it can be easier!
***S**omeone **R**eally **O**ughta **T**ell **Y**ou* (SROTY)...

To the absentee sires, SROTY to you too. But I won't say more than that in print.

To all the dedicated parents out there, I salute you. Pass on your life skills and wiser attitudes to your kids, and to the parents of lesser caliber.

To all kids, and to the kid in all of us, know you can. *Learn and DO.*
Get real, then get smarter. And get the appropriate help when you need it.

Don't fuss and worry. Learn and solve!

Happy Birthdays, and rights of passage

A decade-marking birthday can snap you into reality quicker than almost anything else. A number of years ago, I found myself confused, scared, and embarrassed about my financial situation. (If that's where you're at, I get it.) Then I got fiercely annoyed at my own naïvete and decided to wise up. Yes, it's initially a little intimidating. Yet it's easier than you might think to pick up some really effective money basics and get going in the right direction. Better late than never. But much better way earlier! So now I'm determined to do whatever I can to help young people not make similar avoidable mistakes and to help those who are stuck, as I was, get their feet out of the muck and quicksand and onto solid ground.

Want a good basic GAME PLAN for what to do with your money?

60% of your **Take Home Pay** (THP) goes to your **Living Expenses.**

A little less than half of this goes to housing. (25 to 30% of your THP)

Slightly more than half (max 30 to 35% of your THP) goes to your other living expenses: food, transportation, health insurances, clothing, and so on.

If adequate disability, critical illness, and long term care insurances can't be covered under "living expenses", use a little of the money you'd be putting into your long term goals or your Ouch account. Without adequate insurances, these could otherwise be decimated.

10% goes to **Ouch money** for emergencies.

(1) First, build at least one month's worth of Take Home Pay.

(2) Once that's in place...

½ of this 10% goes into your **Short Term Goals** (Saving for a home, vacation, car, whatever. For motivation, name each account and smile as it grows.)

½ continues to build your OUCH savings until you have three months worth of THP set aside. *As your income grows, top up that emergency income-replacement fund.* Then use this 10% for your long and short term goals, to reduce your debt more quickly, and to help with your living expenses.

10% goes to **reducing debts** as fast as possible.

(1) Pay down your highest interest debts first. (See page 167-168)

(2) Once you have no debt except your mortgage—Yay you!—split this 10%.

½ gets added to your Long Term money (that could include knocking down the principle on your mortgage faster as that's a major savings in itself)

½ goes into your Short Term Goals, Play money, and easing your living expenses.

10% at least, on an ongoing basis, goes to **Long Term** being-kind-to-future-you and freedom-money. (Start early—you'll need to put less in to get much more out. See Chapter 19)

5% goes to **play money** and small indulgences, *guilt free.*

5% goes to **meaningful causes,** whether it's to help the planet, other species, or other humans. Start at 1% if you need to. Work up to 5% or more when you can. Contributions to charities are tax-deductible.

If you prefer, give without giving money: volunteer time instead.

SCENARIO ONE

Perhaps your Take Home Pay (THP) is $ 2000 / month.

60% = $ **1200** a month to Living Expenses (it's going to be a bit tight for now)
< ½ = $ **500** max to **housing** (share an apartment?)
> ½ = $ **700** to all **other living expenses** (forget owning a vehicle, for now)

10% = $ **200** to an **OUCH account** (Build to one month's THP)
Then ½ ($100) goes towards Short Term Goals and living expenses
½ ($100) continues building Ouch Money (to >3 month's worth)
After you have 3 months worth of THP set aside, this 10% ($200) can be divided up as needed.

10% = $ **200** to **Pay Down Debt** as fast as possible. Once the debts are gone,
½ of this 10% ($100) goes to Short Term Goals and Play money
½ of this 10% ($100) gets added to Long Term Money.

10% = $ **200** goes to **Long Term money** for Future-You.

5% = $ **100** to **Play Money**, guilt free.

5% = $ **100** as **Contribution** to causes. Volunteer your time instead, if you prefer, and use this money for your other goals and as needed.

Obviously, housing costs will vary widely depending on where you live. And living expenses will depend on your lifestyle and the number of dependents you have. However, do *not* short-change your Ouch and Long Term moneys. Otherwise, short-term "gain" translates into long-term pain faster than you'd like to think. (At least with this plan, your play money is guilt-free *and* you know you've got your bases covered.)

SCENARIO TWO

Suppose your Take Home Pay or Joint Family Income is $ 5000 / month.
(In 2010 the median household income for Canadian families–couples and single parents–was $69,860.)

60% = $ **3000** a month to Living Expenses
< ½ = $ **1250** to **housing,** total costs (25% of THP)
> ½ = $ **1750** to **all other living expenses** (35% of THP)

10% = $ **500** to an **OUCH account** to build one month's worth of THP
Then ½ ($250) goes into saving for **Short Term Goals**
½ ($250) continues building Ouch Money (to >3 month's worth)
Afterwards, this 10% ($500) is used as needed.

10% = $ **500** to **Pay Down non-Mortgage Debt** as fast as possible.
Once the debts are gone,
½ of this 10% ($250) goes to your long term goals,
e.g. paying off your mortgage faster.
½ of this 10% ($250) goes to Short Term Goals and Play money

10% = $ **500** goes to **Long Term money** for Future-You.

5% = $ **250** to **Play Money**, guilt-free

5% = $ **250** as **Contribution** to causes. Volunteer your time instead, if you prefer.

If you want to compare your income to that of others, check out statscan.gc.ca for Canadians or mybudget360.com for Americans. Search "median" incomes, not "average" incomes. (Median is not as skewed by the incomes of the rich.)

Life is always a work-in-progress.

Let me say it again—no guilt, no blame, no excuses.
Focus on finding solutions and implementing them, a little at a time if need be. Explore what you could do to improve your cash flow choices. What might you be willing to or need to change? Do yourself a huge favour—make those changes.

Don't forget to celebrate the things you are already doing well and are learning to do better. (That's what those revision columns on pages 120-123 are for.)

There are many helpful sites and books. E.g. ynab.com, or quicken.ca or .com.

> You know to take your vehicle in for tune-ups and a diagnostic.
> Do a tune-up and diagnostic on where your money's currently going.
> Have courage. You *can* do this.

Current Realities and Wiser Ways

Get out your paycheck and calculator, and work through the following.

Current Monthly Take Home Pay (after all deductions) = $ ________

60% = $ ________ a month to Living Expenses, divided roughly in half as follows:

< ½ (about 25 %) = $ ________ to total housing costs
> ½ (about 35 %) = $ ________ to the other living expenses

10% = $ ________ to an OUCH account until you have one month's worth of THP

Then ½ ($________) goes to your Short Term Goals
And ½ ($________) goes to continue building your 'Ouch' money.
Once you've got at least 3 month's worth, divide this 10% as needed, between your long and short term goals, helping with your living expenses, and debt reduction. (Include part of your insurance costs here, if they don't fit into your living expenses.)

10% = $________ to pay down non-mortgage debt as fast as possible. (p. 167-168)

Then ½ ($________) to Long Term Goals
(e.g. paying off your mortgage faster, p. 158)
And ½ ($________) to Short Term Goals, and Play money.

10% = $________ to Long Term i.e. Freedom-money and for Future-You.

5% = $________ to Play Money, guilt free.

5% = $ ________ as Contribution to causes. Volunteer instead, if you prefer.

Use the suggested percentages above to estimate "target amounts".
Then revisit Chapter 13, "Getting Real", pages 120-123 and enter your target amounts in the grey boxes in the blank columns on the right hand side.
The "revision" columns can be used to make some gradual modifications.

Congratulate yourself!
No, this isn't easy, but do it anyway.

You're doing this *for* yourself, not *to* yourself.

You've been doing the diagnostic on your finances.
Do your tune-up, and the necessary repairs,
add in some monthly preventative maintenance,
and your trip will be a lot smoother and more enjoyable!

Chapter 18

Investing is not just about the money.

Not everything that pleases and is important is related to dollars and cents. We know but often ignore that fact.

On my kitchen counter, I have a large cookie jar in the shape of a rabbit in a goofy green top-hat. Given that I like as little clutter around me as possible, why would I keep such a silly looking thing? Partly because it is silly looking. It reminds me not to take myself too seriously. And that goofy rabbit reminds me, as well, that life can hand you joys you didn't expect. (What six year old would have expected that Saturday afternoon, indoors, sitting around with a bunch of "old folks" could in any way be fun? "Bingo! Nana, I won!" A full card—and a full cookie jar!) So it reminds me, as well, of the profound value of wonderful people in our lives—in this case, my feisty loving gran whose spunk and humour could brighten any day. The best joys in life are those involving the company one keeps rather than what money can buy. That silly cookie jar probably cost a couple of bucks back then. To me, it's priceless.

On a more serious note, it reminds me that while I can reach for those cookies and those memories whenever I want, as an adult, it's *my* job to put them there.

What is one of your treasured, meaningful possessions?

Why do you value it? Monetary worth? Likely not.
Where, when did you get it? From whom? In what circumstances?
What does it represent to you?
How does it make you feel? How does it make you feel about yourself?
How could you get more of that good feeling?

"Return on Investment" – ROI, is a term usually reserved for money.

When you're considering investing some of your money, be it in a home, in savings, in the market or in a business, you want to know not only what you'd need to put in, but *what* you'll be getting back and *when*.

I'd like to propose that you consider this ROI idea for life in general. No, I'm not cold-blooded. Quite the opposite. I'll say it again—it's *not* just-about-the-money. If you aren't investing time and energy to better your life, why do you expect to get something better back, at any point? The same goes for investing time and energy into bettering the lives of others and into meaningful causes.

You want the world to improve? Do something to improve it.

INVEST in a fulfilling life.

Invest in your ability to generate income: in your education, training, skill development, your energies and your health.

Invest in your happiness, without negatively impacting the future or your ability to earn.

Invest in your ability to make a difference.
Fulfillment and meaning don't come from a huge bank account. There are numerous rich people who are miserable, and many average folks who, in the ways that actually matter, are truly wealthy.

Invest in learning to better appreciate life and the opportunities you have.
As Oprah and many others say, keep a gratitude journal. At least make your waking and falling asleep thoughts about something you're thankful for. We are so much luckier than so very many.

Invest in your relationships. Build trust. Share experiences and thoughts.

Invest in your future by building assets. The future is always closer than you think. Get your money working for you, instead of always the other way around.

Invest time to get wiser about what you do with your resources—your time and energy as well as your money.

What's the ROI, the Return on each Investment?

You invest time and energy into work.
The benefit? The self-respect of a job well done, and a paycheck. And, with a good reputation and better skills, hopefully better income security and the confidence to roll with the punches.

You invest time and energy into family and friends.
The benefit? A sense of belonging, mutual caring, joy and fun.

You invest time and energy into meaningful causes.
The benefit? A sense of satisfaction and a better world to live in.

You invest time and energy into your *being*.
That includes sensible self-care of body, mind, and in whatever way you like to interpret it, spirit. The benefit? A healthier self, inside and out, and a better appreciation for Life and for being alive.

And *when* do you see these rewards?
Every day, on an ongoing basis. And the return on your investment just keeps blossoming. What is that return, that reward? A sense of efficacy and fulfillment at all sorts of levels. What more could you possibly want from any investment, monetary or otherwise?

Chapter 19

Make your money work more, so you can work less.

"What money? You've gotta' be joking. I don't have any extra money!"

Reallocating your present income can at least get you started on the path to confident independence. Let me use an analogy here. A lump of iron sinks. Refashion that iron into a sheet, then a boat. Now it floats. Same amount of iron—it has simply been reformatted. Do the same with your money. Your choice—sink or sail? For each financial decision, ask yourself: "Is this taking me *toward or away from* my goals?"

Meet Sam. Sam just got an inheritance of $10,000. Spend it or save it? If he invests it in a tax-deferred "retirement" plan that averages 5% per year, after 20 years he has over $27,000. Suppose instead that he splurges now on $10,000 worth of toys and doings. These will cost him, not the initial ten grand, but $27,000 or more. Ouch. If he realizes now that's the *actual* cost of splurging, would he make a different choice? Rather than an either/or, how about a compromise? Sam could spend $2000 now and put the rest into building assets. That way, the Now-Sam and Future-Sam are both happy.

Pay yourself first. Pay yourself sooner.
Max your pensions. And build assets along the way.

ONE Pay yourself first.

To be:		
	Dead broke	Spend more than you make.
	Poor	Think "maybe someday...."
	Middle Class	Pay yourself ... 5 to 10 % of your gross income
	Upper middle class	Pay yourself ... 10 to 15%
	Rich	Pay yourself ... 15 to 20%
	Rich enough to retire early? Put aside at least 20%	

(These are David Bach's categories of the lifestyle results of our choices.[1])

Advisors say at least 10% of your income ought to go into long-term asset building. Calling it your **freedom money** is more fun than calling your "retirement money" which feels like a lifetime away. (Some say it should be 10% of our gross income rather than 10% of our take-home-pay, but that's likely a bit rich—haha—for most of us.)

Like gravity, compound interest works whether you acknowledge it or not. Its magic may as well be harnessed to work *for* you, as against you.
(Compounding—you earn interest on your money which thus creates a larger total. The next interest calculation is then done on and added to that larger total. That new and even higher amount, in turn, earns interest and so on, and so on...)

If you've not yet done at least Chapters 15 and 17, please do them now. You need to understand the importance of an Ouch account, the usefulness of targeted short-term savings accounts, and how to respect your now *and* future self.

TWO Pay yourself SOONER.

Ah, the MAGIC of Time ...

Maria contributes $200 a month into an RRSP (in the States, that would be a 401K) starting at age 21, each year for 10 years. She stops and never puts in another cent. Period. Ever. Suppose over the decades it averages 6% interest. At age 61, her investment that cost her $24,000 has grown to over $198,000. That's over $174,380 "donated" in interest. "You gotta be kidding..." Nope. For real.

Patrick starts at age 31. He sets aside $200 a month, *every year* for 30 years. By age 61, his investment, which we'll assume also averages 6%, has produced a nest egg of $201,900. Barely more than Maria, but it cost him three times as much to get there. ($72,000 rather than her $24,000.) The interest? Almost $130,000. Less than Maria's, but still really sweet.

If they were nervous about the markets, they could have invested in Guaranteed Investment Certificates or bonds. They would have gotten less out, but their money would still have been growing slightly and would be safe. And, by paying down debts early, they could save major money in wasted interest costs.

The magic of time will do most of the work of building your nest egg. Start sooner rather than later—you'll need to put much less in and you'll get much more out. Starting in your early 20's? You can set aside 5 to 10% and build a reasonably comfortable future. If you start in late 40's, you'd need to put aside more than 20%. Ouch. But better late than never.

THREE Maximize your pensions.

According to a recent StatsCan Wealth of Canadians survey, 27% of Canadian families in the 35 to 44 age group have no pension assets of any kind. Yikes. On a slightly positive note, I guess that means that 73% of us have a little something set aside, even if it's not enough. According to some experts, in order to maintain a similar lifestyle when we retire, we'll need to be able to generate about 70% of our working income. But how?

There are group retirement pension plans and individual retirement plans. (The latter, in Canada are RRSPs. In the States, there are 401Ks and Roths.)

A *group retirement plan* is a pension plan into which you put, each pay period, part of your earnings in *pre-tax* dollars. Some employers contribute from their funds into your pension, over and above what goes in from your paycheck. Sweet. Free money. You'd have to be nuts to turn that down.

For *individual retirement plans*, the government calculates each year how much you're entitled to pay into yours. If you're self-employed, you're allowed to contribute more. Max that out. (Social security is not going to be enough.) Your professional association or union may have their own group retirement plans which are likely to be reasonably priced in comparison to similar coverage elsewhere. For making your contribution, the government will refund some of your taxes.

You are not taxed on the money in your pension funds until you retire at which point you can take it out, gradually, at a time when your tax rates are usually lower.

In the meantime, the magic of compounding-over-time is at work without any tax bites. There are other details to consider, such as whether your pension is "defined benefit" or "defined contribution". Check with your human resources people at work, then discuss the implications with your advisor.

Some important cautions:

Do not put a lot of your retirement money into buying your own company's stock. Think of Enron. If the company tanks, you've lost your pension *and* your investments. Keep it to less than 10% of your Portfolio.[2] (A "portfolio" is what they call your set-aside-moneys, investments and other assets.)

When you change jobs, voluntarily or otherwise, "roll over" your pension funds rather than cashing them out. If you don't, your nest egg will get seriously dinged by the tax man. Talk to an accountant or your financial advisor now about how to do this before you might need to.

Be careful about getting involved with (i.e. sucked in by) the workshops put on by those less than scrupulous self-proclaimed money-gurus that promise the "solution to all your financial problems". Your gullibility may simply be the solution to *their* problems. And be very cautious about get-rich-quick schemes that seem too good to be true. That being said, there are a lot of honest and wise financial advisors that you do want to listen to. Two of my favourites? Suze Orman and Gail Vaz-Oxlade. Of course there are many wise male advisors as well, but it's important that the female readers realize that money savvy is *not* a man's world.

FOUR Build ASSETS

Do not confuse building assets with having more expensive stuff. And true assets are not necessarily the usual things you might include on a typical Net Worth Statement. Your car, for example, is worth something if you sold it but it loses value each year. It doesn't make you money, so it's not an asset.

Assets produce money for you, over and above their costs, whether you are running them or not. [3]

Some good examples of true assets? [4]

- a business that does not require your ongoing presence,
- income generating real estate,
- financial investments (such as index funds, GICs, mutual finds, etc.),
- royalties from intellectual property (e.g. patents, scripts, music),
- anything else that has value, produces income or appreciates, and has a ready market.

In 2008, the median Canadian family at age 40-ish had a net worth of about $160,000; at age 50, about $265,000; at age 60 about $450,000. After retirement, these figures start to drop significantly as they draw down their funds.

Where would you likely end up if you continue with your previous money habits? Better or worse than "typical"? Remember typical is not optimal. *Go for optimal.* Keep reading and doing.

Where are you now?

You know the dollar value of your current income. And having done Chapters 12 and 13, you now better understand and can more readily orchestrate your cash flow. If you haven't done those chapters yet, get your head out of the sand or where ever else you might have it. Have a good look at what you're doing and where you're going.

To build resiliency and secure your future, build *genuine* assets. Whether you're an employee, or are self-employed or own a business, turn your earned income into "passive income" and "portfolio assets" as fast as you can.[5] Most people's income gets eaten up instead by expenses, liabilities, and that "must have" stuff that seems to multiply like sex-crazed rabbits, taking over your living space and eating up your money. Meanwhile, true assets barely get the crumbs left over after everything else has fed from your income.

Liabilities

Liabilities are a combination of personal debt and the expenses that are associated with generating and maintaining your assets. You want to build assets in a way that is as financially efficient as possible. That's where ROI planning and good unbiased advice comes in (more on that shortly).

> Expenses and liabilities are like the weight in the hold of a sailing ship. Sensible expenses (putting money where it makes you money) you can consider ballast. But the more weight you're carrying, the less maneuverable you are. Too much weight and the slightest storm? Down you go.

Is your cashflow adequate for your present and future needs?

I repeat, where are you now?

Do a Net Worth Statement.

There are numerous how-to examples online. Perhaps start with your bank's version. First, do one the typical way with the typical format.

Then distinguish between the things you simply own and those that are *genuine* assets. Which ones make you money or appreciate in value whether you're working at them or not? That's not your toys, golf clubs, upscale furniture, or vehicle. Remove those posers and imposters. Then you'll know what your current true assets are.

Each year, redo your Net Worth summary using an asset building perspective. That will help you track where you're really at. ("He who has the most toys" is not the one who wins. He's probably just the schmuck with the biggest debt load. That most-toys mindset is the consumption-machine's biggest asset, not yours.)

Suggested reading
moneysense.ca/2009/11/01/the-all-canadian-wealth-test/

`"Money: Spend it foolishly, and you choose to be poor.
Spend on liabilities, and you join the middle class.
Invest in your mind, and learn how to acquire assets, and you will be choosing wealth as your goal and your future." [6] Robert Kiyosaki

Cashflow => Assets
then Assets => Cashflow

Assets—an overview

Gradually, you build your assets. The idea is to eventually have your assets "generate more than enough to cover [their own] expenses, with the balance reinvested into growing more assets".[7] The end goal is that your assets provide you with enough of an income that you don't have to work unless you want to. Nice.

For your long term plans, the Asset Allocation (i.e. what percentage of your money goes into what types of investments) depends mostly on your life stage, partly on your personality. You want, of course, to compare potential-upside with potential-downside. You might choose to include the market as *one* component of your assets. Some advisors suggest that the percentage you put into the market be no more than 100 minus your age. As you get older, you've got less time to recover from volatility and downturns, so you must play it safer. (Some suggest we need to revise our mindset regarding the markets. Chaos theory, discontinuities, and invalid premises and assumptions are as present there as in the rest of reality. No, I'm not telling you to stay away from the markets, just to be very sensible in your approach.)

Kiyosaki suggests you "collect assets you love... If you don't love it, you won't take care of it." [8] His is real estate and start-up companies. Yet he and others don't encourage people to start their own company unless they really want to. Because few have the skills, stamina, and nerve it takes to build a business, for most, it's "better to keep your daytime job and build your asset column". [9]

I mentioned earlier that, whether we're talking sports or money, to be in the game you must get good at the fundamentals. Without these there's no point fussing and futzing about what's going on with the markets or the economy. Control what you can—that's your own behavior and what you do with your other assets. If you don't, you're burnt-toast anyway and you did it to yourself. Ouch.

"Plant seeds in the asset column. Some grow. Some don't.
There is always risk. Financial intelligence improves your odds." [10]

"Sometimes you win, and sometimes you learn. But have fun.
People who do everything to avoid failure also avoid success." [11]

Assessing the potential return on your investments is a skill which can be improved over time as you *learn* and *do*. Obviously, the idea is to minimize expenses and reduce the likelihood and magnitude of any downsides, and to maximize the potential for good cash flow. You plan and put in money and expertise. You want to know, in advance, *what* you'll get out and *when*. What's interesting, to me anyway and maybe to you too, is that a good ROI is not necessarily a result of putting money in the usual places.

What could you do to generate an asset?

Write a song or a movie script, market it and collect royalties?
Paint, sculpt, or sew, and sell your creations?
Create and rent out a bachelor apartment in your basement?
Buy a condo and rent it out so it carries itself while it's building equity?
What could you *upgrade* that will *save* you money in the long run?
(For example, eco your home.)

Indirect assets

An architect friend described the thinking of some of his wiser clients.
(Allan Killin, akarchitect.ca)

- In a safe investment like a GIC, you could make 2 or 3%.
- In the market, you *might* make x%, but you might lose some or all of it.
- On the other hand, if you invest in greening your business or your home, you calculate that you'd consistently save, say, 10% on your utility expenses. The initial cost is perhaps a few thousand (depending on the project), and the upgrade would pay for itself in only a few years. *After that, it's all profit in what you then save.* A good ROI. An upgrade that's indirectly an asset. If it's your home, that's in after-tax dollars so it's an even better investment. If it's your business, the upgrade is tax deductible. **Predictable and with no downside**. Helps you. Helps your bottom line. Helps the planet. Doesn't get much better than that.

Is your home an asset?

Yes. And no. Your house *can* be an investment vehicle, depending on a number of factors some of which are controllable, some not. Home ownership is a great asset-building motivator—most people who buy a home will do pretty much anything not to lose it.

Demographics

Boomers are living longer and healthier and are staying in their homes as long as possible. Young singles are buying their own homes rather than waiting until they get married. With the divorce rates, splitting up means a family needs two homes not one. "Between now and 2020, the passing of the baby boom generation, not just in Canada but throughout North America, is expected to lead to the largest inter-generational transfer of wealth the world has ever seen."[12] The boomers' kids, the "echo" generation, will be inheriting money, including the equity in their parent's homes, and using it as down payments on their own.

Time frames

House values do not always go up over the short-term. (Consider the sub-prime meltdown in the states which, ironically, might make it a good time to buy.) But, long term, real estate usually appreciates considerably. Between 1997 and 2006, the average Canadian house went up 50%. In Toronto and Vancouver, for example, in that time frame values almost doubled. Here in Toronto, prices went up about 10% in 2011 alone. The increase is expected to level off somewhat now.

Do you plan on being in that home for seven to ten years? The longer you're in the home the more equity you build, so there's less impact from a temporary or modest downturn. The trick with real estate is to not have to sell at the bottom of the market.

ROI: Return on investment

When you buy a property, to finance the mortgage you're using other people's money. You gradually pay back the lender (the bank, credit union, or mortgage broker) with interest—that's how they earn their profits. They do not have a stake in the equity that you're building in your home. That's yours, minus real estate fees of course. A decent down payment is best. Not only will you pay less per month, it will cost you less in interest.

Tax considerations

In the States, your mortgage interest is tax-deductible. Here in Canada it's not, but you can claim part of the upkeep costs if you're renting out part of your place. (In either country, rental properties have tax write-offs.) A nice aspect of owning a home in Canada is that you're not taxed on the profit you make when you sell it. That capital gain, i.e. the equity in your principle residence, is pretty much tax-free for Canadians. (See cra.gc.ca for other variations, for example, if you own more than one home or are renting yours out part of the time.) Tax-free profit. Nice. Try that with any other investment. Besides, you need to live somewhere, unless you like the view from under the bridge. You could rent, but then you're paying off someone else's mortgage.

Is it better to put a little extra into your retirement funds or towards paying down your debt or mortgage? Most advisors say to put the money into your *registered* retirement plans (the tax sheltered versions), and put the resulting tax rebate into paying down the debt or mortgage. You win both ways.

Missed opportunities?

Kiyosaki cautions that one of the downsides of home ownership is that opportunities are missed because when "all your money is tied up in your house", you lose "time in other assets which could have been growing."[13]
That assumes you actually would have been putting money into other assets, and that they actually would have grown. Some advisors say that, given the current economic climate, the best investment you likely can make these days is to pay off your mortgage and other debts. The ROI on that is predictable, guaranteed, and in after-tax dollars.

Flips

Some look at houses, not as homes, but as "flips". They're into buying, fixing, and selling, sometimes numerous places at once. Some did well. Others got flushed. Timing, cash flow, location, expertise—how well they planned, or didn't. If you want to invest this way, compromise with yourself. Buy a place, live in it for a couple of years, fix it as you go, then sell it as your principle residence. Again, if you're in Canada, that's tax-free profit. (Check with an accountant about capital gains ins-and-outs and maximums.)

Mixed blessings

Your mortgage will be going down. But your property taxes and utility costs? Not likely. And who knows what future interest rates will do to your payments the next time you need to renew. Yet you are building equity and the place you live is your own. If you're renting, as I said before, your money is building equity for someone else.

Another suggestion?

Don't sell your first home, rent it out. Why? Bach says "Homeowners get rich; landlords get really rich."[14] Use some of the equity in that first home as a down payment on your second. The tenant then finishes paying the mortgage on the first, and the costs of maintaining the place are tax-deductible. (You could even have your tenants automatically deposit the rent into a specified account. If you don't want the responsibilities of being a landlord, hire a property management company.) This is a great way to build equity if you get sensible tenants. And if you're a sensible and conscientious landlord. (That's a whole other discussion I'm not going to get into.)

Vampire fantasies? Don't feed on your home.

As you build equity, you may be tempted to bite into it for those tempting luxuries, doodads and doings. Suck on what you own with home equity loans, and your debt load will come to own you. If you want a ramped up lifestyle, ramp up your assets and your income. Don't drain your own lifeblood by draining your equity.

The Controllable Musts?

- *Location. Location. Location.* A decent neighbourhood or one that's up and coming. Check out the upside potential in the "worst house on the best block".[15] Or start fixing up your corner of your block. ("Nicer" is contagious.)
- Buy a place with "good bones"—one that is structurally sound and that has some aesthetic appeal that's immediately apparent or could be. (Ever watch HGTV or the DIY channel? Personally I'm addicted to both. If I could adopt stray houses I would.) Then put in some sweat equity. And take good care of the place.

> Allow me another small rant here. The core of Canadian cities are vibrant and very livable. Many American cities have abandoned their core in favour of suburbia that ranges from "slob"erbia to "snob"erbia. (It's that "good location" thing. Or so they think.) There are so many cool downtown buildings going to waste, to ruin. They could be rejuvenated into great neighbourhoods! Come on people, put a little more political will and grassroots energies into building in—pun intended—civic pride in your core. What an opportunity going to waste! (Rant. Rant.) You don't like where you're at? *Fix It.* You're not the only one who wants to see positive change. Get together. And get at it. You think others won't join in? Get at it anyway. Lead by example. You'll be pleasantly surprised.

Extraordinary things happen when "ordinary" people get busy.

Elinor Orstrom won the 2009 Nobel Prize in economics for her unconventional economic wisdom. She showed what groups of people can do with their common resources when certain do-able conditions are met. And more "conditions" are do-able than many might think. (For more ideas on grass roots initiatives see David Sloan Brown's book, *The Neighbourhood Project.*)

Financial Investments as Assets

DISCLAIMER! DISCLAIMER! DISCLAIMER! I'm NOT a financial advisor and have zero interest in trying to pretend I am. I'm simply passing along some advice and a few cautions from others who do have their heads on straight about this stuff. (There are things we'd rather *not* have to learn through the school of hard knocks.)

Master your cash flow and the other money fundamentals before you consider messing with the markets.

The first and best investment is to PAY DOWN DEBT. Start there, not here. Once your debt is being reduced, then start further building your assets.

Ready?

Sensible investing means having a sensible long-term plan. So let's look at the long term. Yes, "the market" is having a bad-hair decade. And numerous economies are in rescue mode. Ironically, since prices overall are lower than usual, now *might* be a good time to get into the market. "Buy low, sell high" is the theory. Another theory is to "Buy and hold." Sage advice, too often ignored. Seems we are our own worst enemy. Even when the economy is doing fine, our own silliness can mess us up. Though the market surged forward 16% a year between 1984 and 2000, the average investor in a stock fund made only 5% over that period. That's less than a third of what they could have made. They kept pouncing from one fund to another, chasing what was "in". They were getting in too late then chasing the next "hot" thing.[16]

Investing is *not* about picking stocks and "timing the market". That's just gambling with your money. Booms go bubble and burst. You can't time the markets. It's been shown that even the so-called "experts" can't. Yet our human arrogance lets us think we have more control over external events than we actually do. Focus instead on things you can control, like your own behavior and habits. Focus on having a sensible game plan instead of getting sidetracked and sucked in by day-to-day hype.

The market is *not* where you want to get your adrenaline fix.

Getting smarter...

No matter where you choose to put your money, it's important to keep fees low, diversify, and use dollar cost averaging.

Fees

Fees are what a fund company charges to manage the money in the fund, to juggle the stocks they deal with in response to the market. And there's no evidence that expensive-fee funds outperform the lower-fee ones. Actually, it's quite the opposite. The so-called "actively managed funds" don't do as well as the overall market 75% of the time.[17] You can bet the fund managers try to keep that out of the public eye. Fees are sometimes called loads, or management expense ratios (MER). Keep these as low as possible. Better yet, at zero. There are No-Load Funds. Higher loads simply mean more money in commissions to the sales people and the fund managers, not more money for you.

If the fees for a given actively managed fund are 2.5%, and that fund makes 5.5 % in a good year, then you've really only grown your money 3%. (Not much more than a nice safe GIC. More in a minute.) On a $200,000 RRSP, a 2% fee will siphon off four to five thousand dollars a year. Evidently, 2% a year lost in fees can consume a quarter to a third of your retirement savings over time. Ouch.

Dollar Cost Averaging

The market goes up and the market goes down. If you put a certain amount into a specific investment each month, some months that amount will buy you more, some less. But overall you're more likely to be ahead than by trying to time things or by putting in a lot all at once. Suppose you were to put $200 per month into an Index Fund ("What's that?" I'll explain in a minute). This month that buys you 5 units. Next month, the market's down a touch and your $200 buys you 6.2 units. The following month, it's up again, and the $200 buys you only 4.3 units, but don't forget that what you already own is now worth more. Statistically, dollar-cost-averaging tends to work well for building your money, with less risk. Nice.

Diversification

The idea is to have your money in different *types* of investments (e.g. bonds, GICs, index funds), in different geographical areas (continents or countries), and in different sectors of the market (e.g. tech, resources, banks, etc.) That way, if something slides, it's only part of your portfolio.

WHAT'S WHAT

Here are some painfully oversimplified yet valid descriptions of the typical components of a financial investment portfolio.

Savings accounts have minimal interest rates but your money is safe (see the caution on the next page) and instantly accessible. However, not all savings accounts are created equal.

The Canadian government a few years ago set up TFSAs, **Tax Free Savings Accounts**. Unlike an RRSP (**Registered Retirement Savings Plan**), when putting money into a TFSA you don't get any money back on your taxes. Again unlike an RRSP, if you take money out of a TFSA you're entitled to put it back in at a later date. There are very few circumstances you can do that with an RRSP. (One is borrowing from your RRSP to buy your first home.) When you draw on your RRSP, you are taxed that year on the amount you've taken out. Whenever you pull money out of a TFSA, the interest or profits are tax-free. TFSA contributions are capped at $5000 per year. RRSP contributions are capped as a certain percentage of your taxable income. Regular savings accounts, of course, have no cap.

Bonds are usually related to some level of government. They lock you in for a certain amount of time, say 1 to 5 years, but your money's reasonably safe, particularly if it's national/federal.

Treasury Bills are government secured but have very low interest rates.

Guaranteed Investment Certificates have locked in time frames, which can be months or years, your choice depending on your goals. You're guaranteed the *face value* at maturity, i.e. you'll get out at least what you put in. If you are allowed to make an early withdrawal, there will be a penalty. As with bonds, the interest rates are on the low side, but your money is insured up to a specified amount per institution. (Again, see the caution below.)

Money Market Funds have rates somewhere between GICs and savings accounts. They're *not* insured by the government, but are considered reasonably safe. They're "liquid" in the sense that you can get at the cash in them quickly. (Some advisors suggest not to bother with these.)

Mutual funds are baskets of various stocks, often with a theme of some sort, like technology or health care, small or big companies, domestic or foreign. Mutual funds have NO government guarantee on your money, even if the fund is sold by a bank. And pay attention to the management fees, the "MERs". These will chew down your profits.

Stocks are basically shares in a specific company. There are zillions. In general, they're much riskier than what's listed above.

CAUTION:
There are limits to the financial protection the government will give you. Find out which financial institutions are covered, what types of accounts and investments are (or are not) covered, and to what extent.

Canadians – see the Canadian Deposit Insurance Corporation site.

Americans – see the Federal Deposit Insurance Corporation site.

Don't have more than the limit with any one institution. Nice problem—worrying about protecting lots of money. But given the number of banks that tanked in the States in the last decade, don't neglect to look into this!

Wanting to "play the market"? Are you nuts? This isn't a game. Again, if you're an adrenaline junkie, this is not where to get your 'fix'. Take up skydiving instead. Here you're building your future, and you don't want to hit the ground without a parachute.

Wealth builders take calculated risks, not silly ones, and balance risk and reward. You need to be able to sleep at night. But what if you're too nervous to do anything at all? Unfortunately, doing nothing is, in itself, a risk. Inflation, at about 2 to 3% is busy chewing away at your money, no matter what you're doing or not doing.

Just as eating better and being more active is the smarter way to physical health, having a sensible game plan for your money is the smarter way to financial health.

IF you decide to play with individual stocks, keep that to less than 1% of your overall portfolio. This wishful-thinking money should be divided into several different sectors. That way your ass—sorry, your assets—won't get too badly burned.

A FEW GOOD IDEAS...

Fundamentals first ! Then maybe try these ideas.

Again DISCLAIMER. DISCLAIMER! I'm NOT a financial advisor. Get the advice of a certified unbiased competent financial planner. (see p. 192)

There seems to be a consensus out there that the following approaches to financial investments work well. In order of simplicity of use they are:

- **Lifecycle Funds**
- **The Couch Potato Strategy**
- **The Rainbow Portfolio**

First you need to know about **Index Funds** as they're integral components of each. Index Funds track various segments of the market *as a whole*. Examples (not specific suggestions) would be the Canadian Bond Index or the Asian Stock Index. Index Funds outperform fund managers 80% of the time. And because Index funds don't have fund managers as such, the management fees deducted from what the funds might make are lower—about 1% rather than 2 or 3%—which means more money for you. Over time, lots more.

Lifecycle Funds

Lifecycle funds are highly valued by both advisors and knowledgeable investors. While these funds may not be the gee-wow sparkly versions the adrenalin junkies fall for, they are in comparison, steadily effective in building your asset base.

Lifecycle funds hold a mix of "fixed income" (e.g. bonds and such) and "equities" (e.g. various Index funds). Unlike most other investments, they have a target date, chosen when you buy in, for when you'll pull the money out. As that target date approaches, the asset mix gradually gets more conservative so there's less chance of your investment backsliding in value. Some Lifecycle funds need more money as a start-up than others. Some offer, as well, a "guaranteed maturity value" for group retirement funds.

The Couch Potato Strategy

There are a number of possibilities for how to set up your Couch Potato strategy. Here's one example: divide up your money as 40% bond *Index* funds and 60% stock *Index* funds. These stock Index funds are divided into 3 parts: 1/3 Canadian stock index, 1/3 US stock index, 1/3 European and Asian stock index. Too many numbers?

Try this as an example. Suppose you have $10,000 to invest.
Put $ 4000 (40%) into Bond INDEX funds.
Put $ 2000 (20%) into Canadian stock INDEX funds
Put $ 2000 (20%) into US stock INDEX funds
Put $ 2000 (20%) into say, European and Asian stock INDEX funds.
(This last 20% is based on using a different geography. I wonder—just guessing here—if these days you might want to add a little South America to your mix? Ask your advisor.)

Canadians can check out Canadiancouchpotato.com to learn more.
Americans, see money.msn.com/how-to-invest/the-couch-potatos-path-to-riches.aspx.

Each year you revisit and rearrange your portfolio to keep the proportions roughly the same; sell some of what's gone up and put it into areas that went down, (That may seem a little counter-intuitive, but apparently it works quite well). Over the past 30 years, this strategy has outperformed the vast majority of the actively managed funds. Over the past 10 years, although the "Global Couch Potato" averaged only 4%, it still out-performed 90% of the others. Impressive.

The Rainbow Portfolio

Spencer Sherman outlines in his book *Money Madness* an investment strategy that's also been highly effective. It's based on a specified pattern of diversification and what he calls "witness discipline" and "re-balancing". He puts down the "superfluity of expertise" and the snobbery of so-called "experts". He adds that these self-proclaimed experts sadly even believe their own hype. It's not the timing, agonizing, and juggling that works, but using time and the overall market as index funds whose long-term rise is reliable. [18]

If you had put $10,000 into the equity portion of the Rainbow Portfolio in 1973, that $10,000 would have earned $920,180 by December 31, 2007. That's a gain of more than twice as much as the S&P 500 index and more than three times as much as the average stock fund."[19] Awesome. It's a bit more complex than other strategies to set up, but not complex to maintain. How to make use of Sherman's Rainbow strategy? See curemoneymadness.com.

Again, do the fundamentals first and well.
And remember that *time plus a plan*, not wishful thinking, is the magic.

Help along the Way

A good advisor is like a coach who will help you up your game. You still have to do the doing. And, as with any coach, be careful who you choose.

Financial advisors

Conscientious advisors tell you what's appropriate for various life stages, lifestyles, and particular (sometimes peculiar) situations. They do this for individuals, groups, companies or large pension funds. They can also provide a little advice on tax and estate planning but you should, in addition, see an accountant and an estate lawyer.

Many advisors will say their advice is "free". Only sort of. They are usually paid on commission by the financial institutions whose products they sell. If their commission is paid per-transaction, they may "churn" your money. (That repeated buying and selling then makes money for *their* bank accounts, not yours.) You're better off with an advisor who is not attached to a particular company, and who is paid either on a per-hour basis or as a percentage of what they help you make, in which case they're truly dedicated to building your nest egg. You may, in addition, have access to free and reputable advice through your work's human resources department, your group pension people, or your professional organization. Ask.

Some important cautions:

- Conscientious advisors say it's a BAD idea to borrow against your home for investment purposes. Do not be talked into doing this. Less scrupulous advisors will try to "advise" (read coax or bully) you to "borrow big" using your home as collateral so you can invest that money. Whether the investment grows or tanks and flushes your home with it, they've still made their commissions on what *you* risked. Meanwhile, you're the one on the hook to pay off that loan.
- If your advisor ever asks you to write out an investment cheque in their name, rather than to the investment company, politely decline and leave. Immediately call the company they work for, and maybe even the cops. There's something very amiss. More than one creep has taken off with other people's money.
- Always check the professional registries to see if there are any complaints lodged against an advisor you might be considering.

To find an advisor:

Start by reading Suze Orman's advice at http://biz.yahoo.com/pfg/e29planner/
Follow that up in Canada, by going to fpsc.ca or iafp.ca
For the USA, napfa.org or FPAnet.org.

Phone and visit a few. Get a sense of who you'd be comfortable working with. Once you've chosen an advisor, gather up your paperwork, make an appointment, and GO. It's just fine to start small, even very small. And don't worry about looking or feeling stupid. Naïve or inexperienced is not stupid. What would be stupid? Ignoring that you need to be doing something about your future and your assets.

Fund managers

Fund managers are not financial advisors. It's rare that you would deal with them directly. They're the guys and gals who buy and sell various combinations of stocks in order to make money for the fund they manage. Sometimes what they do works. More often it doesn't. And their loyalty is to the fund company that pays them and to their own bank accounts, not yours. While some are worth what they're paid, here's something they don't much like the public knowing—"the vast majority of actively managed funds lag behind the market".[20] In other words, they usually don't get it right. So what can you do? Again, you get really good at managing your habits and directing your cash flow. Then learn and use, if you wish, strategies such as those described in this chapter. And find an advisor who genuinely has your back. Know too that you can build other kinds of assets not related directly to the market. Explore those possibilities.

Stock brokers

Brokers are sales people, not analysts. They simply implement your choices of what and when to buy and sell. Remember that sensible and effective investing is not the same as playing-the-market. That's more like Russian Roulette but with your money, and with more than one chamber loaded.

If you think you're the new Warren Buffet (uh huh), at least use a discount broker. Comparison shop for these at smartmoney.com in the USA. In Canada, have a look at financialhighway.com/canadian-discount-brokerage-review-and-comparison.

Accountants

These are your tax advisors. They can also help you set up a business, calculate ROIs, plan your estate, and so on. There are differences in the qualifications and tasks of CA's, CAA's, and the people who work in businesses that prepare your tax returns. The more complex your taxes are, the better qualifications you want your tax advisor to have. It may cost a little more, but it'll likely save you a lot more.

Insurance agents

You'll want a savvy insurance agent in your corner. You need to protect your income generating ability, your business if you have one and, obviously, your dependents and your property. (See Chapters 22, 23, 24 for the details.)

Tax and Business Lawyers

These legal eagles can help you structure your business so you avoid problems in the first place. The nuances and implications with businesses can be a minefield. What if your business partner dies? Or is getting divorced, and the soon-to-be-ex spouse is coming after a big chunk of the business? Preemptive planning is crucial and well worth the expense.

Estate planning and Estate lawyers

As a young person, you think your passing is a long way off. And it probably is. But you never know. And then there's your parents. You want the transfer of assets to, or from you, to be as efficient and stress free as possible.

Estate lawyers help you direct your assets to exactly where you want them to go. They can, for example, help you set up *Inter Vivos Trusts* in which you place some of your assets now yet they're still yours until your death, or *Testamentary Trusts* in your will that take effect after you die. Mind you, you can gift money or assets to your heirs before you kick off, but then it's no longer yours if you need it.

Your heirs have to pay an Inheritance Tax on the value of the "estate". (Which does not necessarily have anything to do with real estate.) The details vary somewhat depending on where you live, but it's not a small percentage. Get the help of an estate lawyer now to help minimize the costs of the transfer of assets later. They know the Hows and the What-to-do-whens, and can head off potential problems you likely haven't even thought of. If you own a business or are a partner in one, this legal advice is *vital* in helping arrange the transfer of assets in case of a partner's death. Contingency plans should be drawn up now while you're still in the driver's seat. Make sure your respective fannies are covered.

A person's separate accounts are frozen on death. Joint accounts become the property of the surviving name(s) on the account. Whether married or Common Law, no one can access the contents of separate accounts or a separate safety deposit box until after the will and probate are dealt with. (See also Chapter 25.) If you have a family or other dependents, you must have a back-up plan. How much do you and your spouse want to keep in joint and in separate accounts? Even with adequate life insurance, remember that there's a brief time lag before the payout. In the meantime, your family has to eat and pay the bills.

All estate plans, wills, insurances, and so on must be revised when your life circumstances change, e.g. if you are getting married, going Common Law, having kids, or if you win a lottery. (You wish.)

Real estate agents

Licensed Real estate professionals will assist you with both buying and selling. Their fees generally range from 3 to 6% of the value of the home. Yes, it's a lot, but so is the amount of work you'll do if you don't have the appropriate help. Only when you've done the buy-and-sell thing a few times should you even consider flying solo on this one. There are too many UGLY and very expensive pit-falls possible!

When buying, good agents:

- Help you figure out what you can, in reality, afford.
- Refer you to bankers and mortgage brokers to help you get the best deal.
- Search for the right home in the right area. They need to be very familiar with the neighbourhood you're looking in, and act as a tour guide.
- Check for comparables: how much have similar places sold for?
- Help you decide what to offer and how to strategize the counter-offers.

When selling, good agents:

- Check the comparables and help strategize the offers.
- Tell you what needs to be fixed and spiffed up to get your best price.
- Market and show your home. But it's your job to keep it show-worthy.

In both cases, they can help get you ready for closing. There's a crazy-making amount to do in a very short time frame. You'll want hand holding, especially if it's your first time.

The Canadian Real Estate Association's site is crea.ca.
The American Real Estate and Urban Economics Association: areuea.org.

$$

Here are some useful money sites—there are many more.

For awesome tracking and personal finance software: mint.com or quicken.com.
For financial calculators, you could use dinkytown.net.

For RRSP info and booklets: ccra-adrc.gc.ca - see "forms and publications"
For 401K's in the States, see irs.gov/taxtopics/tc424.html.

The Canada Savings Bonds site for rates and info: csb.gc.ca
For the States: savingsbonds.gov.

For planning and investing:

thesimpledollar.com
morningstar.com
curemoneymadness.com.
allfinancialmatters.com
getrichslowly.org/blog
iwillteachyoutoberich.com

Each day, each dollar, is a choice.

Steer where your money and your life are going.
Images of kayaking come to mind. Paddling rivers. Calm waters or white.
Sometimes you can just glide along. Other times, you need to dig in and paddle hard.
Right now, you're learning how to paddle and how to handle the kayak.
With practice, you'll gain confidence.
You're building money skills.
Be proud of that.

So far in this MONEY section:

- You've gotten organized and gotten real.
- You've put in place a useful Easy-system.
- You've learned how to not flush your money.
- You know better how to handle big-borrowing and other debts.
- You know how to make better use of your money, so you can now show more respect for your current and future needs and wants. And you've learned how to protect your credit rating and your sanity.
- You have a better idea of how to invest in your life and how to build assets.
- You're freeing up your options—you'll get to where your basics are taken care of by your money working for you, instead of the other way around.

Let's face it. You spend 40+ hours a week, more than 160 hours per month for a great many years, earning your money.

Do yourself two favours:

- Choose ways of generating income that please you.
- Invest a couple of hours a month to continue learning how to use your hard-earned money effectively and well.

In the next chapter, you'll explore various options for generating your present and future income. But first, go celebrate. You've already learned a lot.

Chapter 20

Designing and Generating Income

You now have a pretty good idea of how to structure the use of your money. But how do you intend to get that money? Win the lottery? Marry rich? Get lucky gambling? Inherit from a rich old uncle? Rob a bank? Scam nice old ladies? Sell drugs? All of which are a poor bet—risky to your freedom and your karma. What are the better options?

"A job is a means to an end, but you are not personally invested. A career is a paycheck with the ability to advance. And a calling is something you simply have to do."[1] How enthusiastic do you want to be about your work? In 1985, a survey showed that almost 80% of people liked their job. Now it's down to about 50%.[2] That's partly because of the current slump in the global economy, which, in turn, is partly a result of mistakes made in high places and by greedy people. It's also partly because many people don't have the know-how to choose well what they "do for a living", or how to adapt as needed.

You want and need to be utilizing your strengths. (That was Chapter 9.) Find the overlap of your talents, skills, desire and the needs that are out there. One of my favourite resources along these lines is *What Color Is Your Parachute?* It's information that's both timeless and annually updated. The author, Richard Bolles, suggests you ask yourself the following kinds of questions. [3]

- What are your favourite interests and fascinations?
- What personal traits as well as expertise, skill, and knowledge do you already have that you would most like the opportunity to use and build on?[4]
- Where do you like to be?[5] (What climate? What geography? Want to be urban or country?)
- What are your preferred people environments? In what kinds of organizations might you find those? [6]
- What are your favourite working conditions? [7] (Indoors or out? 9-to-5 or otherwise? Alone or in a group?)
- What level of responsibility and what salary do you want? [8]
- And of major importance, what would best serve your values and goals? [9] What do you see as your purpose in life?

Let's add a few more:

- What did you want to do when you were a kid? (Fly a plane? Be a rock star?)
- What would you do if you didn't have to work for money? (Don't say "Nothing". Nothing might feel great until you're rested and relaxed, then it'll get boring rather quickly.)
- In what way, in what context, could you contribute something valuable? (What makes you feel like you matter, and does some good in the world?)
- Do you want to live to work, or work to live? Or both?

So what are your choices?

What do you *really* like to do? Which of these activities could provide a solution of some kind for someone else? That's where you can create an income.
Use your imagination. Look around. Pay attention. Notice the opportunities that others are not seeing or are ignoring. Grab those ideas and run with them.

Know too that it's highly likely you'll have not only multiple jobs, but more than one kind of career. What are the possible variations? Which might you want to do first?

Here are a few possibilities:

- Have a burning passion? Get really good at that, then find someone to pay you to do it. Would it make you enough money to have a lifestyle you'd be comfortable with? Research that. (If it won't, you may find yourself building up toxic levels of envy and resentment.)
- Save your passion for your leisure time. Find something that pays decently and that you are "happy enough" doing. Then you can do your passion, your way, without having to worry about paying the rent.
- If you already have a job or a career, find ways to get happier doing that.
- Work for someone else, at least for now, and build a sideline. See how things evolve. Who would have thought that inventing a squeezable ketchup bottle would make someone rich?
- Pinch hit. Punt. Do some of this and some of that. (Some people make hundreds a day catching leeches in cold lakes or shooting alligators. But that might not be your choice. Or mine. It might not have been their top choice either. But something about that is working for them anyway, at least for now. No boss? It's outdoors? How flexible and inventive are you willing to be?)

Mastering skills

What level of education do you need to get into what you want to do?

A 2004 study showed that the net worth of a university grad is on average 4 times that of someone who only finished high school. And, with all the outsourcing, without an adequate education your job is more likely to disappear from under you.[10] Ouch. However, university or college is not necessarily the best or most appropriate option for smart people. Yes, college grads tend to make more money in salaried positions, but there are lots of highly educated people struggling financially. Unfortunately, when it comes to money most people, even the Ivy Leaguers, think that all they need to know is to "work hard". The skill most still need to learn? Managing their cash flow. Perhaps marketing their skills. Likely both. Neither of which are taught in typical schools. Both of which any interested person, with any education level, can learn. There's more to being smart than being IQ-smart.

Let's look at some USA stats on average annual full time incomes:
With no high school diploma? About $27,000. With high school, $37,000.
A Bachelor's degree? About $68,000. A master's degree? $85,000. A Ph.D.? $113,000. A professional degree? About $140,000. Yet here's a revealing statistic from Skills Canada—the average annual salary for a skilled trades person is 25% higher than the average Canadian wage. ($50,000 compared to $40,000.) The average apprenticeship, according to the Canadian Apprenticeship Forum report, lasts two to five years. Their education costs? About one-third of the cost of university. And about 80% of the time the apprentices are training on the job and getting paid while they're learning. Starting salaries? $45,500 for a university grad, $52,000 for a certified journey person. A journey person's average salary at ages 25 to 34 is about $62,700. In many ways they're ahead of the game since they're less likely to be weighed down by student debt. So, no, university is not necessarily the best route.

What is? The route that helps you become *who you want to be*, both professionally and personally.

Learn how to learn. Know that you need to keep learning. Ask questions. Develop savvy—both head and street smarts—and soft skills. (Again, a good book on that is *The Hard Truth about Soft Skills* by Peggy Klaus.)

What skills are needed to develop excellence in your particular field? Do what that entails. Master one skill at a time. Maybe get a job where you can learn and improve the appropriate skills. Find a mentor to help you with the ins-and-outs of your profession. If you need that piece of paper to be legal and to prove your credibility, get it. Those protocols are in place to protect people—knowledge and skill must be appropriate to the task. I doubt you'd want a bank manager adjusting your spine, or your music teacher in charge of food safety standards where you eat.

Learn to combine focus and flexibility. Focus is necessary to master any skill. Flexibility in how you apply that skill, and in how you apply yourself, enables you to transfer that competency to other contexts. And keep upgrading your skills. Along the way, savour your successes, both big and small.

Mastering yourself

There's lots of competition out there—many people with similar education, similar skills, and varying amounts of relevant experience. So what do you do? Become the person that employers and clients want to hire. I'm not talking about faking or padding your resume. It's more than a resume or skill set that will get you hired. Be reliable and honest, with yourself as well. Integrity matters. Take a long view of your life. *Your character and reputation are at least as important to your success as any skill set you have.*

Don't expect even the "perfect work" to be perfect. And don't expect to stay in one place forever. The average young adult today is expected to have twelve different jobs in as many as four different careers! Wow. But the better you choose your work, by choosing work that has meaning to you and that plays to your strengths, the more likely you are to succeed financially. The wealthy and the financially comfortable got that way, in good part, by being more passionate about what they do. They were, as a result, more consistent in their income path.[11]

Feeling stuck? Or that you're settling for less than you're capable of? Yet, for any number of reasons, you can't change jobs or careers at the moment? Try adapting your attitude, even slightly. No, this is not the same as settling. "If you can find the willingness to endure short term frustrations, to compartmentalize the parts of your work that are not enjoyable and put them in a place where they won't impede your ability to get the good out of the other parts, the overall payoff can be huge." [12] (Chatzky's talking about work. Personally, I think that applies to a lot of life.)

More food for thought ...

- Do not confuse busy-ness with productivity.
- What do you currently focus a lot of your time on? What are the genuinely productive aspects of what you're doing? Focus on those. What tasks, if you had more time for them, would boost your effectiveness?

- What do you like about what you're already doing? How much of your time is spent doing that?
- Look for the overlap between what adds value to your organization *and* what you like to do. How could you start implementing more of this, a little at a time? In what ways might this enable you to be happier and more effective on the job? (See Chapter 9, if you previously skipped it.)
- Perhaps adapting the hours or the location of your work would make you happier. Do you need to spend two hours a day commuting? Perhaps negotiate to work from home (or a local coffee shop) a day or two a week. If all you need is a laptop and good communication gadgets, why not work from the cottage or even from a different continent for a couple of months? Not as unusual as you might think. Saves buying ties at least. But obviously you better have the reputation of getting things done very well and on time.

A little discouraged because you've tried everything you can think of to improve your current context? Instead of totally reinventing yourself or changing careers, perhaps change companies? Or go out on your own? But before you take the plunge, be sure you know how to assess and access your strengths, and how to manage and compensate for your weaknesses.

Do you know what you're worth?

Whether you're a male or female employee, a one-person business or an entire corporation, you need to have a good sense of your competition. Be aware of your strengths, what you have to offer, and your market value. When you're really good at what you do, chances are your current employers (or clients) won't be the only ones interested in hiring you.

Are you getting what you're worth? If you don't care enough to do something about that, why should anyone else? For example, women working full time still earn on average about 75% of what men make. That's partly because men are more likely to negotiate their salary going in and more likely to ask for raises. And partly because of the so-called "glass ceiling". Unfortunately, women too often just accept what they're offered, even when they're highly competent and experienced.[13] Smarten up.
Here more courage => more cash. (For some eye-opening stats on the workplace, see statcan.gc.ca.) There are numerous women's mentoring and networking groups. Join one.

Do you know what you want?

Before you start negotiating your salary or raise, know in advance what your hierarchy of *wants* are. There's more to this than just-the-money. Are you willing to make trade-offs for flexible hours or for certain perks? Decide as well, in advance, what your deal breakers are and whether you're willing to walk away if you don't get these. While it's often not a good idea to burn your bridges, especially these days, you don't need to stay stuck in one place either.

Useful salary sites: salary.com, payscale.com, jobstar.org, monster.ca, or bls.gov (USA)
Some wonderful sources on **how to ask for a raise**:

Richard Bolles – *What Colour Is Your Parachute*
Ramit Sethi – *I Will Teach You to Be Rich,* pages 234-244

Approaches to earning your money

The traditional and most common approach to generating an income has been to get educated, find a job, work hard for the same company for decades, struggle along, and try to save towards a retirement with a sadly downsized lifestyle. The world has changed. Unfortunately, our mindset about how to earn and use money has not. It's now a global economy and loyalty between corporations and employees—in both directions—is in short supply. As individuals we need to be much more agile in our approach.

I love Timothy Ferriss' book, *The 4-Hour Work-week.* He's tapped into and put form to a grass roots revolution/evolution and helped a lot of people redesign their work life. Here are a half dozen of his many gems:

- "Inactivity is not the goal. Doing what excites you is." [14]
- "Boredom is the enemy, not some abstract 'failure'." [15]
- "The blind quest for cash is a fool's errand."[16] "People don't want to *be* millionaires – they want to experience what they believe only millions can buy." What's the true currency of the New Rich? Time and mobility.[17]
- "Alternating periods of activity and rest is necessary to survive, let alone thrive. Capacity, interest, and mental endurance all wax and wane. Plan accordingly." [18]
- To conquer fear? Define the fear. Ironically, "most things just aren't as serious as you make them out to be." [19]
- "Being busy is a form of laziness – lazy thinking and indiscriminate action." Instead be selective. "Identify what pulls the most weight." [20]

We don't have to use the Old-Think of 40 years then and only then retire and finally, maybe, get to do what you want. Instead we can mix and match not only our income generating work styles but our work related time frames. We can take intermittent mini-retirements along the way *if* we plan carefully and well. Why work harder when the solution is working smarter?

No matter what your preferences are for time frames or geography, there are basically **four different ways of generating income.**

(1) As an Employee

As soon as you mention money, most people think "Job". Being an employee is the typical way of earning a living. Working for someone else for a paycheck requires your effort, energy, and presence. It's an exchange of time and skill for money whether you're earning minimum wage, $500 an hour as a legal-eagle, or mega-bucks as a CEO.

You're there to "add value", to perform certain tasks for your employer. Yes, it's supposedly a steady income but these days there are certainly no guarantees of job security. What is guaranteed is that you'll need to be good at whatever you do, so make that promise to yourself. And it's highly unlikely that you'll be in the same job or with the same company for decades as often was the case in the past.

Recent surveys showed considerably fewer employees are happy with their current job than 15 years ago. (For more info, visit careerkey.org.) Perhaps more people need to do the Strengthsfinder.com program, and more bosses need to learn what it takes to genuinely lead and mentor rather than simply micro-manage. (Meoww.) Employers, on the other hand, might say "their people" should be more conscientious and reliable. Perhaps everyone should consider that we're all in this together and through mutual respect build a win-win rather than a dog-eat-dog paradigm.

(2) By being Self-employed

You own your own Job. Technically it's a business but you do most if not all of the work whether you're an MD, a carpenter, or a freelance consultant. And you need to build and maintain a client base. Sure there's a certain kind of freedom, but the downside? If you're not doing the doing, you're not making money. You can't call in sick and still get paid. And, if you are sick, you're still on the hook for the costs of running the business. So make sure you've got good disability insurance. (See p. 211) You're also responsible for your own benefits and for setting aside enough *now* to fund your eventual retirement. But at least, in the meantime, you're not likely to lay yourself off.

> Whether you're an employee, self-employed, or an entrepreneur you're trading expertise for money. You're basically selling solutions to other people's problems, or in some way meeting the needs of your employer, customers, or clients. Treat them as you would want to be treated. Be knowledgeable, highly competent, and friendly. Make doing business with you easy, fair, and maybe even fun. And make doing repeat business with you even easier.

(3) As an Entrepreneur—build or buy a business

You can build your own business from scratch then, once you've got it up and running, set it up so that someone else does most of the work. That's the usual goal anyway. If you were to start your own business, what would be your chances?

Statistics can be boring, but consider these as batting averages. Brace yourself.

- Stats Canada shows that about 145,000 new businesses start up each year. And each year, about 137,000 others declare bankruptcy.
- The U.S. Bureau of Labor Statistics shows that 66% of new small businesses are still in existence after 2 years, 44% after four years.
- Small to medium businesses (less than 20 employees) have a 37% chance of surviving 4 years and only a 9% chance of surviving 10 years. (Dun & Bradstreet)
- New restaurants? Only a 20% chance of surviving 2 years.
- In general, most businesses that do fail do so in the first year. Only half of those survivors are still in business at five years.

Yikes. Franchisees and Licensees have a better track record because there's a proven formula for how to run that particular business. But then you're paying the franchisors or licensors a big chunk of your business income.

If you're leaving your job because you think being an entrepreneur is easier, good luck. It might be more gratifying, but it's certainly not easier. If you're lazy, can't make decisions, or are terrified of risk, being an entrepreneur is not for you.

Guts, creativity, perseverance, and good planning are vital. Chatzky in *The Difference* says that many businesses fail because, right out of the gate, they start with a lousy business plan.[21] The result? They have to work, and work, and work. More planning up front would have helped immeasurably. The financial difficulties associated with poor financial management—and frustration—then tank most of them. Interestingly, of the failed businesses, only 10% closed involuntarily due to bankruptcy. The other 90%? The business did not provide the income they desired. Or the effort, time, and financial outlay was just too much for the meager benefits gained.

> Whether you build or buy a business, you need not only expertise in your particular field but expertise in what it takes to run the business. Develop business savvy or hire it. Have smart, reliable, and highly competent people on hand to help you.

Some prefer the supposed safety of a regular paycheck, not because they aren't good at what they do, but because they don't know how to market their services or they consider sales beneath them. Ha. What are resumes and job interviews? Selling yourself, simply part of what you expect in your career. Similarly, to be in business and stay in business, you must expect that selling your services is just part of what needs doing. Marketing done with integrity doesn't make you a sleaze any more than going to a job interview does. Simply choose not to be one of those bad-apples who tries to con people into spending money on stuff or services they don't need or want.

Think of marketing yourself simply as letting people know that you're there to provide what they need, or do what they need done.

We've justifiably become pretty cynical these days about advertising and corporations. Because of this, the most effective marketing is definitely word of mouth referral—there's an implied level of trust involved. Do what you promised and when. Build trust in your competence and your reliability. *Integrity* is what will build your business. Your reputation and that of the people who work for you, and the networks you develop, will make or break you.

(4) **Build Assets to create Passive Income**

We've already talked about building assets in Chapter 19. Here I'm just reminding you that those assets can come to generate for you a major part of your income.

What if you want to not have to work anymore, ever?
The answer? Assets up + Expenses down => Freedom => True wealth

Wealth is "a person's ability to survive so many days forward without having to work. To become financially independent, your cash flow from your assets, per month, must exceed your monthly expenses – Therefore you're no longer dependent on wages for your livelihood." Buckminster Fuller

Growing money is "like planting a tree, water it for years and one day it doesn't need you any more. Just sit in the shade and enjoy it."[22] Robert Kiyosaki

You work for an income. And it needs to work for you. The good news? Learning to steer your money towards where it'll do you more good takes less time than you think. And learning to develop "passive income"—the kind you don't have to trade your time and effort for—takes a small fraction of the time that you spend earning "active income". To become your own "golden goose", you don't need to become a mega-mogul. Keep it simple. A number of authors suggest that, for most people, it's better to keep your job and build assets on the side. It's less aggravating and, given the odds of business success, less risky. Once your passive income is in place you can, if you want, hire competent and trustworthy people to maintain your assets and your financial portfolio for you. Then you can spend most of your time playing. Sweet.

Now What?

Your realities. Your facts. Your responsibility to deal with what's going on.
Stuck? Get help from the appropriate people to improve the situation.

To improve your income? Working harder and working longer hours is often not the answer. "Once you push yourself past a max of 50 hours per week, efficiency, creativity, and effectiveness all start to shrivel. Don't go there." [23] Instead, be more effective with whatever you do. Be proactive. Get some appropriate help, and improve your current and future realities.

Protect yourself. You already, I hope, set up an Ouch account. Now you need the right insurances. (That's Chapters 22, 23, and 24.)

Protect yourself from yourself. Avoid getting mired down in survival mode. At the other end of the scale, don't get caught up in ego-driven overindulgence. Both can lead not only to income losses, but to physical and emotional health issues.

Protect your future. Build assets sooner rather than later. In the meantime, be as self-indulgent with the non-monetary pleasures as you wish. (Or not. It's your life. Your call. Your consequences.)

Acknowledging to yourself how much control you actually can have over your life, your finances being one example, might be a little daunting. So what? Deal with it. Remember—*no guilt, no blame, no excuses*. Just get on with *solutions*.

Are you doing what's been suggested? Maybe not? At least not *yet*? Think of it this way —you might not feel like working out, but you know you're going to like the results. Get the idea? Same thing here. By becoming more financially literate, you're giving yourself more and better options. Sometimes, like a small push to get a toboggan moving, it's just one or two more skills that will set you up for a really fun ride.

Recommended Reading

The Automatic Millionaire, David Bach
What Colour Is Your Parachute?, Richard N. Bolles
The 4-Hour Workweek, Timothy Ferriss
Rich Dad Poor Dad, Robert T. Kiyosake, with Sharon L. Lechter
Women & Money: Owning the Power to Control Your Destiny, Suze Orman
The Six Day Financial Makeover, Robert Pagliarani
I WILL TEACH YOU TO BE RICH, Ramit Sethi
The Lazy Person's Guide To Success, Ernie J. Zelinski

Chapter 21

Build NON-monetary assets

KNOWLEDGE

Know yourself. Know what truly matters to you. Know how you will recognize when you have your happily satisfying Enough, both in your work world and personal life.

Invest the energy to create a better, more fun, more meaningful life. Why settle for one that's boring and unfulfilling, or one that's defined for you by others?

Learn how to learn. "In today's fast-changing world, it's not so much what you know any more that counts" That becomes outdated fast. "It is how fast you learn. That skill is priceless."[1]

Invest the time to learn the information and skills you need. Or hire someone who's already good at that, and treat them well.

You'll learn faster and with less effort if you find mentors. Find someone who's already good at what you want to do. Inquire as to whether they'll let you ask the occasional question. They're highly regarded and busy—let them know that you're aware of that and that you'll respect their time and energy. Their primary focus needs to be *their* business. And, whatever you do, make sure your reputation will never negatively impact theirs. If you want their help, *earn* their respect.

FRIENDS and ALLIES

Choose your friends carefully. They're your fun social group, your confidants, and you're each other's harbor in a storm. But don't confuse your friends with your network. The latter are your allies in a very different sense. With them, you brainstorm and collaborate to get ahead with your professional and monetary lives. With them, you find solutions, solve problems and, as mutually supportive motivators, hold each other accountable to your respective goals. Mutual respect is vital, but whether you'd choose them as a close personal friend needs to be irrelevant. Instead, deliberately choose each other for your *differences* in strengths and skill sets. Then you can coach each other in whatever needs to get done. "It takes a village".

Be careful of the naysayers. Some people are stuck, afraid, and without even meaning to, they can drain your energy. Yes, pay attention to relevant cautions and to your own fears, but constructively assess and address these. Don't chicken out before you see if what's scattered on the ground around you are simply pebbles or the seeds that could grow your money trees.

YOUR GO-TO PEOPLE

Choose your professionals carefully. Pick people who are not only highly competent, but who walk-their-talk and have your best interests at heart, even if that's mostly because they know that being both competent and conscientious is good for their reputation and hence their business.

If your Go-To people will help you learn what you should know, even better. And don't be cheap. Pay your professionals well. Good information is priceless. These are people with valuable and relevant expertise and experience, and they can help you think outside the box. Even large companies with highly skilled executives have a Board of Directors for this very purpose.

If you haven't yet read Chapter 19, "Making your money work more", visit pages 192-195 for who else to include on your go-to team.

ATTITUDE and ENERGY LEVELS

People often don't do what they can and ought to do for themselves. Why is that? It's not that there aren't solutions. They may be somewhat naïve without realizing it. They may be stuck in denial. Or worse, they may have a somewhat negative attitude or a self-defeating arrogance. (After all, no part of the problem is, even in a *small way,* their fault. Uh-huh.) But let's not blame the victim, even when we're our own victim. No guilt. No blame. No excuses. Please don't let fatigue, and the fear of facing what's going on, get the better of you. Of course, pay attention to sensible cautions but don't succumb to fight-flight-or-freeze on one hand or analysis-paralysis on the other.

When we're afraid of what we don't understand, we have a tendency to cop out, to lie to ourselves. We pretend that "it doesn't matter", or that there are, supposedly, no viable solutions so why should we try?

There are solutions. If you need some help, get it.

Think of learning to take care of yourself as a fun adventure, rather than an imposition or a nuisance.

Design your own life. Learn how to implement your choices.

It's not the effort involved in the initial learning curve that bites, but naïvete and inaction.

Take courage. Be your own best friend.

Covering your Ass...ets

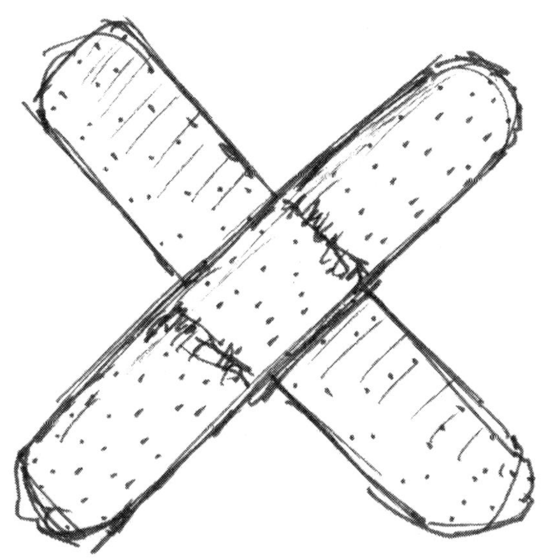

Chapter 22

Insurances

Ironically, this is money you *hope* you're wasting!

You can't afford to be arrogant, obtuse, or naïve here. Bad things do happen to good people. While "the fault" may not be at all yours, the consequences still will be. Some things that happen in life require more than a band-aid.

"Forewarned is forearmed." However, do not assume that others will think to tell you what you need to know and do. They may assume that you already know, or that it's not their job to tell you. This chapter is about getting your safety nets in place.

Here are two examples.

A young teacher, just starting her first contract, assumed that human resources would coach her on the kinds of benefits one should get, and how and when to get them. (That's not an unreasonable assumption.) She got the usual "extended care" benefits and so on. (These had to be signed up for within 30 days of being hired. At least they told her that.) They never mentioned disability insurance and since she'd never heard of it—let alone understood why it's important—it didn't come up in the conversation. (Disability insurance with her board would have provided decent coverage at reasonable rates.) Two years later, at age 28, she's diagnosed with non-Hodgkin's lymphoma. Now she doesn't medically qualify for it. While she has some sick days owed to her in her teaching contract, whether that will be enough to tide her over the chemo and recovery and possible relapses, who knows? Someone really oughta tell you this stuff!

A 32 year old fireman—wickedly fit, health conscious, eats mostly organic food—noticed a small lump on his neck. He too was diagnosed with non-Hodgkin's lymphoma. He's married with one young child and another on the way. Luckily, the people who advise firefighters are more thorough. Thanks to the benefit protocols for firefighters, he had not only good disability insurance to tide them over until he could get back to work, but also "critical illness insurance" which paid off their mortgage. Someone did tell them.

Same disease. Both unexpectedly hitting otherwise healthy young adults.
Two totally different impacts.
She's struggling financially, in her second chemo, and stressed.
He's doing much better. Chemo worked, and his family is mortgage free.

Cover your ass...ets!

Let's look at ...

- Insurances FOR you:
  Health, Disability, Critical Illness, Long Term Care, Powers of Attorney / Living Wills, and Travel Insurance.
- Insurance for your stuff:
  your place, your things, your vehicle (if you have one).
- And insurance ON you.

Insurances FOR you

Health Insurance… a must, immediately and always!

There are substantial differences in how Canada and the USA approach health care benefits. I'm glad I live in Canada. Hooray for quality universal health care that comes out of our collective taxes. I wish Americans could get past the fear-mongered myopia and implement more sensible medical reforms. And yes, contrary to their naysayers, we do have the freedom to choose our doctors and services. And our doctors aren't being told what they can and can't do for their patients by some greedy corporation.

In 2007, high medical costs were a major contributing factor in 60% of American bankruptcies. In 2009, over 16% of the population was still uninsured. And a Harvard study from the same year estimated that each year over 44,000 deaths occurred each year *unnecessarily* because of a lack of health insurance coverage.[1] For a developed country, I find that disgusting. And despite their higher per capita healthcare costs (almost double that for many similar countries) life expectancy in the States lags behind that of the European Union countries. Hopefully, their 2010 "Patient Protection and Affordable Care Act" will start to rectify those pathetic statistics. American health insurance possibilities can be found at http://www.usa.gov (search: "healthcare insurance coverage") and healthcare.gov.

Back to Canada. To cover dental and eye care, prescription drugs, and other extended health services (such as having a private or semi-private room if you have to go into hospital), about 65% of Canadians choose to have supplementary coverage, usually through their employers. Extended coverage for a Canadian 25 year old non-smoker with no dependents might cost about $15 a month. Not bad. The average person otherwise might end up spending about $900 a year.[2] Ask your human resources department for the details of your carrier's benefits. Read the fine print. If you're self-employed and hence buying your own policy, compare companies by reading their detailed "Evidence of Coverage" or the "Certificate of Insurance", not just their "Plan Summary" descriptions. And talk to your professional or trade association. They may have group coverage available to their members. (Group plans usually cost less for the same coverage.)

> Be certain you're comparing apples with apples. You want the best (i.e. most appropriate and highest quality) coverage you can afford, not the least expensive policy. In fact, that's crucial for any insurance policy.

Have a look at such sites as:
insurance-canada.ca or ehow.com/ehow_money-insurance-basics.

Compare the policies of Blue Cross, SunLife, Manulife, and others.

> Keep in mind that—unfortunately—with disability, critical illness, and long term care policies, you don't get to buy as much coverage as you might like. You get only as much coverage as you qualify for. And with all of the following insurances, get a "partial disability" component built in.

Disability Insurance

Your greatest financial asset is your ability to generate income. You must protect it. Unless you're retired or your assets already generate enough income to allow you to not have to work, **you need this.**

Some scary STATS:

- In the USA, every 0.01 seconds (yes, you read that correctly) another disabling injury occurs. Every four minutes an injury is fatal.[3]
- According to a Hartford study, one-third of all Americans will find themselves disabled for at least ninety days during their working years.[4]
- 1 in 6 Canadians will be disabled for three months or more before age 50.[5]
- The average long-term disability lasts about two and a half years.[6]
- One in seven workers can expect to suffer a 5 year or longer period of disability before age 65.[7]
- For a 30 year old, disability is 4 times more likely than death.[8]
- By the time you're 65, the chances of your needing your disability insurance are three times greater than your chances of dying.[9]

Realistically, without disability insurance you'd be in serious financial difficulty!

Waiting Periods

With any Disability, Critical Illness, or Long Term Care policy, there is a span of time immediately after you're ill or disabled before the benefits kick in. These waiting periods are usually 90, 60, or 30 days. The shorter the period, the more expensive the policy. (It's sometimes referred to as an "elimination period". They eliminate their payments, not you.) You need to have something to live on during this period. Here's where your OUCH money (three months worth of your take-home-pay) acts as your lifeboat.

Disability insurance companies are not going to pay you your full salary. (They don't want to get scammed by lazy rip-off artists.) You'll possibly get coverage for about 50 to 70% of your income. And many plans have a dollar-value maximum as well as a percentage value. Try to get enough to at least cover your living expenses.

The best disability policy, but the most expensive:

- Has a 30 day waiting period, rather than 60 or 90.
- Maxes out what they'll pay you according to your occupation (based on your taxable income), and what you think you'll need.
- Maxes the potential years of benefits. It's best to specify "until age 65" rather than cover yourself for only a few months or years. You never know...
- Has inflation protection of at least 5% per year.
- Has premiums that don't increase with age.
- Includes an "own occupation" clause, meaning that you go back to work only when you are able to perform the tasks associated with your own occupation. (I doubt a carpenter, a surgeon, or a CEO would want to sling burgers for a living.) Specify your own occupation or, at least, list defined alternatives.

If you don't, they will cut off your payments if you refuse to go to work, any work. If you're in business for yourself or your income has substantial input from commissions, or you have a highly specialized skill, you need to be particularly concerned about the definition of "own occupation".

- Contains a non-cancelable clause. As long as you keep paying your premiums they can't cancel your coverage if your health starts to deteriorate.

To bring down the cost somewhat, here are a few **compromises** you could make.

- Get a guaranteed-renewable policy instead of non-cancelable.
- Have a 90 day or 60 day waiting period instead of 30 days.
- Bring down slightly what they'll pay you per month.
- Have a modified "own occupation", but specify what work you'd do.
- Skip the inflation protection. (If you're under 50, keep this.)
- Cover yourself to an age slightly less than 65.

Be sure to read the features of good Long Term Care policies on the next page as they are similar.

Group disability insurances

These are likely to cost less, but check the details of the benefits they offer and the conditions attached. You may need to supplement your group policy with an individual policy from an outside source. Since group policies usually end when you leave that particular workplace, it's an excellent idea to set up a policy that goes with you no matter where you work.

The cost of decent disability insurance?

Expect to pay about 1 to 3% of your income for a decent long-term disability policy. Suppose you're a 30-something healthy non-smoker. To get a "my own occupation" policy that would pay out about $3000 a month until age 65 (with a 90 day waiting period) might cost you about $150 a month. If you go for an "any occupation" clause, which I would not recommend, it might be half that.

Remember that disability is much more common than death in working age people.

The younger you are when you start a disability policy, the less it's going to cost. But be sure to add in that inflation clause, and look for a policy whose costs don't increase much as you age.

Some companies will give you the option of a "refund of premiums" if you never have to collect on the policy (nice), or you die (not nice), or if someday you choose to cancel it (not wise, unless you're then retired or rich). "Refund of premiums" is a great feature. Your butt's covered, and you can get your money back. Some Critical Illness policies offer similar perks.

Critical Illness Insurance

"CI" is meant to help if you suffer a major nasty, e.g. a life-threatening cancer, go blind or deaf, have a heart attack or stroke, or are in coma. Again, it's cheaper if you get it—the policy, not the problem—when you're young. Look for a policy whose costs increase minimally as you age. And choose one that includes, as well, a "partial payout" list of less severe conditions.

Rather than paying out a certain amount per month, Critical Illness policies generally pay out a lump sum that you use as you see fit. (Confirm the pay-out conditions and possible exclusions.) You choose the payout dollar value when you take out the policy. Don't short-change yourself here. What you need that money for will, obviously, depend on what condition you find yourself in health-wise and on your particular circumstances.

Long Term Care insurance

LTC Insurance is rather like disability insurance in that it covers you in the event of an accident or illness. It has the added advantage of not being tied to your work-life and it doesn't end at age 65 as do disability policies. LTC is meant to continue until your death, at any age.

Some STATS pertaining to Long Term Care needs:

- 43% of people receiving LTC are *under* age 65. Yikes.
- If you're over 65, you have a greater than 70% chance of needing LTC. [10]
- Overall, according to the American Health Care Association, the odds of your needing your LTC policy are 1 in 2.
- In contrast, the odds of needing to claim on your fire insurance are less than 1 in 1000, but you don't gag on paying that.
- 10% of nursing home residents will be there for 5 years or more. And that care is getting more expensive all the time.

When to start an LTC policy?

Probably the most sensible time is in your late 40's. Before this, you're likely better off with a disability policy and wisely investing the money you would have put into an LTC. After age 49, the cost of premiums for all insurances starts to climb sharply. And chances are you may have the beginnings of health issues that could either disqualify you or trigger more stringent conditions on what they would do for you, at any price.

If you do buy an LTC policy earlier, say in your 30's, the rates are considerably less. Get a "limited-pay option", i.e. you pay for a certain number of years after which you owe them nothing more, yet the policy stays in effect. And look for a policy where the premiums don't increase much as you age. Include that inflation clause.

Maintaining one's independence and continuity of lifestyle are important. That's difficult if we're disabled by illness or accident. And most of us will want to stay in our homes as long as possible. That eventually may become less of an option as a result of increasing frailties. Yet preserving one's dignity—at any age—is crucial.

Be sure that you, your spouse, and your parents are covered. You caring for them, or they for you, could wipe you all out financially. Like that's a fun conversation: "You're going to get decrepit, then die". It's not even an easy conversation to have with yourself. Yes there are publicly funded nursing homes, but they're not likely to be where you or they are going to want to spend the "golden years". And the more years, the more gold it's gonna take.

Ask your folks, tactfully and respectfully, what they would want for that future time. If they don't yet have their financial plans and insurances in place, encourage them to do so. "Immortal" is only for books and movies. If you're financially fit and your parents can't afford a Long Term Care policy, consider paying the premiums for them. Talk with them and with an insurance agent about this possibility. If they become financially dependent on you, this policy could save you money in the long run. And you and your spouse, if you have one, research and implement yours. After all, if you aren't covered, who's your fairy godmother going to be?

To be physically dependent, i.e. to be considered "disabled", a person needs to require assistance to perform two or more of the six "activities of daily living" (bathing, dressing, feeding, transferring, using the toilet, or continence) or to require continual supervision because of a deteriorated mental condition.

The **best LTC policy** would include the following features (some of which are similar to those for good disability policies):

- Coverage for the rest of your life, not just for a certain number of years. (Who knows, you may be a rare one and make it to 100+.)
- An inflation protection of 5%, especially if you buy the policy earlier in life.
- An "income style plan" rather than one that reimburses you for certain expenses and not for others. (You'd have to keep and submit all your receipts.) This is about dignity and choice. It's bad enough that you and your life have gotten messed up. Why put yourself in a position where you have to justify and grovel? Suppose you've been in a nasty accident and won't be able to work for months. You're home from the hospital but can't even get in and out of the tub. You want to be able to pay a family member for caring for you if that's your preference, or get a massage to help ease the aches and pains.
- An option for "return of premiums" on death or on cancellation of the policy. If, for some crazy reason you decide to do that, be sure to use that money for subsidizing your *long-term* goals, not for toys or temporary joys.
- A waiting period of 30 days. You choose the length of this you-pay-first period when you buy the policy—you don't get to change it later. (Some LTC policy pay-outs start only after you've been paying someone out of your own pocket for that waiting period. When comparing policies, check if this is the case, and the particulars of who you'd need to hire and for how long.)
- The monthly premium is waived once you start requiring care. If you're part of a couple, see if you can set up your policies so that if one of you needs your LTC, the other's premiums are also waived.
- "Comprehensive care" which covers home health care, assisted living, and quality nursing facility care.
- It's "guaranteed renewable". There are very few "non-cancelable" policies available. Guaranteed renewable means they can't outright cancel your policy as long as you pay the premiums, nor can they raise your *individual*

rates. They do however have the right to increase premiums for all of their policyholders as a group. And they likely will at some point.

- When does the policy stop paying out? All policies will require that you are reassessed occasionally to see if you are able or unable to perform those specified self-care tasks.
- As with all insurance policies, check the company's long-term viability rating. To do that, Canadians can check dbrs.com (Dominion Bond Rating Service). Both Americans and Canadians can visit ambest.com.

Before purchasing any policy, check the pay-out conditions, the exceptions they won't cover, and who they'll pay and when.

Insurances of a different kind:

Your **Living Will** and your **Power of Attorney for Property**

What happens to you if you're temporarily or permanently incapacitated (e.g. in a coma)? This is generally referred to as your Living Will or Health Care Directive.

What about your finances and other practical matters during that time? What do you want done about those? And who will be in charge of what? This is the "Power of Attorney for Property". (The "attorney" you appoint does not need to be an attorney, i.e. a lawyer, just someone you totally trust.)

Please don't tell me that you're willing to hand yourself over to some government bureaucrat. Or that you're willing to put your family in the upsetting position of having to argue about what to do for and with you. This kind of thing tears families and individuals apart. Don't do that to them. Realistically, *everyone* needs to set up a Living Will and a Power of Attorney. *Draw these up now while you're healthy.* And designate that each is "revocable" so that once you've recovered you can take back your decision-making powers. You, and your loved ones, really need to get on this—now.

The details for Living Wills and Powers of Attorney are beyond the scope of this book since they depend, not only on your wishes, but on the legal requirements for where you live. Start with your government sites and the sites for the various law associations.

Canadians can start with the Canadian Bar Association's cba.org/cba.
Here in Ontario, there's attorneygeneral.jus.gov.on.ca/English/family/pgt/livingwillqa.pdf.
Other provinces have comparable sites.

Americans, check your state government sites, and perhaps agingwithdignity.org and americanbar.org/groups/real_property_trust_estate/resources/estate_planning/estate_planning_faq.html.
For help finding a lawyer or for free legal advice see FindLegalHelp.org.

Some sites offer generic forms. While they may be useful as a place to start gathering ideas, I strongly advise you to see a lawyer to fine-tune and formalize your wishes. You're handing your life over to others and to a piece of paper. Don't screw this up! And don't not-do-it.

What do you want done about *YOU* ?

You decide in advance what kind of medical care and interventions you want under what circumstances. For example, if you're permanently brain-dead, do you want tube feeding for the rest of your could-be-very-long-life, or do you want the MDs to pull the plug? Write out your wishes. Since medical techniques and technologies change quickly specify *intent*, the results you want, not specific procedures. And be sure that if your wishes change, you immediately update your documents. You can, if you want, specify a certain person or persons who will make your healthcare decisions or literally the final decision.

Once this document is ready, discuss it with and give a copy to your doctor and your proxy (the person or persons who would make your health care decisions for you).

What about your finances and other practical issues?

Again, have your ideas vetted and finalized by a lawyer. Risk = chance x damage. Too much risk, too much potential damage here—for both you and your loved ones —to risk messing this up.

Choose a lawyer who specializes in Estate Planning and Wills. It's worth the money. Since lawyers are paid by the hour, be prepared. Think about your preferences and jot down your questions before you go. The lawyer can help with the details and advise on aspects you may not have even thought of. You will need to sign the final document in the presence of two adult witnesses who are not personally involved.

Again, once this document is ready, discuss it with and give a copy to your proxy (the person or persons who, in this case, would make your "practical decisions" for you).

Note: You can choose different people as the decision-makers for your "living will" than for your "power of attorney for property", if you want.

A Living Will and a Power of Attorney are musts.
They keep YOU in control of your life, even when you can't be...

Keep copies of both with your lawyer—let your family know who that lawyer is— and have a copy in your own easily accessible files *not* your safety deposit box. (Or set your proxy up as a co-signer on that box. If you'd trust your proxy with your life and/or your finances, why not your box?)

On a happier note... Travel Insurance

Coverage for YOU

You must assume that your local health care coverage will cover *nothing* once you cross a border. Ask your health insurance providers what is covered, and where. *And* get travel insurance, whether you're going on an extended overseas vacation or just across the border for an afternoon of shopping. Yes, the risk may be small that you'd be in an accident or develop a sudden health issue, but the impact on your financial health could be profound. There's a good chance those bills could financially wipe you out. Get travel insurance! Yes, I'm repeating myself.

Canadians, a two day hospital stay in the States will cost you over $10,000. Your provincial plan might refund you $400. Two weeks in a trauma unit after an accident? Well over $110,000. Your provincial refund might be $5,000. Ouch. We're well covered at home, but your financial health outside our own borders is up to you.

Get coverage that will take care of *all* your medical costs *and* the cost of getting you home. (I once had a mind-numbing 3 a.m. call from half way around the planet— a neurosurgeon in Australia telling me that my gone-walk-about twenty year old daughter had been in an accident and couldn't move or feel anything from the armpits down. Every parent's nightmare. Luckily, she's now fine. The damage, torn ligaments and spinal cord swelling, though intense was not permanent. And luckily, she had good travel insurance or it would have been more than one kind of nightmare.)

Commonly covered? (Ask.)
Your medical, hospital, or dental expenses. Emergency evacuation. Accidental injury or disablement. Accidental death. Even overseas funeral expenses.

Common exclusions? (Ask.)
Pre-existing conditions. Illness or injury caused by alcohol or drug abuse. War. Pregnancy coverage varies. Coverage after the first trimester may not be available.

Options that might be available?
Coverage for some types of previous health conditions if they're considered "stable". Car rental collisions. Coverage for high-risk sports (hang-gliding, diving) or high-risk countries. Natural disasters. War. Maybe even kidnapping or ransom coverage? (Yikes.) Ask. Obviously, some types of coverage will cost more than others.

Ask. Ask. Ask.

Further cautions:

- Is there is a "travel advisory" posted about the country you want to visit? That may impact not only your travels, but your travel insurance options.
  For Canadians: travel.gc.ca For Americans: travel.state.gov
- Get the updated information, not only for the necessary visas, etc., but for which vaccinations and pills, potions and lotions you'll need. (Do this at least several weeks in advance as some vaccinations need time "to take" after they stick you, as do some pills.)
  For Canadians: phac-aspc.gc.ca/tmp-pmv/index-eng.php
  For Americans: wwwnc.cdc.gov/travel

Another caution:

- If you buy your trip or your travel insurance online rather than from a travel agency, the travel industry watchdogs won't cover you if the company goes belly-up. (Here in Ontario that would be TICO, the Travel Industry Council of Ontario.) Search these sites to see what they will cover.

Coverage for the loss of your stuff while traveling

Your baggage and personal items might be covered under your home insurance policy, or through your credit card *if* you used it to book the trip. Check this.

Specify "replacement value". Make a list and maybe take a photo of what you're taking with you. Leave a copy at home and/or upload it to a secure-site.

If your baggage is delayed, you'll need to replace some items in the meantime. Cover that too.

Be sure to make copies of all your ID papers and trip documents. Again, leave copies at home or with a friend, just in case. Do *not* email these. Never, ever. (See Chapter 28.)

Coverage for the trip itself

What happens if the travel company goes under before you leave or while you're away? It's one thing to lose your vacation. It's quite another to be stranded somewhere and fending for yourselves to arrange and pay for getting home. The answer? Don't buy your travel insurance from the same company that booked your trip. The CAA or AAA and some banks, for example, have good coverage at reasonable rates. Good travel insurance will cover your costs if you do get stranded. Again, ask.

Here's where some credit cards earn their keep. Some will cover you for a 60 day window between purchase and "non-delivery". Book well ahead if you want, but pay only the minimum deposit required until you're within 60 days of your leaving date, then pay the rest. If the travel company can't deliver on exactly what you booked, your card will refund your within-60-days money. Ask your card company what their policies are.

Suppose you've booked a European tour that starts in Paris. What happens if, because of weather or some other reason, the airline cancels your flight at this end? To catch up with the tour, would the alternate flight arrangements be paid for by the travel company that booked your tour? Generally yes, *if* they also booked your flights. Ask.

Under what circumstances can *you* cancel and still get your money back? How far in advance must you do this? Ask.

If there's a problem while you're away, do you have to pay up front and then get reimbursed? (That generally takes more time than you'd like.) Or does the travel insurance pay the providers directly? You don't want to have to instantly come up with several thousand dollars for flights to get a sick or injured loved one home fast. Ask.

Generally, people under 55 don't need to fill out medical forms. But check their policies on pre-existing conditions. If you have one, don't lie. They check and they'll deny you coverage after the fact. Ouch.

Ask. Ask. Ask. Have them explain their coverage, in detail. As always, read the fine print. **Confirm you've got the coverage you truly need before purchasing it.** And get everything in writing.

Take your policy numbers, coverage pamphlets, and contact numbers with you. Keep copies in more than one spot: your wallet, your hidden-pocket, your bag, and your carry-on. (No harm in being a little excessive sometimes.) If your luggage gets lost or you get mugged? Just when you most need the info—and right now—it's gone.

The cost? Travel insurance is often only a few dollars a day. A decent travel policy usually costs between 3 to 7 % of trip, depending on your age. If you cross a border frequently, even if only for the occasional evening out, consider a policy that covers you for a whole year and for multiple trips.

Let me say it yet again...

NEVER EVER travel without Travel Health Insurance! Otherwise, having to cancel your trip or losing your stuff might be the least of your worries.

Images of disabled cruise ships come to mind...

Insurances are designed to protect you ...

Much as you'd like to hope otherwise, *it can happen to you*. Life can change in a heartbeat. Don't get lazy about this. You need to protect yourself and those you care about. And they need to protect you.

When choosing any insurance policy, you need unbiased advice. Talk to a financial planner who will not be earning a commission on the policy you purchase, and an insurance *broker* who will have access to a wide variety of policies and companies. (You want to find an advisor you can trust to be both knowledgeable and conscientious. Ask around. Check their credentials and references.) For any and all policies you're considering, read the fine print. What you don't understand, ASK.

Do you have what you need?

Make a list of the types of insurances you currently have and what they cover. (Go through your policies. If there's something you don't understand, ask your advisor.) Compare these to what you oughta have.

- **Health Insurance** is a must. Always.
- **Disability insurance** is a must until you retire or you're rich.
- If you travel anywhere, **Travel Insurance** becomes a must.
- **Critical Illness Insurance** is great but it's a little harder on the budget. Do give it serious consideration—perhaps even before you purchase life insurance. At least you're still alive. (Life insurance is covered in Chapter 24)
- In your 40's consider starting your **Long Term Care** policy soon. Your LTC policy will need to replace your disability policy which ends at age 65. With LTC in place, you can let go of your disability insurance whenever you retire.

Having trouble coming up with the money for your health, disability, and other personal insurances? Revisit Chapter 15. And reduce the cost of your home and vehicle policies by increasing the deductibles. If you need to, use some of the money you've designated as long-term money. (See pages 173 & 175)

You need insurance on your place and stuff, and your vehicle if you have one. That's Chapter 23 coming up.

If you have any dependents or a business, you'll need Life Insurance as well. That's Chapter 24.

Have a full medical check-up *before* you cancel any insurance policy. You may not be aware that you have the beginnings of a health issue that would negate your ability to get another policy. As you age, this becomes even more important.

Chapter 23

Insurances

on your PLACE, your STUFF, and your VEHICLE

The Top Priority

The most expensive problem? Being sued. **Liability Insurance** covers you if you're sued by someone who may be—or claim to be—injured while in or on your property (your place, vehicle, or job site). Good quality liability coverage with an ample dollar value is a must. Otherwise, if there's an accident you could become someone else's "lottery win". Being sued is hideously expensive. Carry at least a couple of million, just in case.

Renting?

It's your responsibility, not your landlord's, to insure your stuff and to provide liability coverage for your visitors. Get a Tenant's Package. They're not expensive.
To cover $30,000 worth of stuff with a $1000 deductible and have a million in liability coverage would cost you, per month, about $25. If you want water-damage coverage, add about another $10. If you have a few rather expensive goodies, have a special "rider" attached for those.

What if you cause damage to your landlord's property? Discuss this with your insurance agent. (Your landlord should have coverage for their place, but they will not cover your stuff.) If the damage is deliberate or your fault rather than normal wear and tear, expect the landlord to come knocking.

You Own Your Own Place?

Insure your place as well as its contents for the "replacement value". Every few years have the value reassessed. You want to stay current with repair and rebuild costs. Remember, even if your home burns down or is in some other way devastated, you're still on the hook for the mortgage. And if you live in a flood, hurricane, tornado or other hazard zone, get that additional coverage spelled out, in detail, in your policy. If you don't, more than your place would be washed or blown away.

Your Stuff

Again, get replacement-value coverage for everything—your clothes, laptop, TV, toys, furniture, kitchen items, etc. Otherwise the insurance company will pay you only the depreciated value, i.e. what the item is worth if you sold it, not what you'll pay to replace it. Pennies on the dollar.

Make detailed lists of everything. Keep the receipts for major items such as furniture and jewelry, include appraisals for antiques, and take photos. Keep a copy of all this info somewhere other than your home. (About a year ago, my neighbours' house went up in a ball of flames thanks to mice eating their wiring. In another two minutes, it would have taken mine with it. You gotta love prompt firemen!) You don't want your list burned along with your stuff. Put a copy in your safety deposit box or upload the list and the photos to a free secure-storage website.

Vehicles

Your policy needs to include "collision", "liability", and "comprehensive" coverage.

Collision repairs crunches to your vehicle. The other driver, if they're driving legally, will have their own insurance. However, in the States apparently there are a lot of drivers without insurance. And they're "I'll-sue-you" happy down there. Carry at least two million in liability! **Liability** covers you if you're being sued for injuring someone, for their "damages", and so on. It's the bulk of the cost in home, tenant, and vehicle insurances. **Comprehensive** covers things like broken windshields, theft, etc.

Vehicle insurance costs for males and females are quite different. The number crunchers know that statistically—brace yourself, guys—women generally are more sensible, and young men the least so. The rates reflect that. So keep your driving record as clean as possible. Avoid speeding tickets. Avoid collecting points.

More expensive cars, newer cars, and sportier cars obviously have higher costs. If you're driving a junker (worth less than say $3000) just carry liability coverage. Eliminate the collision and comprehensive and put the difference towards saving for a newer car.

Reducing the cost of insurance

Insurance is cheaper if you have higher deductibles. The **deductible** is what you have to pay before the insurance company pays anything. It's often $500. If you up it to $1000, you could shave perhaps 3 to 10% off the cost. With some companies, if you pay annually upfront rather than monthly, you could save up to one month's worth of premiums. That's a fairly common but little known treat.

To claim, or not to claim?

Don't claim for small amounts. Claims almost always increase your insurance rates. Some companies will give you one "freebie" claim, especially if you've been with them for years. Why waste your one claim on something small?

A single at-fault vehicle accident may boost your premiums by about 10 to 15% for six years. With homes, a claim can trigger a premium increase of 10% for 3 years. So if you're not facing a loss of well over the $500 deductible, it may not be a good idea to claim. Why not have a $1000 or $2000 deductible in the first place, and save on the cost of the policy? Put the difference into your Ouch account.

If the damage was the result of something definitely outside of your control, and if the repairs are fairly expensive, it's best to claim. If in doubt, discuss it with your insurance agent or with an unbiased insurance broker. Details vary by province or state.

Surprisingly, it's not one huge claim but the **frequency of claims** that'll bite you. Three even very small claims inside of five years can kill your ability to even get home insurance! That's bad. Really bad. You want to be financially resilient enough to avoid having to claim for small amounts. (That OUCH money does come in handy.)

For any insurance, get the best policy you can afford, not the cheapest one!
Some useful sites for comparisons:

Canada:	insurance-canada.ca	kanetix.ca
USA:	carinsurance.com	insure4usa.com

Chapter 24

Insurance ON you...

So now you're dead. Who cares? No, I'm not being sarcastic or nasty.
Who specifically is going to be impacted by your death?
What can you do about that—now—to soften the blow?

When and why do you need Life Insurance?

When it comes to life insurance, "Most people with dependents are underinsured. Most people without dependents are over-insured."[1] When you have a spouse and/or kids, or anyone else who is fully or partially dependent on your income, life insurance is a must. If you have no dependents (at least for now), you're likely better off putting that money into reducing debt and building assets. Yet the older you are, the more it will cost and the more likely it is that you may develop health issues that could prevent you from getting a policy. Give it serious consideration by age 29.

Life insurance is also valuable as a way to pay off estate taxes. And it's a must if you own a business. (Your accountant or business lawyer should have insisted on a good life insurance policy as well as the usual business coverage. If not, get on that now. There could be big bills to pay there if you are not covered. If you have a business partner, he or she must be covered too or you could lose everything.)

Life insurance pay-outs are not taxed. And the money is paid out quite quickly. It takes much longer—months or even years— to access money from "the estate".

How much do you need?

To replace your income?

It's usually recommended that you have 10 to 20 times your family's annual living expenses, or 5 to 10 times your salary. (Your policy should cover at least your family living expenses per year x the number of years they'd need to be covered, plus pay off the mortgage.) That could mean $500,000 to $2,000,000 of coverage, or more. Invested wisely, that should keep things going for them.

You and your mate *both* need adequate life insurance, even if one of you is not working. The mortgage will still need to be paid and now on one salary. And if you have kids to care for, now as a single parent, you'll have higher day care and sitter costs on top of the rest of the bills. (Ask your insurance agent about "joint-last-to-die" policies.)

To pay Estate taxes?

To claim an inheritance (from anything other than an insurance policy), the Estate taxes need to be paid up front. The taxes might be as much as 50% of the value of the estate, if it's a high-value estate. Let's say you're well-off when you kick-off. Lucky them. Well, maybe, maybe not. They may have to sell half the assets, and maybe even the family home, to get the money to pay the taxman. Talk to an accountant and an estate lawyer to figure these out. Make sure your loved ones aren't inheriting a nightmare.

If there's no will, or you're in a Common Law relationship, things can get really messy. (Common Law spouses have NO automatic property rights. You must set up a well thought out Cohabitation agreement, and now.) A little planning saves a lot of unnecessary grief. Be very clear and specific as to who are the beneficiaries of what. (More on this in Chapters 25 and 27.)

What kinds of Life Insurance should you get?

There are two basic types, TERM and WHOLE LIFE, and a mind-boggling variety of in-betweens of which UNIVERSAL is one.

TERM Insurance

TERM covers you for a certain period of time and ends at a specified age. In the past, it used to cover people only until age 65. Now you can even get Term-to-100 policies, if you plan on sticking around that long. You no longer need "Whole Life" to cover you for your whole life. Term is fine for most people and it's less expensive, costing hundreds not thousands per year. However, the premiums increase as you age. (Term insurance prices have come down somewhat because people are living longer.)

$300,000 of term insurance for a healthy 30 year old is about $300 per year. Whole life? About $3000. Wow. (Mind you, there are some advantages to whole life policies. More in a minute.) Some agents will tell you whole life policies are better because they provide "automatic savings" and you can later borrow against the policy. (They also make higher commissions on whole life policies.) You can set up your own automatic savings, thanks. (Hopefully, you already have.) And if you do borrow against the policy, their loan rates are higher than borrowing money from the bank. That's particularly nasty since it's your own money you're borrowing. What you took out as a loan plus the interest you accumulate is deducted from what they'd pay your beneficiaries. If you don't pay it back fast, that pay-out value can be eaten up faster than you'd ever guess.

To cut costs somewhat, look into group rates at work or through your union or professional association. However, these group plans usually end when you change jobs or stop working. So make your own additional arrangements. Some organizations (e.g. the CAA, AAA, and many others) offer group insurance that isn't tied to where you're working. These days, that's a good idea.

Choose a policy with the end-date you want—for the policy, not you. And because Term insurance premiums increase as you age, look for a policy with lower price jumps. Whole life premiums do not go up as you age, but it costs much more to begin with. It may be better to go Term, and save the difference or pay off your debts faster.

Some say that, rather than one big policy, you might want several smaller ones with different time frames or different purposes: one for raising the kids and helping them get through school, another to pay down the mortgage, yet another to pay off the estate taxes. You can gradually eliminate a policy or two, or add another, as your needs shift. Other advisors say that's actually not cost effective, and that one or two larger policies are better. What does your advisor advise? If you want, get a second opinion. (But if you don't trust your financial advisor, maybe it's time to find a new one.)

NOTE: Having a financial advisor that's paid by the hour, or paid according to how well they build your portfolio, is a good thing. That way, they don't have a hidden agenda to steer you towards products on which they'd make a higher commission. Some are more conscientious than others. (Revisit page 192.) However, insurance brokers (or the agents of the various insurance companies) are *not* to be paid by you, but by the companies whose policies you buy.

WHOLE LIFE Insurance

It's also referred to as "permanent insurance" because the policy can be continued as long as you live. The premiums won't increase over your lifetime but, as I said before, it's more expensive to begin with. Here's an example: Sam was paying a certain amount for Whole Life insurance. When he switched over to Term-to-75, he tripled his coverage for less than half the cost. Mind you, his premiums will increase somewhat every five years. So the cost difference between the two types of policies will decrease as he ages. Whole-life costs are stable but high, Term is lower but increases incrementally as you age.

How long will you need that particular policy? What's it for? Though the vast majority of people do not need Whole Life policies, there are special circumstances where it does make sense. Do you have a dependent whose special needs are expensive, and ongoing in the sense that their needs will long outlast you? For these kinds of circumstances, you'll need more specific and specialized advice than can be provided here.

UNIVERSAL LIFE is rather like a mix of Term, Whole Life, and a Fund. Some say it's generally not worth the difference in price unless, for example, you're using it to protect a business. There's no cash value as such to it, but it might be useful in terms of avoiding some probate taxes. Talk to your business advisors.

And the variations go on and on ...
It's easy to get confused, or duped into spending more than you need to.

One size does not fit all.
You want the policy that's most suitable to your needs. And again, rather than one big policy, you may want two or more smaller ones targeting different needs and with different timelines in mind. Or not. Ask your financial advisor what's appropriate for *your particular circumstances*. Then call an insurance *broker* who has access to policies from a wide variety of companies. And choose the companies and policies that best suit each of those needs.

As I said in Chapter 22, when comparing insurance policies be sure you're comparing apples with apples. And go for the best coverage you can afford, not the cheapest policy. (Chances are it's cheap for a reason.) And make sure your policies are **guaranteed renewable**, so that, as long as you pay the premiums, the company can't cancel them.

Reliability and long term viability of the insurance company

How financially solid are the various insurance companies? You want to know the company will still be around when you or your beneficiaries need to collect. There are independent advisories on this:

Canadians, check dbrs.com (Dominion Bond Rating Service).
Both Americans and Canadians can visit ambest.com.

Save yourself a lot of money.

Don't smoke.
Smokers rates, for almost all insurances, can be up to double that for non-smokers. Combine those savings with the money you've been flushing on cigarettes, and pay down your debt and mortgage faster. You'll have more money both for building assets and to play with. Stop burning dead plants in your mouth—your present and future money are burning up right along with them. (Revisit page 141)

Who gets the money when you die?

Your choice. Give the full name of each beneficiary and state clearly the percentage each will inherit from the policy. (See as well Chapter 25)

Do NOT name your Estate as the beneficiary to an insurance policy, or money and time will be lost in the Probate process. (Probate is a legal process, the hoops that an estate must get through before your heirs get what you intended.)

Never make a minor your beneficiary. Insurance companies will not issue a cheque to a minor, and a judge will have to oversee the money *even if you appointed a guardian* for your kid. Instead, set up a Living Revocable Trust and make the trust, not the minor, the beneficiary. (See a lawyer to do that.) That way, the guardian you've chosen is in charge of taking care of the needs of the child according to *your* wishes, not some court's.

How long do you need insurance for?

For your significant other:

Unless and until your assets are capable of generating enough income to give your spouse/partner a decent life without you, protect each other. Both of you need to carry the appropriate insurances until then.

For your kids:

By the time your kids are finished school and have their first job—at the very latest by their early 20's—they should be fully self-supporting. If they're not, they need to smarten up and so do you. This is weaning of a different sort. (You're not doing them a favour by enabling them to be financial parasites, even if they're cute and friendly ones. Paying their bills as well as yours is not only hard on your financial future, it could be hard on theirs. In your old age, do you want to be in a position where you have to return the favour and mooch off them? Ouch.)

A much better gift than, yet again, rescuing them from themselves? Teach them the self-reliance skills that are good for their self-respect. And if you can't do that, help them find someone who can. So much better for all of you… now and later. (Hey, maybe get them their own copy of this book.)

For other dependents:

Individual circumstances vary tremendously. Discuss with your insurance broker and advisor the most appropriate way to meet the ongoing needs of any other dependents.

A few important CAUTIONS:

- When being asked the qualifying questions for any policy, tell the truth or the insurance company legally can and will deny the payout later. Your loved ones will have enough to deal with when you die.
- If, at any point, you're considering switching insurance companies, do not cancel the previous policy until you have the new one confirmed and physically in your hands. Who knows, in only a few hours, something could happen that would negate your getting the new policy. And you could be disqualified for a new policy at the last minute if they find a "pre-existing condition" in your medical files. Then you have neither policy. Yikes.
- Do not be talked into buying life insurance on your kids. Who are they supporting? If anything, you might consider getting them a Critical Illness policy. (If one of your kids becomes seriously ill, it may be difficult for you to continue working.) For someone that young, it's not expensive and they can keep the policy going as they mature.

This is not just about you providing for others.
Have the people in your life made adequate provisions for your needs?
While these are not the most comfortable conversations you'll have, they are necessary.

When it comes to life insurance…

Do you have the right kinds of policies?
How much do you need for what, going to whom?
How long will you need each policy? For now? For the long term?

What companies have the policies that best fit those needs?
The same refrain—comparison shop for the best fit at the best price.
Could you get more coverage of the right kind, with a reputable company, for less cost?

Again, do not cancel anything until you have the new policy already in place. You may not be able to re-qualify!

Further resources:

Pick up some tips at selectquote.com/learning or accuquote.com/learningcenter. And check out the websites of individual companies.

Chapter 25

Directives and Wills

You die first. Or they die first. Ouch.

There are two components to consider—and *now*. That's the Directive and the Will itself. Do this while you're still "of sound mind and body". (Speaking of sound mind and body, if you haven't yet read Chapter 22, I suggest you go over the information there on "Living Wills". We all need one of those.)

Directives

First of all, a Directive is not the same as a Will. And it must not be made part of your Will nor put in the same envelop. (Your Will is just about the last thing that will be dealt with after your death.) Do not store your Directive or your Will in a safety deposit box unless someone else has signing rights on that box, or your wishes won't be accessible when they need to be. (Your body may end up somewhere you didn't want it to go, and your funeral rites may not have gone as you would have liked. Mind you, at that point you probably wouldn't care.)

Keep the original of your Directive with your lawyer and have three copies made. One you give to your Executor, the person you put in charge of what needs doing, legally and practically, after your death. One goes into your important papers file. The third you give to your emergency contact who could be a trusted family member or close friend. (Pick someone who'd likely be one of the first to know you're dead.)

Ask yourself before drawing up your Directive:

- Do you want to donate body parts? Someone who's still here would benefit from your generosity. (You can carry a wallet card for this.)
- Do you want your body to be embalmed or go au naturel?
- Do you want a fancy casket or a pine box?
- Who will your pall-bearers be?
- Do you want to be buried or cremated or something else? Do you want to "live" in an urn, or to have your ashes sprinkled somewhere you enjoyed while you were alive?
- Do you want a gravestone? What do you want on it?
- What kind of memorial service do you want? Do you want a funeral or a big party, or both? Do you want to specify what you'd like for either? You're entitled to get as specific as you want, if you want.

Now actually set up that Directive so your family and friends will know what you want. If they don't know, and they do something you may not approve of, you don't get to come back and haunt them. (Well, probably not.)

Wills

Wills are legal documents used to transfer your money, your assets, and your stuff to various people or organizations after you die. And, sadly, no one's too young to die. In your Will, you outline in detail who gets what. If you want, you can even state *when* they get what, and under what circumstances.

> **Estate:** The combination of all things owned and moneys possessed by a person. It could be a mega-mansion on a private island, or simply the change in your pocket, some family photos, and a favourite childhood teddy bear.

Inheritance taxes may be due on part or all of what you're passing along. How big a bite will these take? Sort out the details with an Estate lawyer and an accountant. You may want to take out an insurance policy to cover these costs. (See Chapter 24, if you haven't already read it.) If you can't afford the cost of the "inheritance tax" policy you want to take out, see if your heirs will pay for it. The taxes are going to come out of their pocket anyway, one way or another.

> **Probate:** The legal hoops the Will and the assets, and hence the heirs, have to go through. This is not a short process. But that time frame can be made a little shorter and much simpler by careful advance planning.

Suppose you're on the receiving end, e.g. someday you'll inherit a house. Until Probate is settled, which can take many months, you can't sell the property to claim the proceeds. Maintaining the place in the meantime could get expensive. And the inheritance taxes, depending on the value of the Estate, could be up to half of what it's worth. Minimize, in advance, both the time needed for the process and the amount of the estate that has to go through probate. The advice of an estate lawyer and an accountant may cost you a few hundred, but could save many thousands.

Ask your folks what they have—or may not *yet* have—set up. A gentle entry into that conversation might be to ask for their advice about setting up *your* Directive and Will. (Frankly, you might want to check out the validity of their advice. They may be less knowledgeable about this than you'd hoped.) If they do have an updated will, it's reasonable to ask who the Executor is. (You may need to be the one that gets in touch with their Executor if/when something happens.) It's *not* reasonable to ask about the details of their will. Be polite. That's their business, not yours. If they don't have a will, encourage them to set one up.

What happens if there's no Will?

The inheritance process will be messy. And slow. For starters, the government will take a big bite. If you're married, your spouse and the kids will inherit some of your estate, but who gets what and how much is determined by the government. Do you really want bureaucrats and the courts in charge of that? Check the laws where you live: proportions and details vary. If there's no will, count on squabbling amongst those who do have a claim on part of the Estate, and quarrels with those who think they might.

If you're living together but not married, unless there's a Will or Cohabitation Agreement stating otherwise, you inherit *nothing*. Even if you've met the Common Law requirements for your location, you have NO entitlement to money or property, unlike in a marriage, unless can *prove* your contribution. You are not automatically co-owner of anything. You *must* keep the receipts for what you paid for or contributed to. (See Chapter 27)

> **Be sure to read page 243 on property and "marital assets".**
>
> And discuss *now* with your financial advisor and your bank how to most sensibly structure your joint and individual accounts. That process isn't complicated. The fallout if you *don't*, could be.

The Will itself

- There are do-it-yourself kits that might suffice *if* your life and your Estate are pretty simple. You could use one of these as a template to gather and organize your facts and wishes—as a place to start, not as your final version. **Estate law is complex and the exact wording is crucial.** Have your intentions formalized by a lawyer. A typical Will might cost you several hundred dollars now, but it could save your heirs a lot of headaches and legal bills later. If your estate is more complex—there's property, a business, or a blended family involved—you really *must* work with an estate lawyer. (Your Net-worth statement would be handy when you're preparing your What's-where list.)
- Proper **witnessing** of any Will is crucial for it to be legally valid, so if you do choose to use a do-it-yourself kit, don't skip that step. Witnessing requires that two people, neither of whom is involved in any way with the Will, sign that it's actually you signing the papers and on that specific date.
- **Keep your will updated**. If you get married, divorced, have kids, whatever, you must revise your will. For example, a marriage automatically invalidates a previous will. A final divorce decree, in most circumstances, cancels out your Ex, but the rest of your wishes should remain valid. (I'd double-check that for your jurisdiction, if I were you.) Simple changes can usually be handled with a "codicil". Again, you *must* keep your will updated *and* update the beneficiaries on your life insurance policies. Don't delay that. It's not just you that your procrastination bites. (Scenario: Guy dies. An 'ex' wife, from almost a decade before, inherits almost everything leaving his beloved and pregnant common-law lady hung out to dry. What do she and their not-yet-here child inherit? A legal mess. He'd "not gotten around to" finalizing his divorce or updating his insurance beneficiaries or his will. The dummy.)
- Choose your **Executor**, the person who will implement the wishes you lay out in your will and deal with the "after-passing" legal hoops. It's often a good idea to choose a more neutral party (a sensible friend or your lawyer) rather than a family member. (That can prevent hard-feelings as the process unfolds.) Always stipulate a back-up Executor "just in case".
- If you have **kids**, specify who will be their **guardian**. And specify to whom, when, and how the money from your estate will be paid out for the costs of raising them. You don't want their caregiver to have to keep running to the courts for permission for this-or-that. (If you don't trust them to follow your guidelines for that money, why would you trust them with your kids?) The courts won't let a minor, i.e. someone under 16 years of age, be a beneficiary directly: they must have a guardian. And stipulate an alternate guardian, "just in case". (See Living Trusts, next page.)

- Make your heirs ***specific* people and/or organizations**, not your Estate, and specify on the policy what **percentage** each beneficiary gets. (Percentages are better because the dollars-in-accounts and the worth of assets fluctuate.) And again, "just in case", plan for contingencies. State who would get what if so-and-so weren't around when you die.
- Check on the various **tax consequences** of what you leave to whom. Talk to an accountant. Some assets, some investments, have different tax implications than bank accounts or insurance policies. Life insurance isn't taxed, and since it doesn't go through probate, it goes more quickly to your heirs.

A Will or a Living Trust?

To avoid Probate costs, you can set up a Living Trust. You transfer your assets to the Trust while you're alive and designate who inherits the various components and when. In the meantime, you're still completely in control. (As a young person, it's unlikely you have bags of money and assets to pass along, at least not yet, but your folks might.) Even with a Trust, you need a Will and you must designate a guardian for your kids. Living Trusts are definitely *not* a do-it-yourself project. The details, pros-and-cons, and implications need to be discussed with a good estate lawyer. It's not inexpensive to do, but it saves a lot of money in the end. Literally.

What about your E-You?

What about your presence online, in cloud-space, in server-land?

- Make a list of what's important.
- What access to what needs to be passed on to whom? (E.g. for your business documents, for family photos, and so on.)
- Is there any monetary value to the digital assets you've created deliberately or otherwise?
- What needs to be shut down? What needs to *not* be shut down?
- Who needs to be notified about stopping the payments for subscriptions, etc.?
- What about your passwords? Set up a document on a safe-server (some are free, e.g. Keepandshare.com) and keep there an up to date list of all of your e-spaces with the appropriate passwords to each. Give your Executor digital access to this document. *Do NOT use email for these!* Realistically, emails are like postcards—they're neither private nor safe. With the safe-server sites, you can give specific people access to specific files, which is both useful and convenient.

See sites such as deathanddigitallegacy.com and legacylocker.com.

Some final thoughts...

"It can't happen to me" is simply a fool's wishful thinking. And death? Hey, we all go there. Some of us sooner than later. Taking care of these very practical issues *now* not only keeps you in control, it makes life simpler and kinder for those who care about you. Get on this. You never know... You owe it to your conscience and to their peace of mind. They'll be in enough emotional pain without added and *avoidable* complications to deal with!

- Research online the legal necessities, and the possibilities for your "last wishes".
- Have a conversation with yourself and your loved ones about your preferences.
- See a lawyer and fine-tune then formalize your wishes. If you can't afford the fees, call Legal Aid or your community legal clinic for free or inexpensive help.

Chapter 26

Living Space...

Rentals, landlords, and roommates

Compromises

For your living space, what will you not compromise on? Think about safety, cleanliness and maintenance of the building, no mold, no roaches...

What are your preferences? What location would be best? Do you need transit availability? How many bedrooms? Want a separate office, a dining room?

List other would-be-nice aspects. A balcony that faces the sunset? Being able to have a pet larger than a goldfish?

What time span are you looking for? A short-term month-to-month, a temporary sublet, a year's lease?

Money-wise?

- Don't pay more than 25 to 30% of your take-home-income for housing. You want a life and some financial resiliency, not just a place.
- You'll need two months' rent saved up for the "first and last". (And sometimes a security deposit that helps protect the landlord from damage to their property.)
- If you can't afford a place you'd actually like, consider sharing a two bedroom, at least for a while. Negotiate this with your intended landlord *before* you sign a lease. (More on this in a minute.)
- If you live with your folks and are old enough to be working, be an adult not a leech. Unless they're millionaires, pay them something. They may be kind-hearted but they already raised you once. "Failure to launch" is only funny as a movie.
- Some folks, some cultures, choose to live as extended families under the same roof, but they're usually sharing expenses as co-operating adults.
- There may be times when you or other family members, though preferring to live on your own, find yourselves in extraordinary or dire circumstances where help and support is truly needed. Being too lazy to get your act together and go it on your own is not one of those.

Finding a place

Word of mouth, on-line sources, and newspaper classifieds, are the usual and best places to start. Try the free sites first.
Some examples:

Canada: kijiji.com, viewit.ca, padmapper.com, mapitat.com
In the States: apartments.com or apartmentguide.com,
In both: craigslist.com

Real estate agents in some areas will find you a place but they'll charge a good chunk of cash to do it, often the equivalent of a full month's rent.

Covering your ass..ets

Get your own liability and replacing-your-stuff insurance. This is *not* the landlord's responsibility. Someone breaks in and your new big screen, laptop and tablet are gone, or a visitor slips in your bathroom and sues you. Your problem, not your landlord's. Tenant's insurance is not expensive. Maybe $30 a month, depending on what and where. Get it. (If you haven't read the previous Insurance chapters, do that.)

Landlord and Tenant Acts

These clarify who is responsible for what, and what happens if such and such occurs. The specifics vary slightly with the jurisdiction you're in (i.e. your province or state). Read up on these.

Landlords are responsible for keeping the place mechanically functional and heated (and in some areas, cooled), and for keeping the common areas of the building clean, well lit, and generally safe (with regard to railings, slippery walks, etc.). They are not responsible for your safety when it comes to crime and so on.

You are responsible for keeping your own place clean, for not damaging the landlord's property or that of others in the building, and for respecting the other tenants and the building's rules, codes and by-laws.

Rental Applications and Credit Checks

Landlords need to know that you can and will pay the rent, and that you aren't going to be a destructive nuisance. They'll ask you to fill out a form outlining your rental history and requesting references. If you won't do that, good luck. And they'll ask for permission to do a credit check on you. (Remember that the more credit checks done on you, the lower your score drops. So only give this permission if you're genuinely serious about the place.) If there are not many decent places available, they may ask you to pay for the credit check. But that's up to you.

Leases

There are standard lease contracts but those might not be what the landlord is asking you to sign. If there's something in the lease that you don't understand, ask the property manager and/or the landlord to explain. And before you sign anything, get the advice of a more lease-experienced friend or relative, perhaps even a lawyer. You may be able to modify the contract a little, but don't count on that if it's a hot rental market and you want to be the one who gets the place.

Ask about the details. Some of these may be deal-breakers for you, or for them. Are there laundry facilities, storage? What about parking? Smoking? Pets? Do *not* make assumptions. *Leases are legally binding contracts.* Once you sign it's too late to start renegotiating or to change your mind.

Leases have end dates. But you need to confirm *well in advance* your intention to stay or go. Even informal or month-to-month rental agreements require more than just a month's notice. In most locations, you must get or give 60 or 90 days notice. Check the laws for your location.

Breaking rather than properly ending your lease can be expensive. And it won't be easy. *You are still legally required to continue paying for the full time frame even if you move out.* Ask *in advance* under what circumstances you would be allowed to end the lease before the end-date (for example, if your job transfers you out of town). Include a "release by mutual consent" clause if possible. If not, ask for the right to sublet to fill the remainder of the term of your lease. Just don't assume they have to give you that consent. Some landlords are more reasonable than others. And so are some tenants. If you decide to trash the place to get out of a lease, they can have you charged and sue you. Then you're paying big legal bills as well as the lease and damages. And good luck ever getting another lease, at least in a place where you'd want to live.

Security deposits

It's not uncommon to be asked to pay a deposit to cover any accidental or willful damage to a rental property. (Again, check the laws where you live.) Get a detailed receipt for this including the following: the date and amount, the person it was paid to, the name of landlord if you're working with a property manager, the address and the apartment number of the rental property involved, and a statement saying that the cheque (or cash) is for the security deposit. Personally, I'd write all that on the cheque as well. Then there's no way that "confirmation of payment" is going to be lost—your bank keeps cashed cheques on file.

As soon as you get the keys, document the place: take dated photos and list any issues so you don't get stuck later paying for pre-existing damage. Notify your landlord and have them fix the problems right away. When your lease is up, be sure to fix any nail holes etc., and clean the place. Again take pictures with dates on them in case you need to go to small claims court to get back your security deposit. As I said before, some landlords, and some tenants, are more sensible than others.

Issues with Landlords

Got any stories to tell? Do your friends or family? Ask around.
Describe two scenarios in which you might encounter problems with a landlord.

Check the appropriate websites for your area (province or state) for the Landlord and Tenants rules and laws that apply to that scenario. Get the answers you would need now. "Be prepared" is a great motto.

For each scenario, what would be the best solution?
What's the worst that could happen?
What could you do to avoid getting into that mess in the first place?

Issues with Roommates

Again, got any stories to tell? Ask friends about roommate-from-hell scenarios they've survived or heard about. How were these resolved?

How could you avoid ending up in a similar situation?

If things seriously blew up with your roommates, what might be the best, worst, or most likely outcome? What leverage or legal recourse would you have?

Platonic Roommates

What's "platonic"? A relationship that's not sensual, sexual, or romantic.

If you're thinking of sharing a place with one or more platonic roommates, you all need to do some practical soul searching about how you like to live. Have an honest conversation about what works for each of you, and what doesn't. *Before* you sign a lease, expectations need to openly discussed. By working together to put these preferences and ground rules down on paper, you'll have a better understanding of what you're getting into, and thus can make a more sensible decision as to whether or not you want to go ahead.

As a place to start, discuss the questions below. Then, *if* you decide to go ahead, detail these agreements *in writing*. This is, perhaps surprisingly, not less but more important if you're already friends. Being friends doesn't mean you'd automatically be compatible roommates. You may want to protect the friendship by having a roommate who is less involved in your life.

I strongly suggest you do a credit check on whoever you're considering taking on. Even if they're a friend, are you sure they're financially able and reliable? Again, you may want to protect the friendship by having a different roommate.

You have a right to privacy, personal safety, noise-free sleep, to expect that you all will respect each other's belongings. And to occasional guests at reasonable hours, as long as the guests follow the household's and the landlord's rules. Again, get all that in writing.

Do you have compatible lifestyles? Be sure to figure this out *in advance*
If one person is into S&M and 3 a.m. drug parties and you're so *not*, or your friend is uptight and a neat freak (they aren't necessarily the same thing) and you're a grouchy slob, you might want to rethink being roommates.

Decide *in advance*...

- Who pays how much, and for what? Maybe the person with the smaller bedroom pays a little less? Or the roomie with the dog pays a little more?
- You want to avoid getting stuck with someone else's unpaid share of the bills. If each person has at least one utility bill in their name, they're less likely to default since you could return the favour.
- Who does what, and when, for routine chores and maintenance of the place? Will you share the cooking and food costs?
- During what hours do you want quiet in the place? How much noise, in general, can you deal with?
- What about overnight guests? Parties? How thin are the walls?
- Do any of you have a medical condition you need to be aware of, such as a peanut allergy or diabetes?
- How will you discuss and resolve issues that might come up?
- Who can boot who out and when, if living together gets weird or uncomfortable? Discuss the legalities and your preferences.
- How good are your communication and negotiation skills? Theirs? Consider some areas of potential disagreements. How would you each want to resolve these?

The common theme through all this?

Know what you're getting into, and what your rights are.
Whether you're the renter, the roommate, or the landlord, figure out who's responsible for what and when. And do that *before* you sign anything. Ever.

> **Caution:**
> There are a lot of self-proclaimed chat-xperts out there who blah-blah a lot of inaccurate advice. The consequences are legal so you want legally valid advice. Go to the proper source for your info, i.e. the government sites and, if you can't afford a lawyer's fees, call the free community legal clinics or get advice from an inexpensive online legal advice center.

A typical situation? Two or more roommates and one lease.

Here are a couple of possible scenarios.

ONE
The landlord wants all of you to sign the lease. You are then all "jointly and severally" liable for the rent and for any damages. That means *each of you* is on the hook to cover the *full cost* of the place, not just your portion. If one of you can't or won't pay their share, and you can't make up the difference, you ALL face eviction. In other words, landlords don't want your problems to become their problems. Fair enough. They have their own bills to pay.

TWO
You, just you, sign the lease, and then sublet rooms to others IF your lease allows that. Negotiate this with your landlord *in advance* of signing the lease (notice a theme here). In many cases, landlords will not let you sublet if you personally are not living there. However, they often will give you permission to take in a roommate. As with all things, get that in writing. Have the roomie sign a *witnessed* Roommate Agreement stating that they too need to abide by all your landlord's rules, and be sure to get their first-and-last and possibly a security deposit. The downside of their not being on the lease? You are responsible to your landlord for their actions. The upside? You're more in control over who's in your space. If a roommate defaults on their share of the costs or they're consistently a major pain, you've got a little leverage. It's generally easier to get rid of a roommate than a fellow tenant. The time frames for tossing someone (or being tossed if you're that not-so-nice roommate) can be a matter of days, not months. (So play nice!)

> Roommate "partial subletting" in many jurisdictions does not fall under the Landlord and Tenant Act. Things can get messy. Check with a lawyer or your local community legal clinic before you sign a lease or an agreement with a roommate. Yes, I'm repeating myself.

Another example:

Suppose you live in Ontario, you own a place that has less than three units in it, *and you personally live there*. If a tenant is a major disruption—they or their guests are a danger, cause damage, are involved in illegal activities, are behaving in "a manner inconsistent with its use as a residential premises", or they have "substantially interfered with your reasonable enjoyment" of your home, etc.—you're legally entitled to serve them with a Notice of Eviction giving them ten days to get out. Not 90 days. Not 60 days. 10 days. (Tenants, play nice. Even if the landlord doesn't live in the building, if you're being an idiot they can still evict you with only a couple of weeks warning.)

What are the rules in your province or state? (In Ontario, see LTB.gov.on.ca)

Some useful sites for renters and landlords:

In the States: rentlaw.com

In Canada see: cmhc.ca/en/co/reho/index.cfm
cba.org (Canadian Bar Association's site which includes, as well, good info on Legal Aid in Canada)

For typical forms that are free or inexpensive:
findlegalforms.com
Lawdepot.ca
Sublet.com

When does being roommates become "living together"?

Throw sex into the mix and there you have it. But who's going to know? You are. "So what?" you say? Well, you're now on the road to Common Law. How long does that trip take? What are the implications that come with it? Keep reading.

Chapter 27

Living under the same roof . . . and more than friends?

Maybe you're roommates, and now you find you've got the hots for each other. Maybe you're "friends with benefits" who decide it's cheaper to share living expenses. Or you're in a loving relationship and can't stand living in separate places any more.

You're thinking about maybe living together?
Before you move in, there are things you must discuss, decide, and do. The implications of sharing a space when you're romantically and/or sexually involved are quite different than when you're platonic roommates.

You already live together?
Whoa. Have the following conversations now, before any more time slides by.

Discuss your intentions and expectations.

Make no assumptions here. Each of you must be open and honest about your intentions. Is this living arrangement playing house, for fun, for now? Is it intended simply to save on housing costs, for convenience, and for convenient sex? Or are you building towards a meaningful ongoing relationship which may or may not have long-term commitment or even marriage papers attached? Will you have each other's back? Or are you just each other's playthings? (Excuse me for being that blunt.) Do you and your mate have compatible views on this? If not...

What are your day to day expectations of each other? As roommates, as friends, as lovers? What are your habits? How do you each like to do things? Are your preferred lifestyles compatible? What will happen if such-and-such occurs...? Together brainstorm and explore some possible scenarios, and how you'd each choose to deal with them.

What obligations, financial and emotional, are you each willing to take on? Who pays for what? What about the roommate pragmatics we discussed in the previous chapter? What baggage are you each bringing to the relationship? These may not necessarily be easy conversations but being clear and honest—with yourself and with each other—will prevent a lot of hassles later. Just be gentle and tactful. And acknowledge if you don't really know what you want, yet.

Please don't mistakenly think that wanting to clarify these aspects is an issue of trust. You're protecting yourself. You're protecting each other. And you're protecting the relationship from life's not-so-fun surprises. By working through these, you'll come to better understand each other's wants and needs, and sooner rather than later.

You like each other. You have each other's best interests at heart. You can hopefully communicate easily. Perhaps you even love each other. But if either of you are reluctant to talk about these things, what on earth are you doing moving in together? Yes, you could "figure things out as you go along", but that too often becomes a crash-and-burn scenario. While relationships, of course, do evolve and people do adapt along the way, it's wiser to sort through your known expectations, preferences, and important differences now, than make lawyers rich later. Even if neither of you are "serious" about this relationship, the consequences of living under the same roof still can be.

When does living together become a Common Law "marriage"? What are the legal criteria?

That depends on where you live. There are different laws in different countries, states, provinces. Check online, and double-check with a lawyer, what the rules are for your area. And if you're planning on moving, know in advance what the rules are in the new jurisdiction. In some areas, you could find yourself already a Common Law couple. On the other hand, some countries don't recognize anything other than conventional Marriage as a legal union, ever.

Usually, not always, the defining criteria for Common Law are a combination of all of the following: (Again, you *must* check the legal criteria for where you live.)

You live together; you have the same address.
You live together for a certain length of time. This time frame will vary with where you live, as will the implications for "interruptions", i.e. various lengths of time apart while "living together".
You present yourself as a couple. You use the same last name, or refer to your mate as your spouse, husband, wife, or in some cases, partner.
You must intend to be married. This is not always a requirement.
You have a child together. Then it's usually instantly a Common Law "marriage".

Generally, two people who live together for a short period of time (say, under a year) have no financial claim on each other.

Unlike married couples, as Common Law you have NO automatic property rights. That may or may not be seen as an advantage. However, there are complicated and potentially nasty palimony (similar to alimony) support issues you both need to take into consideration. Unless you have a formalized Cohabitation Agreement drawn up in advance, don't assume that being common law rather than married simplifies your life. It certainly does not. (More on Cohabitation Agreements in a minute.)

If you become legally Common Law, you must go through regular divorce proceedings to undo the mess. It gets even messier if you later decide you want to marry or even just live with someone else. A lot of issues are in the legally grey not-easily-resolved area, and it can get really expensive to sort things out. Save yourselves a lot of hassle—do a Cohabitation Agreement! (See pages 243-245)

Get PROOF of your intended mate's legal status.

Divorced? Separated? Are there alimony or childcare commitments?
Are there "Baby-mommas" on the side? Other dependents? Other legal obligations? You need to know what you're getting into. If they squirm when you ask about these things, be afraid—be very afraid. Do not fall for the "you don't trust me" nonsense. If they truly are trustworthy, they won't hesitate to calm your very reasonable concerns. Both of you need to disclose your commitments and prove your 'marital status'. It's simply self-protective good sense. If they continue to be evasive or are stubbornly trying to avoid this, run! A few bandages for your heart now are better than a body bag for your emotional and financial future later.

Let me say it again. If one of you is still legally bound to someone else, you are in serious financial and emotional jeopardy. (Even a formalized Cohabitation Agreement between the two of you could be invalidated.) You may find that the not-yet-actually-an-ex is going to get it all. Let me give you an example. You're living with someone. You buy a house together, and put both your names on the deed. Your mate gets killed in an accident. Unless there are legal documents to the contrary, such as divorce papers or a formalized separation agreement, the previous spouse can come after a share of your mate's share of your house, your spouse's accounts and pensions, and part of any business your mate owns, or you own together. That "Ex" could even challenge the Will. Don't be a naïve fool—get proof of each other's legal status and clear up any legal baggage *now*. Otherwise, the legal wrangling and expense you're setting yourself up for could be horrific. Even if the previous relationship was Common Law, if there's a child involved, things will get messy.

Have your lawyer do a search to confirm your mate's marital status and any other legal obligations. Then the two of you need to draw up a Cohabitation Agreement, preferably before you move in together. You already live together? Get on this *now*!

> You're madly in love. Breaking up? It could never happen to you. Ya right. More than 60% of living-togethers split up within 10 years. Of first marriages, the roughly 30% that end, do so within 8 years. If you make it that far, chances are you're likely good for the long run. And there are numerous advantages, both emotional and financial, to being amongst the *more than* 50% of couples who make it. So, both of you, take good care of your relationship. Think of it as a beautiful plant—water it and give it sunlight. Take care of it, consistently and on an ongoing basis—don't let it wither!

Explore each other's money styles.

Evidently, one of the biggest reasons for break-ups is fighting about money.

- What are your spending habits like? Frugal or cheap? Sensible or rather daft?
- What debts are you each carrying? How much? What for? What are the plans to pay it off? How's that going? What's their comfort level with carrying debt? What's yours?
- What is their credit score and credit history like? What about yours?
- What insurances are you carrying? Which ones do you each still need to get?

- What are your banking habits like? How savvy are each of you about this?
- How open are you to improving those skills?
- How organized are their records? Yours?
- What are their long term plans? Yours?
- Do you have any major goals that you share, or that are truly incompatible?
- Who makes how much, and what do your work futures look like? What are your expectations of each other's contribution to living costs, now and later? For example, when you have kids? Do you both want kids?
- Who contributes what to the running costs of your living space? Is it going to be a certain dollar amount, or based on a certain percentage of each of your incomes? Do you each want to be responsible for different bills?

By now you may be wondering if you want to be bothered with "togetherness". If that's the case, you're likely not at the moment in the "thinking long term" group. Ask these questions anyway. If you're sharing body fluids, you ought to be able to share thoughts. Otherwise, put yourselves in the "for now" or "toys" category. (Sorry if that sounds harsh. But better harsh reminders than harsh consequences.)

> Healthy relationships are those where both can think "we" ***and*** "me".
> Talk through these issues. You'll both be better able to relax and enjoy each other, knowing that if something did for whatever reason go wrong, you'd at least be financially okay.

Separate though together

Whether you're married, common law, or living together—in addition to any joint accounts—you must, as well, have separate banking accounts and separate credit cards. Do not be talked out of that. The intention is not to hide things from each other, but to create peace of mind for both of you. The reasons for this?

- It's healthy to maintain that sense of individuality that comes with having your own money in your own account.
- When pissed off, people can clean out joint accounts and leave their mates hanging in the wind. If you're married, you have some legal recourse but, in the meantime, you still need to eat. If you're just living together and, surprisingly, even if you're legally common law, you have *none*.
- If a living-together or common-law partner dies, their separate accounts will be frozen. No one will have access until after probate and the Will are dealt with. Joint accounts pass to the surviving name(s) on the account. That's the simple version. The variations and details for the various jurisdictions are beyond the scope of this book. Explore the ins-and-outs of how to set up your accounts with your financial advisor and your lawyer, or at least your bank manager. Perhaps start by looking at the explanations at ritceyteam.com or about.com.

When you and your mate are discussing how you want to set up the accounts, think win-win. Again, reassure each other that this is not a trust issue. It's a purely practical consideration based on the good sense to know that life can throw curve balls. You're protecting the "We", not just each "Me".

Discuss property

- Who gets to keep your current place of residence if you split up? This applies whether you rent or own.
- How will property you owned before living together and that you accumulate while you're together be split up if you split up? I suggest you stipulate in your Cohabitation Agreement, that property that either of you already owns, be kept separate. If you buy a home together, make sure both names are on the deed not just the mortgage or, believe it or not, you'll end up responsible for half the mortgage without owning any of the property.

The format of the legal title to any property is a crucial decision.

Joint ownership with rights of survivorship -This designation means that if one person dies, the property automatically goes to the other without probate or inheritance fees. "Joint ownership with rights of survivorship" overrides a will. Both names, of course, must go on the deed not just on the mortgage.

Tenants in common - You each own a certain percentage. Spell this percentage out, in writing, before you buy. As "tenants in common", you can will your share to someone other than your mate, for example, to your kids. So can your mate. Set up a written agreement about when and under what circumstances the property would be sold to give the money to the respective heirs. (You could state in your will that your mate can live in the house as long as they want to or can, then the property is sold.) A will is crucial if you are tenants-in-common. You can still, now or later, pass along your share of the property to your mate if you want to. But as tenants-in-common, if you change your mind, you can change who gets your share by simply updating your will.

- If you own a business, either separately or together, discuss the many implications with your business lawyer.
- How will gifts and/or inheritances will be handled? Your parents can stipulate in their will, even if you're married, that your inheritance is not to be part of the "marital assets" but just *for you*. When you get these assets or money, they must be put into an account or portfolio that has *only your name on it. If it even for an instant passes through anything named jointly, it becomes "joint property" and half then belongs to your spouse*, if you're married. A live-in mate who's not yet Common Law has no claim on your money as long as it's in *your* account. Technically, a Common-Law spouse has no right to your property either, but spell out your intentions in writing, i.e. in a cohabitation agreement. Otherwise, the situation could get ugly.

The COHABITATION AGREEMENT

Okay, so you can't stand living apart any longer. Whether it's with long-term intentions or just for now, it is crucial that you set up a Cohabitation Agreement. And each of you needs to get independent legal advice. (For the agreement to be legally valid and binding, you each need different lawyers advising you.) Expensive? Yes and no. It might cost a couple of grand now, but it will save you many times that later if things go sour. Ya, I know, "How romantic".

A better way to look at it? A properly designed Cohab agreement, negotiated with both your best interests in mind, is a genuine gift to the relationship and to each other.

Since lawyers are paid by the hour, the more you can figure out in advance and the better prepared you are with questions, the less it'll cost you.

For an overview of some of the things you need to consider, visit:
In the States:
freeadvice.com or usattorneylegalservices.com/free-legal-advice.html
In Canada:
lawdepot.com, or publiclegalforms.com or
family.findlaw.com/living-together/sample-cohabitation-agreement.html or
docstoc.com/search/cohabitation-agreements-forms-free
(These websites are starting points only.)

Again, the legal requirements for and obligations of Common Law vary from country to country, province to province, state to state, so check the details for your jurisdiction.

The information provided in this book is *not* meant to replace proper legal advice. That's a MUST. The consequences are too profound and far-reaching to get lazy or sloppy. And do not sign ANYTHING, EVER, without reading it in full, AND having it vetted by a lawyer.

A few more strong suggestions:

- Stipulate that you are not responsible for each other's current, future, or past debts, bills, or expenses. (You can still help, if you want to, but it's best to avoid being legally obligated to do that.)
- Put in a clause that states that mediation will be used to resolve disputes and that if that fails, the dispute will go to binding arbitration. This saves you much unnecessary future expense and emotional hassle.
- Spell out whether there will be "support after death". Will there be an arrangement for pension survivor-benefits?
- Will there be palimony, the Cohab version of alimony? Watch out for this one. Time slips by, and you're now Common Law. You've finally clued in that you're living with someone who, in reality, has become a freeloader. If you have a "waiver of palimony" in the agreement, you can escape. If you don't, you'll get caught in the implied-contract stuff because you've been kind enough to help out or even support the *Bleep*. You could find yourself paying palimony to said *Bleep* for life. Yikes. It happens. And to smart people who should have been smarter.
- Carefully document your contribution to any assets, especially the large ones. To have claim on anything, you must be able to prove what you paid for or contributed to. That could be a condo or a car, or something considerably less expensive, like a sofa or Wii. You could choose to each buy certain things on your own separate cards or accounts. If you want to split the cost of something, say a big screen, you could put half on your card and half on your mate's. Don't want to bother tracking the small stuff? Your call. But don't whine if someday you wish you had.

Avoiding doing an Agreement will *not* simplify your life.

As time slides by, you'll get caught in the stickiness of Common Law implications, such as palimony. And without a Cohabitation Agreement, some bureaucrat or judge, not you, is going to dictate what happens to you and yours. In the meantime, you're engulfed in a financial and emotional mess. It's so much simpler to do an Agreement up front. Otherwise, the court will look for those implied-contracts in the patterns of how you've lived together—who did what, who paid what, and so on. And they'll base their judgments on those. And that certainly may not be to your advantage.

What's the difference between Common Law and Marriage?

In general, as a Married couple, you're both better protected: the laws are much clearer about each person's obligations and responsibilities. Yes, divorce can be nasty. So some people think "just living together" or even Common Law is simpler. True? The answer to that? Yes, no, and maybe.

- YES. If you live together for a very short time, and never refer to each other as a spouse, and sign legal papers that you never intend to be married, you may find it's fairly easy to separate. Just watch that time thing—double and triple check the prerequisites for Common Law for your Jurisdiction, especially if you're planning to move. Even with all that, it doesn't mean your soon-to-be-ex won't get vindictive and do their best to make your life miserable. On the other hand, you may be so glad to be rid of each other that you both choose to simplify the exiting strategies. Or not.
- NO. Some assume that Common Law means that you have an automatic right to support or property as you would with Marriage. The usual victims of this all too common self-inflicted assumption? Women. Smarten up!
- NO. If you get caught up in a Common Law dispute such as palimony, it's actually messier than a divorce because the laws are less clear. You can expect the legal bills to be *much higher* than the cost of a Cohabitation Agreement!
- MAYBE. If you have a good and fair Cohabitation Agreement, YES, splitting up is pretty simple. If there's no Co-hab Agreement, NO, it certainly is not. The aftermath will likely end up in the hands of lawyers and you could end up in court. The MAYBE? At that point, you have no control over what happens. Who knows how things might turn out?

Do I need to say it again? Do a Cohabitation Agreement up front!

Prenuptial Agreements?

These are the marriage version of Cohabitation Agreements. You spell out what happens if such-and-such occurs. You can not, however, even in a prenuptial agreement negate or ignore the marriage laws in your jurisdiction. Discuss the details with a family law lawyer *before* you get married.

For scenarios to consider, prenuptialagreements.org is a reasonable place to start.

Your wish-list and deal-breakers...

Do you want a platonic roommate? A for-now lover? A long-term Love?
What is your upside wish-list for the kind of relationship you do want?
What can you do to improve the chances of that being the way things turn out?
What questions would you ask? How would you approach that discussion? (I highly recommend the book *Difficult Conversations*. Learning to resolve differing points of view to get to win-win is pure gold.)

What are your absolute deal-breakers with each of the above kinds of relationships? While you don't want to "have one foot out the door", how could you, if you had to, extricate yourself with the least problems for all involved? (You may not expect that your place will burn down, but it's a good idea to know where the exits are and to carry fire insurance.)

Enough of the dark side!

By addressing these practicalities in advance you protect yourself, each other, and your relationship by minimizing potential misunderstandings and difficulties.

You'll be able to truly relax and enjoy your evolving life together!

You'll better understand what makes your mate tick and know more about what to expect of each other. Let's be realistic, you know that "happily ever after" doesn't mean happy every hour of every day. When, at times, you get a little unnerved because the day's not going as smoothly as you hoped, you'll both have the courage to persevere and solve. Even if your approaches to "the issue" are a little different, you know you're on the same page. If at some point you should, sadly, choose to split up, you'd be more readily able to patch your wounds, heal, and get on with your lives.

So get real with each other. Get smarter. Do the doing.

Then go have fun exploring your new life together!

Chapter 28

Protecting Your Identity

Each year well over 10 million Americans and Canadians become the victims of identity theft. The total financial cost to these individuals? Well over $15 Billion. The emotional costs? Also huge. Paranoia is not only reasonable when it comes to protecting your identity, it's a must. E-crooks and identity thieves have gotten too good at what they do. The following cautions are a good start on self-protection:

- NEVER give anyone who phones you any of your ID—not birth dates, not your SIN or SSN number, passport number, etc. *Never ever.* And don't carry these pieces of ID around with you. Leave them safely at home, preferably in that lockable fireproof "Important Papers" box you've set up.
- No bank, financial institution, or government agency ever contacts you, online or by phone, to ask for confirmation of any numbers or other personal info. If you get a call like that, take their number down. (If there's no number, you know for sure it's a scam.) Then go to the official website, the phone book or directory assistance, and immediately call the organization that supposedly contacted you to confirm "the reason" they called. If it's supposedly a charity calling, do the same thing. If you do want to contribute, call the phone number you know is for-real. A real charity won't be offended by your being careful.
- NEVER give anyone your pin numbers. And cover your hand whenever you punch them in.
- NEVER use predictable answers for the questions used to identify you online or over the phone—never use your mother's maiden name, the kid's birthday, and so on. Anybody can find those out. Think up something only you would know.
- Online, watch out for spelling look-a-likes especially designed to trip you up. Type carefully. And avoid using hyperlinks. Report phishing:
  In USA: antiphishing.com, or ic3.gov
  In Canada: antiphishing.org
- People worry about being hacked, yet more identities are stolen as a result of losing a wallet or by putting paperwork out in the garbage. Buy and use a shredder for credit card offers, outdated bills, old tax returns or anything else remotely related to your ID. Scammers can go through your garbage, pull out bits of credible information, and begin building a profile on you.
- Identity theft can cost you your home. Crooks, using the profile they've built on you, can take out a mortgage in your name and run with the money, or sell your home out from under you. Incredible but true. "Title Insurance" has been invented so that buyers know that what they're buying is actually the seller's to sell. To protect owners? The legal system is in the process of setting up better safeguards. Arrange with your bank and mortgage provider that *face to face contact* with someone there who knows you is a must for all major transactions.
- Banks and credit unions are very rarely hacked and, if their system screws up, they guarantee they'll fix the problem at their expense. If the place you keep your money can't promise you this *in writing* (read your account descriptions), switch to one that's more reliable!

- Most people know to report the loss of a card immediately to the card company. *Immediately* needs to be measured in minutes or hours, not days. What most don't realize is that they should also notify the credit reporting agencies at the same time: Equifax and Transunion and, in the States, Experian as well. See page 163 for their contact information.

> As more and more digital databases are linked, a small error in one can contaminate numerous others. You've got to catch these errors, and quickly.

- Check your credit reports and credit rating at least once a year to be sure they're correct. Once a year, it's free, if you mail it in. If you do it online, or more frequently, there's a small fee.
- Check your bank statements every month. Innocent errors do occur. You usually have 60 days to catch and correct these.
- Credit cards offer better identity protection for online purchases than debit cards. Virtual accounts such as Paypal are good since you don't have to give your card number to a vendor. (Most vendors are honest and legit, but even big-box stores occasionally get hacked.)
- Keep your anti-everything software upgraded and current. And shut off your computer when you're not using it.
- There are now "scare-ware" programs that advertise that they'll clean up your computer. Be wary of these. They may be cleaning *out* your computer, or busy feeding it nasties. Get your programs from well respected companies.
- Lock down, as much as possible, all the privacy settings on whatever social media you use. Yes, these sites have a lot to offer but, unfortunately, they also offer a wider venue to the perverts and crooks out there. (I was once at a workshop for educators, run by the RCMP, on how to help young people protect themselves online. As an example, the officer randomly pulled up a Facebook page of an 18 year old. After a little poking around, and using no tactics available only to police, he accessed a link from this particular page which she was using to apply for a university grant, to her other page. She happened to be a freelance part-time hooker. Oops. Then he sent her an email suggesting she be more careful, gave his badge number and the official number for the RCMP and told her to call them, not him, to get advice on protecting her privacy on the web, and herself. I'm sure that email didn't make her day. It may, however, have saved her a lot of grief in the long run—perhaps even her life.)
- Assume that any electronic communication is a postcard viewable to all. For example, while it's not necessarily legal, companies can and will run a deep-search on you if they want to hire, promote, or potentially fire you.
- A few companies now have the audacity to ask for your social media passwords on job applications. So much for privacy. Do they want to know the colour of your underwear too?

Protecting your Privacy

What is defined, legally, as "publicly available"? Just how do we define "Privacy"?

- Remember that the web *never* forgets, and realistically nothing is truly private anymore. Online, nothing we "delete" is ever truly deleted. It's still out there in server-land. It makes it hard for people to overcome past mistakes when they're dragging around cyberspace baggage.

- Identities and reputations take time to build, yet they can be shattered by BS—that has no factual basis—going viral. Unfounded gossip becomes cyberbullying. Maybe you haven't locked down your social media site adequately, or someone you know innocently links you to someone you don't who has an axe to grind. Or the site changes its privacy protocols without warning or explanation.

- The patterns of our online behavior are being tracked. By the social media people who want to "meet our needs" and by marketers who want to know what sites, what products are popular in your postal code. Who-we-are and what-we-do is being sold to the highest bidder.

- RFID tags—Yo, Big Brother, welcome to my life. Not. The original intention was for convenience and efficiency in inventory tracking. Now these things are everywhere: in clothing and in packaging, in EZ passes, in passports, in your work ID tags, even in car key fobs. They're also the chips in your credit cards. RFIDs were and are designed to be read by scanners, at a distance. Useful, yes. But also rather scary. *There are minimal to non-existent legal safeguards on how this personal or collective information is being used by data miners.* Yikes. And these days a crook can walk by your wallet with a scanner and capture both your ID and your banking information. (Some companies now sell scan-proof wallets.)

It's not just purchasing patterns that can be tracked. It's also where we are when. Which is fine, I guess—*if* it's the "good guys" watching. What about E-crooks? Organized crime? Spy guys? Big brother? And how we are viewed—and judged—is less and less as who we really are, but as a stereotyped facsimile. Even our access to credit may be impacted by such "profiling" now. (I suggest you read the articles in "Life Under Digital Dominance" by Lori Andrews and Somini Sengupta in the New York Times from Sunday, Feb. 5, 2012.)

What do you want to keep private? Your thoughts, your habits? Your sex life? Your genetics? Your medical history? The ideas you may want to patent or copyright? Are there things you don't care about keeping private? What do we want *others* to *not* be able to keep private? Does it make for a better world if we can assume we're *all* open and honest, in *all* things? Is that a "safe" assumption? Who can we, should we, trust?

What are we, as individuals and as a society, willing to put up with? (Yeah, I know, I'm asking too many questions again.) *Who are we willing to give access to what?* As groups? As individuals? How do we control that? In the name of "protecting our country", are we flushing our rights? Canada and many countries in Europe have much better safeguards on personal privacy than does the USA. Land of the Free, continue to protect your *individual* freedoms too!

A little paranoia makes us appropriately careful. When we're pre-emptive, when we watch our own back—and each other's—we enhance our ability to be, not apathetic cynics, but *realistic optimists.* So get out there and push for tighter laws—not on us "average" individuals who make up the many—but on those who want to use us.

For more information see:

In Canada: Priv.gc.ca/fs-fi/02_05_d_10_e.cfm
Rcmp-grc.gc.ca/scams-fraudes/id-theft-vol-eng.htm
And phonebusters.com which is part of CAFC, the scam busting branch of the RCMP.
Cmcweb.ca/eic/site/cmc-cmc.nsf/eng/fe00084.html

In the USA: ftc.gov/bcp/edu/microsites/idtheft
justice.gov/criminal/fraud/websites/idtheft.html

Recommended Reading
Identity Theft Toolkit: How To Recover From and Avoid Identity Theft, John Lenardon
The Net Delusion: The Dark Side of Internet Freedom, Evgeny Morozov

There's lots of useful self-protection information out there.
People just need to get much smarter about actually using that advice.

A Quality Life

Chapter 29

Some Thoughts on Happiness . . .

Finding, creating, and practicing happiness

Just how do you find happiness? Where do you look? Does it just happen—*Kazam!*—like some bolt of lightning? Is it given to you by someone else? Do you have to earn it, as you do respect? Can you grow it like flowers?

Different languages each use a variety of words to describe the many variations of "happiness". And different cultures and different individuals have their own diverse views on what "makes them happy". (In the USA, for example, self-expression and personal success are important components. In Japan, meeting your social responsibilities and self-discipline are high on the list.) It seems that happiness, like love, is hard to define. And, like love, how do you know when you "have it"? You just do.

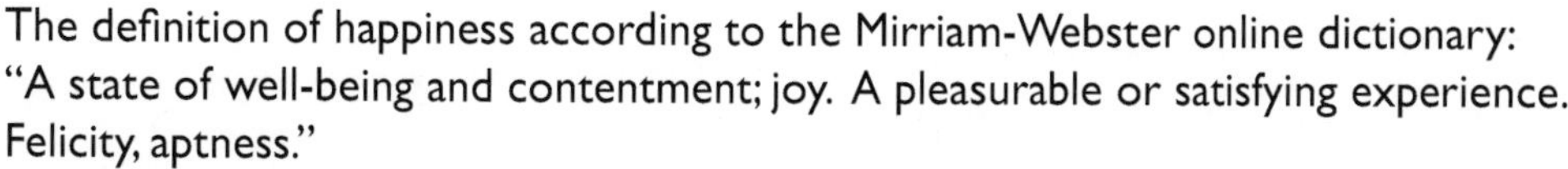

The definition of happiness according to the Mirriam-Webster online dictionary: "A state of well-being and contentment; joy. A pleasurable or satisfying experience. Felicity, aptness."

If you search the research, you'll find many ways that those in-the-know try to explain what happiness is and what it means. There's "positive affect", meaning how are you feeling in the moment; there's "subjective well-being"; and there's "life satisfaction" with its longer time frame. So I asked a well-read, well-written, well-respected philosophy professor friend for his definition. (I expected to hear a prof-like answer.) His reply? "Happiness is a warm puppy. And expenditures of at least a dollar less than you make." I'll add that happiness includes having friends that make you laugh.

The many forms and expressions of Happiness

Here are a few ...

Side-splitting laughter	A quiet chuckle, humor, a smile
Delight, playfulness	A sense of satisfaction, pride
Feeling fortunate	Contentment
Optimism, hope	Interest, enthusiasm, passion
Feeling peaceful, even serene	Bliss, elation
Wonderment, awe	Gratitude

Choose any three of these and think of a time when you experienced that feeling.

Less commonly recognized is the other component of the definition of happiness: "aptness". Something that is "fitting, suitable, appropriate". Don't ignore that one. (There's a Ph.D. thesis for someone, if it hasn't already been done. Compare the various words for happiness in many different languages. The Inuit have almost 30 words for "snow". I wonder how many nuances there are for "happiness" in other languages?)

Finding and recognizing happiness

Personally, I've never liked the "glass half full" analogy, especially when it comes to happiness. If you actually drink from that glass, you're going to get to the bottom at some point. Rather than a glass half-anything, think of happiness as being more like the magic porridge pot in that kid's fairy tale. (It could refill itself whenever asked to do so.) Think of it this way: each morning your potential for a pot full of happiness has renewed itself. Have some. You're entitled to be happy. In fact, the Dalai Lama in *The Art of Happiness* says "the very purpose of our life is to seek happiness". [1]

How much control do we have over our happiness? None, some? Total? (We wish.) Some silly people think it's anyone else's job but their own to "make them happy". So much for free will and freedom. Why voluntarily toss yours?

Perspective is crucial. Think of it this way. Pretend you're walking through life, looking through your camera lens. What you aim it at, focus on, is what you'll get as your picture of life. If you want a better or more interesting view, watch where you point that lens. And adjust your settings appropriately. Experience the moment *and* take the snapshots you want to keep in mind—wide angle and macro—both for now and in retrospect.

Perhaps happiness, like luck, can be thought of as making the most of being in the right place at the right time. Let's go one further. Make a point of making the most of —and making better—whatever situation, place and time you're in. Don't think of it as simply pleasure for now—indulge in creating meaningful experiences for yourself and others, and help do some good in the world. There's more kick to making-a-difference than there is in wanton hedonism.

Creating and Growing Happiness

Fed up with psychology's obsession with the downside, Martin Seligman along with Chris Peterson created an "un-DSM"[2], a diagnostic manual for character strengths, talents, and healthy possibilities, and designed ways to empirically study the for-real upside of life. (The *DSM* is psychiatry's diagnostic manual for unhealthy minds.) As with Maslow who kicked off the study of healthy minds, they took the conversation in a healthier direction.

In *Authentic Happiness,* Seligman says that "Optimistic people tend to interpret troubles as transient, controllable, and specific to one situation. Pessimistic people in contrast, believe that their troubles last forever, undermine everything they do and are uncontrollable." He suggests we need to (and can) change the way we explain and interpret the events that occur in our lives. By doing so, we can shift ourselves into a more adaptive and beneficial way of being, while still acknowledging the facts and realities of the experience. [3]

Jean Chatzky, in *The Difference*, says that "happiness and optimism are not synonymous. Happiness is what you're feeling today about how things are going in the short term...your [current] sense of well-being. Optimism is a way of looking at the future... Happiness is about today. Optimism is about tomorrow." [4]

Speaking of tomorrows—does age impact happiness? Yes. But contrary to what most young people think, older adults are happier. (No, cynic, that is not due to being either daft or senile.) A recent survey was done with young people, average age of thirty-one, and older people, average age sixty-eight. The results? "The surprising truth... is that people get happier as they get older, even though they do not expect it in advance... Learning from your accumulated experience as you age, you screen out the things that used to upset you, focusing instead on whatever is most likely to give you pleasure. As time goes by, you become a better emotional manager. Your good moods last longer, you recover from your bad moods faster." And you become better at letting go of past disappointments. You become more focused on "investing in experiences and relationships that add meaning and fulfillment to your life".[5] Maybe it's partly because once you come to realize you won't be here forever, you more consciously savour each day. Yet Helen Fisher, an anthropologist at Rutgers University, suggests it's more than that. It may have been an important evolutionary advantage to have elders with a calm and more optimistic view in order to settle disputes within our tribes.[6]

"Happy people see the woods, while sad people tend to focus on the trees, it seems."[7] Psychologists Karen Gasper and Jerry Clore showed people a picture then asked them to draw it from memory. The test results showed that "happy people concentrated on the general effect, while sad people went for the detail", and sad people's drawings also looked less like the original.[8] I suggest you may want to not fixate simply on details. Look at the big picture. Write, sculpt, paint your life story with broad stokes, both in design and in retrospect.

Abraham Lincoln said, "Most people are about as happy as they make up their minds to be". Still true apparently. You can choose to be happier with or without that lottery win. Besides, the chances of winning are pathetically small. The chances of a better attitude boosting your happiness? Huge. So, is happiness a choice? Yes.

Research shows that the absence of happiness is very rarely faulty brain chemistry. And recent studies show that less of our day to day happiness is impacted by a genetic "set-point" than was initially thought.[9] It's more a potential range that's quite malleable. So choose your priorities carefully. A twenty-five year long study of 60,000 people found that if you placed career and material success much above altruism and family, your happiness would slide into a long-lasting decline.[10]

> Altruism and self-sacrifice are not synonymous, nor are they necessarily even compatible. Not taking adequate care of yourself (for example, your health) usually translates into being less able to care for anyone or anything else.

Why choose to be happy?

Why would you not? A caution for the misguided—choosing to be cruel may take you to hell, but choosing to wallow in the "wretched martyr" role is no guarantee of getting to heaven or anywhere else you might want to go. And, cynics, choosing to be happy is not naïve, it's productive.

A good mood apparently improves our creativity and problem solving ability.[11] And it boosts our verbal reasoning skills.[12] While fear may help us intensely focus our attention to solve short-term problems, positive states of mind when in non life-threatening situations improve our thinking, and hence allow us to build up our resources for the long term.

"Positive feelings change the way our brains work and expand the boundaries of experience, allowing us to take in more information and see the big picture" And "as positive emotions compound, people actually change for the better."[13]

According to Ed Diener and Robert Biswas-Diener, eminent researchers of "subjective well-being", happier people are much more likely to have more friends and better marriages. (I really admire their work, but my sarcastic side couldn't resist "Gee, Ya think?" I wondered if this is one of those "chicken or the egg" things. Nicer life => happier, or happier => a nicer life?) Evidently, the people in their studies were *choosing* to be happier, in spite of life circumstances that might make others really quite uncomfortable.[14]

Research shows that there are, as well, less obvious benefits of choosing to be happier. Not only will being more light-hearted improve our interactions with others, we'll be more resilient and cope better with difficult circumstances, have higher self-esteem and a stronger immune system, maybe live longer and, surprise, earn more money. Chatzky too reports on the effects of happiness on wealth. Happy people, whether they're Malaysian farmers or typical North Americans, "tend to be more productive, more creative, more dependable, and produce higher quality work"... Although wealth cannot buy you happiness, happiness does seem to be able to 'buy' you money".[15]

Cornell University Professor Alice Isen says that "many people believe that happy feelings make you impulsive. [That] they make you throw caution to the wind. In fact, they do just the opposite. The happy feelings facilitate self-control, the consideration of how well you'll do long term, not jumping to conclusions. In this way, happiness is an astonishing resource."[16]

Humor, with or without obvious laughter, decreases not only emotional but physical pain, even that of post-surgical orthopedic patients. The latter was first noticed in the late 1920's and the effects of humor on pain and healing have since been studied in more depth.[17] Mind you, if you've just had abdominal surgery, you're likely better off keeping it to the quiet smile rather than the rollicking fall-off-the-bed-laughing version. Save joining the Laughter-Yoga club until after you're home and healed.

What does *not* contribute to Happiness?

More and more money. That may come as a surprise to many. Yes, you need to be able to take care of your basic needs such as food and shelter. Yet there are seriously diminishing returns on the ability of more money to improve your day-to-day happiness. That's not surprising—an extra thousand dollars matters less if you're making a six figure income than if you're barely putting food on the table. Studies by a Nobel prize-winning economist, Daniel Kahneman, show that, yes, day-to-day emotional well-being (as researched in the UK) seems to rise up to about $75,000 annual income. Yet the mega-rich are not mega-happy. Subjective "life evaluation" continues to rise to about $115,000 (which is admittedly high in comparison to most people's income). Above that neither happiness nor life satisfaction increase noticeably.[18]

A sensitivity to what we may perceive as "scarcity" is linked to survival fears. That's been burned into our primitive caveman brain over millions of years. The result? Our brains are, unfortunately, hard-wired to slide into deprivation-fear at the slightest and sometimes silliest provocation. These days what we perceive as "deprivation" has really run amuck. "Keep up with the Jones" or we won't survive? Ya right. We let envy, social comparison, and status-seeking ruin our day and our lives.[19] On that one, we really are still walking around on our knuckles.

The social psychologists and others say that we are caught up in how our incomes (and hence our self-perceived "status") compare to those around us. I think it's that we compare ourselves, not so much to those around us, but to what we are being fed (i.e. having shoved down our throats by unscrupulous marketers) about where they want us to think others are at. Create a market for false or ephemeral pleasures by creating ego-insecurity. (No, your teeth do not need to glow in the dark.) We should be paying more attention to genuine financial insecurities and pursuing genuine needs and interests, rather than selling out our well-being to service our mounting debt loads and to pad the bottom lines of big business.

Happiness is now treated as a commodity to be bought and sold. It's stirred into face goops, driven as ego-on-wheels, designer-ed into mega-square-footage. But if your chosen path to happiness is more stuff, it ain't gonna work, no matter how much you spend. Tim Kasser, author of *The High Price of Materialism,* found that young adults who focus on fame and/or riches tend to become more depressed and less physically healthy. He believes too that the more insecure people are, the more materialistic they become.[20]

Let's restate that: insecurity may drive you to being materialistic, but being materialistic won't solve your insecurities. Why? More stuff won't fill the holes left by unfulfilled *genuine* needs. Maybe that's why so many of the rich-and-famous are rich-and-miserable. Don't get so hung up on "The Good Life" that you neglect to create a genuinely good, in the sense of a happy, meaningful, and fulfilled life.

Impediments to Happiness

As long as we don't have faulty brain chemistry (which is relatively uncommon and obviously needs medical help), what can we do to welcome and build more happiness into our lives? Mind you, we're talking about happiness hopefully tempered with conscience and good sense, not crazed hedonism or self-destructive pursuits. (Retail therapy, whether as new clothes or a yacht, bites back as debt-stress later, unless you just won that lottery. And submerging into the slimy quicksand world of substance abuse to hide from or to jolt your current realities is a counter-productive choice.)

Want a little for-sure pleasure now? Or more pleasure, slightly later? What if those pleasures are slightly less predictable? We have a strong tendency to opt for the here-and-now. (It's that caveman survival thing again.) Even the near certainty of much greater gains in the future does not outweigh what we see as a possible loss in the present. Watch that. Don't let the Immediate derail the Important. (Refer back to the decisions chapters if you want to.)

Another thing that can derail us? The mindset of the people we surround ourselves with. We all need companionship. And we need to be supportive of each other through hard times. However, if your friends are consistently pessimistic, lazy, self-pitying, and love to blame rather than solve, you might want to trade them in for some new ones. Connection definitely boosts happiness. But wearing yourself out trying to save others from themselves, when they can't be bothered, does not.

Our interactions with a lifemate, if we have one, have a significant impact. No surprise there. What stage are We at? The intoxicating high-heat but short-burn "passionate love" phase? Or evolving into the deeper strong "companionate love" which is caring and commitment spiced with passion? The shift, which hormone research shows seems to start happening midway through the first year[21], is where mistakes can easily be made. You marry the hottie and shortly wish you hadn't, for any number of reasons. Or you assume that because the dopamine rush of the initial burn is "fading", i.e. calming down, you write off unnecessarily what would have been a wonderful long-term relationship. The health and happiness benefits of those are remarkable. That does not mean, however, that you must have a lifemate to be happy or healthy. What you do need is "close and long lasting attachments to particular others".[22] Interestingly, researchers have found that the level of happiness of our same gender best friend has a more important effect on us than we might think.[23]

Some life changes that have negative consequences are self-imposed. Daniel Gilbert, in *Stumbling on Happiness*, cautions that if you're thinking about major changes, try out the new lifestyle before actually committing to it. (For example, if you're moving to another town or continent, don't buy, rent until you're sure you want to stay there.) His research shows that people tend to overestimate how happy something will make them in the future, and overestimate how long that feeling will last. Ouch. What is less often quoted from his work is that we also overestimate how badly we'll feel under certain circumstances.[24] I like that concept better. Me being an optimist. Most of the time.

There's sensible-optimism and daft-optimism—the kind of stubborn naïvety that can make you reckless and irresponsible. (After all, "Bad things won't happen to me.") There's sensible-pessimism and daft-pessimism—the unrelenting refusal to see and acknowledge the already real and the potential good in life. (That's perhaps an even more pathetic version of "It won't happen to me.") Avoid the "daft" versions. Sensible optimism gets you over the bumps and hurdles—it's a great antidote for lethargy and anxiety. And an occasional sensible dose of mild pessimism makes you appropriately cautious—you look ahead and design appropriate strategies and contingency plans. Being realistic involves both. How much of each you need, and when, is circumstance dependent. Neglecting either? That's definitely an impediment to happiness.

Disappointments and losses come in a range of sizes. Most of them we can repair or roll with, and get on with life. Unfortunately, there are likely to be times when we'll be humbled by what we can't control. There will be the occasional, hopefully infrequent, major kicks in the head that life throws our way, often through no fault of our own. Some of these are hideously painful and complicate life considerably. We must bolster our resiliency, get the appropriate help, and do our best to cope and heal. Ironically, that's when we most need to be able to find fragments of happiness in other parts of our life to keep us afloat until we can find solid ground again. If our lives have multiple dimensions, we're more likely to have multiple flotation devices. What small joys help keep you going on a bad day? What can the people in your life do to give you a hand up when life knocks you down?

Fear, which resides in the part of our primitive brain called the amygdala (sounds like a name for a sci-fi princess), evolved as a mechanism to keep us safe. Medical psychologist Dan Baker, co-author of the book *What Happy People Know,* says that fear, the biggest enemy of happiness, comes in two main forms: a fear of not *having* enough (in terms of evolutionary survival), or of not *being* enough. He outlines several tools to stop that protective-fear running amuck.

Evidently, appreciation is the best antidote, so take the time to notice and perhaps journal what's good in your life. And exercise your choice-making muscles to counteract a sense of powerlessness. Similarly, focusing on our strengths creates energy and drives real change, whereas thinking we need to fix our weaknesses before we're entitled to appreciate ourselves, just generates more fear. [25]

Baker also says "The stories we tell ourselves about our lives eventually become our lives." So be careful, and perhaps more kind, in how you write yourself into your own life script.

Perhaps try this: write out the phrase, "I was given..." (by Life) and complete it in as many ways as you can. (Add this list to your "Gratitudes" notes from Chapter 3.)

Resilience

But what if you're having a bad day? A bad few months? A bad decade? Pain, sadness, depression chewing at you... (Hey, wait a minute. Thought we were talking about happiness here!) Before we visit the dark side (just for a page and a half), you need to know that we're much more resilient than we give ourselves credit for. Research shows that while there is considerable variation in how we deal with a downer (e.g. a major loss, a trauma) we are remarkably, even surprisingly, resilient. Fear and sadness are temporary and are not illnesses. Six months post-trauma, only about 10% of people still have symptoms that significantly impede their functioning. The National Center For PTSD (post-traumatic stress syndrome) has found that many handle things well without intervention. They've found that, for the majority of cases, encouraging people's own coping abilities is more effective than ongoing medication or too much introspection.[26] What people do need is help with the *practical aspects* of what they need to do to get on with their lives. And, yes, having supportive friends and/or family does make a difference.

The value of sadness and discontent?

Terence Ketter, a psychiatrist at Stanford University, reminds us that "emotion is information" so you "don't want to stifle or blunt emotion... Discontent can drive change".[27] It would be great if we make that change for the better. According to Jessica Marshall, numbers of researchers now "fear that the increasing tendency to treat normal sadness as if it were a disease is playing fast and loose with a crucial part of our biology. Sadness, some argue, may serve an evolutionary purpose... It helps us learn from our mistakes...The risk of sadness may deter us from being too cavalier in relationships or with other things we value." In many cases, medicating sadness could "blunt the consequences of unfortunate situations and remove people's motivation to improve their lives", for example, to get out of bad relationships.[28]

The first antidepressant came on the market in the early 50's. Outpatient treatment for "depression" increased threefold between 1987 and 1998.[29] Did life really become three times as bad in that time? Or that bad for three times as many people? Or is there something else going on here? In 2000, the pharmaceutical industry made $7 Billion a year on antidepressants in the USA alone.

The medical definitions of what is "normal sadness" and what is "depression" are pretty vague. In 2007, a study showed that about 25% of people who would have been diagnosed as being "clinically depressed" were actually suffering from normal reactions to unfortunate and major life events such as job loss, divorce, or the death of a loved one. Sadness and/or anxiety are not the same as the incapacitating ongoing emotional flatline of "clinical depression". Depression, like the many shades of gray, is a continuum. And it is, according to numbers of researchers and clinicians, dramatically overdiagnosed. Luckily with rare exceptions depressions, like fevers, do not last forever.[30]

> Allow me a profoundly dark comment here: if you find yourself falling into a seemingly bottomless emotional pit, remember that suicide is a permanent "solution" to what is, in the vast majority of cases, a *temporary* though intense and perhaps very difficult problem. There is help. Get it. Fast.

Pain, whether physical or mental, is a warning. Rather than simply medicating the symptoms, we need to solve the cause. Yes, take some time to regroup. And maybe get some meds for the short term. However, while we need to take the time to examine a problem, relentless ruminating without doing something about the issue, backfires and may sustain the depression. Rather than hide from the problem, face it, dismantle it as best you can with whatever help and advice you need, and learn some coping skills for the long term. Yes, easier said than done, but well worth the effort.

Here's something we all might find surprising. Justin Feinstein, a neuroscientist at the University of Iowa, has found that amnesiacs and patients with Alzheimer's continue to feel distress even though they don't remember the event that triggered it.
So be nice! The ability to store and reflect on—process, not obsess about—emotional events seems to be able to help diffuse the negative emotions. With those suffering from post-traumatic stress disorder for example, it is possible that using drugs or other therapy to block painful memories may actually hamper their recovery.[31]

What does research show as tops for shortening depression? Getting re-engaged in our social life, even if it's a tentative toe-in-the-water for now, seems to much outdo the typical approaches. If you've been withdrawing from life, what might you start doing to gently ease your way back?

> All the emotions are valid in their own context. Life's a colourful and textured sculpture contoured by light and shadow, not a flat monotone wall. After all, no one said you had to always be happy to be happy. But you can make a point of being happier than you may be right now...

Don't get fixated on what you've lost. Be open to unexpected treasures that might be of equal or greater joy.

Let me give you an example from my own life. Towards the end of my interning year as a chiropractor, I seriously damaged my wrist by falling on ice. Needless to say, I had to adapt my clinical techniques. Doubly scary because I had two kids to support, and now on a wimpy wrist. (We had gone through a divorce a couple of years before.)

It takes about two months for the "license to practice" to come through, so I looked for work as a supply teacher. (I had a B.Ed. before applying to Chiropractic, but teaching jobs back then, like now, were painfully scarce. Chiropractic had become, at that point, Plan B.) I took what's called an "LTO" for the interim. Then the woman I was replacing decided not to return to teaching. The school liked my teaching style and offered me the position. OMG. If only that job had materialized before I started the four years of brain-strain and money-drain I'd just finished. (Sometimes, it seems, the "gods" do like to laugh at us.) I took it as a half-time position to give my wrist time to heal and to pay our rent while I built my practice.

Fast forward. Though my wrist eventually healed and my practice was growing, after a number of years I realized I loved teaching more. (Yes, it was a tough decision to let go of my practice.) I switched to full time teaching—senior sciences in an "alternative" high school. And now? Here I am writing a book to hopefully help young people enjoy and better weather the world. Lemons to lemonade. Unexpected joys.

The Practice of Happiness

Think of happiness as a *skill* you can practice, a *muscle* you can strengthen, a *habit* you need to and can develop. It's also a gift you can give yourself and others. Happiness is contagious—it's one of the few things you want to infect others with. "Sick", as the kids say. So catch it. And spread it around.

Where do most of the most-satisfied people live? In countries where there are not only adequate resources for such basic needs as food and water, but also the opportunities for education and health care. A recent Gallup poll shows that the happiest countries seem to be Denmark and the other Scandinavian countries, along with Canada, Australia, and Venezuela. Other sources vary somewhat, depending on their criteria for "happy and satisfied", but Denmark is tops in most and Canada and Switzerland repeatedly make it into the top ten. The USA, sadly, now rarely makes it to the top 20. (Mind you, they're assessing almost 180 countries.) Countries consistently in the top 20 in many indexes? Costa Rica (which spends its money on health care and education rather than a military), Bhutan, Antigua, and Barbuda.

The least satisfied? Not surprisingly, the poorest nations suffering serious environmental issues, natural disasters or food scarcity, and those engulfed in war. Haiti, Sierra Leone, Georgia, and Angola come to mind.

Let's pick up on the criteria-for-happiness idea. Remember those memes we talked about in the decisions chapter? Social construct and expectations will impact how pleased we are with ourselves. Pride, self-respect, self-esteem, whatever you may choose to call it, is a strong component of how we define our criteria for happiness. And how we achieve that self-respect may vary between cultures. For example, Pacific Rim Asians are less concerned with personal happiness than with how their families view their activities. Unfortunately, research shows that they also have a tendency to focus on what's gone wrong rather than right. Hispanics, on the other hand, seem to be happier because they, as a culture, have strong social bonds and tend to look at the "glass half full".

Apparently the Danes are particularly well off in "life satisfaction". They have one of the lowest disparities between the incomes of the rich and poor, and though they pay relatively high taxes, they have amazing free healthcare and education systems, 37-hour work weeks with lots of paid vacation time, extended parental leaves for both parents, and great family services. Not only are the Danes world leaders in actually implementing their cutting edge environmental innovations, the vast majority of the population trust their fellow citizens *and* their government.[32] Other countries should take some lessons from them.

Does increased GDP translate into increased happiness? No. Roberto Foa at Harvard University says that the Chinese people are becoming less happy in spite of their economic boom—they're falling victim to the stuff-as-status and ladder-climbing mentality. People in Columbia and Nigeria are happier than you might think, given their lower GDPs. Both cultures are very family focused. Maybe you'd rather live in Bhutan. The government there has declared itself more concerned with gross-national-*happiness* than gross-national-*product*. They too should talk to a few other governments.

Happiness causes you to be more likely to smile. No surprise there. However, and this may be a surprise, by smiling you can actually cause yourself to be happier. This has been medically documented. You may feel like an idiot smiling "for no reason" (be sure to crinkle your eyes too, as that's what's not there in a fake smile, and your brain will know it), but there's a neural feedback loop between those face muscles and your brain that genuinely does make you feel happier! Unfortunately, the same is true for frowns. So don't let that grinch-grimace get stuck on your face. Maybe try singing or whistling while you go about your day?

Here's another interesting finding. Not only do our memories affect our moods, our moods also affect our memories. Wiseman points out that "when we look back on our lives in a happy mood, we tend to remember life events that worked out well." The opposite is also true. Feeling sad or unlucky draws up memories that are likely to take us down further. Acknowledge and deal with unfortunate events, but don't get stuck back there. Make a point of focusing on whatever is good in your life at the moment. (There's bound to be something.) Deliberately think about something, anything, that has pleased you. That will allow your moods and memories to cycle into each other in a way that boosts your ability to feel happier and luckier.[33]

What if life doesn't turn out exactly as you planned? So? There's more than one route to a good place. In fact, there's more than one "good place" and it might be just over the next horizon. Change is all part of the adventure—you co-create your life and you evolve with it. You learn to adapt, to be resilient, and with experience grow stronger and wiser. So don't hobble your potential for happiness by assuming that change, even unexpected change, is not for the better at least in the long run. Keep your compass, map, GPS handy. Adjust the sails. Enjoy the journey, both the scenic views and the occasional challenges. That storm that blew you off course may land you somewhere more wonderful than you could have imagined.

Expect happiness. But don't expect constant bliss. Ed Diener and Robert Biswas-Diener recommend that "people think of happiness in terms of mildly pleasant emotions" that are felt much of the time, "with intense positive emotions being felt occasionally." From their research they strongly believe it's possible for most people to be happy most of the time.[34] And Sonja Lyubomirsky and her colleagues at the University of California believe that "durable increases in happiness are indeed possible and within the average person's reach".[35] Sweet.

Yes, worry and discontent can motivate us towards our goals. And yes, we'll likely feel some mild stress en route. Yet our goals will pull us, like a magnet, towards a greater sense of "life-satisfaction" which is yet another form of happiness. What do *you* mean by "a satisfying life"? Interestingly, the happier we are the less we care about the "social comparison" which has a strong tendency to bring us down.[36]

It may seem that happiness in its many forms is a moving and blurry target. So don't make it a target. Don't make it yet another thing to chase. Don't add to your stress by thinking you need to *make* yourself happy. Instead choose to *let* yourself be happy. Cultivate a sense of humor, of optimism, of wonderment, curiosity, and gratitude. Let some happiness in. When you want fresh air, you simply open the windows to catch a little breeze—you don't need to create the air molecules or blow the winds around the planet.

Notice and appreciate what genuinely brings you joy. Maybe that's a walk in the sunshine, giving your car a bath, good sex (maybe in the car now that it's clean), qi-gong (that's a martial art, not a position), dancing around the kitchen, meditating, watching funny movies, or playing with the kids, if you have any. Then *do* what makes you, and others, happy—regularly, until it's a habit. (When trying to improve your skill in playing a musical instrument, you expect to have to practice. Why not use the same strategy to build a Happiness Habit?) Turn happiness into an ingrained skill you can count on.

I think we need a word for "happiness" that's a verb, not just a noun. Get on with happy-ing yourself, and others.

The brain chemistry?
Dopamine – the pleasure center's little gift.
Serotonin – the calming post-turkey-dinner buzz.
Oxytocin – the trust-inducing, "warm fuzzies", social bonding neurotransmitter.

The main brain structure involved with happiness?
The left prefrontal cortex, which can be trained and actually expanded with practice. So practice! And grow your happiness...

Practicing Happiness

"Smell the roses". Literally, if you can. Notice the beauty around you.
If you don't have a gorgeous mountain view, pay attention to that gutsy dandelion pushing through the asphalt at your feet. Appreciate its determination.

Today, pay attention to any of the many wonderful sensory inputs. Notice how the shadows play on the wall nearby, the scent of fresh bread at the local bakery, the touch of breezes, the cool of grass in shadow, the textures of leaves...
Notice everything that's red, or any other color you like.

Be physical. Get outside. Sunlight and movement boost your good-feelings body chemistry. Being active calms anxiety because it signals our primitive brains that we are able and capable and therefore more likely to survive. So go DO something!

Let yourself play. Try something new without any thought as to whether or not you'd be good at it. Don't hold back. Don't let Ego get in the way of having fun.

Indulge your curiosity. Try a new genre of music or movies or books. Check out a new food. Maybe visit a comedy club. What else comes to mind?

Boost your sense of wonder. Watch a sunset. Watch the moon rise. Savour the images and perspective that the Hubble telescope gifts to us. (See hubblesite.org or science.nasa.gov.) Listen to silence. Listen to the wind in the trees, the waves crashing on the cliffs. Listen to a sleeping baby's contented sigh, a toddler's laughter.

Meditate. Not necessarily the cross-legged "Omm" version. Just find a way to have some peaceful time to sit quietly, to Not-Think. Let thoughts that poke through just float away. Gently pay attention to only your own breathing for five to fifteen minutes.

Try speed. (No, not the drug.) Research at Princeton University has shown that thinking fast made participants feel more upbeat, creative, and energetic. It turned out that *fast and varied* thinking made people feel more excited, even elated.
Fast but repetitive thoughts tend to promote anxiety. As for slow thinking?
Slow repetitive thoughts drain one's energy and can easily promote feelings of dejection and depression. *Slow and varied* thinking leads to feeling calm and peaceful, similar to the effects of mindful meditation. These effects are independent of what people are actually thinking about. So mix it up a bit.
You want both slow and *varied*, and fast and *varied*. Repetitive thoughts? These can too easily take you down.[37]

Feeling a little bummed out? Or emotionally flat? IF you were feeling happier than you are right now, what might you do differently today? Try that out.

Our brains are hard-wired to get a deep satisfaction from the physical effort needed to produce something tangible and meaningful. So go do something, create something that involves more than pushing buttons or shuffling paper. "By denying our brains the rewards that come with anticipating and executing complex tasks with our hands ... we undercut our mental well-being."[38]

For the next few days, every few hours ask yourself, "how am I feeling right now?" Then ask yourself—and be honest—is it something external that's causing you to feel that way or something going on in your own head? What could you do to improve either?

Design a great endpoint. For example, if you're planning a holiday, save something particularly wonderful for the last day. The emotions associated with a memory seem to be considerably impacted by what happens near the end of that experience.[39]

One of the most potent contributors to happiness is a sense of community. Get outside your own skin. Volunteer.[40] How could you improve the well-being of someone else? In what way could you contribute to a good cause? As well as being good for your community, it's good for your self-respect. A sense of meaning and purpose, of personal effectiveness, of interconnectedness, all have a profound impact on your overall life satisfaction. And when we adopt the mindset of "we're all working together to solve this"—whatever "this" is—a lot gets accomplished. There is joy in both the doing and the result, and in the bonds built. Mutual respect and supportiveness build more happiness into the lives of all involved —whether that's between mates, within a family or a tribe of friends, or a group of diverse citizens working to improve their immediate surroundings or the health of the whole planet.

Let's revisit the definition of happiness.

"A state of well-being and contentment; joy. A pleasurable or satisfying experience. Felicity, aptness."

- Be a well-being. Take care of your health. (Realistically, our bodies and the planet are what we need to consider our true Home.)
- Do what is "apt, appropriate, and necessary" for your best-self *and* for your surroundings.
- Appreciate whatever brings you joy and contentment, now and in the long run.
- Enjoy and create more opportunities for satisfying experiences for yourself and for those around you. Improving your ability to excel in activities that you and others respect is a more effective self-esteem booster than is giving in to the ego-drive to out-compete others.[41]
- Trust, co-operation, and mutual respect go a long way in improving everyone's sense of psychological well-being. By making choices that foster happiness, we create more grace and meaning in our hearts and minds, individually and collectively. Help build a better world.

For creating a happy and meaningful life, *doing and being*, even a sense of *becoming*, are truly much more effective than *having*.[42]

Want more ideas?

Suggested Reading

What Happy People Know, Dan Baker and Cameron Stauth
The Pursuit of Perfect, Tal Ben-Shahar
The Art of Happiness, The Dalai Lama and Howard C. Cutler,
Happiness: Unlocking the Mysteries of Psychological Wealth, Ed Diener & Robert Biswas-Diener
The Brain That Changes Itself, Norman Doidge, M.D.
Happiness Hypothesis, Jonathan Haidt
Lifting Depression: A Neuroscientist's Hands-on Approach to Activating your Brain's Healing Power, Kelly Lambert
Happiness: Use It or Lose It, David Loomis
100 Simple Secrets of Happy People, David Niven

Onions, Pomegranates, and . . .

Some of us think in images more easily than in words. Trying to translate into words the thoughts that generated this book has been a rather daunting process. Please indulge me as I switch to images as well as analogies for this last chapter. Images may better tickle your imagination. Images may stay with you longer and help you sustain your motivation as you ponder "what's next?"

Life as an onion – in layers

The idea of the circles-within-circles of Life is hardly new. But let's play with it a little. Let's use an onion as our image—onions are tastier than circles. Consider that we grow from the inside out, and that our centers are embedded in multiple layers.

You
Is it bad, small, or selfish to consider yourself the centre of your own world? No. Taking care of yourself doesn't make you a narcissistic brat any more than purposely ignoring your own needs makes you a saint. If you don't take care of yourself, how can you be in decent shape to help anyone or anything else? *It's not an either/or thing.* Taking care of yourself does *not* mean you won't, don't, or can't take care of other people and other things that matter. It means you're more able to. After all, of all the things in the world you're entitled to have influence over, it's primarily yourself.

Family and friends, your tribe—your closest layer.
You care about them. They care about you. You enjoy each other's company, at least most of the time, and you help each other out.

Community and societal context
How does *where you are* impact *who you are*? And vice versa?
How can you help build a healthier (in all the meanings of that word) place for all?

Country and continent
I'm not talking about patriotism here, at least not in the usual sense. We may truly appreciate many aspects of where we live. Yet how can we better empower, not only ourselves, but our fellow citizens to be happier and healthier? (We may be diverse individually and culturally, but what's beating inside all of us is a human heart.) And how can we institute and enforce sensible laws that will protect the well-being, not only of our fellow humans, but the many other species entitled to their share of the planet?

Citizen of the planet

Our wee planet? A mere spec in the cosmos. Humans, only one of millions of species. And each of us? Only 1 of 7 billion individuals. And we haven't been around very long, geologically speaking, either as a species or as individuals.
How aware is our consciousness and conscience? How humane our humanity?
Are we stewards of our place in space or gluttons feeding on the future of our young?
Hopefully, we can tame arrogance and greed with a little more wisdom.
The convictions and actions of like-minded individuals are what drive constructive change and compel political will. Let's not leave that power in the hands of those who do not have the best interests of us "average people" at heart.

Spiritual context

There's surprising and intriguing growth in the overlap of spirituality, metaphysics, and physics. Yet we still know so very little about the physics of other dimensions and about what we seem to intuitively sense as "soul". Though there are many variations in personal beliefs and in the expressions and rituals of organized religions, we all seem to be *seeking*. *What,* I suspect, we're likely not sure. (Perhaps that's why some prefer to have what-they-should-believe handed to them as dogma.) Connection? Meaning?

We are curious creatures. And we've barely scratched the surface of the workings of mind, and of space and time. So how do we know *where we fit*? How do we *know*? Why do we matter? Do we? In fact, why *are* we matter? Thanks to the physicists, we do know that matter and energy are interconvertible, inextricably interlinked; that matter is the universe's energy in physical form. And that there are many more dimensions to life, to "reality", than we are currently able to see.

Sorry if I just made your brain ache. Ah well. So does mine. Isn't it nice though, in some awe-inspiring, profound, and humbling way, to know that we are simply a tiny embedded component of that vast energy that's both out there *and* inside us? Describe that energy in whatever way you choose, as *Whatever* or *Whomever*. It is what it is. Whether fundamentalist or atheist we are all still a part of that energy-of-the-universe. So take care of the energy that is You, *and* respect the other energies and entities in the world. Humans are not the only energy forms that matter.

Like pomegranates better than onions?

Think of yourself as a pomegranate seed. Together with multiple other individual seeds, each vivid, lustrous, and bursting with flavour, you are enclosed in your own segment, in close contact, lives touching. Numerous other segments, side by side, each contain their own individual seeds. The delicate boundaries between each and all of these segments are imprinted and sculpted by the shapes of each contained seed and by the shapes of the other segments. Each seed, all segments, are surrounded by a firm finite boundary that is both protector and sanctuary for the whole. Here, think planet not pomegranate.

And as a seed, what do you want to pass forward to the next generation?

Life is about blend, not balance.

For me, *balance* brings up images of teeter-totters, plate juggling, or walking on high wires. Balancing keeps us busy, yes. Yet the effort it takes to maintain that "balance" eventually becomes more draining than entertaining, more confining than productive. We become trapped between the necessity to keep things going, and having to recover from trying. Personally, I think *balance-as-a-life-goal* is a bogus concept. We're far more likely to be effective, healthy and happy if we use *blending* as our strategy. Blending doesn't mean, as with a teeter-totter, that we are up or down. It does not mean, as with juggling plates, that the whole lot smashes down if we miss a beat, or that the high wire is cutting our feet as we wobble. I think "balance" is an unproductive metaphor for improving one's life. Blending is a much gentler and more effective tactic.

With balance, people tend to think too much in terms of either/or. Life is not in "balance" *or* "out of balance". Not this *or* that. Each day is a mix of roles and goals. It's the blending of these ingredients that produces the flavour we seek in our day and in our life. Focus on what matters most, of course, but flexibility is a must. Our focus, and the flavour of our current priorities, can then more readily adapt to what's going on. Why not allow ourselves the gift of possibility and variety? Neither of which are created by being obsessed with "balance".

When I think of blending, I imagine the words in a recipe-on-a-page becoming mouth-watering flavours, ingredients tailored to taste, savoury nourishment. Similarly, a musical score, when lifted off the page as palpable sound, becomes food for the soul. Whether solo or orchestral, energizing or calming, Reggae or Baroque, *the magic is artful blending.* We are surrounded by the sounds and rhythms of the natural world. And, individually and collectively, we blend into that the music of being-human.

The skills and ideas in this book are, for now, merely words. Lift them off the pages and into *your* reality. Want more flavour in your life? More music in your world? *Use what you've learned.* Turn those recipes into nourishment for the journey, those notes into music. And encourage others to do the same.

Influence

Influencing others?

Maybe we don't need to. Maybe all we need to do is invite other individuals to join in "the dance". Do they need a little inspiration? Entice them into enjoying and evolving who they are and could become. How? Let yourself do that. *Live it.* Lead by example. You don't need to be the leader to lead. Realistically, *doing, showing,* often says more than talking.

What about our influence on groups? Their influence on us? Research has shown that "activities performed in unison, like marching or dancing, increase loyalty to the group."[1] Why? The brain releases a little more of the reward chemical dopamine when we fall more in line with the group consensus. We're individuals, yes, but built to be part of a collective. This is useful as a survival tactic. Useful *if* the herd is going in a constructive direction. Otherwise? Change the herd's direction. Or change herds. Or start a new one. (Just don't follow lemmings. Or some manipulative, unscrupulous, self-serving ego-maniac. There's more than one of those out there.)

Want someone to hear and actually pay attention to what you want to say? Think of the conversation as a meal. (I'm thinking food again. I need my lunch...)

- An appetizer whets your listener's pallet. Consider his or her priorities. What are your mutual priorities? Start with what the benefit might be to them. (It may be money to be made in a business deal. Or they may feel enriched by helping something good happen for someone or something they care about.)
- The main course? Discuss the issue and your intentions, and what you *each* see as your preferences, the benefits, and the possible solutions. Listen with your ears and heart.
- Add a dessert—make a nice comment, and be genuine. Leave the person you're interacting with feeling that you're a calm and sensible person that they'd be comfortable dealing with again. By sharing such a "meal", you create an ally rather than an enemy. And you put more trust, mutual respect, and goodwill out into the world.

> You *versus* them, whether as individuals or countries, is so counter-productive! You *and* them facing an issue together to find and implement solutions? Amazingly effective. If we were to all start thinking Me *and* We? The results would be incredible.

Influence your personal context. How?

You want something to change? Change something. If not your intention, your tactics.

Use what's already a good habit to reinforce one you're in the process of trying to build.
Keep forgetting to take your vitamins? Keep them beside your toothbrush.

Harness your engrained mindset for a more beneficial result.
You've been using food (e.g. comfort fatty-carbs) to make yourself feel better. Now you're wearing a lot of pudge. The solution? Oddly, the same mindset: use food to make yourself feel better. Wherever you are, keep *healthy* yummy foods around. Eat those instead, and you *will* feel better.

Deliberately adjust your surroundings so they can help you make better choices.
It's often easier to control your context than your willpower. Trying to quit smoking? Take your break away from the smokers. Want to lose weight? First lose the junk food in your pantry.

Influence your context so that it can, in turn, create healthy opportunities.
You like skiing. There's no snow. That's a no-brainer—go where there is snow. Or try out a few sports that are more appropriate for your climate. Cycling? Rock climbing? Maybe pick an all-seasons activity. Go dancing. Take up kick boxing. You might just find you come to enjoy one of these activities as much as skiing. As more and more people participate, opportunities will expand for healthy active living in your area.

You want more good in the world? Do more good in the world.
Help create a kinder context. Healthy altruism boosts our self-respect, our sense that we matter and that we are effective in the world. *Healthy* altruism is neither self-sacrificial nor self-righteous. And, ironically, it's self-protective. That generous heart-in-motion indirectly encourages kindness in the hearts of others.

Influencing yourself?

It's easier to do the right thing when the right thing is easier to do. That's the main reason I wrote this book—to help make doing-the-doing easier, and to help you avoid the swamps, alligators, and little brown piles on the path. As I said on the first page, some things are best *not* learned the hard way—life then can be a lot kinder and more fun. As for the mistakes you've already made? Don't let them fester. Fix them, as best you can. Get the appropriate help when you need it.

Humans have survived this long because we blend curiosity and ingenuity with learning. We learn from those who have wisdom born of experience, and from those with the appropriate relevant expertise. The combination allows us, as individuals and as a species, to adapt to shifting circumstances and to modify certain situations and our surroundings to better suit our needs.

> Be curious. Ask questions. Watch. Learn.
> Try things out. Practice.
> Enjoy the process.

Resilience

We've spent time looking at some avoidable problems. I'm a realist. What about the unavoidable ones?

Let's revisit the analogy of a **sailing ship** dealing with the weathers of life.

In decent weather and familiar territory, you can happily sail along, enjoying the scenery and the gentle yet energizing breezes. To create an adventure, you can hone your skills, gather up your charts and GPS, and head out into less familiar waters. Either way, there will be the occasional storm. If you know one is on its way, you perhaps can find a way around it. If you know one is likely, you can more readily prepare. (Good sense, not bravado, is the sign of strength.) Improve your sailing skills. Keep your ship ship-shape. Have the necessary instruments and provisions on board. Life rafts are a must. Beacons, a must. An emergency back-up plan, a must. To lie to yourself, to pretend that gales don't exist, could get you ripped apart. Some storms you may not be able to ride out. Some are not predictable. Some are more intense than you could have anticipated. One of these may trash your ship. What if there's only flotsam left to grab onto? You may be in the water, but you're still afloat. You may be miserable, and in desperate need of having someone fish you out, but you're still afloat. Courage is your life jacket. The rescue helicopter? That's the emergency plan and support system you made sure was in place, "just in case", *before* you set out on your adventure.

Thankfully, high seas and rough winds don't last forever. The experiences that challenge or humble us can be useful lessons, even if we'd rather have learned them in a less dramatically painful way.

> A little humility in facing Life encourages and inspires preparation. Preparation improves our ability to be resilient. And that resilience becomes a quiet strength, one that has the confidence to equate humility, not with subdued meekness, but with wisdom. When we add enthusiasm to wisdom, wow!

One last analogy—Origami

Imagine your life as a simple flat piece of paper. As colorful or plain, as shiny or as textured as you want. Want to add some dimension and shape? Create some curves and folds. Haphazardly, if you want—it may turn out to be something you'd like. Or not.

Have an idea for the shape you'd prefer your life to take? One that you'd find interesting *and* appealing? Plan a design, or borrow a similar tried-and-true one and adapt it to suit *your* intentions. (That's why we have coaches, mentors, and experts—to help our initiative and creativity blossom.) Then make those folds, one at a time, to create that shape you want. When, not if, you make mistakes, you can smooth out and better fold that particular part. You may see a few wrinkles, but the overall shape you envisioned is there. What if you aren't pleased with this edge or that corner? Or with the whole thing? No, not all decisions and their consequences are reversible. But more than you might think *are*. You can change the shape of your future by changing your mind—shift your mindset, your habits, your tactics—carefully unfold and refold your paper into something else that better suits your new needs and desires.

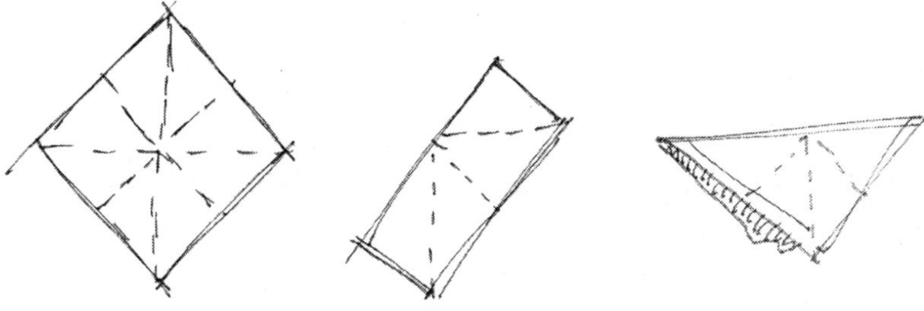

What's next?

Inspiration and initiative,
curiosity, and a dab of courage
A little patience with ourselves, and others
An appreciation for life
for what is, and could be.

We're growing and evolving,
exploring and skill building.
Add some coaching and companionship,
Synergy and serendipity.
It's *your* life. Live it. Love it.

This book? Ideas and skills as words.
Pared down do-able information that works, in readily chewable chunks.
Easy to implement practical tips to help you live life on your terms.
Incorporate even just a few of these—you'll like the results!

You've played with your priorities.
You've built skills to be more effective and joyful with both your time and money.
You've learned how to better protect You and Yours,
and how to improve your happiness, influence, and resilience.
Now it's up to you to design *your* quality journey.

You want to hit a home run? Get off the bench. Pick up the bat.

Appendices

Moving – an example of "Planning Backwards"

Whatever goal you're taking on, ask yourself:

- **What might I need to *know* to help this happen?**
  How, where can I find that out?
- **What do I need to *do* to help that happen?**
  Who might be able to help?
  What can I do now to get started?
  What do I do when?

As for moving?
So far no one's invented a teleportation device, at least not that we know of. And most of us would not put moving at the top of our fun-list. Yes, a new place is a fresh start which is perhaps somewhat exciting, but the process? Ugh. And obviously there's a deadline attached. How do we make the transition as painless as possible?

First of all, is the timing for the move flexible?
To save some money and to make booking trucks and movers easier, move mid-month or off season. Avoid Sept 1, or May and June, if at all possible.

WHAT TO DO WHEN?

At least six weeks in advance:

Do your research and notify the appropriate people

- Call several reputable movers to compare their per-hour rates, and get estimates on how much time they'd need for packing, moving, and unpacking. Ask friends if there's a particular company they'd recommend. and research online, including what previous clients have said.
- Make a decision. Save a little money? Or save your back? If you want to "do-it-yourself", ask a few friends if they'd be willing to help. Book the truck now. Ask if the truck comes with padded blankets to wrap your furniture. Does the truck company rent or sell moving boxes?
- If you decide to hire movers, which tasks do you want them to do for you? Pack? Unpack? Or just the actual truck-and-carry? (The latter's a good compromise.) Lay out *exactly* what you want them to do. Get written estimates detailing what they'll do for what price. Walk around your space with the movers as they compile the list of what they are to move. Book the company you choose.
- Arrange what day you'll get the keys to the new place. And schedule the day you'll actually move in and the approximate time you'll arrive. If you're leaving or going to a high-rise, book the freight elevator.
- If the new place needs painting or some other fix-ups, arrange for those to happen before you move in, if possible.
- Notify the motor vehicle office, post office, banks, credit card companies, etc. of your new address and the date it will take effect.
- In the USA, you may need written permission from a lender to move items not yet paid for out of state, e.g. your vehicle.

- Arrange with each provider the date to shut off the gas, electricity, cable, land-line at old place, and arrange to have these set up at new place.
- If you have kids, start talking with them about the move. Take them to visit the new neighbourhood.
- If you're changing schools, doctors, dentists, vets, and other professionals, call them to make arrangements for the transfer of your files.

Edit and purge your stuff! Starting *now*!

- Don't discourage or overwhelm yourself: do one drawer, one room at a time.
- Create four groups of items: *Give away*, *Sell*, *Throw out*, and *Keep*. To simplify the process, have four containers ready when you start, one for each group.
- Put like-with-like items. Get rid of duplicates. Edit down to your favourites. This is no time for "maybe". That Maybe-pile could end up bigger than all the other piles combined. It's costing you money to move or store this stuff!
- Ask yourself: "Do I actually use it, fairly frequently? Do I totally love it?" If not, let it go. You're making space for your new life, so keep only the things that really matter. If it's too large or the wrong style for the new space, sell or donate it. What if it has sentimental value? Take a picture, and keep that instead. *Chances are it's the memory, not the actual item that matters.*
- Don't keep a gift you didn't actually like just because so-and-so gave it to you. And don't keep things you "might-use-someday". (You haven't worn that jacket in years? What about that kitchen thingy that, realistically, just takes up counter space?) Be kind. Let these go to someone who could make use of them now. Charity does begin at home.

  For donations: goodwill.org, thriftstore.ca, valuevillage.com
  For sales: cashconverters.ca, ebay.ca, playitagainsports.com, craiglist.com, kijiji.com, or ouac.com for kid's stuff
- Finally, where will each of your *Keep* items be put in your new home? Can't think of where and how you'd use that item? You likely don't need it. Edit. Purge. What about the things you won't immediately or frequently use, but that have important sentimental value or ongoing aesthetic appeal? Put them, not in some junky cardboard box, but into nice containers worthy of their contents. If they're not worth doing that, they're not worth storing.
- Let the kids participate in the purging and packing of their things. Their opinion of which items are their favourites, and to be kept, matters. Encourage them to enjoy passing on to other kids their outgrown clothing and superfluous toys.

Two weeks before the move:

- Have some fun fantasizing about your new space. What is the intended use for each area? Which activities will happen where? Which items go where? Arrange to have rugs, drapes, duvets, etc. cleaned before you pack them.
- Pick up your moving supplies: get boxes, thick black permanent markers, packing tape, bubble wrap, packing paper. For items you want to store, get clear plastic bins for quicker viewing of the contents. And label each bin for easy retrieval. (Be honest with yourself: if you won't occasionally need to retrieve these items, get rid of them.) Exactly where will you store these in the new place?
- Label *all* the boxes, as you pack them, with their contents *and* destination. For example, "photos, blue bedroom". This will help the movers, your bank

account (remember they charge by the hour), and your sanity at the other end. You could even number the boxes if you want, and make a list of the general items they contain. E.g. "Box 3, dishes, kitchen". Then, if number such-and-such goes AWOL, you know what's missing.

- Pack the least used items first. Clothes can be left in the dressers on moving day, if they aren't absurdly huge or heavy. Moving companies sell wardrobe boxes for your hanging clothes – these are worth the cost.
- Confirm the date and time with the movers or with your friends and the truck rental company. Confirm the use of the freight elevators.
- Call your insurance agent about the location changes and confirm the extent of your coverage.
- Send out "change of address" notices to friends, relatives, magazine subscription services etc., and include the date you're moving.
- Use up perishable food and freezer items. Minimize the groceries you'll take.
- Get rid of flammables. Drain the gas out of your lawn mower, etc.
- If you're taking your appliances with you, arrange for the disconnection and reconnection at the new place.
- Return library and other borrowed items. Collect those you loaned out.
- Houseplants? If you can't move them yourself, give your green-friends to your human-friends. Movers don't like transporting plants.
- If you've got kids, arrange to send them off with relatives or friends for moving day. Arrange to board the pets for a few days.
- You might want to stay with friends or in a hotel for your first night in the new space. It'll be pretty chaotic. A good rest can start the new day in the new space off on a happier note.
- Prepare the things you'll transport yourself, e.g. in your car. Include delicate breakables and valuables. Include, as well, *all your legal documents such as deeds, and wills, and any identity related documents, e.g. passports, tax returns, etc.* (If you did Chapter 13, that will be easy.)
- Pack a first day survivor-bag containing a change of clothes for everyone, toiletries, etc., and a survivor-box with healthy snacks, your favourite caffeine fix, and a few mugs. If you're staying in the new place the first night, have bed linens and towels handy.
- Arrange the details of the key hand-overs at both ends.

Day before and/or day of the move:

- If you'll be using a different bank branch, pick up the contents of your safety deposit box to transport personally, or arrange for your bank to transfer the contents to the new branch.
- Take the kids and pets off to relatives or friends, or board them—the pets, not the kids.
- Empty the fridge and freezer. Pack what you're taking into coolers.
- Put the garbage and recycling out.
- Walk around with the movers and confirm what does or does not go on the truck. (Perhaps put the items you're taking personally in a separate room.)
- After the truck is loaded, go through the entire place carefully to make certain nothing is left behind. Lock the windows and doors.

- Be nice. Clean the place (at least sweep) for the next people coming in. You hope those at the other end have done the same for you.
- Go through the key hand-over process with your current landlord. (Or, if you've sold your place, the buyers.) Have the landlord sign off that the place is okay and get back your damage deposit.
- In the new place – *before* the movers start unloading your stuff – check that there's been no damage left by the previous tenants. Take pictures, preferably with the date attached, of any damage that is present and call the landlord. Residential damage forms need to be filled out on the day you move in.
- Similarly, make sure the movers haven't damaged any of your things. Again take pictures, and fill out the damage forms then and there. Don't "sign off" with the movers until you've done this for at least the big stuff. (Reputable moving companies will have insurance. And your home or tenant's insurance typically will cover your stuff for 30 days of transportation or storage between homes. Ask them, in advance.)
- Be sure nothing is left in the truck.
- Unpack the survivor-box, and take a break. Don't try to do everything all at once. Pick your own pace to get up and running. Home wasn't built in a day.

Enjoy your new place!

Creating Your Wardrobe

You want a wardrobe:

- **That is comfortable.**
- **That suits your lifestyle.**
  Is it appropriate for your various activities and contexts? (Are your surroundings artsy or corporate, trendy or conservative, urban or country, indoor or outdoor? Some of this, some of that? Something else?)
- **That reflects who you are, suits your personality, and enhances how you are perceived.** Does it help with the roles and goals you've chosen?
- **That flatters your body shape and coloring.**
- **And does all of the above without wasting your money or time.**
  Think ease of care, as well as looks and fit.

Realistically, all we need physically is something to protect our naked cave-selves from the weather. But since we're past the grunt-grunt knuckle-dragging stage (at least most of us), getting a little more deliberate about what we wear and how we present ourselves is actually quite life-enhancing. And we can do that without spending a fortune. How?

Buy less, but buy better quality.
And use and take care of what you do buy.

Where to start?

First, PURGE.

Keep the process simple: start at one end of your closet or with one drawer.

Have three containers handy – one for *Fix*, one for *Give away*, one for *Toss*. You don't need to do this all at once. Until you're finished purging, keep these containers on the closet floor, if you can find it.

What fits? If it almost does and you *love* it, have it re-tailored. Otherwise, let it go. Ask yourself, "Would I buy this particular item *now?* Do I like how it makes me feel? Is it useful?" (When did you last wear it? That might give you some indication of its usefulness.) If it still fits, is useful to who you are now and looks good, put it in a more noticeable place in your closet.

Beware the "maybe someday" things. These can take over your closet like a sci-fi fungus. If it's a once-and-a-while piece like a tux or gown, would you feel good wearing it now? If, in reality, it has only sentimental value, take a picture and keep that instead. Same goes for the 20 concert T-shirts stuffed in your drawers.

Maybe re-purpose some pieces. Got a tired looking but very comfy favourite old shirt? Rather than toss it, save it for days when you're mowing the lawn or lying around reading. But you don't need 10 of these, please. (I'll confess. I had so many socks you'd think I was a centipede, yet numbers of them were in pathetic shape. And enough scarves to outfit a family of giraffes. Silly me.)

Then BUILD your wardrobe.

Think *function*.
Maybe you never do "fancy", so you don't need an opera outfit. But you sure could use a new pair of cross-trainers or an updated jacket for work. And if your Work context is dress-casual, you may have considerable overlap with the Everyday category. You'll notice other overlaps – that's a good thing. Multi-functional clothes truly earn their space in your wardrobe.

Go for mix-and-match for more flexibility. Think in terms of neutrals, both light and dark, and colors that suit *you*. (Yes, consider jeans a "neutral", unless yours are neon or leopard skin.)

Plan for complete outfits rather than random pieces. Using what you currently have, try putting together outfits for specific activities. That will help you figure out what you need to get and fine-tune what you can get rid of.

Purchase items that will enhance and fill gaps in your wardrobe.
Don't buy something just because it's on sale. If it's not something you *will* use and of good quality, it's a waste of both space and money no matter how inexpensive it is.

Experiment a bit. Play a little. In the stores, try on a few styles and colors you wouldn't normally gravitate towards. You never know – maybe there's a more flattering variation of you out there, whether it's in the fit or the spunk or elegance of the outfit.

Whether purging or building your wardrobe, ask yourself:

Do I genuinely need this item? What aspect of my life does it help or enhance? What am I missing to function well? What's just taking up space?

It's not about more, but *more suitable*. And, again, think *less* but *better*.
Put together what lets you function at your best without depleting your resources or the planet's. You *can* have the right things and still do the right thing. Develop your wardrobe, not haphazardly or through random neglect, but deliberately and with self-respect in mind.

These charts are meant to be a tool, not a taskmaster. The idea is to *fill in the blanks in your wardrobe*, not all the blanks on the page. The idea is simply to help you figure out what you consider to be *appropriate, sensible, and fun* for someone who does what you do. (Yes, *sensible* and *fun* do belong in the same sentence.) After purging, see how your current wardrobe compares to what you need to function well *and* feel good. The process is likely to be eye-opening. It definitely will be useful. Have fun as you think your way through this. How much detail you get into is entirely up to you. Your call. It is your wardrobe.

How many of each item? How often do you do laundry?

> A friend of mine told me, with a surprised and surprising expletive, that I've included too many kinds of items. (Guess I was trying to be too thorough. Hey, ignore whatever you want.) Some things to leave blank will be obvious. (For example, you don't need different underwear for work than for everyday. Mind you, that depends on what you do at lunch.) And some categories will cross-over. You have a hot date? Now is that "Dressy" or "Play"? Some distinctions don't matter that much.
> Have some fun with this. ("Useful" and "serious" are not synonyms.)

FUNCTION →	Everyday (Casual)	Work (Regular)	Work (Spiffy)	Dressy	Play & Hobby	Other
TOPS						
Blouses / shirts Long sleeve Short sleeve or Sleeveless						
T-shirts / knits Long sleeve Short sleeve						
Tanks						
Fleeces / Hoodies						
Sweaters Cardigans / Zip-ups						
Jackets / Blazers						
Other						
BOTTOMS						
Pants & Jeans For warm weather For cool weather						
Mid-length pants, capris						
Shorts						
Skirts For warm weather For cool weather						
Active wear Eg track pants						
Other						

FUNCTION →	Everyday (Casual)	Work (Regular)	Work (Spiffy)	Dressy	Play & Hobby	Other
DRESSES						
Sleeveless Short sleeve Long sleeve						
Dressy dresses Long Gowns						
Other						
SUITS / TUX						
Warm weather Cool weather						
Other						
ACTIVE WEAR						
Eg yoga, skiing						
FOOTWEAR						
Warm socks Light weight socks						
Stockings / Leggings						
Sandals						
Everyday shoes						
Athletic						
Dressy shoes						
Rain boots						
Cold weather boots						
Other						

FUNCTION →	Everyday (Casual)	Work (Regular)	Work (Spiffy)	Dressy	Play & Hobby	Other
MISC						
Handbags Wallets						
Briefcase Backpack						
Carry-on bag						
Other						
ACCESSORIES						
Umbrellas						
Sun Glasses						
Other eyewear						
Ties Scarves						
Earrings, studs						
Necklaces						
Armbands, bracelets						
Pins, brooches						
Cufflinks, clips						
UNDERWEAR						
Panties Briefs / Boxers						
Bras						
Camisoles, slips						
Body Shapers						
Other Lingerie						
Undershirts, Tanks						
Thermals						

FUNCTION →	Everyday (Casual)	Work (Regular)	Work (Spiffy)	Dressy	Play & Hobby	Other
SLEEPWEAR						
PJs / Nightgowns						
Robe Light-weight Warm						
Slippers						
OUTER WEAR						
Sun hats, caps Winter hats						
Scarves Light weight Warm						
Mitts / gloves						
Coats & Jackets Light-weight Cold weather						
Rain coat Other rain gear						
SWIM-WEAR						
Swimsuits						
Cover-ups						
OTHER WEAR - LIST any additional HOBBY GEAR and special clothing requirements: E.g. hockey gear, riding or ski boots, golf gloves ?						

Now list specifically what you want to replace or add, or do to your wardrobe.
Some examples:

REPLACE old runners → new cross-trainers
ratty boxers → get 4 pairs of briefs

ADD 3 pairs of black socks
A white dress shirt

DO Have grey pants shortened
Take in green skirt

HOME

Creating your Preferred Personal Context

To help you figure out "what you want", here are a zillion questions to ask yourself.
Play with the ideas in Part A first.
Then *if* you want more detail for specific rooms, continue with Part B.

Part A

Be as specific as you can in describing what you'd like for your present life-stage and for your foreseeable goals.
For starters, is it just you, for now at least? Or are you living with others?
How many? Will that likely change in the future? How, and when?

What matters to you about where you live?

CLIMATE

Describe the climate in which you want to live. Seasonal, temperate, tropical?
Which temperatures do you dislike more – frigid or roasting?
Do you prefer lots of sunshine or the moody beauty of mist and rain?
Are you impacted by low sunlight levels? Suffer from the winter blahs?

GEOGRAPHY

Describe the geography you would prefer. Mountains, prairies, desert, lakeside...?
Crave a salty breeze? Prefer a hillside, a cliff, a sheltered valley, or wide-open spaces?

AREA

Do you want a context that's urban, suburban, rural, forested, exotic?

What indoor and outdoor activities, hobbies, sports do you want access to?
How do you intend to get to these? Walk? Drive? Transit?
Which of these involve other people, groups, or organizations?

NEIGHBOURHOOD

What do you want included in your immediate neighbourhood, i.e. walking distance?
Lots of shops, restaurants and night life, or only trees or farms for miles?

Promote green spaces! Encourage your town and your neighbourhood to plant and care for trees. It's good for your health and the planet's. The health impacts of having access to green spaces, on both children and adults, are remarkable no matter what your socioeconomic status. Living within a kilometre of a green space provides significant decreases in the impact of at least 15 common illnesses.[1]
Some of the effects? Better fitness, decreased stress, lowered cortisol levels, lower blood pressure, less asthma, depression, anxiety, headaches, and even fewer respiratory infections.[2] So if you live in an urban context, be active in promoting the inclusion and use of parks in your area!

FORMAT / STYLE

What type of home do you want? A loft, a condo, a townhouse or a detached?
A mansion, rambling ranch, log cabin? Maybe an adobe, straw-bale, or cliff-dug dwelling?
Or perhaps a tent or motorhome for easy travelling?

How high off the ground do you want to be? Want a 40th floor penthouse or are you okay with a basement apartment, at least for now?

Prefer one, two, three stories?
Want lots of open-concept space or really cosy areas? Or some of each?
Do you like formal or casual living? A little of both?

To avoid frustration, think FUNCTION before aesthetics.

What do you want your home to *enable you to do*, comfortably and well?
What are the functions it needs to be able to handle? Daily? Occasionally?

Sleeping and storage for clothes and personal items
Bathing, grooming
Food prep and eating
Conversation, relaxing, reading
Home business and/or meetings
Laundry, mud-room, etc
Storage for what and where? Specify.
Media/TV watching, games
Hobbies and interests – get specific e.g. Listening to music/making music
Sports – specify.
Children – how many kids, when? Indoor play space?
Guests? How many at once? Overnight? How often?
Parties? For how many? Indoors, outdoors?
Space for pets?
Place for car(s), bikes, etc, and maybe a workshop?
Add any other functions that matter to you.

> Many people are unclear about what they want. Again, you are PLAYING with these ideas and questions. Go with what *feels right* and *functions well*. Pretend. Experiment. Then fine-tune your ideas.

HOME ZONES - What functions go where?

This is rather like a mix-and-match game. Don't use typical room labels if they don't fit your lifestyle. Maybe you don't care about a formal living or dining room – you need space for working out at home, or an office.

Which functions would you like to let flow into each other (open-concept areas) and which need more separation?

Which activity, or inactivity, requires quiet? Does someone work shifts?
Are there drummers in the house? You might want some areas soundproofed.
(Are you comfortable with the sound effects of a toilet stack in the dining room wall, or the bathroom door opening off the living room?)

What about privacy? Do you need a home office where clients can come in without disturbing family life? Do you want a separate space where kids can play? A family room or den, or both?

Which functions need to be mobile, such as trekking your laptop "home office" or a baby, or both, around the house with you?

Which room(s) might be of flexible use as life changes? You could use a formal dining room as the kids' playroom while they're little.

SITE

Whether dream-building or actually building, consider the **orientation** as well as the **location**. Arrange the rooms on the site to get the maximum joy from each. Don't be concerned about details yet. For now, just circle approximate areas.

Where are the views?
Where do the winds, the breezes come from?
Where is north/south/east/west? What orientation would keep heat out in the summer and let in the sun's warmth in winter?
Do you love or hate having the sun wake you up in the morning?
Want to watch the sunset from the living room?
Which rooms do you prefer warmer, which ones cooler?
Want the dining room overlooking the backyard, or maybe a city skyline?
Do you want access to a balcony, deck, BBQ, a garden?

THE FLOOR PLAN

Lay out a possible floor plan. Use graph paper, or a computer program that helps you visualize in 3D what you're putting together. At this point, it's cheap and easy to make changes and mistakes.

What are the daily patterns of traffic flow throughout your space?
How do these patterns vary with the seasons? When you have guests over?

Many homes have two "front" doors, one central and one beside the garage. Design your landscaping to make it obvious to guests which entry you want them to use.

How many stories would best serve your needs? Get a little more detailed here, and more or less to scale. How many square feet, on each level, would your home need to house what you want to do?

A caution here—bigger is usually *not* better, just more expensive. More carefully *tailoring your space,* while still allowing for some flexibility, is what's truly effective in enabling your chosen lifestyle.

Rather than maximize the size of each area, consider appropriate and comfortable human scale. For example, how much space do you need on each side of a bed or around a table to allow for comfortable traffic flow?

Visit some of the many home-design websites. Choose a few places that appeal to you and pretend you live in them. What would you change or add? Use those ideas in yours.

What furniture, equipment, and so on would you want where? Beds, sofas, tables, media/sound systems, fireplaces…? (For more detail, see Part B *later.*)

LIGHTING

Natural light is highly beneficial. With it our bodies build Vitamin D which has numerous health benefits including boosting our mood. Research shows, as well, that windows enable an instinctive sense of time which reduces stress, and that being able to stare at a view increases rather than decreases workplace productivity. [1] (That may surprise your employer.) Circadian rhythms, and adequate levels of the natural frequencies of light, are crucial to our optimal functioning, whether we're students, worker-bees, hospital patients, or just going about our day.

Lighting is crucial to both function and aesthetics.
Which areas need to be brighter? E.g. work spaces need to be well-lit for both safety and productivity. Which areas need dimmers or multiple light sources, spots, or other direct lighting? Where do you most want to have windows – for light and for views?

HEALTH

The EPA cautions that indoor air can be many more times more polluted than outdoor air, so open the windows. Keep air moving with fans, and/or keep the fan on your furnace running all year to prevent stale air pockets.

Have your home and workplace checked for mold, for radon, and for other nasties. Look at Everydayexposures.com and the sites for the Environmental Working Group and the Collaborative on Health and the Environment.

Reduce your use of carpets. New carpets, unless made of natural fibres, off-gas for various lengths of time. Older synthetic carpets eventually stop emitting fumes, but it's not easy to get rid of dirt, dust, mites and so on in any rug, even with regular vacuuming. There can be kilograms/pounds of old microscopic critter-bits in even "clean" carpets. Gross, especially for asthma sufferers. Perhaps use washable rugs. Have others cleaned regularly with non-toxic cleaners.

Avoid the "air fresheners" that actually put into your air more chemicals and micro-materials to inhale into your lungs. Clean air is better than "scented" or de-scented air. Use Hepa filters on everything that uses a filter. And change them regularly. Consider buying an electronic air purifier. Or better yet, *grow fresh air.*
A couple of plants per room make a wonderful difference in air quality. A few useful examples? Bamboo palm, Spider plant, Weeping fig, Areca palm, Australian sword fern, Rubber plant, English ivy, Boston fern, Peace lily, Corn plant and Gerbena.

For more info, see:
epa.gov/
everydayexposures.com
rethinkrecycling.com
davidsuzuki.org
cleanuptheworld.org
And search the "Toxic Taxi" for your area.

SANITY

What is your preferred organizational style? How comfortable are you with clutter? (Some people's cars look like travelling garbage cans.) How neat and organized would you like to be? And the others you live with…?

Your stuff does not pay you rent. Get rid of what isn't necessary, pleasing, or meaningful. Why pay to house it, literally?

What kinds of storage do you prefer – open and visible, or closed door?
What do you need to have – and where – to feel happy and calm, and to minimize the time needed for your various chores and for tidying and cleaning-up?

MECHANICALS and UTILITIES

Let's state the obvious – depending on where you live, you'll need a furnace and/or an air conditioner. You could go natural gas, propane, oil, or whatever – or go geothermal. You could insulate like crazy, use good quality windows, appropriate site placement and roof overhangs, and cut your energy consumption in half.

You may or may not need a water heater, depending on the amount of sunlight you get: roof top water heaters, as black tanks or pipes, are amazingly effective. As are heat-on-demand systems.

Yes, you need electricity. Perhaps go off-grid with solar panels and a mini wind-turbine. Let light in and heat out: use skylights that open yet automatically close when it rains. The list of good sense, both budgetary and planetary, goes on and on.

AESTHETICS

Make collages of what you want each area of your home to look like.
Sketch what you can't find pictures of.

What ceiling heights appeal to you? The usual 8', or do you like the grace and spaciousness of 9' or even 10'?

What colours, textures, shapes would you use? Where?
Choose *natural* scents as flowers, fruit, leaves, or potpourri, not finely misted chemicals.

What about external aesthetics? Curb appeal?
And so on, and so on ...

IMPLEMENTING your CHOICES

What can you do NOW to enjoy even a morsel of your dream-place?
What aspects of where you're currently living might have some resemblance to the preferences you've outlined here? Create your "perfect life-space" in phases. Collect some pictures to start your good-idea collages. Paint a room a colour you'd really like. Rearrange some furniture. Clean out some junk.

Whether you're thinking large projects or small, get creative. What non-monetary resources could you bring to one of the projects you're considering? Do you have a decent design sense? Organisational ability? Construction skills? Who can you call on for help? A friend with an empty garage who could store some salvage finds? Or a relative who's a carpenter?

What is your budget? A hundred, a thousand, or hundreds of thousands?
Don't wait until you can build your dream home from scratch. Make a few changes now, wherever you can. *Create a context that lets you be you!*

**You'll live in multiple places during your life...
You want each one to feel like home.**

Part B More detail for specific areas.

Living room

Do you want a formal living room plus a family room, media room, or some combination?
What activities will go where? What storage would be useful where?
How many people typically use this space? The maximum number you'd accommodate?
What kinds of furniture do you prefer? All club chairs, a couple of sofas, or some of each?
Coffee tables, end tables, game tables?

Kitchen

Are you a spread-out or clean-as-you-go cook? Is there one cook, or more?
Do you like to see your pots, pans, dishes, and foods – or have them hidden?
What kinds of storage do you prefer? Cabinets, open shelving, drawers, a pantry?
Do you want to encourage or discourage guests congregating in the kitchen?
What about the kitchen's connection to the dining or family rooms, and the outdoors?
Want to not see the piles of dirty dishes from another room?
What kind of stove—gas or electric? As one unit, or as a cooktop and wall oven?
You'll need a fridge and a vent hood. And a dishwasher. (Or one that comes on two legs).
What smaller appliances (e.g. coffee maker, blender) matter to you?
Get energy star appliances—for the sake of your budget and the planet.

Dining / Eating area

Want an eat-in kitchen? (A table, an island?) A dining room as well?
What size and shape of table do you want? Extendable? For how many?
Describe how you'd use your dining area. Daily? Or only on special occasions?
Will it be used during non-mealtimes? If so, for what? As an office, for homework?
What kind of storage areas do you need here?

A FLEX room?

Will you have a home-based business? Full or part-time? How much space and what office equipment, furniture, and storage will you need? Will clients, employees, or co-workers be coming in? Do you need a separate entrance and/or a meeting room?
Or will the flex-room be a guest room/hobby room?

Bedrooms

How many bedrooms might you want?
Consider your own needs: What is your typical sleep pattern? Does it vary much?
Are you a heavy or a light sleeper? Morning person or night owl?
Do you like to be awakened by the rising sun? Or need darkening blinds?
Do you like to read in bed or in a comfy chair?
Like to see the stars, moonlight from your bed? Consider a skylight.
How big a bed, a bedroom do you want?
Do you want to include as well a desk, a couple of chairs, a vanity and full length mirror?
How many feet of closet space? Prefer a big walk-in closet for each of you?
Craving a luxurious ensuite bathroom?

Bathrooms

How many bathrooms do you want? Where? One on each floor? Full baths, half baths?
A bathroom beside a mudroom? How many people share each bathroom?
The master bathroom – a simple efficient space or a sensuous place to luxuriate?
Do you want a combined shower & tub or separate ones? How large?
Want a lovely view from a soaking tub? A fireplace beside the jacuzzi? A bidet?
Do you want a separate toilet compartment? (That's common in parts of Europe.)

Laundry

Where do you want the laundry? In the basement? Near the bedrooms, the kitchen, the mudroom, the garage? Are stackables in a hall closet okay?
Or do you want a separate laundry room with side-by-sides. Front or top loading?
What other functions could be in that room? Ironing, sewing?
Do you want a utility sink and a folding area? An outdoor and/or indoor clothesline?
What storage might be useful here?

Entry/Mudroom

Do you want separate entries for family and for guests? (How messy are you?)
With separate entries, what would go into each? How much space would each require?
What closet space and other storage would be useful – for each person, for various activities? What about winter boots, off-season coats, and pets or kids with muddy paws?

Transportation storage (Cars, bikes, and so on.)

Do you need parking? A garage, car port, or turn-around?
How many cars and/or bicycles will be housed? Do you work on your own vehicles?
Do you need a solar charging station or other renewable fuel accommodation?
What other gadgets (e.g. mowers or boats) need to be housed? What are their spatial needs?
Is this where you'll bath the dog? Consider a mini shower in the garage. (Maybe hose off muddy kids there as well?)

Balcony, rooftop, garden, yard?

What outdoor play and relaxing space are you going to create?
Do you want outdoor areas for a BBQ, for entertaining, perhaps sleeping, maybe even bathing?
Are you, or might you want to become, a gardener? A passionate and dedicated one? Or the low-maintenance-only kind? Will you need a toolshed, potting bench, a compost area?

Your home, your hobbies, your life. Enjoy!

Appendix C Endnotes

1 American Journal of Preventative Medicine vol 35, p 547
2 Journal of of Epidemiology & Community Health, vol 63, p 967

What's your TYPICAL WEEK? (168 hours)

Guesstimate how you THINK you spend your time.

Time	MON	TUES	WED	THUR	FRI
midnight					
1am					
2					
3					
4					
5					
6					
7					
8					
9					
10					
11					
noon					
1 pm					
2					
3					
4					
5					
6					
7					
8					
9					
10					
11					

NOTES TO SELF:

(continued)

Time	SAT	SUN
midnight		
1am		
2		
3		
4		
5		
6		
7		
8		
9		
10		
11		
noon		
1 pm		
2		
3		
4		
5		
6		
7		
8		
9		
10		
11		

How long did each of the various tasks take you? Do you want to spend more time, or less, on certain categories?

CATEGORIES of time spent ... Add more if you want—categories that is—you only get the usual 24-7, unless you're in a sci fi movie.

Total hours per day (or week) spent in each category	
Sleeping	
Getting up, getting ready	
Eating	
Commuting	
Paid work List 'typical tasks' if you want.	
For your Living space	
Tidying, organizing	
Cleaning	
Food prep./ Cooking	
Groceries	
Running errands	
Other...	
Doing for/with others	
Romance, dates	
Kids (?)	
Other family members	
Friends	
Community groups?	
Staying Healthy & Fit Getting exercise Sunshine & fresh air	
Taking care of your money Monthly bills Long term strategies	
A-LIST goals Yours are?	
Hobbies List them	
Miscellaneous Online? TV? Games? Other?	

ACTUAL WEEK (168 hrs)

For this coming week, track how you ACTUALLY spend your time.

Time	MON	TUES	WED	THUR	FRI
midnight					
1am					
2					
3					
4					
5					
6					
7					
8					
9					
10					
11					
noon					
1 pm					
2					
3					
4					
5					
6					
7					
8					
9					
10					
11					

NOTES TO SELF:

(continued)

Time	SAT	SUN
midnight		
1am		
2		
3		
4		
5		
6		
7		
8		
9		
10		
11		
noon		
1 pm		
2		
3		
4		
5		
6		
7		
8		
9		
10		
11		

Total hours per day (or week) spent in each category	
Sleeping	
Getting up, getting ready	
Eating	
Commuting	
Paid work List 'typical tasks' if you want.	
For your Living space	
Tidying, organizing	
Cleaning	
Food prep./ Cooking	
Groceries	
Running errands	
Other...	
Doing for/with others	
Romance, dates	
Kids (?)	
Other family members	
Friends	
Community groups?	
Staying Healthy & Fit Getting exercise Sunshine & fresh air	
Taking care of your money Monthly bills Long term strategies	
A-LIST goals Yours are?	
Hobbies List them	
Miscellaneous Online? TV? Games? Other?	

How long did each of the various tasks take you? Do you want to spend more time, or less, on certain categories?

DESIGN YOUR PREFERRED WEEK (168 hrs)

Which of your roles/goals/values might not be getting the time and energy they deserve? Build these in.

Taking charge of how you spend and invest your time is both calming and energizing. It drops your stress levels, builds confidence, and boosts your effectiveness at creating and implementing what you need and want in your life!

Time	MON	TUES	WED	THUR	FRI
midnight					
1am					
2					
3					
4					
5					
6					
7					
8					
9					
10					
11					
noon					
1 pm					
2					
3					
4					
5					
6					
7					
8					
9					
10					
11					

(continued)

Time	SAT	SUN
midnight		
1am		
2		
3		
4		
5		
6		
7		
8		
9		
10		
11		
noon		
1 pm		
2		
3		
4		
5		
6		
7		
8		
9		
10		
11		

Total hours per day (or week) spent in each category	
Sleeping	
Getting up, getting ready	
Eating	
Commuting	
Paid work List 'typical tasks' if you want.	
For your Living space	
Tidying, organizing	
Cleaning	
Food prep./ Cooking	
Groceries	
Running errands	
Other...	
Doing for/with others	
Romance, dates	
Kids (?)	
Other family members	
Friends	
Community groups?	
Staying Healthy & Fit Getting exercise Sunshine & fresh air	
Taking care of your money Monthly bills Long term strategies	
A-LIST goals Yours are?	
Hobbies List them	
Miscellaneous Online? TV? Games? Other?	

Flex Blocks and Found Time

Once you have a better sense of how long things take, you can create a list of various tasks or activities that can fit into certain time frames. This is not commonly done, but it is useful once you get the hang of it. If you have a snow day off work or your dentist appointment gets cancelled, choose something on your list that fits - it could be revamping your resume or just putting your feet up with a cup of tea or a cold one.

Keep your Flex Blocks list in your planner so it's handy.

Time Needed	(Here are a few examples...)
Under a ½ hr	Call dentist & vet
about 1/2 hr	Take out trash for elderly neighbour, call a friend
1 to 2 hrs	Help kids with homework, clean car, get groceries, go for run
2 - 3 hrs	Do some sorting, putter in garden, take kids to hockey Your favourite sport or date night (not necessarily the same thing)
½ day	Redo resume, volunteer somewhere, great date night
full day	Organize a room, go canoeing
2 days	Build a deck, have a romantic weekend

Endnotes

Chapter 1 Where do you want to go with this?

1 Maslow, A.H., "A Theory of Human Motivation", *Psychological Review*. 50, 370-396. 1943.

Chapter 2 What matters?

1 From THE LAZY PERSON'S GUIDE TO SUCCESS: HOW TO GET WHAT YOU WANT WITHOUT KILLING YOURSELF FOR IT by Ernie J. Zelinski, copyright © 2002 by Ernie J. Zelinski. Used by permission of Ten Speed Press, an imprint of the Crown Publishing Group, a division of Random House, Inc., p 99

Chapter 3 Gripes, Grumps, and Gratitudes

1 Barbara Sher, with Annie Gotlieb, *Wishcraft: How to Get What You Really Want*, 1983, Ballantine Books, Random House, Inc., NY. Copyright Year © 1979 by Barbara Sher, p 104
2 Ibid. p 97
3 Ibid. p 96
4 Ibid. p 102

Chapter 4 Creating Luck

1 p 166 from The Luck Factor by Richard Wiseman, published by Arrow Books and Miramax Books, Hyperion. Reprinted by permission of the Random House Group Limited, (UK,) and MIramax (USA)
2 Ibid. p 167
3 Ibid. p 4
4 Daniel H. Pink (interviewer), Dr. RIchard Wiseman (interviewee), "How to make your own luck", FastCompany.com Retrieved from http://www.fastcompany.com/magazine/72/realitycheck.html On: June 30, 2003
5 Wiseman, op. cit. pp 161-162
6 Ibid. p 69
7 Ibid. p 88
8 Ibid. p 102
9 Ibid. p 147
10 Ibid. p 44
11 Ibid. p 43
12 Ibid. p 156, 157
13 Ibid. p 128
14 Ibid. paraphrased from chapters 7 and 8
15 Daniel H. Pink (interviewer), Dr. RIchard Wiseman (interviewee), "How to make your own luck", FastCompany.com Retrieved from http://www.fastcompany.com/magazine/72/realitycheck.html On: June 30, 2003
16 Zelinski, op. cit. p 67

Chapter 5 Effective Decision-making – Conscious and Unconscious

1 Kate Douglas, "Making Your Mind Up", New Scientist, 12 November 2011, pp 39-41 © 2011 Reid Business Information - UK.
2 Adapted from THE THREE BOXES OF LIFE AND HOW TO GET OUT OF THEM: AN INTRODUCTION TO LIFE/WORK PLANNING by Richard N. Bolles, copyright ©1978, 1981 by Richard N. Bolles. Used by permission of Ten Speed Press, an imprint of the Crown Publishing Group, a division of Random House, Inc., Appendix pages 420-423
3 Spencer Johnson, "YES" or "NO" The Guide to Better Decisions, HarperCollins, 1992, Copyright ©1992 by Spencer Johnson, M.D. Reprinted by permission of HarperCollins Publishers, the Margaret McBride Literary Agency, California, and Spencer Johnson. p 4
4 Ibid. p 4
5 Ibid. p 39
6 Ibid. p 7
7 Ibid. p 18
8 Ibid. p 26
9 Ibid. p 28
10 Ibid. p 37
11 Ibid. p 15
12 Ibid. p 27
13 Ibid. p 21
14 Ibid. p 23
15 Ibid. p 40
16 Ibid. p 47
17 Ibid. p 18
18 Ibid. p 46
19 Ibid. p 54 & 56

20 Ibid. p 58
21 Ibid. p 60, 61
22 Ibid. p 52
23 Ibid. p 62, 63
24 Ibid. p 66, 67
25 Ibid. p 65
26 Ibid. p 68
27 Ibid. p 71
28 Ibid. pp 73 & 74
29 Ibid. p 73
30 Ibid. p 82
31 Ibid. p 75
32 Ibid. pp 76, 77
33 Ibid. p 80
34 Ibid. p 82
35 Ibid. p 90
36 Ibid. pp 84,85
37 Ibid. p 89
38 Ibid. p 91
39 Ibid. p 101
40 Ibid. p 12
41 Ibid. p 86
42 Blackmore, Susan, "Memes, Myself, I", New Scientist, 13 March 1999, © 1999 Reid Business Information - UK.
43 Ellwood, Wayne, "On the Road To Zero Growth", *New Internationalist* Magazine #434, July/August 2010, p 11
44 From BLINK by Malcolm Gladwell. Copyright © 2005 by Malcolm Gladwell, By permission of Little, Brown and Company. p 10
45 Ibid. p 44
46 Ibid. pp 35-37
47 John Gottman and Sybil Carrère, as refernced in Malcolm Gladwell, BLINK pp 20-22
48 Gladwell, op. cit. pp 58-60
49 Reprinted by permission of the publisher from STRANGERS TO OURSELVES: DISCOVERING THE ADAPTIVE UNCONSCIOUS by Timothy D. Wilson, pp.6-7, Cambridge, Mass.: The Belknap Press of Harvard University Press, Copyright © 2002 by the President and Fellows of Harvard College.
50 Gladwell, op. cit. pp 59-61
51 Ibid. p 13
52 Ibid. p 52
53 Ibid. pp 64, 69, 52
54 Ibid. pp 71, 181
55 Ibid. pp 85-88, 96 & 233
56 Ibid. p 15
57 Ibid. p 77
58 Ibid. p 91
59 Ibid. p 76
60 Ibid. pp 113, 114
61 Ibid. p 184 and 179
62 Ibid. pp 150-152
63 Ibid. pp 168, 169
64 Ibid. p 173
65 Ibid. p 264
66 Ibid. pp 141,142
67 Ibid. pp 273-274, 250, 254
68 Ibid. p 264
69 Ibid. p 225
70 Ibid. p 229
71 Ibid. p 233 and Keith Payne, et al, Journal of Experimental Social Psychology 38 (2002): 384-396
72 Ibid. p 237
73 Ibid. p 241
74 Ibid. p 97
75 Ibid. p 269
76 Kate Douglas, "Making Your Mind Up", New Scientist, 12 November 2011, pp 39-41 © 2011 Reid Business Information - UK.

Chapter 6 Evaluating and Interpreting our Decisions

1 Barry Schwartz, *The Paradox of Choice*, HarperCollins Publishers, 2004, Copyright © 2004 by Barry Schwartz. Reprinted by permission or HarperCollins Publishers, Paraphrased from Prologue
2 Ibid. p 132

3 Ibid. p 54
4 From THE 4-HR WORKWEEK: ESCAPE 9-5, LIVE ANYWHERE, AND JOIN THE NEW RICH by Timothy Ferriss, copyright © 2007, 2009 by Carmenere One, LLC. Used by permission of Crown Publishers, a division of Random House, Inc., p 323.
5 Schwartz, op. cit. p 7, 130, 72.
6 Ibid. p 125, 126
7 Ibid. p 131, 132
8 Ibid. p 129
9 Ibid. p 48
10 Ferriss, op. cit. p 323
11 Schwartz, op. cit. p 172, 173
12 Ibid. p 179
13 Ibid. p 89 & 79
14 Ibid. p 176, 177
15 Ibid. p 113-115

Chapter 7 Who are You?

1 James March, *A Primer in Decisions Making: How Decisions Happen,* Free Press, New York, 1994 as referenced in SWITCH: HOW TO CHANGE THINGS WHEN CHANGE IS HARD by Chip Heath and Dan Heath, p 153

Chapter 8 Toddler Tactics and Strategies for Change

1 A.Michalos, "Job satisfaction, Marital Satisfaction, and the Quality of life," in F.M.Andrews (ed.), *Research on the Quality of Life,* Ann Arbor, MI: Institute for Social Research, 1986, p. 75.
2 Barry Schwartz, *The Paradox of Choice*, HarperCollins Publishers, 2004, Copyright © 2004 by Barry Schwartz. Reprinted by permission of HarperCollins Publishers, p 183
3 Robert Pagliarini, *The Six-Day Financial Makeover,* St Martin's Press, New York, 2008. Copyright © 2006 by Robert Pagliarini. P 49.
4 Spencer Johnson, M.D., *Who Moved My Cheese?* G.P. Putnam's Sons, Putnam Penguin Copyright © 1998, 2002, by Spencer Johnson, M.D.
5 From SWITCH: HOW TO CHANGE THINGS WHEN CHANGE IS HARD by Chip Heath and Dan Heath, copyright © 2010 by Chip Heath and Dan Heath. Used by permission of Broadway Books, a division of Random House, Inc. and Random House Business Books, Random House Group Limited UK, p 164
6 Ibid. p 169
7 Ibid. p 3
8 Ibid. p 12
9 Ibid. p 15
10 Ibid. p 10
11 Ibid. p 48
12 Ibid. p 15 -17
13 Ibid. p 130 & 131
14 Michael Ramundo and Susan Shelly, The Complete Idiot's Guide to Motivating People, Alpha Books Macmillan, USA, 1999, 2003
15 Heath and Heath, op. cit. p. 7-9; the analogy is Jonathan Haidt's, permission of the author.
16 Kiyosake, Robert T. , with Sharon L. Lechter, *Rich Dad Poor Dad,* Cashflow Technologies Inc., 2000, p 33
17 From STUMBLING ON HAPPINESS by Daniel Gilbert, copyright © 2006 by Daniel Gilbert. Used by permission of Albert A. Knopf, a division of Random House, Inc. p 25
18 Albert Bandura, a Stanford psychology professor, in *Alternative Medicine* magazine, Jan 2003: p30
19 Stephen Covey, *Seven Habits of Highly Effective People,* Fireside, Simon & Schuster, USA, 1990. Copyright Year ©1989 by Stephen Covey. p 100

Chapter 9 Flying frogs? Strengths and Weaknesses

1 Marcus Buckingham, *Go Put Your Strengths to Work*, Free Press, Simon & Schuster, Inc., 2007, Copyright © 2007 by One Thing Productions, Inc., P 90
2 Ibid. p 87 & 90
3 Ibid. p 83 & 90
4 Ibid. p 111
5 Rath, Tom. Strengths Finder 2.0, GALLUP PRESS, New York. 2007. Copyright © 2007 The Gallup Organization. p 20
6 Ibid. p 12,13
7 Ibid. p 7
8 Dobbs, David, "The Orchid Children", *New Scientist,* 28 January 2012, p 42-45. © 2012 Reid Business Information - UK.
9 Linda Gottfredson, Intelligence, *New Scientist #2819,* 2 July 2011, p. i-viii © 2011 Reid Business Information - UK.
10 Rath, Tom. Strengths Finder 2.0, GALLUP PRESS, New York. 2007. Copyright © 2007 The Gallup Organization. p iii

11 Marcus Buckingham, *Go Put Your Strengths to Work*, Free Press, Simon & Schuster, Inc., 2007, Copyright © 2007 by One Thing Productions, Inc., p 164
12 Ibid. p 169
13 Ibid. p 159-160
14 Ibid. p 164
15 Ibid. p 8, 23

Chapter 10 Goals and A-LISTS

1 Zelinski, op. cit. p 147
2 Kathy Kolbe, www.kolbe.com. [Four Action Modes, "Quick Starts", "Fact Finders", "Follow Thrus", "Implementors"] are the trademarks of Kolbe Corp or Kathy Kolbe
3 http://wordinfo.info/unit/1941
4 Sher, op. cit. p 106

Chapter 11 Everyone's got 24 – 7

1 Stephen Covey, A. Roger Merrill, Rebecca R. Merrill, *First Things First*, 2003, Free Press, A division of Simon & Schuster, Inc., New York, Copyright © 1994 by Covey Leadership Center. p 88-90
2 Ibid. p 37 & 205
3 Zelinski, op. cit. p 74
4 Ferriss, op. cit. p 33
5 Morgenstern, Julie. *Time Management From the Inside Out.* Owl Book/Henry Holt & Company,: New York 2000, 2004, p 26
6 Ibid Chapter 2

Chapter 12 Get Sea-worthy

1 From THE DIFFERENCE: HOW ANYONE CAN PROSPER EVEN IN THE TOUGHEST TIMES by Jean Chatzky, copyright © 2009 by Jean Chatzky. Used by permission of Crown Publishers, a division of Random House, Inc., p 16
2 Ibid. p 11
3 Jon Hanson, *Good Debt Bad Debt*, Penguin Group, Copyright © 2005, with permission of the author. p 115
4 Ibid. p 13
5 Mark Buchanan, "Why Money Messes With Your Mind" – *New Scientist* #2700, 18 March 2009, p. 26-30 © 2009 Reid Business Information - UK.
6 Tony Fitzgerald, Toney. *Don't Bitch, Just Get Rich*, Simon & Schuster, Pymble, 2006. p 70
7 Zelinski, op. cit. p 202

Chapter 13 Getting real

none

Chapter 14 Taxes

1 Kiyosaki, op. cit. p 95
2 Ibid. p 99

Chapter 15 Flushing money

1 From I WILL TEACH YOU TO BE RICH, Copyright © 2009 by Ramit Sethi, Used by permission of Workman Publishing Co., Inc., New York. All rights Reserved. p 46
2 Kiyosaki, op. cit. p 45
3 Ibid. p 46
4 Ibid. p 63
5 Ibid. p 60
6 Liz Pulliam Weston, moneycentral.msn.com "The new class divide: debt" 6/9/2009
7 Hanson, op. cit. p 5
8 Schumacher, John, "In Greed We Trust", *New Internationalist* Magazine # 369, July 2004, pp 34,35
9 Graham Lawton, "We Have Ways of Making You Buy", *New Scientist* #2772, 9 Aug 2010, pp 32-35 © 2010 Reid Business Information - UK.
10 Vicki Robin & Joe Dominguez, with Monique Telford, *Your Money Or Your Life*, Penguin Books, New York, 1992, 2008. p 131
11 Ibid. p 109
12 Larry Winget, *You're Broke Because You Want To Be*, Gotham Books, Penguin Group (USA), 2008, p 7

Chapter 16 Big ticket borrowing

1 Sethi, op. cit. p 35
2 Suze Orman, "A Car Guide for the Young, Fabulous, and Broke" on Yahoo, Aug 20, 2010.
3 From THE CURE FOR MONEY MADNESS: BREAK YOUR BAD MONEY HABITS, LIVE WITHOUT FINANCIAL STRESS – AND MAKE MORE MONEY! by Spencer Sherman, copyright © 2009 by Spencer D. Sherman. Used by permission of Broadway Books, a division of Random House, Inc., p 192.

4 Ibid. p 194
5 From THE AUTOMATIC MIILIONAIRE HOMEOWNER A POWERFUL PLAN TO FINISH RICH IN REAL ESTATE by David Bach, copyright © 2006 by David Bach. Used by permission of Broadway Books, a division of Random House, Inc., p 6.
6 Ibid. p 140.

Chapter 17 Using money well

1 Ibid. p. 26
2 Liz Pulliam Weston, Moneycentral.com 3/11/2009
3 Bach op. cit. p 82
4 Kiyosaki, op. cit. p 158
5 Rob Carrick, Globe and Mail, 2009 and Andrew Binet, Globe and Mail, 2010
6 From THE DIFFERENCE: HOW ANYONE CAN PROSPER EVEN IN THE TOUGHEST TIMES by Jean Chatzky, copyright © 2009 by Jean Chatzky. Used by permission of Crown Publishers, a division of Random House, Inc. p 219
7 Robert Pagliarini, *The Six-Day Financial Makeover*, St Martin's Press, New York, 2008. Copyright © 2006 by Robert Pagliarini. p 96.
8 Robin, op. cit. P 176
9 Meadows, Donella L., et al, *Beyond the Limits: Global Collapse or a Sustainable Future*, Earthscan Publications, 1992, p 176
10 Robin op. cit. p 177
11 Kiyosaki, op. cit. p 145
12 Pagliarini, op. cit. p 77

Chapter 18 Investing is not just-about-the-money

none

Chapter 19 Make your money work more, so you can work less

1 From THE AUTOMATIC MILLIONAIRE A POWERFUL ONE-STEP PLAN TO LIVE AND FINISH RICH by David Bach, copyright © 2004 by David Bach. Used by permission of Broadway Books, a division of Random House, Inc. p 76.
2 Ibid. p 114
3 Kiyosaki, op. cit. "back matter"
4 Ibid. p 115
5 Ibid. ch 3
6 Ibid. p 197
7 Ibid. p 99
8 Ibid. p 115
9 Ibid. p 196
10 Ibid. p 159
11 Ibid. p 162
12 From THE AUTOMATIC MILLIONAIRE HOMEOWNER A POWERFUL PLAN TO FINISH RICH IN REAL ESTATE by David Bach, copyright © 2006 by David Bach. Used by permission of Broadway Books, a division of Random House, Inc., p 52
13 Kiyosaki, op. cit. p 96
14 Bach, op. cit. p 16.
15 Ibid. p 142
16 Barbara Hawkins, "Ten Laws of Building Wealth", *Moneysense* magazine, summer 2007, p 30
17 From I WILL TEACH YOU TO BE RICH, Copyright © 2009 by Ramit Sethi, Used by permission of Workman Publishing Co., Inc., New York. All rights Reserved. p 146.
18 From THE CURE FOR MONEY MADNESS: BREAK YOUR BAD MONEY HABITS, LIVE WITHOUT FINANCIAL STRESS – AND MAKE MORE MONEY! by Spencer Sherman, copyright © 2009 by Spencer D. Sherman. Used by permission of Broadway Books, a division of Random House, Inc., material from Ch. 6
19 Ibid. Inside cover.
20 Ian McGugan, "Rich by Next Monday", *Moneysense* magazine, October 2008, p 40

Chapter 20 Designing and generating income

1 From THE DIFFERENCE: HOW ANYONE CAN PROSPER EVEN IN THE TOUGHEST TIMES by Jean Chatzky, copyright © 2009 by Jean Chatzky. Used by permission of Crown Publishers, a division of Random House, Inc. p 86.
2 Ibid. p 77
3 From WHAT COLOR IS YOUR PARACHUTE? A PRACTICAL MANUAL FOR JOB HUNTERS AND CAREER-CHANGERS 2012 40TH ANNIVERSARY EDITION by Richard N. Bolles, copyright © 2012, 2011, 2010, 2009, 2008, 2007, 2006, 2005, 2004, 2003, 2002, 2001, 2000, 1999, 1998, 1997, 1996, 1995, 1994, 1993, 1992, 1991, 1990, 1989, 1988, 1987, 1986, 1985, 1984, 1983, 1982, 1981, 1980, 1979, 1978, 1976, 1975, 1972, 1970 by Richard N. Bolles. Used by permission of Ten Speed Press, an imprint of the Crown Publishing Group, a division of Random House, Inc. The following cited pages are from the 2012 Edition. p 21, 22, 227

4 Ibid. p 200
5 Ibid. p 219
6 Ibid. p 206
7 Ibid. p 210
8 Ibid. p 215
9 Ibid p 224-228
10 Chatzky, op. cit. p 61
11 Ibid. p 78.
12 Ibid. p 89
13 Hilary Lips, "The Gender Wage Gap" womensmedia.com, Retrieved from: http://www.womensmedia.com/new/Lips-Hilary-gender-wage-gap.shtml on: August 20, 2010
14 Ferriss, op. cit. p 20
15 Ibid. p 53
16 Ibid. p 22
17 Ibid. p 7,8
18 Ibid. p 32
19 Ibid. p 42 & 45
20 Ibid. p 75
21 Chatzky, op. cit. p 234
22 Kiyosaki, op. cit. p 73
23 Chatzky, op. cit. p 206

Chapter 21 Build non-monetary assets

1 Kiyosaki, op. cit. p 223

Chapter 22 Insurances FOR you

1 American Journal of Public Health, December 2009, Vol 99, No.12
2 From FIGHT FOR YOUR MONEY: HOW TO STOP GETTING RIPPED OFF AND SAVE A FORTUNE by David Bach, copyright © 2009 by David Bach. Used by permission of Broadway Books, a division of Random House, Inc., p 148.
3 National Safety Council, Injury Facts, 2008
4 Pagliarini, op. cit. p 173
5 Commissioners Individual Disability Table
6 Commissioners Disability Table, 1998, Health Ins Assn of America, NY Times, 2000
7 Pagliarini, op. cit. p 173.
8 Ibid, p 200
9 American Association on Aging, May 2003

Chapter 23 Insurances for your stuff

none

Chapter 24 Insurances ON you

1 From FIGHT FOR YOUR MONEY: HOW TO STOP GETTING RIPPED OFF AND SAVE A FORTUNE by David Bach, copyright © 2009 by David Bach. Used by permission of Broadway Books, a division of Random House, Inc., p 126.

Chapter 25 Directives and Wills

none

Chapter 26 Living space – Rentals, landlords, and roommates

none

Chapter 27 Living under the same roof and more than friends?

none

Chapter 28 Protecting your Identity and Privacy

none

Chapter 29 Some thoughts on Happiness

1 Dalai Lama, the Art of Happiness, Penguin Group USA, First edition, 1998
2 Martin Seligman and Chris Petersen, "Un-DSM"
3 Martin Seligman, Authentic Happiness, pp 9 &10
4 Chatzky. op. cit. p 99

5 Reprinted with the permission of Simon & Schuster, Inc. from YOUR MONEY & YOUR BRAIN by Jason Zweig. Copyright © 2007 Jason Zweig, p 255. (Zweig was reporting on the work done by psychologists Heather Pond Lacey at Bryant University in Smithville, Rhode Island and Laura Carstensen at Stanford University. Carstesen's work is published in the *Journal of Personality and Social Psychology* vol 79, p 644.)
6 Helen Fisher, *The Journal of Neuroscience* DOI: 10.1523/jneurosci.0022-06.2006
7 "In Brief: Picture of Happiness", *New Scientist* 02 Feb 2002 p 25 © 2002 Reed Business Information – UK
8 Karen Gasper and Jerry Clore, *Psychological Science,* vol 13, p34
9 David Lykken, *Psychological Science,* vol 7, p189
10 *Proceedings of the National Academy of Sciences*, DOI:10.1073/pnas. 1008612107
11 *Journal of Personality and Social Psychology,* vol 52, p1122
12 *Proceedings of the National Academy of Sciences*, vol. 104, p383
13 Barbara Fredrickson, *Review of General Psychology*, vol 2, p300
14 Ed Diener and Robert Biswas-Diener, *Happiness: Unlocking the Mysteries of Psychological Wealth*, Blackwell Publishing, 2008
15 From THE DIFFERENCE: HOW ANYONE CAN PROSPER EVEN IN THE TOUGHEST TIMES by Jean Chatzky, copyright © 2009 by Jean Chatzky. Used by permission of Crown Publishers, a division of Random House, Inc., p 96
16 Alice Isen, Cornell University, author's permission and as referenced in Chatzky, p 142
17 as reported by Steve Ayan, "Laughing Matters", *Scientific American Mind*, April/May 2009, p 24-31 PUBI
18 Liz Else, "The Happiness Agenda", *New Scientist,* 16 Apr 2011, p 47
© 2011 Reed Business Information – UK
19 Sonja Lyubomirsky as referenced in Chatzky p 194
20 Kasser, Tim, *The High Price of Materialism,* (MIT Press, 2002)
21 Haidt, Jonathan, *The Happiness Hypothesis: Finding Modern Truth in Ancient Wisdom*, Basic Books, Copyright © 2006 by Jonathan Haidt. pp 126-128 (With permission of the author.) Dr. Haidt is Professor, Dept. Of Psychology, University of Virginia, and Henry Kaufman Visiting Professor of Business Ethics, NYU-Stern School of Business.
22 Ibid, p 131
23 Michael Bond, "How your friend's friends can affect your mood". *New Scientist* # 2689,
30 Dec 2008, © 2008 Reed Business Information – UK
24 From STUMBLING ON HAPPINESS by Daniel Gilbert, copyright © 2006 by Daniel Gilbert.
Used by permission of Albert A. Knopf, a division of Random House, Inc. and Reprinted by permission of HarperCollins Publishers Ltd. © 2006 by Daniel Gilbert
25 Baker, Dan, and Cameron Stauth, *What Happy People Know*, St. Martin's Press, New York, 2003, pp 37-40
26 Gary Stix, "The Neuroscience of Grit", *Scientific American*, March 2011, p 33.
27 T. Ketter, Stanford Univ. as reported in *New Scientist*, p 38, see #28 below
28 Jessica Marshall, "Woes be Gone", *New Scientist,* 14 Jan 2009, p36. © 2009 Reed Business Information – UK
29 "A pill for every ill." *New Scientist* 14 Jan. 2009 p 38. © 2009 Reed Business Information – UK
30 Andrews & Thomson, "Depression's evolutionary roots", *Scientific American Mind*, Jan/Feb 2010, p 57-61
31 Proceeding of the National Academy of Sciences, DOI.10.1073 /pnas.0914054107
32 Biswas-Diener, Vitterso, and Diener, Danish survey, 2010
33 Wiseman, op. cit. p 141,142
34 Diener, op. cit. p 216
35 faculty.ucr.edu/~sonja
36 Schwartz, op. cit. p 194 reporting on research done by psychologist Sonja Lyubomirsky and her colleagues
37 Emily Pronin and Elana Jacobs, "Thought Speed, Mood, and the Experience of Mental Motion". *Perspectives on Psychological Science*, vol 3 No. 6, p 461-482
38 Kelly Lambert, "Depressingly Easy", *Scientific American Mind*, Aug/Sept 2008, p 31-37
39 Reprinted with the permission of Simon & Schuster, Inc. from YOUR MONEY & YOUR BRAIN by Jason Zweig. Copyright © 2007 Jason Zweig, p 259
40 Peggy Thoits and Lyndi Hewitt, *Journal of Health and Social Behaviour*, vol 42, 115; and James Konow, *American Economic Review*, vol 90, p 1072
41 Ed Diener's thoughts as reported by Suzann Pileggi Pawelski in "The Many Faces of Happiness", *Scientific American Mind*, Sept/Oct 2011, p 55
42 Martin Seligman's work as reported by Jason Zweig. (Reprinted with the permission of Simon & Schuster, Inc. from YOUR MONEY & YOUR BRAIN by Jason Zweig. Copyright © 2007 Jason Zweig.) p 265

Chapter 30 Onions, Pomegranates, and ...

1 David Robson, "How to control a herd of humans", *New Scientist* # 2694, 04 Feb 2009, p 13. © 2009 Reed Business Information – UK

Acknowledgements

I'd like to express my heartfelt thanks to the young people who inspired and encouraged me to write this book. (Frankly, your confidence in me is quite humbling, and I deeply appreciate having had the opportunity to touch your lives. You have certainly enriched mine.) And to my two daughters and sons-in-law, and dearest friends, for their support, enthusiasm, and suggestions.

My gratitude also goes out to the following:

Elaine Mitchell for her editing and insightful other-points-of-view.

Robyn York, whose InDesign expertise, good eye, and easy-going manner made translating my vision for the book from brain to publishable page a true joy.

Anna Calleja for contributing the drawings that help make-real the metaphors, and for proofreading the final draft.

Guiomar De Sa for hijacking her own very busy schedule to take the time to help me tweak parts of the financial section.

Dan Pitt, my surrogate "kid brother", for his reading and weeding feedback.

Ken MacMillan and Rosalind Eadie who read segments of the first draft and cheered me on.

David Bunn, whose patient listening to my occasional rant during the oft-times frustrating learning curve of the How-Who-Where copyright permissions process, helped keep me more or less sane.

And Caroline Makar whose tireless encouragement was a real gift.

I'd like to also express my appreciation to the authors and their publishers who generously let me include segments of their works. (A special thanks, in particular, to New Scientist, Reed Business Information, and the Gallup Organization for their remarkably prompt and thoughtful responses.)

And deep thanks to the researchers in the trenches of discovery for unearthing the facts and patterns we humans need to come to see and, hopefully, understand. Individually and collectively, as a human aspiration, wisdom certainly trumps mere survival.

About the Author

Having, like many, learned a few too many things the hard way, Erika Dianne Gibson is determined to do what she can to help others make their life-musts easier and the path to their joys smoother. *Someone really oughta tell us...*

She taught sciences at the college and university levels, then became a Doctor of Chiropractic as a "mature" student. Though she enjoyed helping her patients get back-to-better, she eventually realized that context was not truly where her heart was. She re-invented her work-life yet again—as an "alternative" senior high school teacher. At this point, she has worked enthusiastically with young people for over twenty years. Her passion is to help young adults—and life renovators like herself—shape fulfilling and meaningful lives.

Gibson spent her childhood north of Lake Superior, and much of her adult life in a rural context. She currently lives in Toronto and, though it took time, has come to appreciate the upside of an urban setting. What's next for her? More travel. More time with family. More latin dance. More learning. And more workshops to assist those who may want to design and build—or renovate—their life.

For more information, visit **sroty.org**